THE OXFORD BOOK OF

CARIBBEAN VERSE

STEWART BROWN is a poet and critic, currently the Director of the Centre of West African Studies, University of Birmingham, where he teaches African and Caribbean literature. He taught in Jamaica in the early 1970s, lectured at Bayero University, Kano in Nigeria in the 1980s, and in 2007 was Visiting Professor of Literatures in English at the University of the West Indies in Barbados. He has edited several anthologies of Caribbean writing as well as critical studies of the great West Indian poets Derek Walcott, Kamau Brathwaite, and Martin Carter. His own poetry is collected in *Elsewhere: New and Selected Poems* (2000). A collection of his essays on poetry, *Tourist, Traveller, Troublemaker*, was published in 2007.

MARK MCWATT is a Guyanese poet and critic who studied at universities in Canada and the UK, and is now Emeritus Professor of West Indian Literature at the University of the West Indies in Barbados. He has published many books and essays on aspects of Caribbean literature, with a particular interest in Guyanese writers. He is founding editor and current joint editor of *The Journal of West Indian Literature*. His own poetry is widely published and anthologized, and his collection *The Language of Eldorado* won the prestigious Guyana Prize for Poetry in 1994. His first collection of short stories, *Suspended Sentences* (2005) won both the Commonwealth Best First Book Award 2006, and the Casa de las Americas Prize.

The Oxford Book of
CARIBBEAN
VERSE

EDITED BY

Stewart Brown and Mark McWatt

OXFORD

UNIVERSITY PRESS

OXFORD

UNIVERSITY PRESS

Great Clarendon Street, Oxford OX2 6DP

Oxford University Press is a department of the University of Oxford.
It furthers the University's objective of excellence in research, scholarship,
and education by publishing worldwide in

Oxford New York

Auckland Cape Town Dar es Salaam Hong Kong Karachi
Kuala Lumpur Madrid Melbourne Mexico City Nairobi
New Delhi Shanghai Taipei Toronto

With offices in

Argentina Austria Brazil Chile Czech Republic France Greece
Guatemala Hungary Italy Japan Poland Portugal Singapore
South Korea Switzerland Thailand Turkey Ukraine Vietnam

Oxford is a registered trade mark of Oxford University Press
in the UK and in certain other countries

Published in the United States
by Oxford University Press Inc., New York

British Library Cataloguing in Publication Data

Data available

Library of Congress Cataloging in Publication Data

Data available

Printed in Great Britain
on acid-free paper by
Clays Ltd.,St Ives plc.

ISBN 978-0-19-956159-9

1 3 5 7 9 10 8 6 4 2

CONTENTS

CONTENTS

CONTENTS

vii

CONTENTS

CONTENTS

CONTENTS

CONTENTS

xi

CONTENTS

xii

CONTENTS

CONTENTS

CONTENTS

INTRODUCTION

A hundred years ago it would have been inconceivable that the Caribbean, for centuries the site of some of the worst atrocities of human history, would produce what is arguably the most life-affirming and spiritually uplifting body of poetry of the twentieth century. This anthology presents work by a culturally, ethnically and linguistically diverse collection of poets, representing a century or so of Caribbean literary activity. It chronicles the transition of the Caribbean as a region from an essentially colonial space where poetry and the poetic were defined in European terms, to the situation at the beginning of the twenty-first century when the region's poets have redefined their cultural identities, acknowledging—to a greater or lesser extent—a 'hybrid muse',[1] but writing a poetry that is unequivocally *of* the Caribbean.

Caribbean poetry has grown in both volume and stature through the twentieth century from something that hardly existed—at least as far as the literary mainstream was concerned—into a body of word-culture (embracing both oral and written dimensions) that is generally acknowledged to be among the richest, most accessible, and yet technically adventurous libraries of contemporary verse. Across the region major poets such as Derek Walcott, Edouard Glissant, Nicolas Guillén, Aimé Césaire, René Dépestre, Kamau Brathwaite, and Nancy Morejón have produced poetry that offers both an account of a particular, Caribbean experience and speaks to a wider notion of 'the contemporary world'.

Indeed, West Indian poetry is essentially a twentieth-century phenomenon, for although verse had been written in and of the region almost from the beginning of the colonizing enterprise (Sir Walter Raleigh was, after all, a poet as well as—to steal Derek Walcott's phrase—an 'ancestral murderer'), the best that can really be said of most of the literary material written in the Caribbean before the end of the nineteenth century is that it is interesting in an historical or sociological sense. The voices that spoke out of those early poems were the voices of strangers or exiles, the languages they spoke had been forged elsewhere.

Of course, there was an alternative 'word culture' existing and developing in the region throughout that period: the oral tradition of songs and stories, prayers and performances, versions of history and mythology passed down the generations and remade—adapted and added to—each generation. Obviously much of that material would have derived from African sources during the period of slavery, but there are also Amerindian and European inputs, and later the influx of peoples from China, the Middle East, and particularly the Indian sub-continent added to the range and substance of those oral traditions. Many—probably most—West Indian poets have been conscious of, and to some extent influenced by, those oral forms and the stories spun around figures such as Anancy, the West African trickster, the Amerindian spirits Ol Higue or Mantop, or the 'East Indian' gods Hanuman or Shiva.

Through the nineteenth century, after the abolition of slavery, various other forms of oral presentation developed, ranging from the great West Indian preachers at one level, through to the formalization of various kinds of word play and verbal contestation into calypso and other popular forms, at another. Perhaps combining the skills of both the pulpit orator and the calypsonian were generations of political leaders who used the spoken word as a powerful agent in galvanizing a still largely illiterate population in the struggle for democracy and independence.

Arguably the most significant impact of the oral tradition on West Indian poetry has been in the movement towards the language of speech becoming the language of narration and action—a journey charted in this collection from the experiments of Claude McKay in the early years of the twentieth century through to the fluid handling of voices, speech rhythms, and tones by contemporary poets such as the Jamaicans Michael Smith and Jean 'Binta' Breeze. The device of the literary poem pretending to be a 'told tale' has real political and cultural resonance in the Caribbean context.

The historical experience of the region in those three hundred years between the first European occupation and the turn of the twentieth century was hardly conducive to the cultivation of a literary sensibility: the decimation of the indigenous peoples; the institution and gradual decline of trans-Atlantic slavery, with its concomitant brutalities and the obscenities of the contrasting lifestyles of great house and slave yard. And after abolition the mass indenture of East Indian labourers, their presence further complicating the evolution of a colonialism characterized by the poison of what Edgar Mittelholzer memorably called the 'spite of shade'[2] mentality, an outlook which for so long distorted West Indian society. However, with the end of the Victorian era, with slavery—at least in most places—more than a generation gone, and access to education gradually more widespread, it perhaps became possible to think of a poetry produced by writers who felt themselves identified by their experience as Caribbean people, a poetry that could in some sense be both a commentary on that past and an exploration of its resonances into the contemporary society that would inevitably be the essential subject of a West Indian—indeed a Caribbean—literature.

So, silence and the voices of strangers: it is from such unpromising ground that the contemporary flowering of Caribbean poetry has grown. Through the course of the twentieth century the poets collected here have chronicled the evolving West Indian cultural consciousness, claiming a multi-faceted identity in the process of re-telling the region's history, discovering its land- and seascapes, and giving voice to the dreams and nightmares of its peoples. Since the independence decades of the 1960s and 1970s, West Indian poetry has extended its range both formally and thematically. The chorus of voices modulates the variety of accents, registers, and creoles that distinguishes the islands and territories from each other and reflects the diverse heritage and cultural traditions of all those peoples who came to the archipelago through history. (It is worth reminding ourselves that far from being a simple single space, the term 'the Caribbean' covers the approximately 2000-mile stretch of ocean from Surinam to the Bahamas, and the region includes more than thirty nation states.) Formally too, the diversity of styles is remarkable, from writers who adhere, more or less strictly, to the conventions of European or American verse, to those who experiment with dub, calypso, reggae, or jazz models, reclaiming and reshaping the oral traditions of the region for contemporary circumstances. But in fact most West Indian poets resist easy classification, even in terms of style, shifting across boundaries of the oral and the literary, the private and the public, as the poems they are writing demand. Contemporary Caribbean poets are as diverse and idiosyncratic a fraternity as American or European poets, but insofar as they share a common aesthetic it might be found to some extent in terms of attitudes towards history and authority and—bound up with that—in ways of refashioning versions of the colonial languages to make a poetry that speaks of and into the present in voices that the peoples of the region would recognize as their own. Those elements come out in the wit, the rage, the verbal energy, the delight in linguistic play, and the use of voices and characters and notions of storytelling that derive from the history of the region that are evident in many of the poems included in this anthology.

It is traditional to relegate an account of the hows and whys of making anthology selections to a brief paragraph at the end of the Introduction, but we feel it is important to foreground what we have tried to do with this anthology. Our original brief was to compile a truly pan-Caribbean collection that would represent the poetry traditions in the four major colonial languages of the region: English, Spanish, French, and Dutch.[3] However, the more we struggled with the weighting and balance of such a selection the more dissatisfied we became with that implicit, homogenizing agenda. For while everyone agrees that the different linguistic territories of the region share much in common—'the unity is submarine' as Kamau Brathwaite puts it[4]— it is also true that, notwithstanding their geographical proximity, the culture of, say, Cuba differs in fundamental ways from that of Haiti or Jamaica. At least, within the English language region, British colonialism provided—for better or worse—some degree of shared cultural values, some parameters within which it is possible to compare the achievement of individual writers from places as otherwise distinct as Jamaica and Trinidad, Barbados and Guyana. We decided then that we would try to let the anthology tell the story of that one linguistic tradition while including major poets and poems from the other languages in the general chronological sequence of the selection, so that readers would be continually alerted to those other strands in the Caribbean experience and the fact that collections which began with, say, a Spanish bias would look very different from the one we have produced.

That said, although the 'English language' poetry of the region forms the core of this collection, the distinctive flavour of the anthology derives from the inclusion of poems from across the 'wider Caribbean'. The English language poets represent a formidable tradition, but our perception of Caribbean poetry is enriched by the addition— albeit in translation—of the great poets of the other languages of the region. Presenting the work of the region's poets together in this way allows the reader familiar only with the Anglophone West Indian tradition a much broader perspective on what Caribbean poetry is and what Caribbean poets have achieved. The sense of connection and crossover—formally, thematically, and ideologically—among poets working in such very different cultural and linguistic traditions within the Caribbean is both very moving and very powerful. By tracing those connections back to their roots in the late nineteenth century in the work of (to adapt the metaphor from Nicolás Guillén's great poem) two unlikely grandfathers of Caribbean verse—the aristocratic white-creole Saint-John Perse from Guadeloupe and the black Jamaican 'peasant' poet Claude McKay—and then forward to the contemporary flowering of poetry by women across the region—poets such as Lorna Goodison, Nancy Morejón, Olive Senior, Marilene Phipps, and Judith Ortiz Cofer—we can begin to comprehend the real scope and achievement of twentieth-century Caribbean poetry.

The other major decision that the editors had to make (given that all anthologists must operate within the constraints of available space and the economics of publishing) was whether to concentrate our selection on a relatively few, already well established, poets who would each be represented by a substantial group of poems, or to try to reflect the range and variety of Caribbean poetry by including many more poets but with a consequently reduced selection from their work. We opted for the latter, feeling it important that readers new to Caribbean poetry understand what a vibrant and diverse body of work it is. Of course, the 'big guns' of Caribbean poetry are all here, and, we would argue, their work is better contextualized and understood for being read among the broad spread of the work of their Caribbean contemporaries.

So who counts as a Caribbean poet? If we take a fairly conventional notion of 'nationality' as someone born in the region, who lived and worked for most of their lives there, then a significant percentage of the writers we have included would not have been eligible. Migration has been a fact of Caribbean life—indeed, it is arguably the defining experience of Caribbean 'being'. Historically, with the exception of the few surviving Amerindian communities in the islands (and, of course, in the mainland South American territories), all the peoples of the Caribbean are 'incomers', whether from Africa, Europe, India, China, or the Middle East. So a sense of being 'half home' as Derek Walcott put it, is perhaps part of what it means to be a West Indian. That being so, it's not surprising, then, that so many Caribbean people have been willing to uproot themselves 'again' to pursue economic opportunities or other ambitions. All through the last century West Indians migrated in significant numbers, to Panama, to England, to Canada, and to the

USA. Many writers were among them, most famously the group who ventured to Britain in the 1950s and collectively drew attention to the region's literary ambitions, notably Naipaul, Lamming, Selvon, Salkey, Mittelholzer, and Harris. Hardly any of those writers returned to live in the Caribbean, but all continued to write about the region throughout their careers. Many contemporary writers also spend much of their lives 'elsewhere'—particularly in recent years settling in Florida, New York, or Toronto where they have some opportunity to establish their literary reputations. But today such migrations are not so absolute, and do not entail such a breaking of ties as they did for the emigrants of the 1940s and 1950s who literally crossed the seas; many of today's migrants are able to maintain close links with home and to travel back and forth quite regularly. The twenty-first-century Caribbean aesthetic depends less on a lived geography than on a distinctive perspective on history, a perspective that reflects the creole nature of Caribbean societies. So we have been fairly flexible as regards our definition of a Caribbean writer, considering work by any writer with Caribbean connections whose work somehow 'spoke to' Caribbean experience—as broad and imprecise a concept as that is.

The collection begins with Saint-John Perse (1887–1975), whose poems spring mostly from the relationship between landscape (seascape) and the educated imagination, a relationship that continues to spawn Caribbean poems in the twenty-first century. The Crusoe images of Perse, the Caribbean's first recipient of the Nobel Prize for Literature, were taken up by the Caribbean's most recent Nobel poet, Derek Walcott (in *The Castaway*, for example), who paid tribute to Perse in his Nobel lecture. Walcott's work has always reflected a similar awareness of a 'literary' past inherited from Europe, and of the Caribbean landscape in which it must be accommodated and re-interpreted. A large number of Caribbean poems focus on the physical landscapes of islands and sea and the way these condition and clarify the experience of life. Frank Collymore (in 'Hymn to the Sea', included here), Phyllis Shand Allfrey, Eric Roach, Bruce St. John, Edward Baugh—are all poets in the collection for whom the seascape is an important dimension of their work. Lloyd W. Brown, in *West Indian Poetry*, argues that there is the tendency in earlier writing about the Caribbean to 'perceive the West Indies as mere landscape', in 'unimaginative imitation of popular literary forms of Western Europe'.[5] And in 'The Starapple Kingdom' Walcott reminds us that the picturesque—the 'faded old daguerreotypes' he discusses—is often more important, in the Caribbean context, for what it masks or excludes, for what lies 'beyond its edges', than for what it actually portrays. Excluded are the 'groom' and the yard-boy and the other servants representing the poverty and oppression which enable and at the same time belie the luxury and calm suggested in the picturesque.

Much Caribbean poetry draws attention precisely to that oppression and suffering; to shifting the perspective from that of the comfortable master to that of the marginalized and oppressed colonial subject, the descendant of slaves. To counter the entrenched power and the hegemonic structures of European colonialism in the Caribbean, poets and other intellectuals are drawn towards groups and movements established to oppose these and to voice the claims and concerns of those marginalized within the prevailing political and economic order. Thus the Jamaican poet Claude McKay, the first English-speaking Caribbean poet to achieve international recognition, was one of the leaders of the Harlem Renaissance, perhaps the most prominent black American cultural movement of the twentieth century. McKay did not only write poems of black protest, notably 'If We Must Die' (not included here), which was read into the US *Congressional Record* as an example of 'Negro extremism',[6] but also poems set in Jamaica which expressed his nostalgia for the rural landscapes of the island and his indignation at the treatment of the urban poor—both of which become important themes in later Jamaican poetry, in the work, for example, of Gloria Escoffery, Olive Senior, and Lorna Goodison, on the one hand, and Anthony McNeil, Mutabaruka, and Mikey Smith on the other.

Another such seminal figure, from the French Caribbean, is Aimé Césaire, the Martiniquan poet and politician who founded, together with Leopold Sédar Senghor of Senegal and Léon-Gontran Damas of French Guiana, the hugely influential 'Négritude' movement while they were students in Paris, publishing the journal *L'Étudiant noir*. Négritude, for all its flaws when viewed from perspectives within the Caribbean region, was one of the first clarion calls for people of Africa and the diaspora to recognize and take pride in their race and origin and to resist the oppression of the European colonizers. These concerns are reflected in the poetry of Césaire, where they are often heightened by a wonderfully effective and authoritative poetic voice ('Return to my Native Land'), and of Damas, whose poetic style is spare, often cryptic, and enlivened with staccato rhythms. There can hardly have been a French Caribbean poet, in the years and generations since, who has not been influenced by the Négritude movement, and the effect has been almost as powerful on the poets writing in the other languages. This influence can be seen in the work of Guy Tirolien (represented here by 'Ghetto'), René Dépestre ('Black Ore'), and Édouard Glissant. It is also discernible in the work of Derek Walcott and, especially, Kamau Brathwaite.

In all the linguistic groups of the Caribbean there occurred, in the few decades around the Second World War, a remarkable (and remarkably coincident, given the separation of the islands by language) intellectual awakening to Africa as origin and spiritual home. Nicolás Guillén in Cuba and Luis Palés Matos in Puerto Rico focused their attention and creative energy on the presence of 'Africa' in the societies in which they lived and wrote. Guillén was associated from early on with the Afro-Cuban movement ('Sociedad des estudios afrocubanos') and quickly became its first authentic Afro-Cuban voice. He wrote, in the Prologue of the collection *Sóngoro cosongo* (1931):

I am not unaware of the fact that these verses will be repugnant to many persons, because they deal with issues concerning Blacks, but that does not matter to me. Rather, I am happy.[7]

Guillén's poetry is replete with references to Africa, from litanies of the names of tribes, to references to Santería, to expressions of solidarity with African peoples fighting for freedom, to more personal identifications with Africa, as in 'Ballad of the Two Grandfathers' (included here), a topic taken up by Derek Walcott in a poem of a similar title (not included here). Similarly, Palés Matos is credited with the re-introduction of 'Africanism' in Puerto Rican poetry.

Kamau Brathwaite, a professor of history as well as a poet, has lived and worked in Ghana and has conducted perhaps the deepest and most careful poetic exploration of Afro-Caribbean 'roots' in his poetry, especially in his trilogy *The Arrivants*. This is a haunting account of the black man's original journey across the continent, the rise of West African civilizations, the encounter with the slave trade, and the middle passage and life on the Caribbean islands and the continental mainland—including a look at what the Jamaican poet Louise Bennett calls 'colonization in reverse', the waves of black migration to the metropolitan cities of Europe and North America. Brathwaite not only expresses this African nexus in his poetry, but also reflects critically on it in several of his essays. In 'The African Presence in Caribbean Literature',[8] for example, he discusses four different kinds or levels of response to 'Africa' in Caribbean writing: from the merely 'rhetorical' to 'the literature of recognition', and he illustrates his argument with quotations from the literature. He sees Jacques Roumain's 'Guinée' ('Guinea', included here) as conforming to the 'rhetorical' model, and the poetry of Nicolás Guillén and Louise Bennett, as well as his own, as demonstrating other levels of the response to Africa. Vera Bell's 'Ancestor on the Auction Block' (included in this anthology) he sees as an example of 'the literature of African survival'. Brathwaite thus establishes, in critical argument and poetic illustration, the central importance of Africa in Caribbean poetry, and it is probably true to say that some aspect of this concern is present in the work of a large majority of the poets here, including: Eric Roach, George Campbell, Andrew Salkey, Slade Hopkinson, Frank Martinus Arion, Edward Baugh, Dennis Scott, Opal Palmer Adisa, Nancy Morejón, Grace Nichols, and Mutabaruka.

Brathwaite's poems and critical writings have also influenced Caribbean poetry in the area of language, in two senses. First, there is the question of poetic language and form; the growing awareness of Africa as ancestral/spiritual home can give rise to an instinct to rupture or subvert the conventional forms of poetry and the decorum of traditional poetic language. In this context Brathwaite has discussed the improvisations of jazz as applied to poetry, and his own work demonstrates the effective use of variations and incremental repetitions of sounds; the African drum, the jazz trumpet, and other instruments can frequently be heard in his poems. In addition, the visual impact of the lines of poetry on the page can be arresting and unusual. Both of these techniques are imitated by younger poets. Brathwaite's more recent poetry has taken these methods to another level, with the use of varying computer fonts, font sizes, and symbols. Some of this is reminiscent of Guillén's exuberant repetitions of African words and sounds in imitation of the drum, and his use of the 'son' as a rhythmic vehicle for his poetic expression. Related to all this is the jazz and performance poetry of poets such as Shake Keane (represented here by 'Shaker Funeral' and 'Soufrière'); Louise Bennett, who performs her dialect poems to packed audiences (represented here by 'Dutty Tough' and 'Jamaica Oman'); the call-and-response dialect poems of Bruce St. John; and the work of the dub poets: Mutabaruka ('dis poem'), Linton Kwesi Johnson ('Dread Beat An Blood'), Michael Smith ('Mi Cyaan Believe It'), and Jean 'Binta' Breeze ('Riddym Ravings'). The sample of 'performance' poems in this anthology, including those mentioned above, suggests the power and prominence of this particular form of working with words within the broad range of styles adopted by contemporary Caribbean poets.

The other area of Caribbean language in which Brathwaite has been influential is that of what he calls 'Nation Language'—the various creoles of the Caribbean. Brathwaite's writings on the subject have made discussions about language more common and more available, and the phrase he coined is very widely used these days, but all this should perhaps be seen in a wider context. At various but proximate times around mid-century—and as part of the awakening to origins and identity—there arose a concern with identifying and documenting the spoken languages of Caribbean peoples. It was a highly charged topic, because the ability to speak properly the European languages was highly prized in colonial societies as a key to acceptance and upward social mobility; any move towards recognizing the validity of local dialects or patois was viewed with great suspicion, especially in education, where it was considered as an undermining of the potential advancement of Caribbean students. Nevertheless, lists and pamphlets began to appear in various islands—glossaries of creole words and expressions. Some of these were brief and informal, others more ambitious and detailed. One thinks of Frank Collymore's 'Glossary of Words and Phrases in Barbadian Dialect', which appeared in several issues of the magazine *Bim* from 1952, and of the later work in Jamaica of Cassidy and Le Page, which resulted in the *Dictionary of Jamaican English* in 1967.[9] It will probably be some time before as many people in the English-speaking Caribbean become as fully literate in their creole languages as in, say, the French Caribbean, but it is clear that a start has been made. In 1996 Richard Allsopp published his *Oxford Dictionary of Caribbean English Usage*,[10] which is quickly and steadily enhancing its reputation as an important tool and resource, not only for Caribbean writers and students, but also in many households across the region.

Apart from the performance poets and a few others who write predominantly in creole, others use that end of the Caribbean language continuum most tellingly for special effects within their work, in which the creole works partly through its sharp contrast with the language in the rest of the poem(s). This is true of Walcott, for example, in one of the sonnets of his early sequence, 'Tales of the Islands' ('Poopa da' was a fête'), or again in the way the calypsonian, the Mighty Spoiler, resurrected from Hell, is brought wonderfully to life in a dramatic monologue in Trinidadian creole in Walcott's much later poem 'The Spoiler's Return'. Trinidadian creole is also an important aspect of 'The Schooner Flight', the long poem by which Walcott is represented here. Another example of the use of creole to reveal character in a dramatic monologue is Edward Baugh's 'The Carpenter's Complaint' (included here).

Often the creole can be used to great effect in just a few words or phrases within a poem, as in some of the poems of Martin Carter, or in Mervyn Morris's 'Valley Prince' (included here). In some poems the effect of the creole is achieved through the incongruity between the solemnity of the situation or occasion being described and the language in which it is rendered. An extended example of this is Pam Mordecai's *De Man*, which is a creole rendering of the Passion of Christ. A more specialized creole, perhaps, is that of the Rastafarians, and this too finds its way into the work of several poets, represented here.

In many of the islands of the English-speaking Caribbean, there existed, long before independence, 'literary' groups and circles, which tended to be peopled by 'colonial' writers who remained externally focused, taking their cues from what was fashionable in the mother-country—and therefore very careful about the subjects, forms, and 'rules' of good poetry. Perhaps the best known of these was the Poetry League of Jamaica, led by J. E. Clare McFarlane and a subsidiary of the Empire Poetry League. One member of the Poetry League whose work is included here is Vivian Virtue; his poem, 'Landscape Painter, Jamaica', embodies the two most important values of the group, the beauty of nature and the desire to produce distinctively Jamaican poetry. With the political awakening of the 1930s and 1940s, and as the younger writers grew restless and needed to express their political views and commitments, new literary groups and movements arose to challenge, or simply supersede, what might have existed in the past. In the case of Jamaica, it was the *Focus* group—centred around Edna Manley—which published (beginning in 1943) the literary magazine *Focus*. *Focus* celebrated the new poetry of awakened social consciousness. Several of the poets included in this anthology were associated with *Focus* including George Campbell, Basil McFarlane (the son of Clare), and A. L. Hendriks. Of the three, Campbell's was the strongest voice, both politically and in terms of poetic craft, as can be seen in 'Negro Aroused' (included here).

The earliest of the literary magazines to be produced by a group of politically informed Caribbean writers were *Trinidad* and *The Beacon* (1929–1933) in Trinidad, centred around the figures of C. L. R. James, George Mendes, and Albert Gomes. Although 30 issues were published in all (2 of *Trinidad* and 28 of *The Beacon*), these were more important for the prose fiction and the political opinion published than for poetry—and indeed the three figures mentioned all went on to write novels. The political fervour of the *Beacon* movement, however, fed into the labour movement in the oilfields in the late 1930s, which was part of the Caribbean-wide upheaval that launched the march towards independence.

The most important—and the most enduring—of the little literary magazines that arose in this period were *Kyk-Over-Al*, in Guyana, edited by the poet A. J. Seymour from 1945 to 1961 and then revived in the 1980s by Seymour and Ian McDonald, and *Bim* in Barbados, edited by Frank Collymore (and later John Wickham) from the 1940s through to the 1990s. *Kyk-Over-Al* and *Bim* published submissions from Caribbean writers working either within or outside of Guyana and Barbados, respectively, and they were responsible for facilitating the literary development of a generation of Caribbean writers, especially poets. Walcott and Brathwaite were published in *Bim* in their early days, and Wilson Harris and (especially) Martin Carter in *Kyk-Over-Al*, along with many others. At roughly the same time that these magazines were launched in the Caribbean, there also began the 'Caribbean Voices' series of broadcasts by the BBC in London, under the direction of Henry Swanzy. This was an important outlet, affording a greatly enlarged audience for readings of the work of many Caribbean writers, both those 'in exile' in London and those still at home in the islands and territories of the West Indies.

The success of the BBC's 'Caribbean Voices' programme was due in part to the large number of Caribbean writers living in London at the time, and in fact 'exile' from the Caribbean had been an important feature of the literature and its creation and publication from the very beginning. Perhaps the term 'exile' is not as relevant for all Caribbean writers: the French writers from Martinique and Guadeloupe who lived, studied, and worked in France, for example, did not technically leave their countries, since these islands are 'overseas departments' of France. It is nevertheless true, however, that in the heady years around the mid-century, it was necessary for such writers to travel to metropolitan France in order to meet fellow writers and to realize their ambition to publish their work. There is a sense in which several writers only discovered the 'West Indies' or 'the Caribbean' after they had travelled to the metropole. A 'West Indian community' in the sense of a group from various islands living together and meeting and interacting was possible only in metropolitan cities—such as London in the 1950s, when 'Caribbean Voices' was at its height.

We have already seen that early poets such as Saint-John Perse and Claude McKay did most of their writing—and achieved their reputations—abroad: Perse was twice an exile, so to speak, since he fled to the USA from war-time France. Nicolás Guillén was, for a time, a member of the famous colony of exiled writers in pre-World War II Paris. Césaire and Damas started their journal and their careers as poets in Paris, and Kamau Brathwaite was a student in Cambridge and went on to live in Ghana before returning to the Caribbean. The only major stay-at-home poets of the Anglophone Caribbean who came into prominence in the mid-century were Derek Walcott and Martin Carter: Walcott studied at the then new University College of the West Indies in Jamaica, before living for several years in Trinidad (a kind of internal exile, perhaps); and much of Carter's poetry grew out of his participation in an unfolding political drama in Guyana.

It is important to remember that most of the 'exiled' poets of the Caribbean—especially those from the English-speaking islands—were not romantic wanderers, but rather, along with hoards of other migrants at the time seeking employment and a better life in New York and London, they were in quest of a market for their skills and talents, as there was no commercial literary publishing in the West Indies at the time. Nevertheless, there were a few poets from the non-English-speaking Caribbean who could be said to have been forced into exile by circumstances at home. Among these was Pedro Mir of the Dominican Republic, who fled the Trujillo dictatorship and lived for several years in Cuba, Mexico, and Guatemala before returning home to become his country's official 'national' poet in 1984. He is represented here by the poem 'Meditation on the Shores of Evening'. Somewhat similar was the experience of René Dépestre of Haiti, a spokesman for the radical young generation in the 1940s and 1950s and a writer of polemical Marxist poetry, who was forced to flee the Duvalier regime in his homeland. He moved to Cuba in 1958, where he helped found the *Casa de las américas* organization. More recently several Cuban poets—at odds for various reasons with the Castro regime—have settled 'in exile' elsewhere, most notably of course in Miami.

There came a time, after independence, when several Jamaican poets felt that they had to leave home with their families because life had become very difficult under the socialist government of Michael Manley in the 1970s; poets who had established their reputations in Kingston literary circles, notably George Campbell and Vivian Virtue, ended up living (and in many cases, dying) abroad. It is ironic that some of the more nationalistic poetic voices—of those who contributed to the struggle for independence—ceased to be heard in political and literary circles in their independent homelands. It is true today that Caribbean poets living and writing abroad far outnumber those who remain at home—although the reasons for exile may have changed somewhat in the last quarter of the twentieth century.

After the break-up of the ill-fated West Indian Federation in 1962 (the poet Phyllis Shand Allfrey of Dominica was a member of the Federal cabinet), the larger West Indian territories, Jamaica, Trinidad, Guyana, and Barbados, all achieved independence by 1966, with the smaller islands following suit at various dates during the next decade and a half. Montserrat, represented here by the poets Howard Fergus and E. A. Markham, along with a very few smaller islands and groups of islands, are the only remaining British territories in the Caribbean—although they all enjoy some kind of internal self-government.

In addition to the Jamaican example mentioned above, independent Guyana, under the Forbes Burnham regime, also proved to be unfriendly to large numbers of its inhabitants, who departed in droves, mostly for North American destinations and for London—but also, in some cases, for more prosperous and stable neighbouring Caribbean islands. These emigrants included several poets whose work appears in this anthology: Michael Gilkes, Cyril Dabydeen, Slade Hopkinson, David Dabydeen, Fred D'Aguiar, John Agard, Grace Nichols, Brian Chan, Mark Mathews, and Mark McWatt.

Independence should not be seen, however, only in terms of these negative aspects. One positive outcome was that independence seemed to herald an extraordinary chorus of women's voices in all areas of creative writing. These included several fine poets who achieved recognition and prominence in the 1970s and thereafter. With very few exceptions (most notably the Jamaican Louise Bennett, who has been actively crafting and—one way or another—publishing her poems since the 1940s), West Indian poetry was dominated by men through most of the twentieth century. That in itself isn't so surprising, given what we know about attitudes towards gender roles, access to education, control of publishing opportunities, and so on. What is so strik-ing is that in the last couple of decades so many powerful and accom-plished women poets should have emerged on the West Indian poetic stage: Lorna Goodison, Grace Nichols, Jean 'Binta' Breeze, Merle Col-lins, Olive Senior, Mahadai Das, Velma Pollard, and Marlene Nourbese Philip, to name just some who have established international reputa-tions. Together they have certainly changed the focus and the tenor of West Indian poetry. That said, the themes and issues that have pre-occupied West Indian poets over time—history, exile, identity, roots, landscape, childhood, race—remain as primary concerns, but are now presented from different perspectives and augmented by other themes directly linked with women's experience and values, including ques-tions around gender itself.

But women's voices have been heard in Caribbean poetry from the outset, beginning, perhaps, with Una Marson in the 1930s. Hers was a distinctive and important female voice, as she was an innovator who did not shy away from explicit references to race in her work, and in fact Philip Sherlock at the time considered that it was she who first raised this 'new issue'.[11] Alongside Louise Bennett in Jamaica, there was also Vera Bell, another strong feminine voice, concerned with the past and with racial identity. The Puerto Rican poet Julia de Burgos was also a controversial nationalist and feminist figure who flouted the rules of social decorum long before the women's movement got going in the 1960s. She is represented here by the poems 'To Julia de Burgos' and 'Poem with the Final Tune'. Thus the full flowering of the female poetic voice in the 1970s did not spring from nowhere, but rather those poets were building on and amplifying a clear and significant minor strain present in Caribbean written poetry from the beginning. Per-haps too it was the rediscovery—as it were—of the voice, the spoken word, the oral tradition, which had for so long been disregarded by the literary 'great tradition', that helped direct attention to the areas of 'word culture' that women had nurtured and developed over the centuries.

Certainly two of the most prominent and accomplished of the con-temporary women poets of the Caribbean, Nancy Morejón of Cuba and the Jamaican Lorna Goodison, have been very aware of the oral dimension of Caribbean word culture. Morejón grew to maturity as the Cuban revolution was taking root and her poems, though never strident, express her strong commitment to the revolution and to the importance of the women within it. In both poets there is a strong sense of shared experience with the poor and oppressed and an unself-conscious mastery of poetic form and language. Another important poet in this category is Olive Senior, who is also one of the Caribbean's leading writers of short stories. Her poems here include the wonderful 'Thirteen Ways of Looking at Blackbird (after Wallace Stevens)'. Other significant contributors to the sense one has of the dominance of women's voices in the Caribbean poetry of the later years of the century are Merle Collins ('Nearly Ten Years Later'), Grace Nichols ('The Fat Black Woman Remembers' and 'Blackout'), Jane King ('Fellow Traveller'), Pam Mordecai ('Last Lines'), and Velma Pollard ('Beware the Naked Man Who Offers You a Shirt').

Another positive outcome of independence, and the nationalism it fostered in the English-speaking islands, is the fact that there has been the institution of national and regional cultural festivals which celebrate the creative and performing arts of the Caribbean. Perhaps the most important of these is *Carifesta*, a regional festival of the arts, the first of which took place in Guyana in 1972. The plan was to have the festival at regular intervals and in different islands as a permanent institution, but some governments found it difficult to finance the event in times of economic downturn, and although there have been subsequent *Carifestas* in Trinidad, Barbados, Jamaica, and even Cuba, these have not all followed the proposed regular schedule, and most people agree that the initial festival in Guyana was the best. This was the first event to bring together writers, artists, musicians, and performers from the various language groups of the Caribbean for a week-long celebration of the arts. At least two of these festivals produced important anthologies of creative writing,[12] and they generated a pan-Caribbean literary awareness and creative ferment, especially among the young 'performance' poets, who were travelling to display their wares for the first time, and whose work was well suited to the format of the festival. *Carifesta*, along with regular national festivals of the arts in some islands, helped to promote and popularize poetry as public performance. The eventual nexus with the recording industry has now, particularly in metropolitan cities, begun to produce CDs, such as the re-issue of Linton Kwesi Johnson's 'Dread Beat and Blood' CD on the *Caroline* label in 2001.

In introducing this anthology, with its predominant emphasis on black Caribbean writers and their history, identity, and concerns, it is important to draw attention also to a growing number of Indo-Caribbean poets and their works, emerging mostly in Trinidad and

Guyana, where large percentages of the population (52 per cent in Guyana) are the descendants of Indian indentured labourers who arrived to work on the sugar plantations after emancipation. Indo-Caribbean writers of fiction, such as V. S. Naipaul, Samuel Selvon, Shiva Naipaul, Ismith Khan, Neil Bisoondath, and David Dabydeen (all but the last-named from Trinidad), have risen to greater regional and international prominence than their counterparts who write mainly poetry, although the poets may have had an earlier start. There was an *Anthology of Indian Verse* published in Guyana in 1934, edited by C. E. J. Ramcharitar-Lalla, although none of the poets therein are included here—or indeed much remembered today. Rooplal Monar (represented here by 'The Cowherd') has lived mostly in Guyana, just as his counterpart Jit Narain ('Working all day, dreaming at night') has remained in Surinam, but most of the others live in England or Canada. Perhaps the most important of these is David Dabydeen (also a recognized novelist), who left Guyana for England at the age of twelve, and whose first collection, 'Slave Song', won the Commonwealth Poetry Prize in 1984. 'Coolie Odyssey', the long title-poem of his second collection (1988, and included here), is an evocation of Indo-Caribbean historical and contemporary experience, somewhat along the lines of Brathwaite's first trilogy. Cyril Dabydeen ('Returning') and Sasenarine Persaud ('Postcard to a Sister in South America') live and write in Toronto. Three important Indo-Caribbean women's voices are Trinidadians Rajandaye Ramkissoon-Chen ('Still My Teacher') and Jennifer Rahim ('Leaving the Coast'); and, from Guyana, Mahadai Das ('They Came in Ships').

Even if it might be considered then, given this range of cultural contexts and histories, that this is a collection in which poems have been somewhat randomly chained together, like a coffle of slaves moving uphill into the cane-field at dawn (to choose a metaphor from Caribbean history), then perhaps that too is appropriate, as it echoes the fortuitously chosen ingredients that have resulted in Caribbean societies. Also, as some writers have told us, such coffles of chained beings, as they moved into the fields of the past, were known to voice their feelings in song. Might one not hope, therefore, that in this particular singing coffle the authentic voice of the Caribbean will be heard and recognized? For if anything can be said to define Caribbean poetry—including the work of the poets represented in this anthology—it is their sense of an engagement with the diverse and often hidden sources of Caribbean history and culture, and the determination to refashion those materials into a poetry that speaks of and into the present in voices that the peoples of the region would recognize as their own.

It is timely, then, at the beginning of the twenty-first century, that there should be a major anthology 'validating'—in the way that (for better or worse) an 'Oxford Book of . . .' still does—the region that has produced what is arguably the most vigorous and exciting body of poetry in our time.

NOTES

1 The phrase is somewhat contentious but part of the current critical/theoretical debate. See particularly Jahan Ramazani, *The Hybrid Muse: Postcolonial Poetry in English* (Chicago: University of Chicago Press, 2001).

2 See Mittelholzer's poem 'Island Tints' in the anthology *Caribbean Voices* edited by John Figueroa (London: Evans, 1971). See also Mittelholzer's autobiography of a Guyanese childhood, *A Swarthy Boy* (London: Putnam, 1963).

3 In addition to those colonial languages it is important to acknowledge the other languages of the Caribbean: the Amerindian languages still spoken in Guyana and a few of the islands; the East Indian and Chinese languages retained by the descendants of the indentured labourers who came to the Caribbean at the end of the nineteenth century, and the creole languages of the former Dutch colonies, such as Papiamento and Sranan. All across the Caribbean the languages of life are predominantly creoles evolved from the meeting of the European colonial languages and the African languages spoken by the slaves brought to the region over three hundred years.

4 Edward Brathwaite, *Contradictory Omens* (Mona, Jamaica: Savacou Publications, 1974). See also Bridget Jones' essay ' "The unity is submarine": aspects of a pan-Caribbean consciousness in the work of Kamau Brathwaite', in S. Brown (ed.), *The Art of Kamau Brathwaite* (Bridgend: Seren Books, 1995).

5 Lloyd W. Brown, *West Indian Poetry* (Boston: Twayne, 1978).

6 By senator Henry Cabot Lodge Senior in 1919: see Lloyd W. Brown in *op. cit.*

7 Nicolás Guillén, Prologue to *Sóngoro cosongo* in Richard Jackson, *Black Writers and the Hispanic Canon* (New York: Twayne, 1997), p.83.

8 Kamau Brathwaite, in *Roots* (Ann Arbor: University of Michigan Press, 1993).

9 F. G. Cassidy and R. B. Le Page, *A Dictionary of Jamaican English* (Cambridge: Cambridge University Press, 1967).

10 Richard Allsopp, *Oxford Dictionary of Caribbean English Usage* (Oxford: Oxford University Press, 1996).

11 Philip Sherlock, in his Introduction to Una Marson's *The Moth and the Star*, quoted by Laurence A. Breiner in *An Introduction to West Indian Poetry* (Cambridge: Cambridge University Press, 1998), p.154.

12 *Carifesta'72: New Writing in the Caribbean,* edited by A. J. Seymour (George-
town, Guyana: Lithographic Co., 1972); and *Carifesta Forum: An Anthology of
20 Caribbean Voices,* edited and with an introduction by John Hearne (King-
ston: Institute of Jamaica, 1976).

The Oxford Book of

CARIBBEAN
VERSE

SAINT-JOHN PERSE

1887–1975

from *Pictures for Crusoe*

Translated by Louise Varese

The Bells

Old man with naked hands,
   cast up among men again, Crusoe!
   you wept, I imagine, when from the Abbey towers, like a tide, the
sob of the bells poured over the City . . .
   O Despoiled!
   You wept to remember the surf in the moonlight; the whistlings of
the more distant shores; the strange music that is born and is muffled
under the folded wing of the night,
   like the linked circles that are the waves of a conch, or the amplifica-
tions of the clamours under the sea . . .

The Wall

The stretch of wall is across the way to break the circle of your dream.
   But the image cries out.
   Your head against one wing of the greasy armchair, you explore your
teeth with your tongue: the taste of grease and of sauces taints your
gums.
   And you dream of the pure clouds over your island, when green
dawn grows clear on the breast of the mysterious waters.
   . . . It is the sweat of saps in exile, the bitter oozings of plants with
long pods, the acrid insinuation of fleshy mangroves, and the acid
delight of a black substance within the pods.
   It is the wild honey of ants in the galleries of the dead tree.
   It is the sour taste of green fruit in the dawn that you drink; the air,
milky and spiced with the salt of the trade winds . . .
   Joy! o joy set free in the heights of the sky! Pure linens are resplen-
dent, invisible parvises are strewn with grasses and leaves, and the
green delights of the earth are painted on the century of a long day . . .

3

The City

Slate covers the roofs, or else tiles where mosses grow.
　Their breath flows out through the chimneys.
　Grease!
　Odour of men in crowds, like the stale smell of a slaughter-house!
sour bodies of women under their skirts!
　O City against the sky!
　Grease! breaths rebreathed, and the smoke of a polluted people—for
every city encompasses filth.

On the dormer-window of the little shop—on the garbage cans of
the poor house—on the odour of cheap wine in the sailors' quarter—
on the fountain sobbing in the police courtyards—on the statues of
mouldy stone and on stray dogs—on the little boy whistling, and the
beggar whose cheeks tremble in the hollow of his jaws,
　on the sick cat with three wrinkles on its forehead,
　the evening descends, in the smoke of men . . .
　—The City like an abscess flows through the river to the sea . . .

Crusoe!—this evening over your Island, the sky drawing near will
give praise to the sea, and the silence will multiply the exclamation of
the solitary stars.
　Draw the curtains; do not light the lamp:

It is evening on your Island and all around, here and there, wherever
arches the faultless vase of the sea; it is evening the colour of eyelids, on
roads woven of sky and of sea.
　Everything is salty, everything is viscous and heavy like the life of
plasmas.
　The bird rocks itself in its feathers, in an oily dream; the hollow
fruit, deafened by insects, falls into the water of the creeks, probing its
noise.
　The island falls asleep in the arena of vast waters, washed by warm
currents and unctuous milt, in the embrace of sumptuous slime.
　Under the propagating mangroves, slow fishes in the mud have dis-
charged bubbles with their flat heads; and others that are slow, spotted
like reptiles, keep watch.—The slime is fecundated—Hear the hollow
creatures rattling in their shells—Against a bit of green sky there is a

sudden puff of smoke which is the tangled flight of mosquitos—The crickets under the leaves are gently calling to each other—And other gentle creatures, heedful of the night, sing a song purer than the signs of the coming rains: it is the swallowing of two pearls swelling their yellow gullets . . .

Wailing of waters swirling and luminous!

Corollas, mouths of watered silks: mourning that breaks and blossoms! Big moving flowers on a journey, flowers alive forever, and that will not cease to grow throughout the world . . .

O the colour of the winds circling over the calm waters,

the palm-leaves of the palm-trees that stir!

And no distant barking of a single dog that means a hut; that means a hut and the evening smoke and the three black stones under the odour of pimentoes.

But the bats stipple the soft evening with little cries.

Joy! o joy set free in the heights of the sky!

. . . Crusoe! you are there! and your face is proffered to the signs of the night like an upturned palm.

Friday

Laughter in the sun,

ivory! timid kneelings, and your hands on the things of the earth . . .

Friday! how green was the leaf, and your shadow how new, your hands so long toward the earth when, beside the taciturn man, you moved in the light the streaming blue of your limbs!

—Now they have given you a cast-off red coat. You drink the oil of the lamps and steal from the larder; you leer at the skirts of the cook who smells of grease and is fat; you see in the mirroring brass of your livery your eyes grown sly and vicious your laughter.

The Parrot

Here is another.

A stuttering sailor had given him to the old woman who sold him. He is on the landing near the skylight, where the darkness is mixed with the dirty fog of the day, the colour of alleys.

5

At night, with a double cry he greets you, Crusoe, when, coming up from the latrine in the courtyard, you open the door of the passage and hold up the precarious star of your lamp. To turn his eyes, he turns his head. Man with the lamp! what do you want with him? . . . You look at his round eye under the putrid pollen of the lid; you look at the second circle that is like a ring of dead sap. And the sick feather trails in the water of his droppings.

O misery! blow out your lamp. The bird gives his cry.

CLAUDE McKAY
1889–1948

The Harlem Dancer

Applauding youths laughed with young prostitutes
And watched her perfect, half-clothed body sway;
Her voice was like the sound of blended flutes
Blown by black players upon a picnic day.
She sang and danced on gracefully and calm,
The light gauze hanging loose about her form;
To me she seemed a proudly-swaying palm
Grown lovelier for passing through a storm.
Upon her swarthy neck black shiny curls
Luxuriant fell; and tossing coins in praise,
The wine-flushed, bold-eyed boys, and even the girls,
Devoured her shape with eager, passionate gaze;
But looking at her falsely-smiling face,
I knew her self was not in that strange place.

A Midnight Woman to the Bobby

No palm me up, you dutty brute,
You' jam mout' mash like ripe bread-fruit;
You fas'n now, but wait lee ya,
I'll see you grunt under de law.

You t'ink you wise, but we wi' see;
You not de fus' one fas' wid me;
I'll lib fe see dem tu'n you out,
As sure as you got dat mash' mout'.

I born right do'n beneat' de clack
(You ugly brute, you tu'n you' back?)
Don' t'ink dat I'm a come-aroun',
I born right 'way in 'panish Town.

7

Care how you try, you caan' do mo'
Dan many dat was hyah befo';
Yet whe' dey all o' dem te-day?
De buccra dem no kick dem 'way?

Ko 'pon you' jam samplatta nose:
'Cos you wear Mis'r Koshaw clo'es
You t'ink say you's de only man,
Yet fus time ko how you be'n 'tan'.

You big an' ugly ole tu'n-foot
Be'n neber know fe wear a boot;
An' chigger nyam you' tumpa toe,
Till nit full i' like herrin' roe.

You come from mountain naked-'kin,
An' Lard a mussy! you be'n thin,
For all de bread-fruit dem be'n done,
Bein' 'poil' up by de tearin' sun:

De coco couldn' bear at all,
For, Lard! de groun' was pure white-marl;
An' t'rough de rain part o' de year
De mango tree dem couldn' bear.

An' when de pinch o' time you feel
A 'pur you a you' chigger heel,
You lef' you' district, big an' coarse,
An' come join buccra Police Force.

An' now you don't wait fe you' glass
But trouble me wid you' jam fas';
But wait, me frien', you' day wi' come,
I'll see you go same lak a some.

Say wha'?—'res' me? —you go to hell!
You t'ink Judge don't know unno well?
You t'ink him gwin' go sentance me
Widout a soul fe witness i'?

LÉON LALEAU

1892–1979

Betrayal

Translated by Ellen Conroy Kennedy

This haunted heart that doesn't fit
My language or the clothes I wear
Chafes within the grip of
Borrowed feelings, European ways.
Do you feel my pain,
This anguish like none other
From taming with the words of France
This heart that came to me from Senegal?

FRANK COLLYMORE

1893–1980

Hymn to the Sea

Like all who live on small islands
I must always be remembering the sea,
Being always cognizant of her presence; viewing
Her through apertures in the foliage; hearing,
When the wind is from the south, her music, and smelling
The warm rankness of her; tasting
And feeling her kisses on bright sunbathed days:
I must always be remembering the sea.

Always, always the encircling sea,
Eternal: lazylapping, crisscrossed with stillness;
Or windruffed, aglitter with gold; and the surf
Waist-high for children, or horses for Titans;
Her lullaby, her singing, her moaning; on sand,
On shingle, on breakwater, and on rock;
By sunlight, starlight, moonlight, darkness:
I must always be remembering the sea.

Go down to the sea upon this random day
By metalled road, by sandway, by rockpath,
And come to her. Upon the polished jetsam,
Shell and stone and weed and saltfruit
Torn from the underwater continents, cast
Your garments and despondencies; re-enter
Her embracing womb: a return, a completion.
I must always be remembering the sea.

Life came from the sea, and once a goddess arose
Fullgrown from the saltdeep; love
Flows from the sea, a flood; and the food
Of islanders is reaped from the sea's harvest.
And not only life and sustenance; visions, too,
Are born of the sea: the patterning of her rhythm

Finds echoes within the musing mind.
I must always be remembering the sea.

Symbol of fruitfulness, symbol of barrenness,
Mother and destroyer, the calm and the storm!
Life and desire and dreams and death
Are born of the sea; this swarming land
Her creation, her signature set upon the salt ooze
To blossom into life; and the red hibiscus
And the red roofs burn more brightly against her blue.
I must always be remembering the sea.

LUIS PALÉS MATOS

1898–1959

Forbidden Fruit

For the loved one of fire

Translated by Ian Craig

It was the prodigal night of a radiant delirium,
it was a somnolent, fragrant indifference:
the mute indifference of the stars, awake
like a shower of open, winking eyes.

It was a haze of perfume of woman in the garden,
beneath the creeper of white jazmine;
and they, the stars, looked tremblingly upon us;
and the eden of yearnings came sighing;

and desire of first woman came,
and the chaste creeper shuddered in shock;

and in the feverish blaze of our young age,
you undone with scruples, I with ardent love,
we tasted the sweetness of the red apple,
and saw how the serpent whistled with bliss . . .

H. A. VAUGHAN

1901–1985

Revelation

Turn sideways now and let them see
What loveliness escapes the schools,
Then turn again, and smile and be
The perfect answer to those fools
Who always prate of Greece and Rome,
'The face that launched a thousand ships',
And such like things, but keep tight lips
For burnished beauty nearer home.
Turn in the sun, my love, my love!
What palm-like grace! What poise! I swear
I prize thy dusky limbs above
My life. What laughing eyes!
    What gleaming hair!

MARIE-MAGDELEINE CARBET

b. 1902

Would I Deny?

Translated by E. Anthony Hurley

Would I deny, could it be true,
The vermilion of your clay,
Your beaches, your cool shades,
Your smell, your salt, O my island?

Would I be so ungrateful as to forget
Your long casuarinas in music,
The flavor of the midday punch,
The whip of the wind on the Atlantic?

Would I no longer know the song
Of the little crayfish seller,
His catch swarming in his
Shiny woven bamboo basket?

And were I to lower my eyelid,
Would I no longer see the humming bird,
Powdered in a dusty rainbow,
Sucking at the hibiscus' heart?

At my bedtime, my house
Latches would I fasten,
Would I fall asleep in a bed
Under heavy blankets,

Without returning to the calm evenings
Where, in the blue velvet of the air,
Among the rustling of the palms,
The green lighted firefly dances.

It matters little to me to expose
The petty dramas of my life

14

Under this sky of pale loves,
But, to confess nostalgia for you,

My country, kneaded from my flesh,
All sensual in your poverty,
My country, golden sea food
Bathed in azure and in light.

How would I tell of your gentleness,
Your sudden fits of violence?
Where to find the sounds, the colour,
To express your opulence?

Like a woman whose charm
Masks valour and passion,
In your modesty, you want your tears
To adorn your rags with pearls.

You want our laughter, our songs,
Poignant or not, to give rhythm to your life,
And every last one of your children,
Branded with the fire of your genius,

To give proof to the universe
That we, your barefoot bastards,
Are in your trials forging for ourselves
Fierce pride and haughty hearts.

NICOLÁS GUILLÉN

1902–1987

from *The Great Zoo*

Translated by Robert Marquez

Senora

This enormous lady
was harpooned in the street

The daring fisherman who caught her
looked forward to her oil,
her slender and flexible down,
to her fat . . . (*to carving her skillfully*).

Here she is.

Convalescing.

The Usurers

Ornithomorphous monsters
in wide black cages,
the usurers.

There is the White Crested (*Great Royal Usurer*)
and the Buzzard Usurer, of the open plains,
and the Common Torpedo, that devours its offspring,
and the ash-colored Daggertail,
that devours its parents,
and the Vampire Merganser,
that sucks blood and flies over the ocean.

In the forced leisure
of their enormous black cages,
the usurers count and recount their feathers
and lend them to one another for a fee.

Hunger

This is hunger. An animal
all fangs and eyes.
It cannot be distracted or deceived.
It is not satisfied with one meal.
It is not content
with a lunch or a dinner.
Always threatens blood.
Roars like a lion, squeezes like a boa,
thinks like a person.

The specimen before you
was captured in India (*outskirts of Bombay*)
but it exists in a more or less savage state
in many other places.

Please stand back.

Cyclone

A thoroughbred cyclone,
recently arrived in Cuba from the Bahama Islands.
It was raised in Bermuda,
but has relatives in Barbados.
It has been to Puerto Rico.
It tore the great Jamaican palm up by the roots.
It was going to ravage Guadeloupe.
It succeeded in ravaging Martinique.

Age: two days.

KKK

This quadruped originates
in Joplin, Missouri.
Carnivorous.

It howls long in the night
without its usual diet of roast Negro.

It will eventually succumb.
Feeding it is a *(n insoluble)* problem.

*　　　*　　　*

Bars

Translated by Robert Marquez

I love those bars and taverns
by the sea,
where people chat and drink
merely to drink and chat.
Where John Nobody goes and asks
for his favorite drink,
where you'll find John Rowdy and John Blade
and John Nosey and even John
Simple, that's all, simply
John.

There the white wave
foams in friendship,
the friendship of the people, without rhetoric,
a wave of 'Hey there!' and 'How ya doin'?'
There it smells of fish,
of mangroves, of rum, of salt,
and sweaty shirts hung in the sun to dry.

Look for me, brother, and you will find me
(in Havana, in Oporto,
in Jacmel, in Shanghai)
with the ordinary people
who merely to drink and chat,
fill the bars and taverns
by the sea.

NICOLÁS GUILLÉN

Ballad of the Two Grandfathers

Translated by Jill Netchinsky

Shadows I alone can see,
my two grandfathers go with me.

Skin drum of wood, bone-pointed spear:
my black grandfather.
Broad neck with ruff, gray battle gear:
my white grandfather.

Torso rockhard, and feet are bare,
those of the black;
antarctic glass from pupils stare,
those of the white.

Africa of the humid forests
and the great, stilled gongs . . .
'I'm dying!'
(says my black grandfather.)
Waters dark with alligators,
mornings green with coco-palms
'I'm tiring!'
(says my white grandfather.)
Oh bitter wind that fills the sails,
oh galleon burning gold
'I'm dying!'
(says my black grandfather.)
Oh glass beads hung in deceit
'round necks of virgin coasts
'I'm tiring!'
(says my white grandfather.)
Oh pure metal-hammered sun
Imprisoned in the tropics' ring;
oh round, clear moon
above the monkeys' dream!

So many ships, so many ships!
So many Blacks, so many Blacks!
Such vast glow of sugarcane!

Such a whip has the slaver!
Rock of grieving and of blood,
and half-opened veins and eyes,
and empty dawns,
and sugarmill dusks,
and a great voice, strong voice,
shattering the silence.
So many ships, so many ships,
so many Blacks!

Shadows I alone can see,
my two grandfathers go with me.

Don Federico shouting,
and Taita Facundo hushed;
both dreaming in the night,
they walk, they walk.
I unite them.

       —Federico!
Facundo! The two embrace.
The two of them sigh.
Two strong heads raised,
both the same size,
beneath stars on high;
both the same size,
black anguish, white anguish,
both the same size,
they shout, they dream, they cry, they sing.
They dream, cry, sing.
They sing!

Wake for Papa Montero
to Vincent Martinez

Translated by Langston Hughes

You burned the dawn
with the flame of your guitar,
juice of the sweet cane in the gourd

of your dusky quick flesh
beneath a dead, white moon!

Music poured from you
as round and mulatto as a plum.

Drinker of tall drinks,
gullet of tin,
boat cut loose in a sea of rum,
horseman of the wild party:
what will you do with the night
now that you can no longer drink it,
and what vein will give you back
the blood you've lost,
gone down the black
drain of a knife wound?

They certainly got you this time,
Papa Montero!

They were waiting for you in the tenement,
but they brought you home dead;
it was a drunken brawl,
but they brought you home dead;
they say he was your pal,
but they brought you home dead . . .
nobody could find the knife,
but they brought you home dead . . .
Baldomero's done for—
Attaboy, you old dancing devil!

Only two candles are
burning a little of the shadow;
for your humble death
two candles are too many.
But brighter than the candles
is the red shirt
that lighted your songs,
the dark salt of your music,
your glossy straightened hair!

They certainly got you this time,
Papa Montero!

Today the moon dawned
in the courtyard of my house;
it fell blade-wise to earth,
and there it stuck.
The kids picked it up
and washed its face,
so I bring it tonight
to be your pillow!

PHILIP SHERLOCK

1902–2000

Trees His Testament

Trees his testament
Daley's dead; dust now, gone for good
Far over Jordan side
Left his body this side.
Of the cold river,
Dead now, gone for good
Nobody see him till Kingdom come
And the trumpet call beyond the river
And the roll call.
Gone for good,
Lips greedy once for a woman's breast
Still now and silent
Pasture for the worm
Then dust.

Daley was a plumber,
Served his time to Hard Up,
Hungry Belly walked beside him
Never left him quiet
Through the slum he had for home
From door to door he asked
If they wanted toilets fixed
And they laughed for the toilet wasn't theirs anyway
Walked and tramped from door to door
Raising cash for peace of mind,
Pocket full is belly full
Belly full is peace of mind.
Hungry Belly never left him,
Grinned and gnawed and never left him
Who would mend what wasn't his anyway?
Plumber's dead now, gone for good
Daley's dead.

Hungry Belly restless talked
When he saw his Daley buy

Paint and canvas for a picture
For a picture when a plumber had to live
But the painter was a-seeking
For the something that he couldn't tell about
That he knew inside himself he must search and search
     and find.
Knock and knock until he find
Past the questions and divisions
Past the doubtings and the troubles
Past the doors and rows of doors
Till at last he saw it all in the trees.

They were quiet and at peace in the pastures
And beside the waters still
And upon the mountain side
Where the drought would parch the root
And the hurricane would walk in the Summer,
Trunks and roots were hard and torn
Branches broken short, and twisted,
Just to keep a footing there
Just to be a living tree.
Plumber's hand and painter's eye,
Plumber's dead and gone for good,
Daley's dead.

Over now the search for silver
Gone away is Hungry Belly
Off to find a fresh companion;
Dust the feet that walked beside him,
Turned to dust the plumber's hands
But the trees still stand together
Like they're shouting over Jordan,
And, look see how cedar trees

Do shade a garden in that place.
And upon that skull-shaped hill top
When the eye of day is clean
Stand two trees with bitter bearing
And between the two a tree
One between the two that lifts
Bright flowering.

ALBERT HELMAN

1903–1996

Lullaby

Translated by Francis R. Jones and E. A. Markham

Dudu, it's past your bedtime, eh?
Now shut your eye. One-foot
Jumbie gonna want you favor him
Or go turn you white

So shut you eye, don't cry, son,
I still here; I not going away.
The yards dark dark long time now;
But tomorrow you can play.

Dudu, what foolishness it have in your head?
Sleep, you little scamp, shush.
You hear what happen to them not in bed
Catching fright out in the bush?

The cold and wind they not playing game
Outside the front door; and who know
What jumbie dress up in rags go claim
To work obeah on you?

Dudu darling, go sleep now, be good:
Your eyes shut? You dreaming?
That's right, sugarcake; my skin, my own blood.
Just a little kiss, till morning.

ROGER MAIS

1905–1955

All Men Come to the Hills

All men come to the hills
Finally. . . .
Men from the deeps of the plains of the sea—
Where a wind-in-the-sail is hope,
That long desire, and long weariness fulfills—
Come again to the hills.

And men with dusty, broken feet
Proud men, lone men like me,
Seeking again the soul's deeps—
Or a shallow grave
Far from the tumult of the wave—
Where a bird's note motions the silence in. . . .
The white kiss of silence that the spirit stills
Still as a cloud of windless sail horizon-hung
    above the blue glass of the sea—
Come again to the hills. . . .
Come ever, finally.

UNA MARSON

1905–1965

Cameo

Blue Skies
    White clouds
      Bluer seas
        White sea-foam
          Coconut palms
            Blue mountains
            And beyond
            More
              Blue mountains
              Soft Shadows
                On the mountains
              Soft Shadows
                Moving Gently

Cool Breezes
    From the sea
      White roads
        Old women
          Breaking stones
            By the roadside
            A truck
              Heavy laden
              With bananas
                Rounding the curve
                Of the white road
              Leaving dust
              And noise—

                    Then once more
                    The everlasting song
                    Of the sea

VERA BELL
b. 1906

Ancestor on the Auction Block

Ancestor on the auction block
Across the years your eyes seek mine
Compelling me to look.
I see your shackled feet
Your primitive black face
I see your humiliation
And turn away
Ashamed.

Across the years your eyes seek mine
Compelling me to look
Is this mean creature that I see
Myself?
Ashamed to look
Because of myself ashamed
Shackled by my own ignorance
I stand
A slave.

Humiliated
I cry to the eternal abyss
For understanding
Ancestor on the auction block
Across the years your eyes meet mine
Electric
I am transformed
My freedom is within myself.

I look you in the eyes and see
The spirit of God eternal
Of this only need I be ashamed
Of blindness to the God within me
The same God who dwelt within you

The same eternal God
Who shall dwell
In generations yet unborn.

Ancestor on the auction block
Across the years
I look

I see you sweating, toiling, suffering
Within your loins I see the seed
Of multitudes
From your labour
Grow roads, aqueducts, cultivation
A new country is born
Yours was the task to clear the ground
Mine be the task to build.

JACQUES ROUMAIN

1907–1944

Guinea

Translated by Langston Hughes

It's the long road to Guinea
death takes you down.
Here are the boughs, the trees, the forest.
Listen to the sound of the wind in its long hair
    of eternal night.

It's the long road to Guinea
where your fathers await you without impatience.
Along the way, they talk,
They wait.
This is the hour when the streams rattle
    like beads of bone.

It's the long road to Guinea.
No bright welcome will be made for you
in the dark land of dark men:

Under a smoky sky pierced by the cry of birds
around the eye of the river
    the eyelashes of the trees open on decaying light.
There, there awaits you beside the water a quiet village,
and the hut of your fathers, and the hard ancestral stone
    where your head will rest at last.

PHYLLIS SHAND ALLFREY

1908–1986

Love for an Island

Love for an island is the sternest passion:
pulsing beyond the blood through roots and loam
it overflows the boundary of bedrooms
and courses past the fragile walls of home.

Those nourished on the sap and milk of beauty
(born in its landsight) tremble like a tree
at the first footfall of the dread usurper—
a carpet-bagging mediocrity.

Theirs is no mild attachment, but rapacious
craving for a possession rude and whole;
lovers of islands drive their stake, prospecting
to run the flag of ego up the pole,

sink on the tented ground, hot under azure
plunge in the heat of earth, and smell the stars
of the incredible vales. At night, triumphant,
they lift their eyes to Venus and to Mars.

Their passion drives them to perpetuation:
they dig, they plant, they build and they aspire
to the eternal landmark; when they die
the forest covers up their set desire,

Salesmen and termites occupy their dwellings,
their legendary politics decay.
Yet they achieve an ultimate memorial:
they blend their flesh with the beloved clay.

JEAN BRIÈRRE

b. 1909

Here I Am Again, Harlem

In memory of those lynched in Georgia,
victims of white fascism.

Translated by Carrol F. Coates

Black brother, here I am, neither poorer than you
Nor less sad and no greater. In the crowd, I am
The anonymous passerby who swells the procession,
The black drop that joins your wave.

Look, your hands are no less black than our hands,
And our steps across centuries of misery
Mark the same knell on the same route:
Our shadows embrace along the ways of calvaries.

For we have already fought side by side.
When I tripped, you picked up my weapons,
And with your great body, sculpted by toil,
You protected my fall and smiled through your tears.

A profound silence arose from the jungle
Broken at moments by unspeakable suffering.
In the acrid odor of blood, I raised my head
And saw you towering on the horizon, immense.

We both knew the horror of the slave traders,
And often, like me, you feel the aches
Of waking up after murderous centuries,
And the old wounds bleeding in your flesh.

But we had to say goodbye toward 1600.
We had looked toward the dancing mirages,
Epic visions of battle and blood:
I see once again your silhouette in the shadows of the ages.

Your trace is lost on the banks of the Hudson.
Summer in Saint-Domingue welcomed my anxiety
And the echo told me in strange songs
About the wistful Redskins who were undone.

The centuries changed numbers with time.
Saint-Domingue, breaking its chains and thongs,
—The conflagration spreading its Titan's canvas—
Waved its bloody flag in the light.

Here I am again, Harlem. That flag is yours,
For the pact of pride, glory, and suffering
Was contracted by us for yesterday and tomorrow:
Today I shred the shrouds of silence.

Your shackles still wound my most fertile cry.
Just as yesterday, in the hold of somber agony,
Your call is torn by the bars of prisons,
And I cannot breathe when you are suffering.

We have forgotten our African dialects,
You sing in English of my dreams and suffering,
My former griefs dance to the rhythm of your blues,
And I relate your anguish in the language of France.

The scorn hurled at you lands on my cheek.
The person lynched in Florida casts a shadow on my soul,
And from the bloody pyre, protected by the law,
The same flame ascends toward your heart, toward my heart.

When you bleed, Harlem, my handkerchief turns crimson.
When you suffer, your cry is prolonged in my song.
With the same fervor and on the same evening,
Black Brother, we both experience the same dream.

HAROLD M. TELEMAQUE

1909–1982

In Our Land

In our land,
Poppies do not spring
From atoms of young blood,

So gaudily where men have died:
In our land,
Stiletto cane blades
Sink into our hearts,
And drink our blood.

In our land,
Sin is not deep.
And bends before the truth,
Asking repentently for pardon:
In our Land,
The ugly stain
That blotted Eden garden
Is sunk deep only.

In our land,
Storms do not strike
For territory's fences,
Elbow room, nor breathing spaces:
In our land,
The hurricane
Of clashes break our ranks
For tint of eye.

In our land,
We do not breed
That taloned king, the eagle,
Nor make emblazonry of lions:
In our land,
The black birds
And the chickens of our mountains
Speak our dreams.

VIVIAN VIRTUE

1911–1998

Landscape Painter, Jamaica

for Albert Huie

I watch him set up easel,
Both straddling precariously
A corner of the twisted, climbing
Mountain track

A tireless humming-bird, his brush
Dips, darts, hovers now here, now there,
Where puddles of pigment
Bloom in the palette's wild small garden.

The mountains pose for him
In a family group
Dignified, self-conscious, against the wide blue screen
Of morning; low green foot-hills
Sprawl like grandchildren about the knees
Of seated elders. And behind them, aloof,
Shouldering the sky, patriarchal in serenity,
Blue Mountain Peak bulks.

And the professional gaze
Studies positions, impatiently waiting
For the perfect moment to fix
Their preparedness, to confine them
For the pleasant formality
Of the family album.

His brush a humming-bird
Meticulously poised . . .
The little hills fidgeting,
Changelessly changing,
Artlessly frustrating
The painter's art.

LÉON-GONTRAN DAMAS

1912–1978

S.O.S.

Translated by E. Anthony Hurley

Then and only then
will all of you understand
when the idea occurs to them
soon this idea will occur to them

to want to have you gobble up negroes
just like Hitler
gobbling up jews
seven fascist days
a
week

Then and only then
will all of you understand
when their superiority
is flaunted
from one end of their boulevards to the other
and then
you will see them
really doing whatever they want
not being satisfied any more just to laugh with
restless forefinger
when they see a negro pass by
but
coldly beating up

but
coldly knocking down
but
coldly laying out
but coldly
beating up

knocking down
laying out
and
cutting off negroes' penises
to make into candles for their churches

So Often

Translated by Ellen Conroy Kennedy

So often my feeling of race
strikes the same fear
as the nighttime howling of a dog

at some approaching death
I always feel
about to foam with rage
against what surrounds me
against what prevents me
ever
from being
a man

And nothing
nothing would so calm my hate
as a great
pool
of blood
made
by those long sharp knives
that strip the hills of cane
for rum.

AIMÉ CÉSAIRE

b. 1913

from *Return to My Native Land*

Translated by Clayton Eshleman and Annette Smith

To go away. My heart was pounding with emphatic generosities. To go away . . . I would arrive sleek and young in this land of mine and I would say to this land whose loam is part of my flesh: 'I have wandered for a long time and I am coming back to the deserted hideousness of your sores.'

I would go to this land of mine and I would say to it: 'Embrace me without fear . . . And if all I can do is speak, it is for you I shall speak.'

And again I would say:
'My mouth shall be the mouth of those calamities that have no mouth, my voice the freedom of those who break down in the prison holes of despair.'

And on the way I would say to myself:
'And above all, my body as well as my soul, beware of assuming the sterile attitude of a spectator, for life is not a spectacle, a sea of miseries is not a proscenium, a man screaming is not a dancing bear . . .'

And behold here I am!
Once again this life hobbling before me, what I am saying life, *this death*, this death without sense or pity, this death that so pathetically falls short of greatness, the dazzling pettiness of this death, this death hobbling from pettiness to pettiness; these shovelfuls of petty greeds over the conquistador; these shovelfuls of petty flunkies over the great savage, these shovelfuls of petty souls over the three-souled Carib, and all these deaths futile
absurdities under the splashing of my open conscience
tragic futilities lit up by this single noctiluca
and I alone, sudden stage of this daybreak
when the apocalypse of monsters cavorts
then, capsized, hushes
warm election of cinders, of ruins and collapses

—One more thing! Only one, but please make it only one: I have no right to measure life by my sooty finger span; to reduce myself to this little ellipsoidal nothing trembling four fingers above the line, I a man, to so overturn creation, that I include myself between latitude and longitude!

Lost Body

Translated by E. Anthony Hurley

I who Krakatoa
I who much better than monsoon
I who chest open
I who Laëlaps
I who bleating better than a cloaca
I who off-scale
I who Zambezi or frenetic or rhombus or cannibal
I would like to be humbler and humbler and lower
always graver with neither vestige nor vertigo
until I lose myself fall
into the living semolina of well opened soil.
Outside a beautiful mist instead of atmosphere
would be not dirty
each drop of water in it making a sun
whose name the same for all things
would be TOTAL AND COMPLETE
ENCOUNTER
so that one could not be sure what is passing
whether a star or a hope
or a petal from the flamboyant tree
or an underwater retreat
streaked by the torches of the medusa aurelias
Then life I imagine would bathe me all over
better would I feel it touching me or biting me
As I lie I would see approaching me scents finally free
like helpful hands
and they would find a way to pass within me
to swing their long hair
longer than this past that I cannot reach.

Things move aside make space between you
space for my rest that bears like a wave
my terrible crest of anchoring roots
looking for somewhere to hold on to
Things I probe I probe
I the burden-bearer I am the root-bearer
And I weigh and I force and I arcane
      I omphale
Ah which takes me back towards the harpoons
      I am very weak
I whistle yes I whistle very ancient things
of snakes of cavernous things
I gold now wind be still
and against my cool unstable muzzle
place against my eroded face
your cold face of canceled laughter.
The wind alas I shall hear it still
nigger nigger nigger from the depth
of the immemorial sky
not quite as loud as today
but too loud yet
and this mad howling of hounds and horses
that it sets on our ever-runaway trail
but when my turn comes into the air
I will raise up a cry so violent
that I will spatter the sky utterly
and by my shredded branches
and by the insolent jet of my solemn wounded bole

     I shall command the islands to exist

lagoonal calendar

Translated by Clayton Eshleman and Annette Smith

    I inhabit a sacred wound
    I inhabit imaginary ancestors
    I inhabit an obscure will

I inhabit a long silence
I inhabit an irremediable thirst
I inhabit a one-thousand-year journey
I inhabit a three-hundred-year war
I inhabit an abandoned cult
between bulb and bulbil i inhabit the unexploited space
I inhabit not a vein of the basalt
but the rising tide of lava
which runs back up the gulch at full speed
to burn all the mosques
I make the most of this avatar
of an absurdly botched version of paradise
        —it is much worse than a hell—
I inhabit from time to time one of my wounds
Each minute i change apartments
and any peace frightens me

        whirling fire
        ascidium like none other for the dust
        of strayed worlds
        having spat out my fresh-water entrails
        a volcano i remain with my loaves of words and
        my secret minerals

I inhabit thus a vast thought
but in most cases i prefer to confine myself
to the smallest of my ideas
or else i inhabit a magical formula
only its opening words
the rest being forgotten
I inhabit the ice jam
I inhabit the ice melting
I inhabit the face of a great disaster
I inhabit in most cases the driest udder
of the skinniest peak—the she-wolf of these clouds—
I inhabit the halo of the Cactaceae
I inhabit a herd of goats pulling
on the tit of the most desolate argan tree
To tell you the truth i no longer know my correct address
Bathyal or abyssal

I inhabit the octopuses' hole
I fight with an octopus over an octopus hole

>Brother lay off
>wrack rubbish
>I hook on like devil's guts
>or uncoil porana-like
>it's all the same thing
>which the wave rolls
>which the sun leeches
>which the wind flogs
>sculpture in the round of my nothingness

The atmospheric or rather historic pressure
even if it makes certain words of mine sumptuous
immeasurably increases my plight.

The Automatic Crystal

Translated by Clayton Eshleman and Annette Smith

hullo hullo one more night stop guessing it's me the cave man there
are cicadas which deafen both their life and their death there also is
the green water of lagoons even drowned I will never be that color to
think of you I left all my words at the pawn shop a river of sleds of
women bathing in the course of the day blonde as bread and the
alcohol of your breasts hullo hullo I would like to be on the clear
other side of the earth the tips of your breasts have the color and the
taste of that earth hullo hullo one more night there is rain and its
gravedigger fingers there is rain putting its foot in its mouth on the
roofs the rain ate the sun with chopsticks hullo hullo the enlarge-
ment of the crystal that's you . . . that is you oh absent one in the
wind an earthworm bathing beauty when day breaks it is you who
will dawn your riverine eyes on the stirred enamel of the islands and
in my mind it is you the dazzling maguey of an undertow of eagles
under the banyan

Wifredo Lam . . .

Translated by Clayton Eshleman and Annette Smith

> Mantonica Wilson, my godmother, had the power to
> conjure the elements . . . I visited her in her house
> filled with African idols. She made me the gift of the
> protection of all these gods: of Yemanja, goddess of
> the sea, of Shango, god of war and companion of
> Ogun-Ferraille, god of metal who gilded the sun
> every morning, always at the side of Olorun, the
> absolute god of creation.
>
> Wifredo Lam

To report: nothing less than
the kingdom under seige
the sky precarious
relief imminent and legitimate

Nothing except that the cycle of geneses has just without warning
exploded as well as the life that gives itself
without filiation the barbarous password

Nothing except the shivering spawn of forms liberating themselves
from facile bindings
and escaping from too premature combinings

imploring hands
hands in orison
the face of the horrible cannot be better indicated
than by these shocking hands

diviner of violet entrails and destiny
reciter of macumbas
my brother
what are you looking for throughout these forests
of horns of hooves of wings of horses

all punctuate things
all bipunctuate things

avatars however of a god keen on destruction
monsters taking flight
in the combats of justice I recognized
the rare laughter of your magical weapons
the vertigo of your blood
     and the law of your name.

PEDRO MIR

1913–2000

Meditation on the Shores of Evening

Translated by Donald D. Walsh

So many, the peoples of the Caribbean, silent
some of them, others sad and nameless, and some
risen from the fountain of oblivion, as happens
      every time night pauses at a bend in the road
      before a beckoning window,
                      they are asleep.

They are asleep. Perhaps unforgettably, with tender
words upon an unsung marble stone. 'Here satisfies
her eternal restlessness a countless soul.' And it is any
one of the Caribbean peoples. No, not just any one.
It is the illusory shore on which a heel slips
or struggles. A key dangling beside a wounded note.

A savage note of drum or leather.

Watchful of everything, a powerful windmill thrust.
Situated upon these mortal verges, unwillingly
he calls on everyone to raise the lance,
and the nag and the burro must rear up
because we are all knots of a single stem
and our hungers and our dreams
sense each other through the same gestures and same
works. We must understand each other implicitly
facing the windmill. Emaciated, crazed, penniless
and grimacing, not knowing from what harsh discipline
this mark and this struggle befall us, but bound as one.
Always bound as one facing the windmill.

Always the windmill and this time with its silent
insinuating crossed arms, its banker's belly,
its registrar's flower, nontransferable, its cool
branch offices the world over like a waning moon.

But here we all are with the same
knees driven into our lands. Ancient gold
that has cursed us ever since, ever since
those flowering caravels shaped like seagulls,
has run through these same veins joined by habits,
wounds and colors, gold received in the kiss
of our poor and century-old knees,
in the abrupt arch of our backs; gold, ancient gold
ages the windmill, suffocates it, works it to death,
and because of us the colt rears up
and a young burro sniffs at sayings, plays Sancho,
when a raised lance rings against the wall of air.

We shall be happy, we peoples of the Caribbean.
Our simple families will return from the dream
We shall bear all the names gathered up, suddenly,
like a floating wisp rolling in with the foam
at the journey's end. We shall be happy, there is
no doubt. None whatsoever. We must clean our house.
Everywhere a certain beast of cleanliness is roaring.

It is right and just that we rejoice and decide.
Our emancipated, mestizo name is victorious.
Yes, of course! We have suffered much and our blood
has enriched many. It was time! Let us greet
the hour. Yes, let us greet the hour and the day,
and let the month and the whole calendar come, too.

This moment pleases and attracts. It is our moment.
From this moment on we shall transform the blood of
business into the blood of martyrdom or victory's flower.

So this is that tranquil meditation that I'm telling you
at peace and on the shores of evening
face to face with the immense torrid lap of the Caribbean Sea.

JULIA DE BURGOS

1914–1953

To Julia de Burgos

Translated by Jack Agueros

Already the people murmur that I am your enemy
because they say that in verse I give the world your me.

They lie, Julia de Burgos. They lie, Julia de Burgos.
Who rises in my verses is not your voice. It is my voice
because you are the dressing and the essence is me;
and the most profound abyss is spread between us.

You are the cold doll of social lies,
and me, the virile starburst of the human truth.

You, honey of courtesan hypocrisies; not me;
in all my poems I undress my heart.

You are like your world, selfish; not me
who gambles everything betting on what I am.

You are only the ponderous lady very lady;
not me; I am life, strength, woman.

You belong to your husband, your master; not me;
I belong to nobody, or all, because to all, to all
I give myself in my clean feeling and in my thought.

You curl your hair and paint yourself, not me;
the wind curls my hair, the sun paints me.

You are a housewife, resigned, submissive,
tied to the prejudices of men; not me;
unbridled, I am a runaway Rocinante
snorting horizons of God's justice.

You in yourself have no say; everyone governs you;
your husband, your parents, your family,
the priest, the dressmaker, the theatre, the dance hall,
the auto, the fine furnishings, the feast, champagne,
heaven and hell, and the social, 'what will they say.'

Not in me, in me only my heart governs,
only my thought; who governs in me is me.
You, flower of aristocracy; and me, flower of the people.
You in you have everything and you owe it to everyone,
while me, my nothing I owe to nobody.

You nailed to the static ancestral dividend,
and me, a one in the numerical social divider,
we are the duel to death who fatally approaches.

When the multitudes run rioting
leaving behind ashes of burned injustices,
and with the torch of the seven virtues,
the multitudes run after the seven sins,
against you and against everything unjust and inhuman,
I will be in their midst with the torch in my hand.

Poem with the Final Tune

Translated by Julio Marzán

Are you asking where I'm going with these sad faces
and the bubbling of wounded veins on my forehead?

I'm going to cast roses into the sea,
to vanish under waves higher than the birds,
to pull out roads that by now had burrowed through me like
roots . . .

I'm going to give up stars,
and dews,
and the brief rivulets where I loved the passion that ravaged
    my mountains,

and a special cooing
of doves,
and words . . .

I am going to remain alone, without songs or skin,
like the inside of a tunnel,
where its own silence goes crazy
        and kills itself.

A. J. SEYMOUR

1914–1989

There Runs a Dream

There runs a dream of perished Dutch plantations
In these Guiana rivers to the sea.

Black waters, rustling through the vegetation
That towers and tangles banks, run silently
Over lost stellings where craft once rode
Easy before trim dwellings in the sun
And fields of indigo would float out broad
To lose the eye right on the horizon.

These rivers know that strong and quiet men
Drove back a jungle, gave Guiana root
Against the shock of circumstance, and then
History moved down the river, leaving free
The forest to creep back, foot by quiet foot
And overhang black waters to the sea.

Sun is a Shapely Fire

Sun is a shapely fire turning in air
Fed by white springs
                      and earth's a powerless sun.

I have the sun today deep in my bones
Sun's in my blood, light heaps beneath my skin.
Sun is a badge of power pouring in
A darkening star that rains its glory down.

The trees and I are cousins. Those tall trees
That tier their branches in the hollow sky
And, high up, hold small swaying hands of leaves

Up to divinity, their name for sun
And sometimes mine. We're cousins.

Sheet light, white power comes falling through the air,
—All the light here is equal-vertical—
Plays magic with green leaves and, touching, wakes
The small sweet springs of breathing scent and bloom
That break out on the boughs.
                                        And sun has made
Civilisation flower from a river's mud
With his gossamer rays of steel.

These regions wear sharp shadows from deep suns.

The sun gives back her earth its ancient right
The gift of violence.
Life here is ringed with the half of the sun's wheel
And limbs and passions grow in leaps of power
Suddenly flowing up to touch the arc.
Upon this energy knit to the sun
To learn the trick of discipline and slow skill,
Squaring in towns upon an empty map
Hitching rivers to great water wheels,
Taming the fire to domesticity.

Sun is a shapely fire floating in air
Watched by God's eye. The distance makes it cool
With the slow circling retinue of worlds
Hanging upon it.
                                Indifferently near
Move other stars with their attendant groups
Till the enormous ballet music fades
And dies away.

Sun is a shapely fire
Turning in air
Sun's in my blood.

ERIC ROACH

1915–1974

Love Overgrows a Rock

Only the foreground's green;
Waves break the middle distance,
And to horizon the Atlantic's spread
Bright, blue and empty as the sky;
My eyot jails the heart,
And every dream is drowned in the shore water.

Too narrow room pressed down
My years to stunted scrub,
Blunted my sister's beauty
And my friend's grave force,
Our tribe's renewing faith and pride:
Love overgrows a rock as blood outbreeds it.

We take banana boats
Tourist, stowaway,
Our luck in hand, calypsos in the heart:
We turn Columbus' blunder back
From sun to snow, to bitter cities;
We explore the hostile and exploding zones.

The drunken hawk's blood of
The poet streams through climates of the mind
Seeking a word's integrity
A human truth. So, from my private hillock
In Atlantic I join cry:
Come, seine the archipelago;
Disdain the sea; gather the islands' hills
Into the blue horizons of our love.

The World of Islands

Watch from a journey close to cloud
A shoal of sea-beleaguered lands,
Siblings of the glaring sun
Grin their dolphin teeth at heaven.

A difficult country to inherit:
Guilt is humid in the glittering air;
Grafted at every branch the human wood
Blooms a bewildering scent, fruits bittersweet;
Indigenous blood still stains the grass;
Dragon's teeth still rattle under root,
And under stone the cold snake's coiled asleep,
Rapt in its murderous dream.

Those whom bondage bit to bone,
Who early learnt to sieve black grief
Through hardihood and song and prayer,
Repaint the tragic mask.
The shattered man sewn in the rock
Arises smiling like the surf,
Reaching to kiss each wind,
Groping to clouds for love.

The drummer with his father's knuckles
Knocks the torrid drum of the sun;
The dancer shakes her castanet the moon
To the loud rhyme of love, calling:
Come, come I am the phoenix Eve,
The mingled wine of the world's grapes;
I am the supple rhythm of the seas;
I recreate the world on islands.

GEORGE CAMPBELL

1916–2002

Negro Aroused

Negro aroused! Awakened from
The ignominious sleep of dominance!
Freedom! off with these shackles
That torment, I lift my head and scream to heaven
Freedom! Now my body is strong, strong!
Now the blood rushes through my veins
And boils up in my head at their insult.
The spirit of freedom is resurrected in me,
I lift my head and cry to heaven defiance,
Freedom! Let them beat down this house,
Muscle built, stifle this screaming voice,
Let them! We are aroused! Fear made us shut our eyes
Once; made us give up Freedom to save our flesh
But my eyes now flash to the very heavens defiance; and
My skin is hard; lash it, O world, and
Bring your battering-rams of insults and discomforts
You that hate others to live! We are no longer
Stampeding cattle, no! The hot fire of new blood
Bubbles under this skin; the heart shouts Freedom!
I lift my face to heaven, awakened, shouting louder, louder
With triumph, with a new found strength—
Freedom! We cry only freedom—we were dead when
Sleeping—now we live! live! We are aroused!

TREFOSSA

1916–1975

A true poem . . .

Translated by Vernie A. February

A true poem is a thing of awe.
A true poem is a struggle unto death.
A true poem is another land
where one sojourns
when one is past death's door.

A true poem is made of words that linger on
when all the others in one's life are washed away:
one single kernel,
but one from which can sprout
life all anew.

Stream then all over me
Arusubanya* of the world.
Perhaps one day, one day,
my mouth will burst asunder
to utter but two words for simple souls
which, as they grow, will sprout ripe stars
which even now I am searching for.

* A rapid in the Suriname river: 'It loosens the ribs.'

GUY TIROLIEN

1917–1988

Islands

Translated by Nick Caistor

This is the low house
in which my race has grown.
Twisting and lifting, the road
takes off beyond.
Will it reach the weary waters
beneath the distant mango trees?

Smells of burnt earth and salt cod
Wafting under the muzzle of thirst.
A smile splitting the ripe coco-plum
of an aged face.
The vague prayer of smoke-trails.
Lament of a prolonged neighing
that scales the sides of the ravines.
Voices of rum
with their breath
warming our ears.

Clatter of dominoes rifling the birds' repose.
Calypso rhythms
in the warm belly of our banjos.
Laughter of desire in the deep insides of the night.
Mouths starved of bread
swilling the cheap alcohol
of words.

The island pushing towards morning
its weight of humanity.

Ghetto

Translated by Ellen Conroy Kennedy

why would I shut myself up
in that image of myself
that they'd like to petrify?
have mercy I say have mercy!
I am stifling in the ghetto of exoticism

no I'm not that ebony
idol
inhaling the profane incense
that is burned
in the museums of exoticism

I'm not that fairground
cannibal
rolling ivory eyeballs
to make kids tremble with fright

and if I let out the cry
that burns my throat
it's because my belly boils
from my brothers' hunger

and if at times I bawl my suffering
it's because my toe is caught
under the boot of others

the nightingale sings in several notes
no more of my single-chorded laments!

I'm not the actor
all smeared in soot
sobbing out his sorrow
arms raised to the sky
as the cameras watch

neither am I
a frozen statue of a revolutionary
or of damnation
I'm a living animal
a beast of prey
always ready to pounce

to pounce on life
that laughs at the dead
to pounce on joy
that has no passport
to pounce on love
that passes in front of my door

I will speak about Beethoven
deaf
amid the turmoils
for it's for me
for me who can better understand him
that he lets loose his storms

I will sing about Rimbaud

who wanted to become a negro
to better speak to men
in the language of geneses

and I will praise Matisse
and Braque and Picasso
for rediscovering under the rigidity
of elemental shapes
the old secret of the rhythms
that make life sing

yes I will exalt man
all men
I will go to them
my heart full of songs
my hands heavy
with friendship
for they are made in my image

MARIE-THÉRÈSE COLIMON

1918–1988

Encounter

Translated from the French by Betty Wilson

I'd say: 'How are you?'
And you: 'Fine, thanks.'
I'd say: 'We don't see you anymore.'
And you: 'I'm very busy.'

A pause . . . I'd begin again very softly
'Tell me . . .' And you, not hearing
My mumbled words
Would go right on unsuspecting
Oh, (politely) you don't have your big straw hat anymore!
But . . . No, not anymore. I'd answer
And you, do you still like sugared almonds?
—Listen to that tune from the house opposite.

Then we would each go off across the city
Carrying in our hearts, full with silent sobs,
The bitter burden of unspoken words
And the empty pride of having kept our pain.

AIDA CARTAGENA PORTALATIN

1918–1994

A Woman Alone

Translated by Daisy Cocco De Filippis

A woman is alone. Alone with herself
With open eyes and open arms.
With a heart opened by a wide silence.
She awaits in the desperate and despairing night,
                    without losing hope.
She believes herself to be in the leading vessel
lit by creation's saddest light.
She has sailed away.
fleeing from love,
the North wind guiding her flight.

A woman is alone. Binding her dreams with dreams,
the remaining dreams and the open blue Antillean skies.
Thoughtful and quiet,
she faces a stony, aimless world,
lost in the meaning of its own word,
its own useless word.

A woman is alone. She believes everything to be nothing.
And no one speaks to her
of the joy and sorrow to be found
in the blood that leaps, that flows,
in the blood which nourishes or dies of death.
No one comes forward to offer her clothing to dress
her naked, self-defining, weeping voice.

A woman is alone. She feels
and her truth drowns in thoughts which speak
of the beauty of a rose, of a star,
of love, of man and of God.

LOUISE BENNETT

b. 1919

Dutty Tough

Sun a shine but tings no bright;
Doah pot a bwile, bickle no nuff;
River flood but water scarce, yaw;
Rain a fall but dutty tough.

Tings so bad dat nowadays when
Yuh ask smaddy how dem do
Dem fraid yuh teck it tell dem back,
So dem no answer yuh.

No care omuch we dah work fa
Hard-time still eena we shut;
We dah fight, Hard-time a beat we,
Dem might raise we wages, but

One poun gawn awn pon we pay, an
We no feel no merriment
For ten poun gawn awn pon we food
An ten poun pon we rent!

Salfish gawn up, mackerel gawn up,
Pork an beef gawn up same way,
An when rice an butter ready
Dem just go pon holiday!

Claht, boot, pin an needle gawn up;
Ice, bread, taxes, water-rate;
Kersene ile, gasolene, gawn up;
An de poun devaluate.

De price a bread gawn up so high
Dat we haffi agree
Fi cut we yeye pon bread an all
Tun dumplin refugee!

An all dem marga smaddy weh
Dah gwan like fat is sin,
All dem-deh weh dah fas wid me,
Ah lef dem to dumplin!

Sun a shine an pot a bwile, but
Tings no bright, bickle no nuff.
Rain a fall, river dah flood, but
Water scarce and dutty tough.

Jamaica Oman

Jamaica oman cunny, sah!
Is how dem jinnal so?
Look how long dem liberated
An de man dem never know!

Look how long Jamaica oman
—Modder, sister, wife, sweetheart—
Outa road an eena yard deh pon
A dominate her part!

From Maroon Nanny teck her body
Bounce bullet back pon man,
To when nowadays gal-pickney tun
Spellin-Bee champion.

From de grass root to de hill-top,
In profession, skill an trade,
Jamaica oman teck her time
Dah mount an meck de grade.

Some backa man a push, some side-a
Man a hole him han,
Some a lick sense eena man head,
Some a guide him pon him plan!

Neck an neck an foot an foot wid man
She buckle hole her own;
While man a call her 'so-so rib'
Oman a tun backbone!

An long before Oman Lib bruck out
Over foreign lan
Jamaica female wasa work
Her liberated plan!

Jamaica oman know she strong,
She know she tallawah,
But she no want her pickney-dem
Fi start call her 'Puppa'.

So de cunny Jamma oman
Gwan like pants-suit is a style,
An Jamaica man no know she wear
De trousiz all de while!

So Jamaica oman coaxin
Fambly budget from explode
A so Jamaica man a sing
'Oman a heaby load!'

But de cunny Jamma oman
Ban her belly, bite her tongue,
Ketch water, put pot pon fire
An jus dig her toe a grung.

For 'Oman luck deh a dungle',
Some rooted more dan some,
But as long as fowl a scratch dungle heap
Oman luck mus come!

Lickle by lickle man start praise her,
Day by day de praise a grow;
So him praise her, so it sweet her,
For she wonder if him know.

BARBARA FERLAND

b. 1919

When They Come from the Island

When they come from the Island
I say to them, Talk to me of home.
    They tell me
Of buildings, knee-high skyscrapers.
They speak of a North Coast, white-bleached by tourists;
Of night-clubs, hotels, of Discotheques,
And black American cars, riding the roads with power.
They declare that Independence has created a new nation,
And they are proud of their prosperity.

    But no-one will say
If the agave still blooms on Long Mountain.
Or if the market-women hills, swinging blue hips down to the plain,
Still sweat their springs,
And smell of ginger lilies.

    No-one has told me
Whether
In the holy caralillo season
Sun candles set poinsettias afire
Under taut skies, a Norther blowing.
They say,
        You should see the new houses, the glaze-tiled swimming pools,
        The Self-Service Plazas. And, of course,
        The air-conditioned flats. Press a button, and you're cool, man,
        All the year round.

    And no one
Remembers Strawberry, Miss Kizzie, or Adinah,
Who used to walk barefooted down the fern-lined paths
Into a good morning,
Their tin cans, wet-sugar lined, capturing cold spring water,
Spendthrift of the flow.

    And no one,
Not one of them, knows
What happened at Mattie's Corner.
Or why a donkey, mindful of a clay pipe smouldering,
Nozzles a shadow, awaiting her return.

JOHN FIGUEROA

1920–1999

Christmas Breeze

Auntie would say 'Ah! Christmas breeze
as the Norther leapt from the continent
across Caribbean seas,
across our hills
to herald Christmas,
ham boiling in the yard
plum pudding in the cloth
(Let three stones bear the pot;
and feed the hat-fanned fire).

This breeze in August cools a Summer's day
here in England.
In December in Jamaica
we would have called it *cold*,
Cold Christmas Breeze,
fringing the hill tops with its tumble
of cloud, bringing in
imported apples, and dances
and rum (for older folk).
For us, some needed clothes, and a pair
of shoes squeezing every toe.
And Midnight Mass:
Adeste Fideles!

     Some Faithful came—
and why not?—a little drunk,
some overdressed, but
ever faithful.
Like Christmas breeze
returning every year, bearing
not August's end, nor October's
wind and rain but, Christmas
and 'starlights'

and a certain sadness, except for Midnight Mass
and the Faithful
('The Night when Christ was born')

    I miss celebrations, but I miss most
the people of faith
who greeted warmly every year
the Christmas breeze.

This Tree My Time Keeper

is brown with berries now.

When last I looked it had
no leaves, was stiff and white
with frost.

Now green leaves and brown berries toss,
toss and bob in the whipping wind.

It is not Spring beyond the horizon
that the bucking boat is heading for,

'It is not Spring with its false hopes,
it is not Spring,' says my time keeper,

'but bitter berries, bitter and brown
and full of wisdom.'

Only in hard winters, they tell me
will the birds touch these berries.

WILSON HARRIS

b. 1921

Behring Straits

The tremendous voyage between two worlds
is contained in every hollow shell, in every name that echoes
a nameless bell,
in tree-trunk or cave
or sound: in drowned Asia's bones:
a log-book in the clouds
names the straits of eternity: the marbles
of ocean and indomitable tides.

So life discovers the remotest beaches in time
that are always present in action: the interior walls of being
Open like a mirrorless pool, the ocean's nostalgia
and the stormy communication of truth turn still deeply
like settlement and root.

Untangled the trees mount to the sky
and the silence is filled with a different wave like sound
That alters dimension. The cool cave of ship
is sudden beached with sun
is drowned in a fluid ecstasy that devours and is devoured in turn,
external still profound.

The voyage between two worlds
is fraught with this grandeur and this anonymity. Who blazes a trail
is overtaken by a labyrinth
Leading to many conclusions.

               The valleys of ocean
are spent
and the mountains stand cloudlike and August, solid and bent
To the sailor on his round. Until they figuratively drown
in an overwhelming sea or a spiritual
mound. So the incomplete discovery of the world

in the blueness of its delicacy
is broken on the beach of its lofty ground
Like a wave that meets resistance and must rise unerringly
into an outline or alienation or history
into a bond that both strengthens and severs in the movement of life:
since heaven deepens the immortal sea
like eternity that disguises
a wound,
But earth waits for the continual voyager
who dances on mortal ground.

A. L. HENDRIKS
1922–1992

The Migrant

She could not remember anything about the voyage,
Her country of origin, or if someone had paid for the passage:

Of such she had no recollection.

She was sure only that she had travelled;
Without doubt had been made welcome.

For a while she believed she was home,
Rooted and securely settled,
Until it was broken to her
That in fact she was merely in transit
Bound for some other destination,
Committed to continue elsewhere.

This slow realisation sharpened,
She formed plans to postpone her departure
Not observing her movement en route to the exit.

When she did, it was piteous how, saddened,
She went appreciably closer towards it.

Eventually facing the inescapable
She began reading travel brochures,
(Gaudy, competitive, plentiful)
Spent time considering the onward journey,
Studied a new language,
Stuffed her bosom with strange currency,
Nevertheless dreading the boarding announcements.

We watch her go through
The gate for *Embarking Passengers Only*,
Fearful and unutterably lonely,
Finger our own documents,
Shuffle forward in the queue.

BASIL McFARLANE

b. 1922

Arawak Prologue

We cross many rivers; but here is no anguish; our
dugouts have straddled the salt sea. The land
we have found is a mountain, magical with birds'
throats, and in the sea are fish. In the forests are many
fleet canoes. And here is no anguish, though storms
still the birds and frighten the fish from inshore shallows. And
once it seemed the mountain moved, groaning
a little.

    In the sunless wet, after
rains, leaves in the tangled underbrush (like cool hands
of children on face and arms) glisten. I
am not one for society, and think how the houses throb with the noise
of women up to their elbows
in cassava milk, when the dove-grey sea's breast is
soft in the lowering light—and the land we found
fairest of women.

    That bright day, the light
like clusters of gold fruit, alone, unknown
of any, the dugout and I fled the shore's
burning beauty; the first wave's shock
an ecstasy like singing, oh, and the sea's strength
entered these arms. All day
we climbed the hill
of the sea.

    It seemed I died
and found that bleak Coyaba of the wise. The dugout
faltered in a long smooth swell. There were houses on the
water, aglow with light and music and strange
laughter. Like great birds, with
ominous mutterings and preenings, they

hovered on every side. Flat on the dugout's
bottom, I prayed deliverance. Where was the land, the
houses throbbing with the noise of women
up to their elbows in cassava milk?

                                        The towering birds
floated majestically on, dragging me a little in their
fabulous wake.
                      I tell this story in the evening, after
the smoke of pipes has addled the elders'
brains, and I am assured at least of the children's respectful
silence. I am no longer certain it happened to me.

GLORIA ESCOFFERY

1923–2002

Shelling Gungo Peas

Happiness is
sitting in one's own chair, in one's own living room
and shelling green gungo from one's own backyard tree.
On the low book table to my right I have placed
the broken-branches on a newspaper;
there is another newspaper on the floor to catch the debris.
In my lap there is a comely bowl for the chosen ones
and on the table a smaller bowl for the dry peas.
You may not think it, but there are decisions to be made,
for instance, are some of the tiny, sticky ones
too insignificant for admission to Elysium?
Will they blow a breath of green sickness through
tomorrow's rice and peas?
And what of the brownish ones, who seem a bit
too self-contained? Is their special, interior glow
an asset or a liability?
The bowl in my lap fills to overflowing
for the crop is good this year and I have caught it in time.
The fat peas with the brightness and glow of corn grains
seem to appraise their neighbours and say,
you, you and you, it is clear you are still too green,
why, may we ask were you admitted?
As for you, you are as brown as a nut. We don't need you!
And what should I do about the mischievous ones
who insist on rolling under my chair?
Let them lie there, I say, helpless as widow's groats.
More charity may be shown to those who simply nestle
in the mountainous landscape of my person.

Happiness is pouring out the green or greenish globes
measuring cup by measuring cup, the glory of the gleaning.
A pint and a half of tiny worlds flow
shimmering back into the great abyss of the bowl.

The slightly shrivelled ones view the homely ritual
with old wive's grimaces, but no evidence of malice.
As they and I know, from earth they came
and to earth they will return. Willy nilly,
it is they, the despised and rejected,
who are the cupbearers of the future.

CECIL GRAY

b. 1923

On the Road

On the road to Sav-la-Mar or through
the Rio Cobre gorge to Port Antonio
there could be no pause to consider
the question that sometimes arose
and smiled calmly and knowingly
in his mind. It was rush, rush, rush
with the tyres hissing when the rain
wet the skin of the asphalt. Then,
when the sun lit up the leaves and
the road was a shining, twisting ribbon,
making up time for the bell. Sandwiches
or a slab of bread pudding lay on
the seat in a bag next to the small coffee
flask. Munching them, later, he might
cross-examine himself about where
the roads led, how far into the future
they would take what he said. But
the buffeting wind would dissolve
the query like drops of rain. So for now
only the sun's quick flashes catching
the windscreen mattered.
                                    Now the low
roar and screech of the tyres cried out
that loaded with freight every moment
attaches its couplings to others to pull
the whole train of change its own way.
It made him afraid of the present, yet
the present was all that he had to steer
with, looking for signposts, keeping
hands on the wheel, going around
blind corners, mounting the long hills
of the island. He drove hard between
the season's plumed sea of canefields

where green waves swayed and swished
with the breeze. The far-off mountains
kept him in sight like watchful Maroons
wherever he turned. In the rearview mirror
old journeys receded like mileposts with
fingers of warning held up. Will pages
he opened today blow about like dry
leaves loose on the ground, spinning
away like the car wheels? It was true
he wanted to know what it was all worth,
but not very often. There were cylinders
with pistons that always fired and kept him
going regardless. Neither rain nor sunshine
determined the distance. All he wanted
was the hope a *cul de sac* did not swallow
the road he was on. At the end
of the trip he would measure the visit
and count up the miles he covered. He
would darn his faith if it was damaged,
fitting a patch with all of the others
around it.

The air was like glass just
polished. Its radiance lifted his eyes
to the sky's high patience. Passing vehicles
tooted and went on, bringing his thoughts
back to the curves, the crossings, bridges
and roundabouts.

Threading the Needle

My grandmother's arm turned the silver wheel
of her sewing machine sometimes so fast
the spokes made one. An unravelling reel
shimmied on its spigot as the thread passed

down to the needle's thrusting eye. The drone
always gave comfort. With a child's wonder
at how it was done I saw one stitch clone
another in the moving cloth. Thunder

might have rolled its far presence but only
the deep chirr of her bent toil in that room
entered my memory. Hers was a lonely
labour, unadorned, uncapped with a plume

of honour. She steered the fabric along
the shuttle, her glasses down on her nose
for zooming. I watched her veined brown hands, strong
with resolve, tirelessly plant rows

in rayon or cotton for bearing buds,
however minute, that flowered the days
for us. She would just take limp shapeless yards
and scissor and baste in magical ways

inherent forms and curves. I was called on
at times to work the handle or apply
my young eyes to threading the needle, one
of the joys that take a whole lifetime to die.

Hymns helped her hemming the end of a dress,
her contralto devoted to bringing
eternal salvation and gifts that bless
her day's work with the praise in her singing.

It was in that happy job being her aide
I most basked in love and noted her stern
grasp of a task. So in seaming I've prayed
she would firmly steady my hand and turn.

BRUCE ST. JOHN

1923–1995

Lighters

Dead for some time, if wood can die
In sickly green water, if water's mortal
Lanky palm trees with broken scabby skin
Watch over you your grave with wither'd look.

No one erected you a monument
They left you here to rot.

Around the corner the water's alive,
Huge liners, freighters safely
Tugged into the man-made harbour,
Machines empty and fill their holds,
The atmosphere reeks with progress.
Thanks to enormous shapeless
Boulders lugged from disembowelled quarries,
They have a port, they don't need you.

But I choose you
You are my paradox
Feather that never flew
Half shell of giant snail
With monstrous oars
Fit only for a tropical Cyclops.

Barbados had no Misters then
But only masters of bodies beautiful
Of ebony lit by the glistening
Sweat of honest toil could move you
Major pectorals deltoids and biceps

Bulged to crowd the wharf
With clothing food and shelter,
Gastrocnemius trapezius and others well defined
Elicited silent awe and smiling admiration
Not boisterous jeers or envious handclaps
Or empty silver trophies.

O Solid lightermen
Walking the sunburnt plank
Gone to your silent home

But not forgotten
May these dead lighters resurrect you
As the poet dips his tiny paddle
In sea-blue ink, that some of the chosen
May behold, commune with you
Before you vanish, disappear once more.

LOUIS SIMPSON

b. 1923

Working Late

A light is on in my father's study.
'Still up?' he says, and we are silent,
looking at the harbor lights,
listening to the surf
and the creak of coconut boughs.

He is working late on cases.
No impassioned speech! He argues from evidence,
actually pacing out and measuring,
while the fans revolving on the ceiling
winnow the true from the false.

Once he passed a brass curtain rod
through a head made out of plaster
and showed the jury the angle of fire—
where the murderer must have stood.
For years, all through my childhood,
if I opened a closet . . . bang!
There would be the dead man's head
with a black hole in the forehead.

All the arguing in the world
will not stay the moon.
She has come all the way from Russia
to gaze for a while in a mango tree
and light the wall of a veranda,
before resuming her interrupted journey
beyond the harbor and the lighthouse
at Port Royal, turning away
from land to the open sea.

Yet, nothing in nature changes, from that day to this,
she is still the mother of us all.

I can see the drifting offshore lights,
black posts where the pelicans brood.

And the light that used to shine
at night in my father's study
now shines as late in mine.

JAMES BERRY
b. 1924

Cut-Way Feelins

Yu know him gone.
Children we know him gone.
Him gone lef de sun
fi walk tru yard
widdout him back-a it.

Yu know him gone.
We know him gone.
Him gone lef stars like spears
from roof holes in we eyes.

Naked big shoulda not here—
dohn come an eat we food,
dohn come an mek mi curse
a-beg a lovin look.

Yu know him gone.
Children we know him gone.
Clay bowl dohn av
shavin suds pon Sunday now.
Logs dem alone hol up a house.

Letter to My Father from London

Over the horizon here
you say I told you
animals are groomed like babies
and shops hang wares
like a world of flame trees in bloom

Lambs and calves and pigs hang empty
and ships crowd the port

You say no one arrives back
for the breath once mixed becomes
an eternal entanglement

You say unreason eats up the youth
and rage defeats him

Elders cannot be heroes
when the young wakes up centrally
ragged or inflated on the world
and the ideal of leisure does
not mean a bushman's pocketless time

An enchanter has the face of cash
without sweat
and does not appear barefooted
bursting at elbows and bottom

He has the connections and craft
to claim the sun in gold
and the moon in diamond

You cannot measure the twig-man
image you launched before me
with bloated belly
with bulged eyes of famine
insistent from hoardings and walls
here on world highstreets
holding a bowl to every passerby

You still don't understand
how a victim is guilty as accomplice

RENÉ DÉPESTRE

b. 1926

Ballad of a Little Lamp

Translated by Ellen Conroy Kennedy

> *Thy dusky face I set among the white*
> *For thee to prove thyself of highest worth;*
> *Before the world is swallowed up in night*
> *To show thy little lamp: Go forth, go forth!*
> Claude McKay

There is no salvation for mankind
Except through a great dazzling
Of man by man I affirm it
Me an unknown Negro in the crowd
Me a wild and solitary blade of grass

I shout it to my century
There will be no joy for man
Except by a pure radiance
Of man by man a proud
Leap of mankind toward his destiny
Which is to shine very high
With the star of all men
I shout it I do that defamation
Of the harelip has
Relegated beasts of prey to the last row
I toward whom the lie always
Points its poisoned claws
I whom mediocrity night and day
Pursues with wild boar hoofs
I at whom hatred in the streets
Often aims the finger
I proceed the shepherd of my revolts
I advance with great diamond steps
I clasp to my wounded heart
A faith so human that often at night

Its crying wakes me
Like some newborn babe's that
One must soothe with lullabies and milk
And tenderly at night I rock
My Helen my sweet faith my life falls
In springtime waters on her body
I cherish human dignity
And give to it the rhythm of the rains
That fell my child nights through
I move forward the bearer of an
Insular and bearded faith, the sower
Of a faith untamed untamable
No great poem on bended knees
Before the altarstone of pain
But a little Haitian lamp
That wipes its tears away with laughter
And with a single flex of wings
Rises to the edges of the sky
To be a man forever

Standing tall and free
As the verdant innocence
        of all mankind!
Christian West my terrible brother
Here is my sign of the cross:
In the name of insurgency
and tenderness
and justice
        May it be so!

Black Ore

Translated by Nick Caistor

When all of a sudden the stream of Indian sweat was dried up by the
    sun
When the gold-fever drained out the final drop of Indian blood in the
    marketplace

And every last Indian vanished from around the mines
It was time to look to Africa's river of muscle
For a changing of the guard of misery
And so began the rush to that rich and limitless
Storehouse of black flesh
And so began the breathless dash .
To the noonday splendour of the black-skinned body

Then all the earth rang out with the clatter of the picks
Digging deep in the thick black ore
How many a chemist all but turned his mind
To making some new precious alloy formed
With this black mineral how many a lady almost
Set her heart on finding pots and pans
Of black Senegalese or a fine tea-service
Of stocky Caribbean pickaninny
Who knows what parish padre somewhere
Almost gave his solemn word
To get a churchbell cast in the sonority of black blood
Or what nice Santa Claus almost dreamed
Of little black tin soldiers
For his yearly rounds
Or what valiant man at arms
Would have gladly hewn his blade from this ebony metal
The earth rang out with the shake and shatter of the drills
Deep in the entrails of my people
Deep in the black man's muscled mineral bed
For centuries now they have dug from the depths
The wonders of this race
O mines of ore that are my people
Limitless vein of human dew
How many pirates have plunged their weapons deep
To probe the dark recesses of your flesh,
How many plunderers have hacked themselves a path
Through the lush illumined vegetation of your body
Strewing over your passing days dead stalks
And pools of tears
O pillaged people dug up from top to bottom
Like land beneath the plough
People harrowed to enrich

The great markets of the world
Store up your firedamp deep in your body's secret dark of night
Then none will dare to cast more cannons and more golden coins
From that black metal of your fury's rising flood.

NEVILLE DAWES

1926–1984

Acceptance

I praise the glorious summers of pimento
Sun-purple, riper than the wet red clay-smell
Of my youth by cornlight and river-run
As dog and I, we screamed the small green hill
And the salt smooth wind from the leaping sea
Sang in the yellow sunflower.

I praise the dumb scared child made me
In coffee-groves, and the barbecues of graves.
Smelling of ghosts' old country flesh, laid
By my father for his tribe (fictitious as angels);
A small all-alone boy riding to harvest hymns
In the green of the day as the shackle-bell tongued
On the churchy hill-top.

I praise the legends we made
When the drunk hawks and worse were merry
Waltzed up the day
Haloed the mountains of birds and the nestling curve of the reeling
    river
Swam, those eyes reading the first garden's blush and Adam's.
When weathers twisted the old thunder-voice
I was King Arthur's irrelevant steed on the lightning page
Castling
All races, all men, the drunk hawks and worse
Climbing together the top of the colourless rain
To the dappling sun.

I praise all this
Returning in a shower of mango-blossoms—
The creaking village, the old eyes, the graves, the sun's kiss—
And lonely as ever, as the bare cedars,
I walk by the stream (where boys still plash

Dusking and falling in a star-apple sunset)
And find her there, ancient as the lost lands,
Bandannaed and gray and calling:
Then I read the monumental legend of her love
And grasp her wrinkled hands.

NYDIA ECURY

b. 1926

The Visit

There were bougainvillea flowers
strewn upon the carpet
when the two of you walked in.

My soul turned a sudden somersault,
skipped a beat or two.

There were flowers dancing
on the carpet
as the trade winds
whispered through my house
caressing our sapodilla skins.

When ceremoniously,
we spilled the wine
for the spirits,
Francisca, my great-grandmother,
invisibly,
yet tangibly arrived,
and the four of us,
we formed a chain.

There were scarlet flowers
trembling on the carpet . . .
The blood!
The blood claiming a sisterhood
that began
in the depths of a slave ship
way back when . . .

MARTIN CARTER

1927–1997

University of Hunger

is the university of hunger the wide waste.
is the pilgrimage of man the long march.
The print of hunger wanders in the land.
The green tree bends above the long forgotten.
The plains of life rise up and fall in spasms.
The huts of men are fused in misery.

They come treading in the hoof-marks of the mule
passing the ancient bridge
the grave of pride
the sudden flight
the terror and the time.

They come from the distant village of the flood
passing from middle air to middle earth
in the common hours of nakedness.

Twin bars of hunger mark their metal brows
twin seasons mock them
parching drought and flood.

is the dark ones
the half sunken in the land.
is they who had no voice in the emptiness
in the unbelievable
in the shadowless.

They come treading on the mud floor of the year
mingling with dark heavy waters
and the sea sound of the eyeless flitting bat.
O long is the march of men and long is the life
and wide is the span.

is air dust and the long distance of memory
is the hour of rain when sleepless toads are silent
is broken chimneys smokeless in the wind
is brown trash huts and jagged mounds of iron.

They come in long lines toward the broad city
is the golden moon like a big coin in the sky
is the floor of bone beneath the floor of flesh
is the beak of sickness breaking on the stone
O long is the march of men and long is the life
and wide is the span
O cold is the cruel wind blowing.
O cold is the hoe in the ground.

They come like sea birds
flapping in the wake of a boat
is the torture of sunset in purple bandages
is the powder of fire spread like dust in the twilight
is the water melodies of white foam on wrinkled sand.

The long streets of night move up and down
baring the thighs of a woman
and the cavern of generation.
The beating drum returns and dies away.
The bearded men fall down and go to sleep.
The cocks of dawn stand up and crow like bugles.

is they who rose early in the morning
watching the moon die in the dawn.
is they who heard the shell blow and the iron clang.
is they who had no voice in the emptiness
in the unbelievable
in the shadowless.
O long is the march of men and long is the life
and wide is the span.

Poems of Shape and Motion

Shape and Motion One

I was wondering if I could shape this passion
just as I wanted in solid fire.
I was wondering if the strange combustion of my days
the tension of the world inside of me
and the strength of my heart were enough.

I was wondering if I could stand as tall,
while the tide of the sea rose and fell.
If the sky would recede as I went,
or the earth would emerge as I came
to the door of the morning, locked against the sun.

I was wondering if I could make myself
nothing but fire, pure and incorruptible.

If the wound of the wind on my face
would be healed by the work of my life
or the growth of the pain in my sleep
would be stopped in the strife of my days.

I was wondering if the agony of years
could be traced to the seed of an hour.
If the roots that spread out in the swamp
ran too deep for the issuing flower.

I was wondering if I could find myself
all that I am in all I could be.
If all the population of stars
would be less than the things I could utter
And the challenge of space in my soul
be filled by the shape I become.

Shape and Motion Two

Pull off yuh shirt and throw 'way yuh hat
Kick off yuh shoe and stamp down the spot

Tear off yuh dress and open yuhself
And dance like yuh mad
Far   far.

Oh left foot, right foot, left—Ah boy!
Right foot, left foot, right—Ah boy!
Run up the sky
Run down the road
But run like you mad
Far   far.

Jump off the ground
Pull down a star
Burn till you bleed
Far   far.

Oh right foot, left foot, right—Ah boy!
Left foot, right foot, left—Ah boy!
Oh right foot, right foot
Left foot, left foot
Dance like you mad
Far   far.

Shape and Motion Three

I walk slowly in the wind,
watching myself in things I did not make:
in jumping shadows and in limping cripples
dust on the earth and houses tight with sickness
deep constant pain, the dream without the sleep.

I walk slowly in the wind,
hearing myself in the loneliness of a child
in woman's grief, which is not understood
in coughing dogs when midnight lingers long
on stones, on streets and then on echoing stars,
that burn all night and suddenly go out.

I walk slowly in the wind
knowing myself in every moving thing

in years and days and words that mean so much
strong hands that shake, long roads that walk
and deeds that do themselves.
And all this world and all these lives to live.

I walk slowly in the wind,
remembering scorn and naked men in darkness
and huts of iron rivetted to earth.

Cold huts of iron stand upon this earth
like rusting prisons.
Each wall is marked and each wide roof is spread
like some dark wing
casting a shadow or a living curse.

I walk slowly in the wind
to lifted sunset and gold and dim
a long brown river slanting to an ocean
a fishing boat, a man who cannot drown.
I walk slowly in the wind
and birds are swift, the sky is blue like silk.

From the big sweeping ocean of water
an iron ship rusted and brown anchors itself.
And the long river runs like a snake
silent and smooth.

I walk slowly in the wind.
I hear my footsteps echoing down the tide
echoing like a wave on the sand or a wing on the wind
echoing echoing
a voice in the soul, a laugh in the funny silence.

I walk slowly in the wind
I walk because I cannot crawl or fly.

Proem

Not, in the saying of you, are you
said. Baffled and like a root
stopped by a stone you turn back questioning
the tree you feed. But what the leaves hear
is not what the roots ask. Inexhaustibly,
being at one time what was to be said
and at another time what has been said
the saying of you remains the living of you
never to be said. But, enduring,
you change with the change that changes
and yet are not of the changing of any of you.
Ever yourself, you are always about
to be yourself in something else ever with me.

Being Always

Being, always to arrange
myself in the world, and the world
in myself, I try to do both. How
both are done is difficult. Why,
I have to ask, do I have to
arrange anything when every
thing is already arranged
by love's and death's inscrutable
laws, mortal judiciary, time's
doll house of replaceable heads,
arms and legs? In another
house, not time's, time itself arranges
mine and the world's replacement.

E. McG. 'SHAKE' KEANE

1927–1997

Shaker Funeral

Sorrow sin-
bound, pelting din
big chorusclash
o' the mourners;
eyes red
with a shout for the dead,
yelling crash-
ing sadness in
the dusty tread
o' the mourners.

> Sweet Mother gone
> to the by and by,
> follow her to the brink o' Zion.

Wave wave
as they roared to grave
a drench song—
soulthunder—
was *aymens* through
the wind, shrieks flew,
and eyes were strong;
for 'twas madness gave
them dirge, that grew
made thunder.

Drums, flags,
pious rags o'
robes stenching
sweat;
mitre o' tattered
straw, bamboo crozier
wagged by wind's clenching—
deathwind that bragged

sorrow, smattered
o' sweat.
    Saints in blue
    bathrobes flew
    about the ranks o'
the sinners,
and froth-lipped virgins
with powdered skins
and frocks that stank
with the slime and the stew
from the purged away sins
o' the sinners.

And heads were white
in starched cloth . . . Bright
was the blood from the eyes
o' the candles;
and the 'horn of the Ram
of the great I Am'
spoke hoarse in cries . . .
and crowned with the light
o' the Judah Lamb
were the candles.

    Lord delivered Daniel
    from shame's mouth,
    (o strong, o strong roll Jordan).
    Lord deliver our Mother
    gone to the Glory Home,
    gone to the Glory Home, gone to Zion.

All God's brothers
were loud, and the ten
holy lampers were
reeking in smoke;
and the 'valley of sod-
and-shadow,' Staff-Rod,
was blenched as the canker-
ing sweat o' men
and the reeking o' God
in the smoke.

His willing be,
Mother gone,
Jordan deep,
but her soul is strong.
Follow her to the brink o' Zion.

And now the grave
was washed in a wave
o' wails and a
city o' stars

that dribbled and burned
in the tears that turned
hot sins, on the smoke-white pillars . . .
But their sorrow was yells,
and their faith was brave
as the blood-blemished lambs
piled big on the grave
their city o' wax and stars.

Sweet Mother gone,
King o' Mansions-over-Jordan.
O strong . . .
Leave her safe on the brink o' Zion.

Soufrière (79)

The thing split Good Friday in two
and that good new morning groaned
and snapped
like breaking an old habit

Within minutes
people
who had always been leaving nowhere
began arriving nowhere

entire lives stuffed in pillow-cases
and used plastic bags
naked children suddenly transformed
into citizens

'Ologists with their guilty little instruments
were already oozing about the mountainsides
bravely
and by radio

(As a prelude to resurrection and brotherly love
you can't beat ructions and eruptions)

Flies ran away from the scene of the crime
and crouched like Pilate

in the secret places of my house
washing their hands

Thirty grains of sulphur
panicked off the phone
when it rang

Mysterious people ordered
other mysterious people
to go to mysterious places
'immediately'
I wondered about the old woman
who had walked back to hell
to wash her Sunday clothes

All the grey-long day
music
credible and incredibly beautiful
came over the radio
while the mountain refreshed itself

Someone who lives
inside a microphone
kept things in order

Three children
in unspectacular rags
a single bowl of grey dust between them
tried to manure the future
round a young plum tree

The island put a white mask
over its face
coughed cool as history
and fell in love with itself

A bus travelling heavy
cramped as Calvary
thrust its panic into the side of a hovel
and then the evening's blanket
sent like some strange gift from abroad
was rent by lightning

After a dream
of rancid hope and Guyana rice
I awoke to hear
that the nation had given itself
two hundred thousand dollars

The leaves did not glisten when wet

An old friend
phoned from Ireland
to ask about the future
my Empire cigarettes
have lately been tasting of sulphur
I told her that.

JOHN LA ROSE
b. 1927

Not From Here

You were not born here
    my child
    not here.

You saw daylight
among our islands
the sun was always there.

None could tap the light
from your eyes
or dictate roofs into space
    for your colour.

There in the middle of a hemisphere
you and I were born
    down there.

We were not in the exodus,
there was no Moses
and this was no promised land.

You may not know this yet
    my son;
I sense that you sense it.

Yet what we leave
    we carry.
It is no mud
    we dry
on our boots.

The saliva we swallow
must ever dwell
    down there.

ÉDOUARD GLISSANT

b. 1928

November

Translated by Betsy Wing

And the oar is earthen expecting a new land Oceania love of you is a bandanna topping a mast Oceania love of you a coconut-palm of fog in your presence Oceania in the shadow of your cathedral shrine to savagery and I am taming the foam of your robes Asia and Europe in our childhoods Asia is a coral dwelling within itself and gnawing at itself between skies and battle and as for Europe it is a field of nails. No longer to hear the red stirring of wild butterflies and a heavy day. More and more fierce the elections of murderers in the lovely cancerous rain. Oh the loveliest where our skins are crammed in the loveliest oh in the desert cowbell fingers of lianas from the bush, Africa. The final mission was to lead the word astray into teeming deafness scorched Tropics. Like an addition of fruits drunk with memories in the banana-trees' mute desire.

Wild Reading

Translated by Betsy Wing

From the hill direction a whole expanse suddenly shoves its cart into
   dizzying splendor
In the factories' mill my poverty smiles over powers of the earth
In the cane scars in shins forever black
The water so often called for reddens to my caressing voice
Rebel now from irascible depths of embrace my leap into the standstill.

Like the hougans leafed out in patience
ah the sole evidence I desire is the last voyage of my lassitude among
   the dry leaves of a monsoon

the flowering of islands the frothy geography of islands on eviscerated
   seas
our hymns our brows barred from sources our feet crammed with
   storms

Cut cut with your long stroke of dawn where birds try in vain to nest
Between the tom-tom's links in spite of me the earth capsizes

From the wind direction like a gash shoulders thrusting into the sparks
Nights of impressment all night.

Slow Train

Translated by Betsy Wing

Words I have fed with fire laid with the flesh of men and the lianas of
   scrub forest
scrub brush that grows in flesh exposed to the sun of clearings now
I have opened the blazing pod of a louvre lying in wait for frozen
   orangutan eyes of mine

It is land when peacocks between boas and giant brambles dare no
   longer fan
by dint of thinking land I explode land is when you gather up brains
   splattered in the trash bin of the new ocean
rivers imagine games where my veins are a hopscotch of freshwater for
   the spring to run dry
I feel myself a child in the trough of terrestrial sound doomed to
   plunderings and solitudes
the sea carves out a friendship where I lay my joy down, word
reviling the snow of streets as slave ships' armor
They provided us amphorae in the frigid heart of this last day we have
   slept in torrents and moons slept in the skies
They have cut us back driving tetanus into the scrubgrowth of pores
Of course the canals were dry and the auvergne beard of rain merged
   with despair
shiver house brine of rough diamond
fish in the cage
asleep

Walkway of Lonely Death

Translated by E. Anthony Hurley

The sad bay on a lake of roses
Has not moved, strewn
With corpses grown pale in the rosetrees
A bay of death it has remained

The shore wavers the sea passes
The boats are women washing water
Black is the sand, colour
Is obvious in this place

Birds clothe in grey
The murky azure of their flights
The first wave to be wrecked
Has been driven mad by this evidence

Waves from madness to madness
Have wanly followed the others
The rosetrees have kept the alms
Of the suicides, in their surplices

The white race of the frigates
Never comes to these meals
They go to toll other knells
Where the wind wears no gloves

No movement here but the stir
Of memory and this loud cry
Heard one August noon
On the cliff and its flock

The cry of a land unfurling
The nervures of its summer
Because love dug it up
Or because rain is pleasant

The cry of a woman ploughed
To the very limit of her fallows
Her nubile breasts shared
Between poverty and moss

Cry of bolts and an eagle's cry
And this people was asleep
The bird of prey makes its nest
On the live ashes of the tree

And still no movement but the milk
Of wracks this smell
Death gives life to death
A bay of death it has remained

But sad it has not moved
On its lake of hate, strewn
With corpses grown pale in the thickets
That forgive you, O rosetrees.

ANDREW SALKEY

1928–1995

History and Away

For Elsa Goveia

What we do with time
and what time does with us
is the way of history,
spun down around our feet.

So we say, today,
that we meet our Caribbean shadow
just as it follows the sun,
away into the curve of tomorrow.

In fact, our sickle of islands
and continental strips are mainlands
of time with our own marks on them,
yesterday, today and tomorrow.

RALPH THOMPSON

b. 1928

Dinner Party

The dignitaries gather for a dinner party,
a long table on the lawn under the stars,
serviettes folded into tall lilies,
place cards between the silver and the crystal.

As each guest arrives, a breathless hostess
feels obliged to break the news—
he had died suddenly that afternoon,
found by his wife slumped in the bathroom.

'They were invited for tonight', the host
explains. A guest gasps, eyes wet with tears.
'I can't believe that he is gone. He sounded
so enthusiastic on the phone this morning'.

The Governor of the Central Bank extols
his splendid innings, praises his achievements
scrolled by degrees, earned and honorary,
knighted by the Queen, beloved by all who knew him.

The Chief Justice clears his throat, issues
an opinion. 'Perhaps that's how he wished to go—
quickly, no prolonged suffering.
His work will be his greatest monument.'

This Canadian High Commissioner disagrees.
'I want a week', she says. 'At least a week
. . . for contrition, to get my soul prepared,
to see my husband, the children, one last time.'

'Amen' mumbles the chorus as the host
hurriedly rearranges the seating plan,
a waiter surreptitiously removing
two place settings, two surplus chairs.

The wine does its work, conversation
like phosphorus flashing around the table,
flaring into laughter. Then silence—
overhead, a curious sky listening.

At seventy he is careful not to drink
too much. Goodbyes said, he strides to the car,
opens the door with a flourish for his wife.
The engine kicks instantly to life.

He checks the rhythm of his heart—no pain, no flutter,
no hint of trouble. His weight and hands are steady,
his bowels regular. The dashboard glows,
all systems go. Ample gas, battery

fully charged, speed within the limit.
He will be home soon. As the lights change
to green, the conviction grows that he has time,
will not die—not tonight, anyway.

DENNIS CRAIG

1929–2004

Trader

(Decades of the seventies and eighties)

You can't have it, says
the god that rules the formal economy

Toilet paper, sweet-soap, fancy perfume
cheese, chocolate with nuts, sundries in tins
textiles and shoes art-crafted in far places—

You can't have it, says the god. So I say
But if foreigner have it, why can't we?

For less than that—for the fun of it really
I Gaiseric, vandal,
razed Rome with fire

But today, the law of the economy
bites more deeply than the sword.

Today, when my people's mouth waters
no plundering follows; the mirage becomes
our foreign debt on the horizon

and I must go buy bring and sell
The god strips me naked before I go:

foreign dollars are crimes leaving the airport
The miracle is how they metamorphosed
from the white-belly shrimp of the sea-coast

thyme, and the dried bushes that are potent—
like from caterpillar to butterfly

after riding the road of the sky
from Georgetown to Port-of-Spain, or Miami.
Or is it from Kingston to Port-au-Prince Haiti?

No matter—into all our bosoms
dollars come first from the earth and the sea.

My big thing is the bundles I bring back.
Always overweight, I push and quarrel.
I am the embarrassment in the seat

beside you on the plane, the minus sign
on social class in air travel

huckster, higgler, the parallel one,
the mongrel tail that wags the dog (or
is it the g-o-d?) of the formal economy.

KAMAU BRATHWAITE

b. 1930

The visibility trigger

And so they came up over the reefs

up the creeks and rivers
oar prong put put
hack tramp silence

and i was dreaming near morning

i offered you a kola nut
your fingers huge and smooth and red
and you took it your dress makola blue

and you broke it into gunfire

the metal was hot and jagged
it was as if the master of bronze

had poured anger into his cauldron

and let it spit spit sputter
and it was black spark green in my face

it was as if a maggot
had slapped me in the belly
and i had gone soft like the kneed of my wife's bread

i could hear salt leaking out of the black hole of kaneshie
i could hear grass growing around the edges of the green lake
i could hear stalactites ringing in my cave of vision

bats batting my eyes shut
their own eyes howling like owls in the dead dark

and they marched into the village
and our five unready virginal elders met them

bowl calabash oil carafe of fire silence

and unprepared and venerable i was dreaming mighty wind in trees
our circles talismans round hut round village cooking pots

the world was round and we the spices in it
time wheeled around our memories like stars

yam cassava groundnut sweetpea bush
and then it was yams again

birth child hunter warrior
and the breath

which is no more

which is birth which is child which is hunter which is warrior
which is breath

that is no more

and they brought sticks rods roads bullets straight objects

birth was not breath
but gaping wound

hunter was not animal
but market sale

warrior was child

that is no more

and i beheld the cotton tree
guardian of graves rise upward from its monument of grass crying
aloud in its vertical hull calling
for crashes of branches vibrations of leaves

there was a lull of silver

and then the great grandfather gnashing upwards from its teeth
of roots.   split down its central thunder

the stripped violated wood crying aloud its murder.   the leaves
frontier signals alive with lamentations

and our great odoum
triggered at last by the ancestors into your visibility
crashed

into history

South

But today I recapture the islands'
bright beaches: blue mist from the ocean
rolling into the fishermen's houses.
By these shores I was born: sound of the sea
came in at my window, life heaved and breathed in me then
with the strength of that turbulent soil.

Since then I have travelled: moved far from the beaches:
sojourned in stoniest cities, walking the lands of the north
in sharp slanting sleet and the hail,
crossed countless saltless savannas and come
to this house in the forest where the shadows oppress me
and the only water is rain and the tepid taste of the river.

We who are born of the ocean can never seek solace
in rivers: their flowing runs on like our longing,
reproves us our lack of endeavour and purpose,
proves that our striving will founder on that.
We resent them this wisdom, this freedom: passing us
toiling, waiting and watching their cunning declension down to the
    sea.

But today I would join you, travelling river,
borne down the years of your patientest flowing,
past pains that would wreck us, sorrows arrest us,
hatred that washes us up on the flats;
and moving on through the plains that receive us,
processioned in tumult, come to the sea.

Bright waves splash up from the rocks to refresh us,
blue sea-shells shift in their wake
and *there* is the thatch of the fishermen's houses, the path
made of pebbles, and look!
small urchins combing the beaches
look up from their traps to salute us:

they remember us just as we left them.
The fisherman, hawking the surf on this side
of the reef; stands up in his boat
and halloos us: a starfish lies in its pool.
And gulls, white sails slanted seaward,
fly into the limitless morning before us.

Milkweed

1

But my father has gone out on the plantation
he used to make us windmills
spinnakers of trash when the crack of cane was in the air

the brown stalks wrinkled and curled in the wind like scarecrows of
    orange angels
and butterflies flickered as the clipped straw clicked
on its pin as it picked up speed

but for years he has brought us nothing
for years he has told us nothing
his verbs shut tight on his briar

while my mother watches him go
with his cap and his limp and his skillet of soup
and we never look at his hands

2

look at his hands:
cactus cracked, pricked,
worn smooth by the hoe,

limestone soil's colour:
he has lost three fingers
of his left hand falling
asleep at the mill:
the black crushing grin
of the iron tooth'd ratchets
grinding the farley hill cane
have eaten him lame
and no one is to blame

the crunched bone was juicy
to the iron: there was no difference
between his knuckle joints
and ratoon shots: the soil
receives the liquor with cool flutes:
three fingers are not even worth a stick
of cane: the blood
mix does not show, the star-
gaze crystal sugar shines
no brighter for the cripple blow:
and nothing more to show
for thirty years' spine
curving labour in clear
rain, glass eyed, coming off
the sea, fattening up the mud
in the valleys, cours-
ing down hillsides, caus-
ing the toil of the deep,
well-laid roots, gripping soil,
to come steadily loose, junction and joint
between shoot and its flower to be made nonsense of:
and the shame the shame the shame-
lessness of it all: the name-
less days in the burnt cane-

fields without love: crack of its
loud trash, spinn-
ing ashes, wrack
of salt odour that will not free
his throat: the cutlass fall-

ing, fall-
ing: sweat, grit between fingers,
chigga hatching its sweet nest
of pain in his toe
and now this and now this:
an old man, prickled to sleep by the weather, his labour,
losing his hands . . .

from *Sun Poem*

11

i

There are certain dreams that boys
have living by the sea
that they will become infamous sailors

see galleons whales
find treasure at the bottom of the ocean
tree; in the hills that they will climb

the mountain; in the desert ex-
orcize their god; in
my backyard that i will shift the boulder

brought years and years before
by the wet shoulder of torn
waves: grown older now and darker

no longer mossy
and in the jewel case of earth beneath
it: there would be this crab: tick-

ing scarlet: petties purple
frothing fromits from its shellac shell and shelter.
this was our vision of the ancient sun

squatting upon the sandy redge of memories
this crab knew ancient histories
old harbour cartagena tenoctitlan half

moon fort plantation grasses; re-
leased its scrapers scuttled with us back
to prisoned childhoods hintless of the world

of banks and bombs now voiceless auction blocks
but instincts fished for lay below the surface
with held and shining breaths that dived us down to truth

of ship retreating coastline dumbless origins

ii

mosquito one mosquito two
mosquito jump in de ole man shoe

mosquito two mosquito tree
mosquito stick stick miss sally knee

mosquito tree mosquito four
mosquito knock in de donkey door

mosquito four mosquito five
mosquito six and de poor get lix

mosquito six mosquito seven
de man in de moon isnt livin in heaven

mosquito seven mosquito eight
mosquito nine rape de girl in de pine

mosquito nine mosquito ten
de monkey jump up and jump dung agen

aeyae yae jin jin *aeyae yae* jin-jin
monkey eat tobacco an shit

white lime

12

i

For this was the summer the blue egg'd blackeyed summertime.
red combs and proud bronze spurs now flared themselves in the
yards. blue white black brown fluffy and bare-necked hens scut-
tled and clucked in the seaside sun while slowly and tall/ly above
them turned and man/oeuvred the golden galleon cocks. for this
was the summer the blue egg'd blackeyed summertime. over the
fence of the seaward yards came the

sea-weed salt-sea sea-moss smell; and far away, where the fisher-
men were, the flying fish flew like corn that was tossed through
the drizzling air . . . sun streaks spread like webs over rock and
the patterned carpets of green purple grass where a crab scuttled
spotted with coral and pink and a starfish closed its eye. the whole
wild floor of the bay was like flowing so the dark rocks breathed
and the lighted seaweed

trembled. and there, cushioned and nested bright in the moss and
cracks of the deep green rocks, were the eggs you were diving to
find. and this was the difficult part: the picking. you had to be still
like a bee by a flower or a hummingbird over a fruit. then care-
fully cupping the palm a your hann so it wouldn't be pricked by
the prickles, you pressed on the sea-egg and pulled

it

lifting the white blue little hedgehog head from the rock like a cup
that is stuck to a saucer. *but hole it! doan mine if it tickle de palm
a you hann*: all the prickles are living: *but hold it*, don't mind if it
tickles the palm of your hand and down back down for another.
in the end you should have from two to tree pairs cradle into the
crook a you arm, each pair like de firs' one: face-touchin-face.

you is ress for a minit, holdin on to de rockin boat an yu breathin:
one two tree: and den down: is back dung under de water: all de
sky blue air you cud hole in you chess in you chess and de ress
store up in yu belly: eyes wide: eyes red: body curve down de
spine to hole de air better an give yu head time: *so is dung back*

dung for annudda: rock bruise prickle finger: rippin an robin an
rapin the ripenin blue egg blackeyed summertime sea

ii

and *tap tap tap* went the spoons off-shore: the men in the moses boats
   sitting off-shore breaking the sea-eggs shells

tap tap tap all the flat day long all in a row off shore

tap tap tap the men sitting cross-legged moored to the close-in shore

tap tap tap and the eggs were split opened lifted and turned
   upside-down so the

sea-moss salt-stale inside-shell fell onto the spattered floor
and the pure gold pale gold sea-egg roe were veins of the sea-egg
   shell

tap tap tap from the blue black boats blazed with the white
   living white waving light

of the heaped-up sea-egg shells and they cracked the egg through
   its one black
watery eye and their spoons raked the gold core clean. a full tin tot
was passed

to the shore with its conical gold-core head
and given a grape-leaf covering hat
by the sea-egg women who sat near the boats on the sloping
   browns beach shore.

and they rose from the sand when their trays were full and

sea-eggs . . . they sang
   eyes looking down as they balanced their trays . . .

     sea-eggggggggggg . . . looook me heyyyyyyyy
      swinging full sails of their hips from the shore . . .

The SilverSands Poem

how is the sound of this south sea so soft
of the hurricane
how so in a hurry to alter the landscape . to let fish slip
under the silence
of nets . to let the sand flurry this afternoon
where we walk on the dunes
waiting for the fisherfolk of ourselves to return
to the land . to recover the harbour

the trip-feeted ipomea catches my foot in its green
upon white as i turn
from all this loud & this labour of water
the glittering blue
of this southernmost coast of our island

and as i enter the grotto
of casuarina seagrape & memory . all that sound
is lost . the sea tossing & glittering .
the wind blowing across it . the reefs of white horses .
how gentle & slow the sand now under my feet
soft as sorrow

and this grotto receives me like water . breathing
the light green of the casuarine . the sharp curled ear
of the seagrape . the cave of these ancient trees
deep underwater where i raise my hands slowly
like swimming . my hands and then my lost
feet moving into this pendulum

the long hard body of the rocky coast now softly floating
away into space .
my eyes lifted upward to where the light of the world is
. like a fish at last of release .
tracing itself thru the hallow . climbing thru time
to millennium

ROBERTO FERNÁNDEZ RETAMAR

b. 1930

How Lucky, the Normal

Translated by J. R. Pereira

How lucky the normal, those peculiar creatures.
Those who didn't have a mad mother, a drunk father, a delinquent son,
A house in nowhere, an unknown disease.
Those who have worn all seventeen smiling faces and more,
Those well-heeled, angelic types,
The complacent and fat and creole,
The Rin-tin-tins and their cronies, the ones who 'But certainly, this
    way',
Those money-makers, beloved to the toe,
Pipers with their rats in tow,
Merchants and customers,
Gentlemen just a shade super'.uman,
Men dressed in thunder, ladies in lightning,
The delicate, sensible, elegant ones,
The kind, sweet, edible, potable ones,
How lucky they are birds, dung and stones.

But just let them step aside for the others, those makers of worlds and
    dreams,
Illusions and symphonies, words that tear down

And rebuild us, crazier than their mothers, drunker
Than their fathers, more delinquent than their sons,

More eaten away by corrosive loves.
Let them leave these their place in hell, and call it quits.

Where's Fernández?

To the other Karamazovs

Translated by Paul Bundy

Now he comes in, to my surprise.
I was his favorite son and I'm sure my brothers
Know that's how it was and won't be put out if I say so.
In any case his preference was at least fair.
When Manolo was still a kid, he said to him, pointing at me
(I can see the marble-topped table in Los Castellanos café
We were sitting around, and the dark wooden chairs.
And the bar in the background with the big mirror and the long rows
    of bottles
That now and again I only see in old films):
'Your brother gets the best grades, but you're the brightest.'
Later, much later, he told him, always pointing at me:
'Your brother writes the poetry, but you're the poet.'
Needless to say, he was right on both counts,
But what a strange way to show preference.
It wasn't his liver that killed him (he'd been a heavy drinker, but it was
    his brother Pedro who was hit with liver trouble),
But his lung, where the cancer spread because they said he chain-
    smoked.
And the truth is I can hardly remember ever seeing him without a
    cigarette between his yellow-stained fingers.
Those long fingers of his hand that is my hand now.
Even in the hospital, dying, he begged us to light him a cigarette.
Just for a minute. Just for a minute.
And we lit it for him. It didn't make any difference by then.
His main mistress had a Shakespearean heroine's name,
That name we couldn't utter at home.
But (I think) that's as far as the connection to the Bard went.
However, his real woman (not his spouse and certainly not his good
    wife)
Was my mother. When she came to from the anaesthetic after the
    operation that eventually killed her,
It wasn't he, but I who was at her side.
But as soon as she opened her eyes, she asked, thickly, 'Where's
    Fernández?'

I no longer remember what I said. I went to the nearest telephone and
    rang him up.
He, who had always had the courage to face things, couldn't bring
    himself to say good-bye to her,
Or wait until that operation was over.
He was at home, alone, surely pacing from one end to another,
I know so well because I do it myself, surely
Reaching out with a shaky hand for something to drink; searching
For the little pistol with the pearl grips that mama had hidden from
    him and in any case
He would never have used it for that.
I told him mama had come through okay, that she'd asked after him,
    that he should come.
He arrived restless, quick and slow. He was still my father, but at the
    same time
He had already started being my son.
Mama died a bit later, that brave heroine.
And he began to die like the Shakespearean character he really was.
Like a strange, old, moving, provincial Romeo
(But Romeo was a provincial, too).
The thunder went out of him, life lost its meaning. His girlfriend
From the boarding house no longer existed, that little brunette
He had almost frightened to death walking on the edge of the roof in
    the hurricane of '26;
The girl with whom he'd spent a honeymoon in a little hotel on
    Belascoaín Street,
And she trembled, kissed him and gave him sons
Without losing her modesty of that first night;
With whom he shared the death of their eldest, 'the little one' for
    always,
During the doctors' strike in '34;
With whom he had studied for the finals; and whose jet-black hair
    turned gray,
But not her heart, that burned against injustice,
Against Machado, against Batista; the one who welcomed the
    Revolution
With eyes bright and pure, and was lowered into the ground
Wrapped in the Cuban flag of her Cerro school, the little public school
    for girls,

Like the boys' school where her brother Alfonso was a schoolfriend of
    Rubén Martínez Villena;
Who didn't smoke or drink, wasn't glamorous and didn't look like a
    film star,
Because she was a real star;
Who while she washed at the stone wash place,
Worked up the soap suds and improvised poems and songs,
Filling her children with a rare mixture of admiration and pride and
    embarrassment, too,
Because other mothers they knew weren't like that
(They didn't know yet that no mother is like another, that every
    mother,
As Martí said, should be called a marvel).
And old man thunder began to go out like a candle.
He sat hours in the living room of a house that had become enormous.
The bird cages were empty. The plants in the patio had dried up.
Newspapers and magazines piled up. Books went unread.
Sometimes he would talk to us, his sons,
And would tell us things about his modest adventures,
As if we weren't his sons, but those old cronies of his
Who were all dead, who he'd get together with to drink, conspire and
    recite,
In cafés and bars that no longer existed.
On the eve of his death I finally read The Count of Montecristo, by the
    sea,
And I felt I was reading it through his eyes,
In the dining room of the somber Catholic school
Where he consumed his orphan's childhood, with no other happiness
Than reading books like that one, that he talked to me so much about.
That's what he wanted to be like out of captivity: just (more than
    vengeful) and gallant.
With some wealth (which he never had, because he was as honest as
    the sun's rays,
And he even became famous because he once resigned from a post
    when he realized he was supposed to steal).
With some love affairs (which he was fortunate enough to have,
    although they didn't always turn out so well in the end).
Rebellious, picturesque, rhetorical like the Count, or better yet,
Like a musketeer. I don't know. He lived literature, the way he lived
    ideas and words,

With an authenticity that's overwhelming.
And he was courageous, very courageous, when confronted with police
    and thieves,
When confronted with hypocrites, liars and assassins.
Near the end he asked me to wipe the sweat from his brow.
I picked up the towel and did so, but I realized then
That I was wiping away his tears. He didn't say anything.
He was in horrible pain and was dying. But the Count,
Gallant, eighty- or ninety-pound musketeer that he was, only asked me
To please wipe the sweat from his brow.

DEREK WALCOTT

b. 1930

The Schooner Flight

1 *Adios, Carenage*

In idle August, while the sea soft,
and leaves of brown islands stick to the rim
of this Caribbean, I blow out the light
by the dreamless face of Maria Concepcion
to ship as a seaman on the schooner *Flight.*
Out in the yard turning grey in the dawn,
I stood like a stone and nothing else move
but the cold sea rippling like galvanize
and the nail holes of stars in the sky roof,
till a wind start to interfere with the trees.
I pass me dry neighbour sweeping she yard
as I went downhill, and I nearly said:
'Sweep soft, you witch, 'cause she don't sleep hard,'
but the bitch look through me like I was dead.
A route taxi pull up, park-lights still on.
The driver size up my bags with a grin:
'This time, Shabine, like you really gone!'
I ain't answer the ass, I simply pile in
the back seat and watch the sky burn
above Laventille pink as the gown
in which the woman I left was sleeping,
and I look in the rearview and see a man
exactly like me, and the man was weeping
for the houses, the streets, that whole fucking island.

Christ have mercy on all sleeping things!
From that dog rotting down Wrightson Road
to when I was a dog on these streets;
if loving these islands must be my load,
out of corruption my soul takes wings,
But they had started to poison my soul

with their big house, big car, big-time bohbohl,
coolie, nigger, Syrian, and French Creole,
so I leave it for them and their carnival—
I taking a sea-bath, I gone down the road.
I know these islands from Monos to Nassau,
a rusty head sailor with sea-green eyes
that they nickname Shabine, the patois for
any red nigger, and I, Shabine, saw
when these slums of empire was paradise.
I'm just a red nigger who love the sea,
I had a sound colonial education,
I have Dutch, nigger, and English in me,
and either I'm nobody, or I'm a nation.

But Maria Concepcion was all my thought
watching the sea heaving up and down
as the port side of dories, schooners, and yachts
was painted afresh by the strokes of the sun
signing her name with every reflection;
I knew when dark-haired evening put on
her bright silk at sunset, and, folding the sea,
sidled under the sheet with her starry laugh,
that there'd be no rest, there'd be no forgetting.
Is like telling mourners round the graveside
about resurrection, they want the dead back,
so I smile to myself as the bow rope untied
and the *Flight* swing seaward: 'Is no use repeating
that the sea have more fish. I ain't want her
dressed in the sexless light of a seraph,
I want those round brown eyes like a marmoset, and
till the day when I can lean back and laugh,
those claws that tickled my back on sweating
Sunday afternoons, like a crab on wet sand.'
As I worked, watching the rotting waves come
past the bow that scissor the sea like silk,
I swear to you all, by my mother's milk,
by the stars that shall fly from tonight's furnace,
that I loved them, my children, my wife, my home;
I loved them as poets love the poetry
that kills them, as drowned sailors the sea.

You ever look up from some lonely beach
and see a far schooner? Well, when I write
this poem, each phrase go be soaked in salt;
I go draw and knot every line as tight
as ropes in this rigging; in simple speech
my common language go be the wind,
my pages the sails of the schooner *Flight*.
But me tell you how this business begin.

2 *Raptures of the Deep*

Smuggled Scotch for O'Hara, big government man,
Between Cedros and the Main, so the Coast Guard couldn't
    touch us,
And the Spanish pirogues always met us halfway,
but a voice kept saying: 'Shabine, see this business
of playing pirate?' Well, so said, so done!
That whole racket crash. And I for a woman,
for her laces and silks, Maria Concepcion.
Ay, ay! Next thing I hear, some Commission of Enquiry
was being organized to conduct a big quiz,
with himself as chairman investigating himself.
Well, I knew damn well who the suckers would be,
not that shark in shark skin, but his pilot fish,
khaki-pants red niggers like you and me.
What worse, I fighting with Maria Concepcion,
plates flying and thing, so I swear: 'Not again!'
It was mashing up my house and my family.
I was so broke all I needed was shades and a cup
or four shades and four cups in four-cup Port of Spain;
all the silver I had was the coins on the sea.

You saw them ministers in *The Express*,
guardians of the poor—one hand at their back,
and one set o' police only guarding their house,
and the Scotch pouring in through the back door.
As for that minister-monster who smuggled the booze,
that half-Syrian saurian, I got so vex to see
that face thick with powder, the warts, the stone lids
like a dinosaur caked with primordial ooze

by the lightning of flashbulbs sinking in wealth,
that I said: 'Shabine, this is shit, understand!'
But he get somebody to kick my crutch out his office
like I was some artist! That bitch was so grand,
couldn't get off his high horse and kick me himself.
I have seen things that would make a slave sick
in this Trinidad, the Limers' Republic.

I couldn't shake the sea noise out of my head,
The shell of my ears sang Maria Concepcion,
so I start salvage diving with a crazy Mick,
name O'Shaughnessy, and a limey named Head;
but this Caribbean so choke with the dead
that when I would melt in emerald water,
whose ceiling rippled like a silk tent,
I saw them corals: brain, fire, sea-fans,
dead-men's-fingers, and then, the dead men.
I saw that the powdery sand was their bones
ground white from Senegal to San Salvador,
so, I panic third dive, and surface for a month
in the Seamen's Hostel. Fish broth and sermons.
When I thought of the woe I had brought my wife,
when I saw my worries with that other woman,
I wept under water, salt seeking salt,
for her beauty had fallen on me like a sword
cleaving me from my children, flesh of my flesh!

There was this barge from St. Vincent, but she was too deep
to float her again. When we drank, the limey
got tired of my sobbing for Maria Concepcion.
He said he was getting the bends. Good for him!
The pain in my heart for Maria Concepcion,
the hurt I had done to my wife and children,
was worse than the bends. In the rapturous deep
there was no cleft rock where my soul could hide
like boobies each sunset, no sandbar of light
where I could rest, like the pelicans know,
so I got raptures once, and I saw God
like a harpooned grouper bleeding, and a far
voice was rumbling, 'Shabine, if you leave her,

130

if you leave her, I shall give you the morning star.'
When I left the madhouse I tried other women
but, once they stripped naked, their spiky cunts
bristled like sea-eggs and I couldn't dive.
The chaplain came round. I paid him no mind.
Where is my rest place, Jesus? Where is my harbour?
Where is the pillow I will not have to pay for,
and the window I can look from that frames my life?

3 *Shabine Leaves the Republic*

I had no nation now but the imagination.
After the white man, the niggers didn't want me
when the power swing to their side.
The first chain my hands and apologize, 'History';
the next said I wasn't black enough for their pride.
Tell me, what power, on these unknown rocks—
a spray-plane Air Force, the Fire Brigade,
the Red Cross, the Regiment, two, three police dogs
that pass before you finish bawling 'Parade!'?
I met History once, but he ain't recognize me,
a parchment Creole, with warts
like an old sea-bottle, crawling like a crab
through the holes of shadow cast by the net
of a grille balcony; cream linen, cream hat.
I confront him and shout, 'Sir, is Shabine!
They say I'se your grandson. You remember Grandma,
your black cook, at all?' The bitch hawk and spat.
A spit like that worth any number of words.
But that's all them bastards have left us: words.

I no longer believed in the revolution.
I was losing faith in the love of my woman.
I had seen that moment Aleksandr Blok
crystallize in *The Twelve*. Was between
the Police Marine Branch and Hotel Venezuelana
one Sunday at noon. Young men without flags
using shirts, their chests waiting for holes.
They kept marching into the mountains, and
their noise ceased as foam sinks into sand.

They sank in the bright hills like rain, every one
with his own nimbus, leaving shirts in the street,
and the echo of power at the end of the street.
Propeller-blade fans turn over the Senate;
the judges, they say, still sweat in carmine,
on Frederick Street the idlers all marching
by standing still, the Budget turns a new leaf.
In the 12:30 movies the projectors best
not break down, or you go see revolution. Aleksandr Blok
enters and sits in the third row of pit eating choc-
olate cone, waiting for a spaghetti West-
ern with Clint Eastwood and featuring Lee Van Cleef.

4 *The* Flight, *Passing Blanchisseuse*

Dusk. The *Flight* passing Blanchisseuse.
Gulls wheel like from a gun again,
and foam gone amber that was white,
lighthouse and star start making friends,
down every beach the long day ends,
and there, on that last stretch of sand,
on a beach bare of all but light,
dark hands start pulling in the seine
of the dark sea, deep, deep inland.

5 *Shabine Encounters the Middle Passage*

Man, I brisk in the galley first thing next dawn,
brewing li'l coffee; fog coil from the sea
like the kettle steaming when I put it down
slow, slow, 'cause I couldn't believe what I see:
where the horizon was one silver haze,
the fog swirl and swell into sails, so close
that I saw it was sails, my hair grip my skull,
it was horrors, but it was beautiful.
We float through a rustling forest of ships
with sails dry like paper, behind the glass
I saw men with rusty eyeholes like cannons,
and whenever their half-naked crews cross the sun,
right through their tissue, you traced their bones

like leaves against the sunlight; frigates, barkentines,
the backward-moving current swept them on,
and high on their decks I saw great admirals,
Rodney, Nelson, de Grasse, I heard the hoarse orders
they gave those Shabines, and the forest
of masts sail right through the *Flight*,
and all you could hear was the ghostly sound
of waves rustling like grass in a low wind
and the hissing weeds they trailed from the stern;
slowly they heaved past from east to west
like this round world was some cranked water wheel,
every ship pouring like a wooden bucket
dredged from the deep; my memory revolve
on all sailors before me, then the sun
heat the horizon's ring and they was mist.

Next we pass slave ships. Flags of all nations,
 our fathers below deck too deep, I suppose,
 to hear us shouting. So we stop shouting. Who knows
 who his grandfather is, much less his name?
 Tomorrow our landfall will be the Barbados.

6 *The Sailor Sings Back to the Casuarinas*

You see them on the low hills of Barbados
bracing like windbreaks, needles for hurricanes,
trailing, like masts, the cirrus of torn sails;
when I was green like them, I used to think
those cypresses, leaning against the sea,
that take the sea-noise up into their branches,
are not real cypresses but casuarinas.
Now captain just call them Canadian cedars.
But cedars, cypresses, or casuarinas,
whoever called them so had a good cause,
watching their bending bodies wail like women
after a storm, when some schooner came home
with news of one more sailor drowned again.
Once the sound 'cypress' used to make more sense
than the green 'casuarinas,' though, to the wind
whatever grief bent them was all the same,

since they were trees with nothing else in mind
but heavenly leaping or to guard a grave;
but we live like our names and you would have
to be colonial to know the difference,
to know the pain of history words contain,
to love those trees with an inferior love,
and to believe: 'Those casuarinas bend
like cypresses, their hair hangs down in rain
like sailors' wives. They're classic trees, and we,
if we live like the names our masters please,
by careful mimicry might become men.'

7 The Flight Anchors in Castries Harbor

When the stars self were young over Castries,
I loved you alone and I loved the whole world.
What does it matter that our lives are different?
Burdened with the loves of our different children?
When I think of your young face washed by the wind
and your voice that chuckles in the slap of the sea?
The lights are out on La Toc promontory,
except for the hospital. Across at Vigie
the marina arcs keep vigil. I have kept my own
promise, to leave you the one thing I own,
you whom I loved first: my poetry.
We here for one night. Tomorrow, the Flight will be gone.

8 Fight with the Crew

It had one bitch on board, like he had me mark—
that was the cook, some Vincentian arse
with a skin like a gommier tree, red peeling bark,
and wash-out blue eyes; he wouldn't give me a ease,
like he feel he was white. Had an exercise book,
this same one here, that I was using to write
my poetry, so one day this man snatch it
from my hand, and start throwing it left and right
to the rest of the crew, bawling out, 'Catch it,'
and start mincing me like I was some hen
because of the poems. Some case is for fist,

some case is for tholing pin, some is for knife—
this one was for knife. Well, I beg him first,
but he keep reading, 'O my children, my wife,'
and playing he crying, to make the crew laugh;
it move like a flying fish, the silver knife
that catch him right in the plump of his calf,
and he faint so slowly, and he turn more white
than he thought he was. I suppose among men
you need that sort of thing. It ain't right
but that's how it is. There wasn't much pain,
just plenty blood, and Vincie and me best friend,
but none of them go fuck with my poetry again.

9 *Maria Concepcion & the Book of Dreams*

The jet that was screeching over the *Flight*
was opening a curtain into the past.
'Dominica ahead!'
                              'It still have Caribs there.'
'One day go be planes only, no more boat.'
'Vince, God ain't make nigger to fly through the air.'
'Progress, Shabine, that's what it's all about.
Progress leaving all we small islands behind.'
I was at the wheel, Vince sitting next to me
gaffing. Crisp, bracing day. A high-running sea.
'Progress is something to ask Caribs about.
They kill them by millions, some in war,
some by forced labour dying in the mines
looking for silver, after that niggers; more
progress. Until I see definite signs
that mankind change, Vince, I ain't want to hear.
Progress is history's dirty joke.
Ask that sad green island getting nearer.'
Green islands, like mangoes pickled in brine.
In such fierce salt let my wound be healed,
me, in my freshness as a seafarer.

That night, with the sky sparks frosty with fire,
I ran like a Carib through Dominica,
my nose holes choked with memory of smoke;

I heard the screams of my burning children,
I ate the brains of mushrooms, the fungi
of devil's parasols under white, leprous rocks;
my breakfast was leaf mould in leaking forests,
with leaves big as maps, and when I heard noise
of the soldiers' progress through the thick leaves,
though my heart was bursting, I get up and ran
through the blades of balisier sharper than spears;
with the blood of my race, I ran, boy, I ran
with moss-footed speed like a painted bird;
then I fall, but I fall by an icy stream under
cool fountains of fern, and a screaming parrot
catch the dry branches and I drowned at last
in big breakers of smoke; then when that ocean
of black smoke pass, and the sky turn white,
there was nothing but Progress, if Progress is
an iguana as still as a young leaf in sunlight.
I bawl for Maria, and her *Book of Dreams.*

It anchored her sleep, that insomniac's Bible,
a soiled orange booklet with a cyclops' eye
center, from the Dominican Republic.
Its coarse pages were black with the usual
symbols of prophecy, in excited Spanish;
an open palm upright, sectioned and numbered
like a butcher chart, delivered the future.
One night, in a fever, radiantly ill,
she say, 'Bring me the book, the end has come.'
She said: 'I dreamt of whales and a storm,'
but for that dream, the book had no answer.
A next night I dreamed of three old women
featureless as silkworms, stitching my fate,
and I scream at them to come out my house,
and I try beating them away with a broom,
but as they go out, so they crawl back again,
until I start screaming and crying, my flesh
raining with sweat, and she ravage the book
for the dream meaning, and there was nothing;
my nerves melt like a jellyfish—that was when I broke—
they found me round the Savannah, screaming:

All you see me talking to the wind, so you think I mad.
Well, Shabine has bridled the horses of the sea;
you see me watching the sun till my eyeballs seared,
so all you mad people feel Shabine crazy,
but all you ain't know my strength, hear? The coconuts
standing by in their regiments in yellow khaki,
they waiting for Shabine to take over these islands,
and all you best dread the day I am healed
of being a human. All you fate in my hand,
ministers, businessmen, Shabine have you, friend,
I shall scatter your lives like a handful of sand,
I who have no weapon but poetry and
the lances of palms and the sea's shining shield!

10 *Out of the Depths*

Next day, dark sea. A arse-aching dawn.
'Damn wind shift sudden as a woman mind.'
The slow swell start cresting like some mountain range
with snow on the top.
                              'Ay, Skipper, sky dark!'
'This ain't right for August.'
                              'This light damn strange,
this season, sky should be clear as a field.'

A stingray steeplechase across the sea,
tail whipping water, the high man-o'-wars
start reeling inland, quick, quick an archery
of flying fish miss us! Vince say: 'You notice?'
and a black-mane squall pounce on the sail
like a dog on a pigeon, and it snap the neck
of the *Flight* and shake it from bead to tail.
'Be Jesus, I never see sea get so rough
so fast! That wind come from God back pocket!'
'Where Cap'n headin? Like the man gone blind!'
'If we's to drong, we go drong, Vince, fock-it!'
'Shabine, say your prayers, if life leave you any!'

I have not loved those that I loved enough.
Worse than the mule kick of Kick-'Em-Jenny

Channel, rain start to pelt the *Flight* between
mountains of water. If I was frighten?
The tent poles of water spouts bracing the sky
start wobbling, clouds unstitch at the seams
and sky water drench us, and I hear myself cry,
'I'm the drowned sailor in her *Book of Dreams.*'
I remembered them ghost ships, I saw me corkscrewing
to the sea-bed of sea-worms, fathom pass fathom,
my jaw clench like a fist, and only one thing
hold me, trembling, how my family safe home.
Then a strength like it seize me and the strength said:
'I from backward people who still fear God.'
Let Him, in His might, heave Leviathan upward
by the winch of His will, the beast pouring lace
from his sea-bottom bed; and that was the faith
that had fade from a child in the Methodist chapel
in Chisel Street, Castries, when the whale-bell
sang service and, in hard pews ribbed like the whale,
proud with despair, we sang how our race
survive the sea's maw, our history, our peril,
and now I was ready for whatever death will.
But if that storm had strength, was in Cap'n face,
beard beading with spray, tears salting the eyes,
crucify to his post, that nigger hold fast
to that wheel, man, like the cross held Jesus,
and the wounds of his eyes like they crying for us,
and I feeding him white rum, while every crest
with Leviathan-lash make the *Flight* quail
like two criminal. Whole night, with no rest,
till red-eyed like dawn, we watch our travail
subsiding, subside, and there was no more storm.
And the noon sea get calm as Thy Kingdom come.

11 *After the Storm*

There's a fresh light that follows a storm
while the whole sea still havoc; in its bright wake
I saw the veiled face of Maria Concepcion
marrying the ocean, then drifting away
in the widening lace of her bridal train

with white gulls her bridesmaids, till she was gone.
I wanted nothing after that day.
Across my own face, like the face of the sun,
a light rain was falling, with the sea calm.

Fall gently, rain, on the sea's upturned face
like a girl showering; make these islands fresh
as Shabine once knew them! Let every trace,
every hot road, smell like clothes she just press
and sprinkle with drizzle. I finish dream;
whatever the rain wash and the sun iron:
the white clouds, the sea and sky with one seam,
is clothes enough for my nakedness.
Though my *Flight* never pass the incoming tide
of this inland sea beyond the loud reefs
of the final Bahamas, I am satisfied
if my hand gave voice to one people's grief.
Open the map. More islands there, man,
than peas on a tin plate, all different size,
one thousand in the Bahamas alone,
from mountains to low scrub with coral keys,
and from this bowsprit, I bless every town,
the blue smell of smoke in hills behind them,
and the one small road winding down them like twine
to the roofs below; I have only one theme:

The bowsprit, the arrow, the longing, the lunging heart—
the flight to a target whose aim we'll never know,
vain search for one island that heals with its harbour
and a guiltless horizon, where the almond's shadow
doesn't injure the sand. There are so many islands!
As many islands as the stars at night
on that branched tree from which meteors are shaken
like falling fruit around the schooner *Flight*.
But things must fall, and so it always was,
on one hand Venus, on the other Mars;
fall, and are one, just as this earth is one
island in archipelagoes of stars.
My first friend was the sea. Now, is my last.
I stop talking now. I work, then I read,

cotching under a lantern hooked to the mast.
I try to forget what happiness was,
and when that don't work, I study the stars.
Sometimes is just me, and the soft-scissored foam
as the deck turn white and the moon open
a cloud like a door, and the light over me
is a road in white moonlight taking me home.
Shabine sang to you from the depths of the sea.

HEBERTO PADILLA

1932–2000

In Trying Times

Translated by Alistair Reid and Andrew Hurley

They asked that man for his time
so that he could link it to History.
They asked him for his hands,
because for trying times
nothing is better than a good pair of hands.
They asked him for his eyes
that once had tears
so that he should see the bright side
(the bright side of life, especially)
because to see horror one startled eye is enough.
They asked him for his lips,
parched and split, to affirm,
to belch up, with each affirmation, a dream
(the great dream);
they asked him for his legs
hard and knotted
(his wandering legs),
because in trying times
is there anything better than a pair of legs
for building or digging ditches?
They asked him for the grove that fed him as a child,
with its obedient tree.
They asked him for his breast, heart, his shoulders.
They told him
that that was absolutely necessary.
They explained to him later
that all this gift would be useless
unless he turned his tongue over to them,
because in trying times
nothing is so useful in checking hatred or lies.
And finally they begged him,
please, to go take a walk.
Because in trying times
that is, without a doubt, the decisive test.

RENÉ PHILOCTÈTE

1932–1995

Misery by Sunlight

Translated by Cheryl Thomas and Carrol F. Coates

The city lights its fires,
even by day
With the sun above
that makes a great broth of gold and light.

Then the sparkling misery of the people
shines, sings, leaps on the roofs and in the streets,
on the piers and the public squares,
in glances and voices,
from courtyards to markets.

The saucy gal put-puts about, making curtsies
to the statutes, the principles,
the state secrets, the contracts,
the controversies, the dialectics,
that allow her to have a view on death
and pain.

She rattles, the gravelly balladeer,
delighted that her flies encircle sad children
with their aureoles
and that her pestilence blooms like the mimosas.

She goes by, thumbing her nose
at the tractors, at the chimneys,
and quickly takes her seat at the Council of Secretaries of State
to manipulate their signatures to the advantage of investors.

Oh, the irresistible little thing;
misery in the sun,
when, with a look of innocence,
she piles her shadows on speech
and the song of men!

MICHAEL GILKES

b. 1933

The Lighthouse

Before it shrank into the logo for Lighthouse matches
and then went out, a blackened stick, it was something to see.
Sun glinted on its bright encircling brass, a small
version of the seawall bandstand elevated, held
up by a concrete red-and-white-striped column, like a tall
bandsman in uniform topped by his tuba's shining bell.

There was a British fortress on that Dutch seawall:
brown surf, brown sand, brown sea habitual as the whiskey
Captain Henwood downed, licking his Errol Flynn moustache.
Horseguards inspection at four, roundhouse cannon at six
firing the street lamps first in Fort Street, Barrack Street,
and then, when Main Street caught, igniting the town. They built
the lighthouse to warn of mud banks and just for fun,
refashioning in English what the Dutch had done.
The thing looked like a stick of Brighton rock candy,
O.H.M.S. ER II stamped on the top
and running (I guessed) all the way through.
Decked with Christmas lights it was a pierside dandy, pissed,
a swaggering Pearly King, nostalgic pink and white reminder
of the seaside towns and fish-and-chips shops they missed.
By day it stood sober, imperially red and white
against the blue, the lighting cue for sunsets to come on,
its strict, right-wheeling lamp impartial as the match
whose methylated-blue green flash once set the town alight.

The spill from its beam catches the leaning torso of a girl
who begins to glow in the lamp of a Demerara window
at the top of a tall house. A boy on a bicycle is leaving
the darkness under the house. She waves as he rides away:
dark, light-light, then dark, the lighthouse semaphore.

He thinks of that rusting flagship, the Key Holt,
once Sandhurst-shine, marooned far out from shore

and waves, straight-armed, hand cocked like a man firing a flare,
looking back until the window goes dark and the glare
of the lighthouse beam is left stroking the space where her light had
   been.
He will not sleep tonight, thinking of lighthouse beams.
She will sleep thinking of him.
He will find her entering his dreams.

EDWARD LUCIE-SMITH
b. 1933

Your Own Place

Invent it now. Your own place,
Your own soil. All inferior
Localities are done with.
Yet how is it to be made
Without things remembered? Sun
Thrown in fistfuls, and the sand
Of that ripe apricot; wind
Spiced with thyme and lavender
Blowing from one hill, at one
Season. But these bring with them
Disasters—the imperfect
Friendship broken, and the perfect
Love unconsummated. Sand
Which burns the foot, hill blocking
The view. So invent it now,
And arrive after the long
Voyage, alone, having left
A companion at each
Port, a lover in all the
Hot bedrooms, all the stifling
Cabins.
        It is before dawn.
There is a cove with a few
Bare rocks. Your feet cling to them,
Naked, as the rest of you
Is naked. Women come laughing
Down to the shore. You call out,
Expecting to be embraced.
They strip and bathe, brush by you
Without a glance or a cry
As the light swells and brightens.

JOHN LYONS
b. 1933

Crusoe's Thursday

No room to swing a macajuel
in this survival struggle
of creepers and tall trees.

On the forest floor
wild bananas with their sucker young
stood spotlit from where the high sun
blasted a hole in the roof of green;

he heard Arawak ghosts whispering
as the wind blew
through the bananas' dried leaves,

and when he stopped running,
the forest cleared to a wide grin
of sand, a salty growth of sea almonds
fringing the land end of its lips.

He stood there, face quivering,
shouting to the sea:
'I shall survive this wilderness
with my wit. There is nobody here
but me. That footprint in the sand
is only an illusion.'

But at the first hint of darkness
he was scaling the parapet of tall stakes
at the entrance of his cave.

That night he slept close to the wall
in the farthest corner of his cave
dreaming of tomorrow.

IAN McDONALD
b. 1933

Forest Path, Nightfall

Paths cut last month to open up new timber
Are lit with streams of late slanting sun:
Beneath a canopy of green crowns of mora trees
Shadows gather except where float tall pillars
Of thick golden light that sets the green dark shining.
So evening falls, I walk this forest path,
Shadowy nave of an immense cathedral:
When Chartres is finest dust, this still will stand,
It stretches far, never-ending in its beauty,
Shines with its own green and gold-stained glass.
When a wind comes the stained windows shiver
A myriad alternating, dark then gleaming, pieces
That never reach the floor but float suspended,
Shimmering arcs of velvet-black and emerald.
One mile from here I found, below its cleansed white beak,
A swarm of ants eating the entrails of an eagle.
Night-shadows begin to rise, mist shaken
From hidden censers in this holy place.
Stars and fireflies, candles lit by ancient priests,
Fill the huge cavern with glowing taper-lights.
In childhood even joy seemed permanent:
I feel cold as if earth was cathedral-stone
Chilled for centuries before the age of man.
In this immense god-theatre night after night brings on
A sense of never-ending mystery vast as time
That swallows man, all his art and legends.
You cannot walk in great forests without diminishment.

The Sun Parrots are Late This Year

For Chico Mendez, murdered Brazilian environmentalist

The great forests of the world are burning down,
Far away in Amazon they burn,
Far beyond our eyes the trees are cut
And cleared and heaped and fired:
Ashes fill the rivers for miles and miles,
The rivers are stained with the blood of mighty trees.
Great rivers are brothers of great forests
And immense clouds shadowing the rose-lit waters
Are cousins of this tribe of the earth-gods
Under the ancient watch of the stars:
All should be secure and beautiful forever,
Dwarfing man generation after generation after generation,
Inspiring man, feeding him with dreams and strength.
But over there it is not so; man is giant
And the forest dwindles; it will soon be nothing,
Shrubs sprouting untidily in scorched black earth.
The sun will burn the earth, before now shadowed
For a hundred thousand years, dark and dripping,
Hiding jewelled insects and thick-veined plants,
Blue-black orchids with white hearts, red macaws,
The green lace of ferns, gold butterflies, opal snakes.
Everything shrivels and dust begins to blow:
It is as if acid was poured on the silken land.

It is far from here now, but it is coming nearer,
Those who love forests also are cut down.
This month, this year, we may not suffer:
The brutal way things are, it will come.
Already the cloud patterns are different each year,
The winds blow from new directions,
The rain comes earlier, beats down harder,
Or it is dry when the pastures thirst.
In this dark, over-arching Essequibo forest
I walk near the shining river in the green paths
Cool and green as melons laid in running streams.
I cannot imagine all the forests going down,

The great black hogs not snouting for the pulp of fruit,
All this beauty and power and shining life gone.
But in far, once emerald Amazon the forest dies
By fire, fiercer than bright axes.
The roar of the wind in trees is sweet,
Reassuring, the heavens stretch far and bright
Above the loneliness of mist-shrouded forest trails,
And there is such a feel of softness in the evening air.
Can it be that all of this will go, leaving the clean-boned land?
I wonder if my children's children, come this way,
Will see the great forest spread green and tall and far
As it spreads now far and green for me.
Is it my imagination that the days are furnace-hot,
The sun-parrots late or not come at all this year?

STANLEY GREAVES

b. 1934

Knees

Oh! the knee,
    wondrous bone
    of flex and stern stasis
    happy to serve conscious form,
    potential moral weight or astute pretender.

Look! by that microphone
    flying flags as god-sent signals.
    Political knees accepting
    words dangerous to truth.

Someday such knees will bend
    inevitable as any hinge,
    when messages take form
    as burden of stern hope.

Streets will sound to marching knees
Parents will dream for their children

    and all will be right, perhaps,
    in that dream if not this,
    where knees of a weary people
threaten petty politics.

SLADE HOPKINSON

1934–1993

The Madwoman of Papine

Two Cartoons with Captions

(1)

Four years ago,
in this knot of a village north of the university,
she was in residence
where a triangle of grass gathered the mountain road,
looped it once, and tossed it to Kingston,
where grampus buses, cycling students,
duppies of dust and ululations in light
vortexed around her.
Ritualist, she tried to reduce the world,
sketching her violent diagrams
against a wall of mountains which her stare made totter.
Her rhythmic ideas detonated into gestures.
She would jab her knee into the groin of the air,
fling her sharp instep at the fluttering sky,
revise perspectives with the hooks of her fingers,
and butt blood from the teeth of God.

She cooked and ate anything. But, being so often busy,
she hardly ever cooked or ate.

What of her history?
These are the latitudes of the ex-colonised,
Of degradation still unmollified,
Imported managers, styles in art,
second-hand subsistence of the spirit,
the habit of waste,
mayhem committed on the personality,
and everywhere the wrecked or scuttled mind.

Scholars, more brilliant than I could hope to be,
advised that if I valued poetry,
I should eschew all sociology.
Who could make anything of a pauper lunatic
modelling one mildewed dress from year to year?
Scarecrow, just sane enough occasionally
to pick-up filth and toast it on a brick.
She would then renew
the comic mime of her despair.

Clearly something was very wrong with her
as subject.   Pedestrian.   Too limited
for lyric literature.
I went away for four years.   Then returned.

(2)

One loaf now costs what two loaves used to.
The madwoman has crossed the road
and gone behind the shops
nearer the university,
oriens ex occidente lux,
the light of scholars rising in the west.
She wears the same perennial dress,
now black as any graduate's gown,
But stands in placid anguish now,
perfects her introverted trance,
with hanging arms, still feet,
chin on breast, forehead parallel
to the eroded, indifferent earth,
merely an invisible old woman,
extremist votary at an interior altar,
repeatedly rinsing along her tongue
a kind of invocation, whispered, verbless:

'O
Rass Rass Rass
in the highest,'

ROBIN DOBRU

1935–1983

Jani (MP)

jani
why you move to a new house
you tire of the kerosene oil
or the standpipe too far
a paved street
with neon lights
where you live
is no bread for us
or are afraid of the cockroaches

jani think of us
when you are in parliament
you ride along
so now and then
if you have time
in your big american car
but don't bring too many sweets for the children
and also not too much tobacco
for the old woman to wash she mouth

tell the speaker
i have enough of my bigfoot
tell him
that the leaks in the roof
already filled all the buckets
and that my boss wants to fire me
for five dollar raise

FRANK MARTINUS ARION
b. 1936

I fell in deep snow . . .
Translated by Paul Vincent

I fell in deep snow
If you cannot save me
Then lie down beside me
Help me weep

If only you spoke Papiamentu
I would call you my lover
Ask for a kiss that would save me
But you can never be black

They told me
They all begged me
If you marry a white woman
You can't return to your black homeland

I fell in deep snow
If you cannot save me
Then lie down beside me
Help me weep

EDWARD BAUGH

b. 1936

The Carpenter's Complaint

Now you think that is right, sah? Talk the truth.
The man was mi friend. *I* build it, *I*
Build the house that him live in; but now
That him dead, that mawga-foot bwoy, him son,
Come say, him want a nice job for the coffin,
So him give it to *Mister* Belnavis to make—
That big-belly crook who don't know him arse
From a chisel, but because him is big-shot, because
Him make big-shot coffin, fi-him coffin must better
Than mine! Bwoy, it hot me, it hot me
For true. Fix we a nex' one, Miss Fergie—
That man coulda knock back him waters, you know sah!
I remember the day in this said-same bar
When him drink Old Brown and Coxs'n into
The ground, then stand up straight as a plumb-line
And keel him felt hat on him head and walk
Home cool, cool, cool. Dem was water-bird, brother!
Funeral? *Me*, sah? That bwoy have to learn
That a man have him pride. But bless mi days!
Good enough to make the house that him live in,
But not good enough to make him coffin!
I woulda do it for nutt'n for nutt'n! The man
Was mi friend. Damn mawga-foot bwoy.
Is university turn him fool. I tell you,
It burn me, it burn me for true!

EDWARD BAUGH

Sometimes in the Middle of the Story
for the drowned Africans of the Middle Passage

Sometimes in the middle of the story something
move outside the house, like
it could be the wind, but is not the wind
and the story-teller hesitate so slight
you hardly notice it, and the children
hold their breath and look at one another.
The old people say is Toussaint passing
on his grey horse Bel-Argent, moving
faster than backra-massa timepiece
know to measure, briefing the captains
setting science and strategy to trap the emperor.
But also that sound had something in it
of deep water, salt water, had ocean
the sleep-sigh of a drowned African
turning in his sleep on the ocean floor
and Toussaint horse was coming from far
his tail trailing the swish of the sea
from secret rendezvous, from councils of war
with those who never completed the journey,
and we below deck heard only the muffled
thud of scuffling feet, could only
guess the quick, fierce tussle, the
stifled gasp, the barrel-chests bursting
the bubbles rising and breaking, the blue
closing over. But their souls shuttle
still the forest paths of ocean
connecting us still the current unbroken
the circuits kept open, the tireless messengers
the ebony princes of your lost Atlantis
a power of black men rising from the sea.

ANSON GONZALEZ
b. 1936

Tabiz

Long time ago they used to say
How jumbie used to walk the road

this poem is to cut maljo
is to save you from the blight
of overloving eyes that conceal hate
from over-generous eyes that subsume
the bitter bile of envy
from judas-friendly eyes that shut
bestowing the betraying kiss

like a blue bottle on a stick
it will ward off whatsoever evil
may try to wither the bounty
of your blooming life's garden
keep it there and no beetle
no bug no worm no fly no snake
will invade and your life
will be a blossoming eden

then you'll sing your happy songs
in the peaceful harmony you wish
and all your joys will be unsullied

or wear it like a mystic amulet
or a ringlet of blue-black beads
or yet like a blessed ankh
and feel your confidence rise

as you scale the unsurmountable
wear it and you'll climb your everests
as easily as your el tucuches

or make of it a magic circle
to protect and comfort you
step into it as my friend's mother once
IN HOC VINCIT and with signs
defied her enemies
and the evil ones
we'll chant the aves the halleluias
the hosannas the alaikums and oms
we'll bring the greater glory
to your assistance and you will
rise and soar

or make it a stole of blue
draping your possessed shoulders
making all your ancestral contacts
give you great strength

encircled by the indigoed words
you will bravely step through
legs of phantoms
put salt on soucouyants' skins
make douens disappear
and you'll dance in life's moonlight
safe from all harm

RAJANDAYE RAMKISSOON-CHEN
b. 1936

Still My Teacher
(Miss S. S.)

I saw the opening flower
Still fastened with dewdrops
And I remember how she said
'In nature there is excellence:
Two reclining clouds
On a bed of sunset sparkle,
A drop of ocean,
Rainlines picking bubbles
On a path'.
And she became my teacher,
Once more.

She had dusted her books
After the croptime,
When burnt sugarcane drops
Like wisps of feathers
To mark her shelves
With curlicues of ash.
And her heart, like with angina, ached
To make a gift.

'For you' she wrote. The cover jacket
Showed gaps like nibbled-out knowledge,
Daubs of fingers, tears
That looked like moth-tracks running.
The aged pages were the sanctum
To some poets' most inner thoughts.

'Shine! like him' she commanded
'With that heaven-light'.
And I saw me
A coiled cotton wick of flame
Again, from her, drawing oil.

HOWARD FERGUS

b. 1937

Behind God Back

You come from a two-be-three island
hard like rock
black you have another handicap
and you come from Long Ground
way behind God back.

They taught you like a fool
never told you miles of cotton
went to Liverpool
to line the Bank of England
from Long Ground behind God back
he shoulda turned round
and catch the thieves white-handed
white and black

They took you for an imbecile
never told you Montserrat tobacco
made W.D. and H.O. Wills
rich testators of Bristol University
lighting their names on the crest of history
with Long Ground tobacco
bought behind God back

Never told you how your mother strong
to carry buckra cotton
and his seed
fertile like Long Ground soil
strong to carry bales of history
and buckra deeds heavy like a sack
of cotton picked behind God back

People in the town
didn't know off-white and brown were black

until they went to England
Powell vote to pack them back
rejected like stained cotton
didn't know when God turned round
his smile like a rainbow
lit Long Ground with hope
and cotton children weave boot strap
to pull themselves up
from behind God back

CLAIRE HARRIS
b. 1937

Child   this is the gospel on bakes

first   strain sunlight through avocado leaves
then pour into a dim country kitchen through bare
windows   on a wooden table freshly scrubbed
I'm warning you   a lazy person is a nasty
person   flurry of elbows
place a yellow oil cloth   on this   a bowl
a kneading board   a dull knife   spoons
then draw up an old chair   have a grand-father carve
birds flowers   the child likes to trace sweep of petals
curve of wings   to tease a finger along
edges softened by age   and numberless polishings
the initiate kneels on the seat
afterwards there will be a pattern of cane left
around her neck tie the huge blue apron
so that only her head   thin bare arms are visible
place a five pound milk can painted green
with yellow trim and full of flour
tall salt jar   salt clumping together
fresh grated nutmeg   sugar in a green can
butter in a clay cooler   red enameled
cup brimming with cold water
have someone say 'be careful now
don't make a mess'
the child takes one handful of flour   makes a hill
outside a humming bird whirrs   sun gleams
on her hill   she adds another handful   another   another
she makes a careful mountain   lightly walks
her fingers to the top   flattens the crest   old
voice in her ear   *'don't you go making yourself out*
special   now'   she watches as flour sifts down
sides of her mountain   then scoops out a satisfactory
hollow   she can see humming birds at red
hibiscus   beyond   a small boy barefeet

162

on the plum tree his voice shrilling king
of the mountain threats   old voice eggs him on
Into the hollow   Daughter   put a pinch of salt
a little sugar for each handful of flour
as much butter as can be held in a nutshell
'ready' she calls   waits
even if she looks straight ahead she still sees
from the corner of her eye   lamps   their bowls full
gathering sunlight   the way girls should
waiting patiently for evening
behind her there is always some one preparing pastry
on a grey marble-topped table
the rolling pin presses dough   thinner
and thinner towards round edges
maker pushing pastry
to transparency   ices
the pin folds pastry over butter
begins again   finally the last stretching roll
till it seems skin must break into a ragged O
she is rigid with apprehension   this
is something to do with her
so she does not hear the voice over her shoulder say
'drizzle this baking powder all over'
handing her a spoon   until she is tapped lightly
starts to the chorus   'this child always dreaming yes
but what you going to do with her'
her mother saying ever so carefully 'let her dream
while she can' she begins to knead
butter into flour   the mother sprinkles grated lemon
peel   and when she has crumbs she makes another hollow
adds water while someone clucks warnings
she begins to knead the whole together
not forgetting the recurring dream in which she climbs
through a forest of leaves she kneads   stepping
bravely from branch to branch   miles above ground
she kneads and kneads trying to make it smooth
she finds a bird that talks
but flies away just as she is beginning
to understand   she kneads   finally someone says
'that's good enough' she kneads just a little more

she is watching the bird   which is flying
straight into the sun
                              where it lives bravely
a rum bottle full of water is thrust into her hands
which she must wash again   then flour the bottle
to roll out her dough which she has made into a ball
outside the high-pitched yelling of small boys at cricket
she is better at cricket than at bakes
she will never be as good at bakes as her mother is
or her aunt   or her great aunt   or her grandmother
or even the kitchen maid who is smiling openly
because the child's bakes are not round
her mother says gently 'I'll show you a trick'
she rolls the dough out for her again   takes a glass
cuts out perfect rounds of bakes
together they lay them out on a baking sheet
'we'll decorate yours with a fork   dad will be proud'
together they cover her bakes with a wet cloth
when the oven is ready her mother will test the heat
sprinkling water on a tin sheet

MARK MATHEWS
b. 1937

Mortal

Why should there be
an engineering of this
to be immortal
like some fierce cancer
to be imperishable
among perishables,
to gobble all others
forever feeding itself?

rather let be of this
now, with those that share
this present,
and like them, when its
time has come, go
having lived as they
do, with hunger, pain
mauled hopes, fears, struggle:
wear its fingers to bone,
its soul case as theirs
falling home
let it burn through slander
strike back at injustices
as some do

let it be real,
of real time
let it flame, flare its
explosive moment
then die at end of usefulness;
then, should needs be,
it will
resurrect different, yet
the same.

MERVYN MORRIS

b. 1937

Valley Prince

for Don D.

Me one, way out in the crowd,
I blow the sounds, the pain,
but not a soul
would come inside my world
or tell me how it true.
I love a melancholy baby,
sweet, with fire in her belly;
and like a spite
the woman turn a whore.
Cool and smooth around the beat
she wake the note inside me
and I blow me mind.

Inside here, me one
in the crowd again,
and plenty people
want me blow it straight.
But straight is not the way; my world
don' go so; that is lie.
Oonoo gimme back me trombone, man:
is time to blow me mind.

Peelin Orange

Dem use to seh
yu peel a orange
perfec
an yu get new clothes

But when mi father try
fi teach mi
slide de knife
up to de safeguard thumb

I move de weapon like
a saw inna mi han
an de dyamn rind
break

An if yu have de time
yu can come see mi
in mi ole clothes
peelin

Muse

When you woo her
she will fade

This is how
the game is played

Smilingly
she leads him on
He approaches
Whereupon

the figure in the
evening air
begins to
slowly disappear

Extraordinary
trade
When you woo her
she will fade

This is how
the game is played

VELMA POLLARD
b. 1937

Beware the Naked Man Who Offers You a Shirt
(African Proverb)

that people who read books and dress in suits
could give a child a gun
just so
and tell him use it to drop that mister man and that
just so

'for dem de man fi ded'

that people who read books
could think it was gwine done
just so
and children's back yards would fill up with gun graves
where the gun bones stay
just so

But no
gun hills
like yam hills
grow gun
shoots
so

Now man a rent out gun like how dem rent out bed
Now dis a serious trade who tell you crime dont pay
wen so much man fi ded?

(seem like black people turn fool fool jus like white
people who think after cotton done
plant nigger would jus turn round and go

just so

swim back to Africa

some even wonder how so many blacks
who come without passport
and winter coat

still walking under Uncle Sam
just so

like guns that came our way
without their licenses)

Gun toting children
now gun men decide
which crimes will pay

No longer hired hands
'we is de boss'
they say

And when your friend
your son
your father
falls some ordinary evening in his blood
do you perhaps . . .

you men who still read books and dress in suits?

LOURDES CASAL

1938–1981

Poem

Translated By Timothy J. Keating

I had to reinvent everything.
With you everything has been like the first time:
The first kiss, the uncertainty,
Not knowing what to do,
The forgotten noise of adolescence.
I had to rediscover love's space,
Compile the bodies' geography,
Rewrite the ritual, choreograph it.
And find myself one more time,
One more first time,
With ecstasy and with mystery.

E. A. MARKHAM
b. 1939

A History Without Suffering

In this poem there is no suffering.
It spans hundreds of years and records
no deaths, connecting when it can,
those moments where people are healthy

and happy, content to be alive. A Chapter,
maybe a Volume, shorn of violence
consists of an adult reading aimlessly.
This line is the length of a full life

smuggled in while no one was plotting
against a neighbour, except in jest.
Then, after a gap, comes Nellie. She
is in a drought-fisted field

with a hoe. This is her twelfth year
on the land, and today her back
doesn't hurt. Catechisms of self-pity
and of murder have declared a day's truce

in the Civil War within her. So today,
we can bring Nellie, content with herself,
with the world, into our History.
For a day. In the next generation

we find a suitable subject camping
near the border of a divided country:
for a while no one knows how near. For these
few lines she is ours. But how about

the lovers? you ask, the freshly-washed
body close to yours; sounds, smells, tastes;
anticipation of the young, the edited memory
of the rest of us? How about thoughts

higher than their thinkers? . . . Yes, yes.
Give them half a line and a mass of footnotes:
they have their own privileged history,
like inherited income beside our husbandry.

We bring our History up to date
in a city like London: someone's just paid
the mortgage, is free of guilt
and not dying of cancer; and going

past the news-stand, doesn't see a headline
advertising torture. This is all
recommended reading, but in small doses.
It shows you can avoid suffering, if you try.

Hurricane, Volcano, Mass Flight

The five eggs in the dining-room
Must be turned each day to keep them fresh.
Their dish, still unchipped
Draws the eye of visitors. If the hens

Lay today, add washed eggs
To the prize and remove the first laid
For breakfast. Remember to dust all
Glassware and wipe the surface of the cabinet.

If there's no one left for housework
Leave one of the children behind to see
To things: the horse won't live forever
And pigs and goats are things of the past.

But fruit in the garden must be picked,
Picked up; rabbits out of the hutch
Kept down; the lawn cut, yard swept.
This house of your mother's can't be protected

By priest or jumbie or de Lawrence.
So do what you can inside and out.
Someone who grew here sniffing new bread
From the kitchen or bat-droppings in the attic

(Puzzled at the great drawing-room library
Shrunk to this size, casting the world
For family out there with a memory;
Or a neighbour alive and interested)

Will guard from afar a dining-room,
Still with its layered, breakable vase, egg-
Crowned, white on blue on white which
Like the piano upstairs, has travelled far.

DENNIS SCOTT

1939–1991

Uncle Time

Uncle Time is a ole, ole man . . .
All year long 'im wash 'im foot in de sea,
long, lazy years on de wet san'
an' shake de coconut tree dem
quiet-like wid 'im sea-win' laughter,
scraping away de lan'. . .

Uncle Time is a spider-man, cunnin' an' cool,
him tell yu: watch de hill an' yu se mi.
Huhn! Fe yu yi no quick enough fe si
how 'im move like mongoose; man, yu tink 'im fool?

Me Uncle Time smile black as sorrow;
'im voice is sof' as bamboo leaf
but Lawd, me Uncle cruel.
When 'im play in de street
wid yu woman—watch 'im! By tomorrow
she dry as cane-fire, bitter as cassava;
an' when 'im teach yu son, long after
yu walk wid stranger, an' yu bread is grief.
Watch how 'im spin web roun' yu house, an' creep
inside; an' when 'im touch yu, weep . . .

Epitaph

They hanged him on a clement morning, swung
between the falling sunlight and the women's
breathing, like a black apostrophe to pain.
All morning while the children hushed
their hopscotch joy and the cane kept growing

174

he hung there sweet and low.
                    At least that's how
they tell it. It was long ago
and what can we recall of a dead slave or two
except that when we punctuate our island tale
they swing like sighs across the brutal
sentences, and anger pauses
till they pass away.

Apocalypse Dub

At first, there's a thin, bright Rider—
he doesn't stop at the supermarket, the cool
red meats are not to his taste.
He steals from the tin on the tenement table,
he munches seed from the land
where no rain has fallen, he feeds
in the gutter behind my house.
The bread is covered with sores
when he eats it; the children
have painted his face on their bellies

The second rides slowly, is visiting, watch him, he smiles
through the holes in the roof
of the cardboard houses.
His exhaust sprays pus on the sheets,
he touches the women and teaches them
fever, he puts eggs under the skin—
in the hot days insects will hatch and hide
in the old men's mouths,
in the bones of the children

And always, behind them, the iceman, quick,
with his shades, the calm oil of his eyes—
when he throttles, the engine
grunts like a killer. I'm afraid,
you said. Then you closed the window

and turned up the radio, the DJ said greetings
to all you lovely people.
But in the street the children coughed like guns.

In the blueblack evenings
they cruise on the corner
giggling. Skenneng! Skenneng!

MARIA ARRILLAGA

b. 1940

To the Poets of My Generation

Translated by Tracey Huggins

I shall die with my dreams
It's a desert
The lights can be seen at a distance
My hair grows
I let it loose, I comb it, I pull it back
I pull myself back, I let myself loose
I run away
I come back slowly
I walk
I think of myself as the road for all my people
including those who are
enemies
How much and how little we know
How little we say, how much we think
I suffer your coldness with you, with me
What a shame that we lack love!
To talk to you, touch you; to touch me and talk to me
To listen to you, to listen to me
To know your beauty, that you may know mine
that you may think it, say it; that I may think it, say it
The snow that falls builds silences
creating the emptiness
It isn't yours nor mine, it isn't ours
There is no way that I know, dear woman
but to prick your body, that you may prick mine
with your trinitarians, with my trinitarians*
to build the world that belongs to us
while we revive the myth of the fire that
kills the dragon, to liberate us and go in
search of what lies unfinished as long as

---

* Trinitarians are flowers with strong, thorny stems like the bougainvillea.

it isn't done in valiant solidarity
the world challenges our poetry
that holds steady and cures, that cures and charms
that charms and rises secure—it will intercept
Icarus—to establish the happy flight
where we are:
the kites of the people, the kites of the tropics,
woman wonders of an indigenous symbol
from our land that we will clitoricize
with the construction of our truth.

MALIK
b. 1940

Instant Ting

For Michael Smith

Was an instant ting
When ah sight im

Swift as ah hawk
With ah hop an drop walk
Limber like ah whip
For ah hop an drop lick
An im face lookin grim
Like im out pon a limb
Was an instant ting
When ah sight im

Im cut a picture
Of trouble in store
Im look familiar
To de days of yore
Was an instant ting
When ah sight im

Was an instant ting
When ah hear im
'S-a-y-y Nattie Nattie
doe Baddar dash way yo culture'

Im paint a picture
Of trouble in store
Im sound familiar
To de days of yore
Was an instant ting
When ah hear im

Was an instant ting
When dem sight im
'—Babylon to mih right
Babylon to mih left
Babylon in front of I

And Babylon behind I
an I an I alone
Like ah Goliath
wid ah sling shot—'

Im cut ah picture
Of trouble in store
Im look familiar
To de days of yore
Was an instant ting
When dem sight im

Was an instant ting
When dem hear im
'I MAN FREE TO WALK ANY PART OF JAMAICA'

Im paint a picture
Of trouble in store
Im sound familiar
To de days of yore
Was an instant ting
When dem hear im

Was an instant ting
When dem stone im
It paint ah picture
Of trouble in store
It look familiar
To de days of yore
An de words of Jah say
'Touch not the Lord's anointed
And do his prophets no harm'
And the voice of the whirlwind say—

MALIK

S-EEEEE
A-AAAA
GA
Was an instant ting
When dem kill im

OLIVE SENIOR
b. 1941

Birdshooting Season

Birdshooting season the men
make marriages with their guns
My father's house turns macho
as from far the hunters gather

All night long contentless women
stir their brews: hot coffee
chocolata, cerassie
wrap pone and tie-leaf
for tomorrow's sport. Tonight
the men drink white rum neat.

In darkness shouldering
their packs, their guns, they leave

We stand quietly on the
doorstep shivering. Little boys
longing to grow up birdhunters too
Little girls whispering:
Fly Birds Fly.

Brief Lives

Gardening in the Tropics, you never know
what you'll turn up. Quite often, bones.
In some places they say when volcanoes
erupt, they spew out dense and monumental
as stones the skulls of *desaparecidos*
–the disappeared ones. Mine is only
a kitchen garden so I unearth just
occasional skeletons. The latest

was of a young man from the country who
lost his way and crossed the invisible
boundary into rival political territory.
I buried him again so he can carry on
growing. Our cemeteries are thriving too.
The newest addition was the drug baron
wiped out in territorial competition
who had this stunning funeral
complete with twenty-one-gun salute
and attended by everyone, especially
the young girls famed for the vivacity
of their dress, their short skirts and
even briefer lives.

Thirteen Ways of Looking at Blackbird
(after Wallace Stevens)

I

The ship
　　　trips
into sight of land. Blackbird
is all eyes. Vows nothing but sunlight
will ever hold him now.

II

Survivor of the crossing, Blackbird
the lucky one in three, moves
his eyes and weary
limbs. Finds his wings clipped.
Palm trees gaze and swoon.

III

Swept like the leaves on autumn wind,
Blackbird is bought and sold and bought
again, whirled into waving fields
of sugar cane.

IV

Blackbird no longer knows
if he is man or woman or bird or simply is.
Or if among the sugar cane he is
sprouting.

V

Blackbird's voice has turned rusty.
The voice of the field mice
is thin and squeaky.
I do not know which to prefer.

VI

Blackbird traces in the shadow not cast
the indecipherable past.

VII

Blackbird finds thrilling
        the drum beats drilling
        the feet of
men of women into
utterance.

VIII

To Blackbird rhythm
        is inescapable
Fired to heights alchemical
the immortal bird consumed

Miles Davis

wired.

IX

Blackbird once again
attempts flight. Crashes into
the circle's contracting edge.

X

Even the sight of the whip makes
Blackbird cry out sharply.
No euphony.

XI

Pierced by fear, Massa and all his generation
mistake Blackbird for the long shadow.

XII

Blackbird strips to reduce gravity's pull
readying for flight again. Fate hauls him in
to another impetus.

XIII

In the dark
     out of the sun
Blackbird sits
     among the shavings
from the cedar coffins.

ANTHONY McNEIL
1941–1996

Ode to Brother Joe

Nothing can soak
Brother Joe's tough sermon,
his head swollen
with certainties.

When he lights up a s'liff
you can't stop him,
and the door to God, usually shut,
gives in a rainbow gust.

Then it's time for the pipe,
which is filled with its water base
and handed to him for his blessing.
He bends over the stem,
goes into the long grace,
and the drums start

the drums start
Hail Selassie I
Jah Rastafari
and the room fills with the power
and beauty of blackness,
a furnace of optimism.

But the law thinks different.
This evening the Babylon catch
Brother Joe in his act of praise
and carry him off to the workhouse.

Who'll save Brother Joe? Hail
Selassie is far away
and couldn't care less,
and the promised ship

is a million light years
from Freeport.
But the drums in the tenement house
are sadder than usual tonight

and the brothers suck hard
at their s'liffs and pipes:
before the night's over
Brother Joe has become a martyr:

but still in jail;
and only his woman
who appreciates his humanness more

will deny herself of the weed tonight
to hire a lawyer
and put up a real fight.

Meantime, in the musty cell,
Joe invokes, almost from habit,
the magic words:
Hail Selassie I
Jah Rastafari
But the door is real and remains shut.

The Kingdom of Myth

A Fable in 32 Lines

Dog-heart's dis-
respect of the cold
Jungle or Tivoli don

left the youth dead—
from the waist down;
left the youth dread—

from the waist up;
Made him push night
with his right wrist

or else he was
a left-handed gun
like

the ghost of Paul Newman;
Made him cry to his woman
Go with Jah-blessings

my nature is gone:
Made him flex with his Bible

in search of a key

unlocking
Red City;
built skull on skull,

in the image of Hell;
Made him turn
and stay

one with the fallen:
pious; touched; angry;

fatally slick; in
their crypts ruth
for the stretch.

His dust will inherit
His dust will inherit the kingdom of myth

ARNOLD HARRICHAND ITWARU
b. 1942

body rites
(chant five)

in this festival of darkening light
i have made many fires

they glimmer in distant evenings
in the shadowed warmth and cold
of uncertain insistent unrememberings

old embers
a needy heat

the nights are long and far
and between them you and i
other things have happened   but here we come
to touch and feed and heal
in the root of our gaze

my bones ache
and something drags about the confessionals and lachrimatories
of me bearing no deliverance

once i played in the grass
i ate berries and fruit grown
in the footpaths of my dreaming
i drank in streams the earthen flow of hope

i nestle in you
a stranger you and i
touch me
feed me
heal me
rooted in the root of our gaze

away for a moment from the burning labyrinths
the assassin's articulate and ready wait
the columns of bodies too terrified to feel
authority fattened in hypocrisy

we are a disapproval   you and i
as we touch and feed and heal
even as of each other we approve
in yet another trial by fire

BELKIS CUZA MALÉ

b. 1942

My Mother's Homeland

Translated by Pamela Carmell

My mother always said
your homeland is any place,
preferably the place where you die.
That's why she bought the most arid land,
the saddest landscape,
the driest grass,
and beside the wretched tree
began to build her homeland.
She built it by fits and starts
          (one day this wall, another day the roof;
from time to time, holes to let air squeeze in).
My house, she would say, is my homeland,
and I would see her close her eyes
like a young girl full of dreams
while she chose, once again, groping,
the place where she would die.

PAM MORDECAI

b. 1942

Last Lines

This is the last line I draw.
Alright. Draw the last line.
But I tell you, yonder
is a next. No line ever last,
no death not forever.
You see this place? You see it?
All of it? Watch it good.
Not a jot nor a tittle
going lost. Every old
twist-up man you see,
every hang-breast woman,
every bang-belly pickney,
every young warrior
who head wrench
with weed, white powder,
black powder, or indeed
the very vile persuasion
of the devil—for him not
bedridden you know—
every small gal-turn-woman
that you crucify on the
cross of your sex
before her little naseberry
start sweeten,
I swear to you,
every last one shall live.
Draw therefore, O governor,
prime minister, parson,
teacher, shopkeeper,
politician, lecturer,

resonant revolutionaries,
draw carefully
that last fine line
of your responsibility.

JOSEPH POLIUS
b. 1942

There are those who . . .

Translated by E. Anthony Hurley

There are those who claim to be afro-this
Afro-that
Those who say they are
not entirely black
not completely white
There are the it's-not-nice-to-speak
creole-in-front-of-Whites
there are those who say they are
European-black like you say American-black
those who put France
on the right side of the father
those who listen to Wagner
and read the financial pages of the newspaper
those who change sidewalks
so as not to pass
a Congolese street-sweeper
those about whom Whites say
'They are nice guys'
there are those who pretend to be serious

and those who are a pain in the neck
there are those who hold forth
and those who ramble on
those who do econ
like you do the dishes
there are those who are decorated
those with their hearts on the right
and their heads red-white-and-blue
there are the daddy's boys
those who are old at fifteen
those who know they're educated
there are those who try to outdo one another

lutherkingizing
on every boulevard in France
there are all those

those to whom we say
shit

CHRISTINE CRAIG
b. 1943

St Ann Saturday

Saturday afternoons. So many shades
of black swinging down the road.
funeral time
Nice afternoon she get eh!

If.

An so many smaddy turn out
like a ole days funeral

Dats right.

Imagine her time come
so quick. Well de Lord giveth
an de Lord taketh away.

Sure ting.

Children walk lightly, plaits
floating with rainbows of ribbons
beside auntie's strong hips, uncle's
suit so dark his body is held in tight,
moves only back, front, back.
Auntie's hips roll sedately, heave
like waves beside the dancing plaits

You see her big daughter come from
Canada. Me no like how she look
at all. No sir. She look a way.
Me never memba say she look so mawga.
Me mind tell me she catching
hard time over dere.

Imagine is six pickney Miss Martha
raise, she one bring dem up an
send dem out into de world.
Six pickney, she one
an is one degge, degge daughta
come home to bury her.

Still an all, dem neva come
when she was hearty, no mek sense
de come when she direckly dead.

A dat too.

Starapple leaves, double toned
bend quiet over the steady walking,
walking for Miss Martha gone to rest.
The path she walked, food to market
children to school, Sunday to Church,
steady walking. In the end, alone
under the starapple leaves a hush
fell over her, silence of age
of no names left to call
to table. Of no news from
Delroy or Maisie or Petal
or Lennie or Edith or Steve.

Nice turn out Miss Martha have.
See Mass Len clear from Topside.
An no Granny Bailey dat from Retreat?
Well I neva. Tink seh she dead
long time. Time passing chile
we all moving down de line.

HEATHER ROYES
b. 1943

I No Longer Read Poetry

I no longer read poetry.
I read obituaries,
horoscopes,
the classified ads, telephone directories
and notes to myself.

I no longer read poetry.
The images of Neruda,
Lao Tzu, Walcott and Senior
are curling,
yellow photographs, vaselined vignettes,
sepia scenes frozen in my memory.

I no longer read poetry.
I read Carl Stone's Polls,
political speeches, Letters-to-the-Editor,
volumes of technical reports.
Even The New York Times
is a flight of fancy.

Mesmerised by the present,
forsaking the past, my mind
a jealous lover holds each moment
much longer than it lasts.
Time slips away and with it
dreams.
I no longer read poetry.

PEDRO PÉREZ SARDUY

b. 1943

the POET

Translated by Jean Stubbs

the POET is the type with class
    who is born on some insignificant day
    like October 20 on which Arthur Rimbaud
    was born in 1854
the POET is the curiously irresponsible type
    practically what has been called
    a serious pathological case
    because he's a city mole and changes
    his skin constantly
    with rare exceptions he always ends up
    being militant for some non-just cause or other
    professing the latest ideas that are *engagées*
    and giving up that self-worship of his
    which is an expression thought up
    by some other poet
    because
the POET that is he who goes about ordering
    or discovering street poetry is the kind
    who likes to preserve
    his private life to the full
    and will go to all lengths to defend it
    and always has a pretext
    because
the POET is the type who doesn't use firearms
    unless they're the harquebuses used
    in the age of enlightenment
    but that's beside the point
    for example if he is born under Libra
    like old Arthur was
    he's unkempt phlegmatic
    neurotic as hell
    hypersensitive

fit to play golf
and listen to Swan Lake
but if he's born under Taurus
he's the kind with a violent streak wild
who never thinks twice
about joining the guerrilla struggle
in any part of the world
—even in the most colossal
of Babel's hotels in the West—
and he's a real Don Juan
even when he's not handsome
because

the POET is in love with love
and knows how to make it only too well
he practices yoga meditates Zen Buddhism
and ceremoniously drinks tea
and ejaculates different colored stars
with each orgasm . . . fabulous . . .!
because

the POET is the COPYRIGHT type who has no faith
in his glory
or that of anybody else and much less
that of the Nobel Prize
he knows other languages specially
Western ones
and buries himself in the country
to study Oriental philosophy
he eats frog's legs and is a connoisseur
of drinks and aromatic herbs
because

the POET is a paranoid with copious atomic neurons
and makes no literary bones about rejecting
all that is troglodyte and socially calcified
beat par excellence in his latter years
of lyricism he likes to love
as much as he denies all signs of frigidity
in his lover
because

the POET is a mythological being almost sacred
as he has been ever since prehistoric times

when he rode on his mammoth
with supernatural powers to presage disasters
he never augurs happiness
because he's a doubting dilemma
just like his day and age
although at times he prefers to go off
into the country
to cleanse himself of the refined oil
to the strains of a thin flageolet
and he's so incredulous as to consider
his work superior to that of the singular kind
unmultipliable by two
almost impossible to believe
that he came from a mother's womb
—sorry [Author's note] it's just that
the POET is the type who is born where
night finds him
what's more
the POET is the type who always believes in someone
or something and therein lies the contradiction
no ifs and buts
and he's so soft that each day
in his solitude
he goes over all his small failures
so as to build the one-and-only-indivisible-
    collective
for when it's time for the enchanted dream
because
the POET is the type to be pitied
but he likes to savor international dishes
and frequently visits
the Volga (Russian food)
the Yang-Tse (Chinese food)
the Saint John (American food)
the Fish & Chip Shop (English food)
the Montecatini (Italian food)
the Polinesio (Polynesian food)
the Monseigneur (French food)
the Wakamba (African food)
the Centro Vasco (Spanish food)

la Carreta (Creole food)
because
the POET is the embittered type who courts trouble
and is always the one to sacrifice himself
to be fucked over and over again
by apocalyptic existence
that is his lot . . . BAM!
until the moment he acquires
(no, not a Prize . . . that's not enough)
social standing and holds
his own in space
(not in a spaceship either)
he often holds it in diplomacy
(as a diplomat) that is
he becomes according to historical materialism
a being who sells his intellectual power
at a high price and the crises start
in his work of creation
(I don't mean Jesus Christ or Buddha
who saw to it that
the poet is subject to the law of the incessant flow of
    dharma)
because he wavers in his beliefs and . . .
well, to continue:
that according to him demand of him
certain standards and make him attached to life
(to transform the WORLD to change LIFE)
but there are others who if they adapt perfectly
and like their new life as a function-ary
(not from Aryan)
start to travel with importance
or go on their important travels
because
the POET is the type made for the clouds
which doesn't mean that
he's up in the clouds
but that he needs to fly to travel
that is to get to know people
swap emotions and people too
and he always maintains as he does now that

there should be an airline
specially for poets
something like POETA DE AVIACION or
POETANA AIRLINES CORPORATION
with Boeings Ilushyns and Super DC-10s
to take them no problem at all
to any corner of this world
as the desire or the inspiration moves them
with no other passport than one of their books
translated into at least five languages
[OK . . . OK, we'll bear you in mind for the next Congress. . .]
because
the POET is the type who needs love affection
and concern more than any one else in the world
and he needs to meet lord fog madame notre dame
mademoiselle le louvre monsieur d'eiffel
and take a spin on the air metro and sit down
and enjoy himself in the gardens of Rome
and drink port and take a minibath in the
Fontana de Trevi think about Botticelli
Michelangelo or the genius of Dante
and throw three coins in so as to sing
three coins in the fountain
to visit the ruins of Pompeii
and those of the old Roman Empire
(seat of incredible battles) to go see
underdevelopment and compare it with his own
his cosa nostra
and that's something else
because
the POET is the type to detest underdevelopment
and yet he doesn't help eradicate it
he thinks that by carrying unforgivably
silken lectures in his bags
he's going to de-underdevelop himself
but it does NOT always happen that way
it's a joke
because
the POET is the thoroughly untrusting
right down to the fallout shelters

because he knows that when all's said
and done he'll not be of much use
when the hour of the comics comes around
and he's had to emigrate on safari
most of the time although not to Africa
but to live in some big old house in
MONTparnasse-pellier-martre
well one or other of those mounts or
along the banks of the Thames
because
the POET is the metaphysical type caught up in
the cycle of rebirth and he goes far very far
to meet with hunger nostalgia and revolution
but he's a globetrotter
knows his way around cities like
Stockholm Geneva Zurich
Moscow Indianapolis Peking Athens
Mexico City Brussels New York
Berlin Havana Barcelona
because
the POET is an internationalist
not of the proletarian but of the poetarian
he's a being who fights like hell
for the collective freedom
and he likes to be steeped in heartache abroad
but he writes the most although to no avail
to justify his being—the rest is bullshit—
HIS BEING
and it's the worst paid
[this thesis is not universal—Author's note]
but he has more feelings than cats have
because
the POET is a scaffold across which the sun creeps
barefoot and naked
he returns in one piece
barefoot
dissipating the illusion that comes
out of materialist desires
I am a beggar
an inoffensive kind of being

not needed anywhere
but to quote Walt Whitman..
'Don't cry over me . . .'

WAYNE BROWN
b. 1944

The Witness

Always when the warring tides
ebb at sunset, someone comes.
At first you can hardly see
him: a black nut in the surf

of the advancing skyline,
or as if the dusk congealed
to fleck that darkening iris:
your eyes widen in terror,

you hate him, mock him as he moves
among the shrapnel of chipped stones,
the palm trees' tattered flags, the stiff
trunks flung face down in the sand. . . .

Later, on the well-lit train
to a colonial future
narrow as rails, you ask 'Who
was that stranger by the sea?'

Man, he is your memory,
that each sunset moves among
the jetsam of the tribe, the years,
widowed past grief, yet lingering,

Even as the murmuring
sea unwraps and wraps its arms
in turn around each dead, loved thing:
and the gesture may be fruitless, but is made.

FAUSTIN CHARLES
b. 1944

The Red Robber

From the depths of burning Hell
I came
Cast out because I raped Satan's daughter
My rage is a millionfold
My mother was a dragon
And my father a Griffin
I can drink a river
And belch an ocean
When my name is called in vain
My belly blows rain
Flooding villages, towns, and cities
I eat countries boiled in vinegar
Emperors and kings tremble
At the sound of my name
Snakes hiss! Wolves howl!
Volcanoes split fire exploding
Damnation scattering the sun
Watch me
As I devour these islands
Watch me
As I drink the Caribbean sea
Brain-washing minds hatched
From a rotten egg circling
The plague-ridden universe
I was the conqueror, slave-driver
And slave
My body grew in the passing
Of centuries
I can destroy
And I can create
Watch me
Reshaping islands from sea-spray
Sweat and grass.

AMRYL JOHNSON

1944–2001

Far and High

(The first song they learnt)

Far and high
far and high
We have set our sights up to the sky
There is no mountain we can't climb
Oh we ain't coming down
Our feet won't touch the ground

Blood or wine
blood or wine
We have drunk both grief and joy
We have drained the dregs of both
Either one caused us pain
Now both taste the same

Love or hate
love or hate
We have chewed their jagged edges
'till they were powder in our mouths
From today our crying's done
Emotions take a back seat now

Weak or strong
weak or strong
We have danced with demons in our dreams
We have cowered from a breeze
Every battle has to be fought
Certain victory is never won

Far and high
far and high
We are climbing up the mountain side

to where the air is sweet and the eagles fly
A-n-d we ain't coming down
No we ain't coming down

We're going
Far and high

JEANNETTE MILLER

b. 1944

Because Death is This Feeling

Translated by JoAnne Engelbert

Because death is this feeling of emptiness and nothing,
this voice that arrives like a whirlwind blowing everything away,
when they killed that woman
when they shot that man
we just stood there silent in the smoke.
Shame for the bones that multiply with every dreaded dawn,
shame for frozen fingers,
for guts that stiffen hidden from the sun, from roaring air.
Tide of blood
licking feet with names and surnames
photo angles
a final red smile like any crimson blossom.
Song of a woodcutter from far away,
cries of a mechanic to accompany it,
and the work grows steadily in fears and silences,
and the street is a risk,
you think twice before going out for groceries or a meal
or to stretch like a wounded seagull
on the island, preserve of predators
where blood gets cheaper every day.

NANCY MOREJÓN

b. 1944

Black Woman

Translated by Kathleen Weaver

I still smell the foam of the sea they made me cross.
The night. I can't remember it.
The ocean itself could not remember that.
But I can't forget the first gull I made out in the distance.
High, the clouds, like innocent eye-witnesses.
Perhaps I haven't forgotten my lost coast,
nor my ancestral language.
They left me here and here I've lived.
And, because I worked like an animal,
here I came to be born.
How many Mandinga epics did I look to for strength.

       I rebelled.

His Worship bought me in a public square.
I embroidered His Worship's coat and bore him a male child.
My son had no name.
And His Worship died at the hands of an impeccable English *lord*.

       I walked.

This is the land where I suffered
mouth-in-the-dust and the lash.
I rode the length of all its rivers.
Under its sun I planted seeds, brought in the crops,
but never ate those harvests.
A slave barracks was my house,
built with stones that I hauled myself.
While I sang to the pure beat of native birds.

       I rose up.

In this same land I touched the fresh blood
and decayed bones of many others,
brought to this land or not, the same as I.
I no longer dreamt of the road to Guinea.
Was it to Guinea? Benin?
               To Madagascar? Or Cape Verde?

          I worked on and on.

I strengthened the foundations of my millenary song and of my hope.

                    I left for the hills.

My real independence was the free slave fort
and I rode with the troops of Maceo.

Only a century later,
together with my descendants,
from a blue mountain

               I came down from the Sierra

to put an end to capital and usurer,
to generals and to bourgeois.
Now I exist: only today do we own, do we create.
Nothing is foreign to us.
The land is ours.
Ours the sea and the sky,
the magic and the vision.
Compañeros, here I see you dance
around the tree we are planting for communism.
Its prodigal wood resounds.

April

Translated by Jean Andrews

These leaves which fly beneath the sky,
want to say the language of the homeland.

These birds which breathe in
the hostile slowness of the squall,

already know that in April
all the aggressions precipitate.

Oh people into which I was born,
thus I look at you fierce, by the sea;
this dust on which I tread
will be the magnificent garden of all.
And if we fall once more
our bones will rise up in the sand.

Here our souls are
in the unforeseen month, in April,
where the Island sleeps like a wing.

Mother

Translated by Jean Andrews

My mother didn't have a garden
only cliff-edged islands
floating, under the sun,
on their delicate coral.
There was no clean branch
in the pupil of her eye only lots of garottes.
What a time that was when she used to run, barefoot,
on the whitewash of the orphanages
and she didn't know how to laugh
and she couldn't even look at the horizon.
She didn't have the ivory bedroom
nor the wicker-furnished drawing-room,
nor the silent stained-glass of the tropics.
My mother had her singing and the scarf
to rock the faith of my insides,
to lift up her head of an unheard queen,
and leave us her hands, like precious stones,
in the face of the cold remains of the enemy.

Grenadian Woman

Translated by Jean Andrews

I am a Grenadian woman.
I sowed nutmegs
beneath the fixed shelter
of the wild flamboyant tree
and I cast the nets again
into the blue of the summers.
Grasses, rocks and conch shells
cradled the heart of my villages
and the sky was witness
to how all my sons
hungered around the port.

I am a Grenadian woman.
I saw the smoke, suddenly,
alive now among the dead,
between the fury and the lightning.
I have discovered the essential morning
while I dig the grave of a marine
who dared to dig mine after stalking unpunished
a girl from Saint George.
I am a Grenadian woman
and here you lie, stretched out,
waiting for the response of the serpents.

JESUS COS CAUSSE
b. 1945

I Could Say

Translated by J. R. Pereira

Here stood the house; I know these ruins despite the dust.
Now only memories and reminiscences of those times remain.
I could say with my eyes shut: here stood the patio where my mother
would wash the neighbours' clothes and weep at times with sorrow,
                                                                with cause:
here the guango shade and the fowl-house with its cracked eggs: here
the innocent lamp with no light save hope: here the corner of the
    room
where Zenaida and I would exchange sweets, songs and secrets
                                                        of childhood:
here the room where grandpa spent that night so solemnly between
                                                        four candles
with the rain pelting the roof and us shifting him around because of
                                                        the drops
falling on the coffin's glass and his face: here the rocker by
the window where grandma would tell me this her simple dream:

Cuba is a white horse galloping
galloping from the shore to a distant palm grove.
And it's also a nightingale winging blue
through the land and wind. A horse
galloping between sea-shells and corals
and an approaching nightingale winging blue.

I could say just as if I were touching the past with my hand: here was
the table with hunger always seated there its stare fixed on the
                                                        empty plate.

I could say so many things: but now we are building another
    memory,
another childhood for the future and other hands and other eyes
                                                to see and touch life.

CYRIL DABYDEEN

b. 1945

Returning

Where I came from
I do not know—
you, there

Upsetting the town or village;
this Goa, you say—
marked by other terrain.

I am bound to it:
my Ganges of years,
talking to you

Baring all. . .
this ocean's memory,
voyages undiscovered—

Or my archive of ancestry,
beginnings or disappearance?
still here, as I am a shadow

Of my former self,
breathing hard and imagining
other ruins, hibiscus,

A sacred cow rampaging
across a wide-open field;
a petal wind, gods with many arms

And legs—such reverences;
mind pulverizing
with other forms: reggae

Of garlanded time—
a lurid understanding
of further loves, conquests;

The plantation's
cauldron in an eye—
my creole sun's

Distancing.

McDONALD DIXON

b. 1945

Roseau—The Forgotten Village

The road unwinds like a ball of twine,
A crude zigzag pulled by teeth
from flour bag seams. Threading
                as we cross the bridge
Where a river in happier times
                    marched seaward.
On its banks shacks multiply.

Misery is an old woman's face nailed
to her windowsill. Behind her,
a fading banner fans the wind;
            its gothic scroll proclaims:

*'Bless this house and
all who dwell in it.'*

In two bold lines screaming from a mildew rag.

Here, desolation is complete. Thrives
In caves that were once eyes, straggling
Down a midday street where dust
            has lost its zeal to fly.

Poverty clothes the toothless grin
            on old men
Etherized by the flamboyant's glare.
The young, city bound, shake wings and soar,
Swearing never to return to this place
Where symbols fade and faith is a blessing
Shared with a sign of the cross
over a bowl of rice and silver-blue
                flying fish:
The smell of the sea still fresh in it.
Here no one starves. Hope is named after
                a motorboat.

ROOPLAL MONAR

b. 1945

The Cowherd

And the fragrance of dusky afternoon!
She clings, she spins, she sings

    Of the tranquility,
    the music,
    and the eternal blessings.

There is dust on his feet,
His body is sunburnt,
And his eyes of a peaceful song!
He thinks not of power,
    he is ambitionless
    as wind;

For he broods behind his cows,
And Nature smiles with serenity,
Through the dust that scatters
the haunting zooms of Evening.

I can see cows,
Silently treading,
    chewing their cud
    and smelling that
    there is Evening.

And I can hear music like a flute,
It reminds me of Krishna
    when he blows
    and he sings
    and the distant plains
    stood up with cows

When the milkmaids dance
    and poetry flung
    from his lips divine!
My! There is music of perfection
    of the soul
    of the passion!
Though the heavens became
    angry . . .
        for beauty sits
        Where there is beauty

O Music! It plays silently!
Seeing him with his cows,
Coming to the village,
How at peace he is,
Satisfied with Life's play
    not knowing about the expression
    but thinking of sleep
    when his golden dreams
    will enchant a tomorrow
    growing beautiful by bliss,
    fashioning by the fields,
    the sun, the crops;
    and the 'will' that is willing
    To live in the happy sentiments
    Of everlasting happiness.

MICHELLE CLIFF

b. 1946

The Land of Look Behind

On the edge of each canefield or 'piece' was a watch house, a
tiny structure with one entry. These were used for the babies
of nursing slaves who worked in the fields. An older woman
was in charge of the infants and the mothers came there for
feeding time.

                    tourist brochure of the Whim Great House

A tiny structure with one entry
walls guttered with mortar
molasses   coral   sand
hold the whole thing fast.

One hundred years later
the cut limestone
sunned and salted
looks like new.

And feels like? And feels like?
I don't know.
Describe it.
Sad? Lost? Angry?
Let me get my bearings.

Outside
A tamarind tree with a dead nest in the first crotch
Dense mud construction.
Immense. The inhabitants long gone.
Hard brown pods crack underfoot
The soursweet flesh is dried.
Inedible.

Inside
One thin bench faces a blank wall.

No message from the watchwomen here.
No HELP ME carved in the mortar or the stone.
Try to capture the range—

What did their voices sound like?
What tongues? What words for day and night?
Hunger? Milk?
What songs devised to ease them?

Was there time to speak? To sing?
To the riverain goddesses
The mermaids bringing secrets
To bring down Shàngó's wrath.

No fatting-houses here.
Nowhere to learn the secrets
except through some new code
in spaces they will never own.

How many voices? How many drops of milk?
How many gums daubed with rum to soothe the teething
or bring on sleep?

How many breasts bore scars?
Not the sacred markings of the Carib—
but the mundane mark of the beast.

How many dropped in the field?
How many bare footfalls across the sand floor?
How many were buried?
I leave through the opening and take myself home.

LORNA GOODISON

b. 1947

For My Mother (May I Inherit Half Her Strength)

My mother loved my father
I write this as an absolute
in this my thirtieth year
the year to discard absolutes

he appeared, her fate disguised,
as a Sunday player in a cricket match,
he had ridden from a country
one hundred miles south of hers.

She tells me he dressed the part,
visiting dandy, maroon blazer,
cream serge pants, seam like razor
and the beret and the two-tone shoes.

My father stopped to speak to her sister,
till he looked and saw her by the oleander,
sure in the kingdom of my blue-eyed grandmother.
He never played the cricket match that day.

He wooed her with words and he won her.
He had nothing but words to woo her,
on a visit to distant Kingston he wrote,

'I stood on the corner of King Street and looked,
and not one woman in that town was lovely as you.'

My mother was a child of the petite bourgeoisie
studying to be a teacher, she oiled her hands
to hold pens.
My father barely knew his father, his mother died young,
he was a boy who grew with his granny.

My mother's trousseau came by steamer through the snows of
Montreal
where her sisters Albertha of the cheekbones and the
perennial Rose, combed Jewlit backstreets with French-
turned names for Doris's wedding things.

Such a wedding Harvey River, Hanover, had never seen.
Who anywhere had seen a veil fifteen chantilly yards long?
and a crepe de chine dress with inlets of silk godettes
and a neck-line clasped with jeweled pins!

And on her wedding day she wept. For it was a brazen bride in those
days
who smiled.
and her bouquet looked for the world like a sheaf of wheat
against the unknown of her belly,
a sheaf of wheat backed by maidenhair fern, representing Harvey River
her face washed by something other than river water.

My father made one assertive move, he took the imported cherub
down
from the heights of the cake and dropped it in the soft territory
between her breasts . . . and she cried.

When I came to know my mother many years later, I knew her as the
figure
who sat at the first thing I learned to read: 'SINGER,' and she breast-fed
my brother while she sewed; and she taught us to read while she sewed
and
she sat in judgment over all our disputes as she sewed.

She could work miracles, she would make a garment from a square of
cloth
in a span that defied time. Or feed twenty people on a stew made from
fallen-from-the head cabbage leaves and a carrot and a cho-cho and a
palmful
of meat.

And she rose early and sent us clean into the world and she went to bed
in
the dark, for my father came in always last.

There is a place somewhere where my mother never took the younger
   ones
a country where my father with the always smile
my father whom all women loved, who had the perpetual quality of
   wonder
given only to a child . . . hurt his bride.

Even at his death there was this 'Friend' who stood by her side,
but my mother is adamant that that has no place in the memory of
my father.

When he died, she sewed dark dresses for the women amongst us
and she summoned that walk, straight-backed, that she gave to us
and buried him dry-eyed.

Just that morning, weeks after,
she stood delivering bananas from their skin
singing in that flat hill country voice.

she fell down a note to the realization that she did
not have to be brave, just this once,
and she cried.

For her hands grown coarse with raising nine children
for her body for twenty years permanently fat
for the time she pawned her machine for my sister's

Senior Cambridge fees
and for the pain she bore with the eyes of a queen

and she cried also because she loved him.

Ground Doves

Small querulous birds
feathers like swatches of earth
graced with wings,
opt for walking.

The female ones
sport surprising underslips
trimmed with stunning passementerie.
Braided arabesques

scalloping round their hems
but that is rarely shown, except
when they bend to scramble
for stale bread crumbs

they have come to expect as due.
Ground doves make you uneasy
because there was a time
when you too walked

and saved your wings
and would not reach high
for the sweet risk
inside the lips of hibiscus

but saved your wings,
and scrambled for used bread
and left over things . . .

The yard man: An election poem

When bullet wood trees bear
the whole yard dreads fallout
from lethal yellow stone fruit,

and the yard man will press
the steel blade of a machete
to the trunk in effort to control

its furious firing. He will dash
coarse salt at its roots to cut
the boil of leaves, try slashing

the bark so it will bleed itself
to stillness, and yet it will shoot
until the groundcover is acrid

coffin colour, the branches dry
bones. Under the leaves it lives,
poverty's turned-down image

blind, naked, one hand behind
one before. The yard's first busha
was overseer who could afford

to cultivate poverty's lean image,
but good yard man says since we
are already poor in spirit, fire for it.

Praise to the mother of Jamaican art

She was the nameless woman who created
images of her children sold away from her.
She suspended her wood babies from a rope
round her neck, before she ate she fed them.
Touched bits of pounded yam and plantains
to sealed lips, always urged them to sip water.
She carved them of wormwood, teeth and nails
her first tools, later she wielded a blunt blade.
Her spit cleaned faces and limbs; the pitch oil
of her skin burnished them. When woodworms
bored into their bellies she warmed castor oil
they purged. She learned her art by breaking
hard rockstones. She did not sign her work.

JEAN GOULBOURNE

b. 1947

Sunday Crosses

The rastaman
came
to the door
that Sunday
and said
'Broom'

Sun overhead
as hot as hell
gate burnt brown
grass grey
under violent
Sunday Sun—
Head wrapped
with cotton closet
of lice and worms—
Death squawking at squaw
and children
nimbling worms—
bellies banged
when hunger
clanged its bell—

Rastaman stopped
at brown
sun baked door
and said
'Broom'.

Door opened Hope
and brown skinned man
with curly hair
a bank account
and good solid credit

at every bank
in town,
poked head out
wrinkled nose
at sweaty sun
day smell
and said

'No broom'

Door closed doom
and sun went out
like a light
grass grew greyer
dark clouds bleaker
man looked at speaker
at the blank mass
of a brown skinned
uncaring futile face
and sighs.

Proud man
pickney down gutter
waiting
commonlaw wife
breeding

son succeeding
at nothing—
moves slowly cross
concrete
on a Sunday full
of crosses
and calls
'Broom'.

MARK McWATT

b. 1947

Nightfall: Kangaruma

Arriving at Kangaruma
I was surprised by a new resthouse,
beds and an inexplicable sadness
in the afternoon light burning low
behind the trees. Off the river
came the coldest breeze that ever sliced
my fifteen years of life.

In a corner of the clear-
ing a red man with wild hair
squatted before a fire—porknocker,
someone surmised. I went over to inquire.
We talked as the sun died
about the river 'topside'; he showed me
a small cloudy diamond and
his manner warmed me,
reminded me of my father
—a foolish thought, for
he suddenly clutched my arm
with a hand as old and hard as diamond:
'life not easy on the water top.'
My nervous chuckle only fanned his fire:
'You think is fun?' he cried
'you think is fuckin' fun!'
His wild green eyes pierced
my foolish little life and I ran from him
with the last rays of the sun.

I sat alone on the verandah,
outside the circle of light
where the others talked loudly about women.
My porknocker's fire still burned
and once I saw his scarecrow shape

move across its light. I decided
I'd forgiven him, but I knew,
as the dark river wreathed us all,
that I had forgiven only myself;
and even that—in this hellish place—
was not beyond recall.

That night I dreamt about a man
—not my porknocker, this was black
as the river, yet an ordinary man;
shorter than I, perhaps
and certainly better dressed.
He had a sinister determination
to be good to me and pressed
a covered basket into my arms,
'Gifts,' he said: buxton spice,
avocado pear, cassava bread—
and a human heart.
When I recoiled he laughed:
'It's only a heart—just like yours'
And I remember being careful not to say
'I've never seen my heart,'
in case he felt he should oblige . . .

I woke in panic
to a darkness deeper than my dream;
covered in sweat I reached
into an adjoining bed and clutched
a sleeping arm: the first time
I'd let fear betray me . . .
'O God,' I breathed as I willed my heart to stop,
'Life is sheer terror on the water top.'

MARLENE NOURBESE PHILIP
b. 1947

Fluttering Lives

Fluttering lives
among shuffled papers
sunstained, sunstarved
for the earth black blue
and the poui
blazing on the hungered edge of pain
yellowing with vengeance
the frangipani
scent-pinking the air
and the earth black blue,

bubbling larva brown laughter
black throat eruptions
brush with delicate green
the coconut
that gently palms the clouds
and the earth black blue,
fluttering lives
Among shuffled paper

fierce fluttering.

HAZEL SIMMONS-McDONALD
b. 1947

Parasite

That tree has died.
Its topmost branches reach starkly heavenward
In seeming terror or mute supplication
To be rid of this vine that has clung
And drained it of existence.
Now its tendrils drape
The lifeless limbs to give itself
As gift in death a shroud
To the thing that gave it life.

How careless are the adornments of death.
Such irony
That in sustaining its own life
This vine has drained the very life it thrived upon.
It must be in all nature
To desire a death-in-life existence—
As we, shrouded in the foilage of passion,
Seek evanescent joy that
Must only end in death.

But there's this vine
Affixed upon a tree
That in death gave its life
To sundry branches.
It must forever be our
Hope in life and
Life in death

MIRTA YAÑEZ
b. 1947

The Duties of Womanhood

We learned the duties of love and silence,
of obdurate loneliness and anguish,
our duty to witness fear and death
and the arduous task of structuring dreams.

We learned the duties of twilight and desolation
the labour of poetry
of Gregorian chants
the mysterious firmament of the stars
the inexorable rituals of waiting
the ceremonies of terror and valour
the secrets of the bow and its invisible arrow
of the night and the fires illuminating it.

We learned of joy
of smiles
light and shadows
magic and science
a tree, an apple, a paradise,
the serpent, a flight of birds,
Mythology and enigma.

We learned men's ways
and seized others meant only for gods.

CYNTHIA JAMES
b. 1948

Woman Descendant

Tanty Merle
Vibert Mother
Miss Clothilda
Mother Eva

this is your daughter
your eyeball and treasure
garden of pleasure
landscaped and landscaped
from nanny to granny
feeled-up and softened
in my sapodilla-sweet belly
handmaid for the legacy
faithful beyond duty
ribbed as ivory
durable as ebony
my womb is eternity
my backbone is history
but drunk from astonishment

asking permission
to banish the myth
that I best bear sorrow
in the tallow of my body
bountiful in recovery
to be free from fixations
that commend me and degrade me
disrespect me in respect
mock me with praise, canonize
iconize, idealize, immortalize
treating me worse than the enemy
mark me as martyr
impale me in literature
climbing down my rockstone

CYNTHIA JAMES

for mine is
the power
the glory
to live

JOHN ROBERT LEE

b. 1948

Vocation

For Patrick Anthony, priest and folklorist

And so, despite the whisperings
behind hands clasped in fervent unbelief,
despite the stale, old lady's scent
of righteousness that crawls from

under French soutanes;

despite all that, and more

this is yours, you, your claim on love.

They could have asked. They could have asked
the blue-smoked hills, the country mandolins;
old trembling-nosed, broad-voiced chantwelles
they could have asked; they could have asked tracks lost
but for some village's dying song;
    and belle-aire drums
    and violons
    and moonlit, ragged choirs,
    could have told and would have told
of what they'd always known:
that like a hidden mountain stream
caught patient swirling past the ages of the land
nothing dims that vision waiting gently:
    of calm clean pools below the waterfall.

And I
who share a common celibacy
that priests and poets must endure,
search the purity of syllable
seeking truths you've found;
incensed with love, I make too
that ritual of Word and Gesture,

wrists uplifted, fingers plucking
outward, scratching at this altar,
daring faith and hope, changing them
into some clarity.

Lusca

For Derek Walcott

> . . . in you, the forever lost has berthed
> the might-have-been is beached
> and glimpses anchored . . .

Caught in my private limbo, my
youth lost in a ravine somewhere
between town and suburb,
I never knew anyone like you,
my Lusca.

Moonlit rings I never knew,
their songs, or dances, chances for first gropings in the dark;
never had I known, like you, grandmothers and their days of pride,
chantwelles for this feast-day or that . . .

Dropping behind the crossed bars
of my parents' pride and poverty,
I sailed alone to meet my heroes
on Europe's passages of glory.

And you, your early gods were rum-soaked banjo-players,
wanderers of hills and towns, story-tellers, gossip-mongers,
to whom you gave your heart up captive, new each time, to each new
    chord,
to each sweet tongue of flute that whistled you past long canoes,
down lonely tracks, to rivers hiding naked among rocks
and frowning rain forests.

   While wolves and wicked wizards held
me rigid and afraid to move
on nights when hell itself had seemed

to choose our roof for lechery
unimagined,
you knew, my little Lusca, of old crones dégagéd;
of strange and silent single men who, they said, might have mounted
  you,
you dear Lusca, in their magec noire! You knew as I did not
of soucouyants and loup-garous, of kélé and kutumba,
of chembois and of obeah!

  Books could make me fear the dark, but your grandmother,
head scarved, nostrils flaring, could flame her mist-ringed eyes and
  send you
quick to bed or straight to father-priest's confessional:
              —duh lajablesse is coming!
                  —M'sieu Luwoi et Papa Bois!
                      —Look! duh screaming faceless Bolom
                      searching for Ti-Jean and Lusca!
        Aieee!
                          —poor jab, poor Lusca.

And so dear Lusca I have a loss to claim:
my friends must know that town bred as I am,
my hands are soft, my feet cling poorly to the land;
my fingers scratch in vain, my toes itch for shoes to wear;
here, I am Lusca's lover, nice boy, but still from town;
the earth will not be entered by my hoe, it cannot conceive
that I can truly want its syllables of roots, its language of
firm green shoots that climb from it with confidence and with
  trust.
A stranger here, my seeds grow weak-kneed, if they grow, and lack
  truth;
no one believes them, their garbled language making them the village
  idiots.

And this is why dear Lusca I must remain a lover
and have but safe acquaintance with your past;
or every image in your dusty album
will fill me with a morbid lust
when each deserves my gratitude.

My plot of ground is dry and hard
as sidewalks are; at nights street lamps
block out the stars and hi-fi sets
replace the country violons;
and I must dig foundations deep,
plunge steel and concrete shafts into
this city's dirt, and hope for structures firm,
and spare, no space for flair or show,
each entrance, passage, exit, clear and marked,
each section storing much within a little space.

Perhaps dear Lusca we should build our house
somewhere on a valley's side, a valley moving
with its riverbed, between the country and the town;
then we would see the city's lights
and hear the dying belle-aire drums;
comb the dust of highways off our hair
and smell the burners' blue-smoked pits.
Perhaps.

EDGAR CAIRO

1948–2000

Child of a New Tide

Translated by Francis R. Jones

what are rivers without shores, shores without you,
a promise to me, still unredeemed?
that's why you and I are parted.

beneath the night of empty talk, caught in words,
a canoe is waiting to leave,
in the parting, filled with truth from this life.

let's not go! no, let's be bound into
each other's heart: you my current, I your channel!
how can such a voyage be, with no growing in us both?

child of a new tide! this is the way that time drifts by,
away to the coast! where in the turn
of tidings, life and love rise to the flood.

JIT NARAIN

b. 1948

Working all day, dreaming at night

Translated Paul Vincent

Working all day, dreaming at night—
Aja's appearance is something like mine.

My ship was not called Lalla Rookh
and my country's name became Holland, meneer.

I flew KLM, I left Surinam.
When the memory of you arose,
I went in search of history.

The sap of this story is not sacred nectar,
the feeling it gives holds my mind in its grip.

Why he left India, that I can fathom;
that India never left him, is the burden I bear.

CHIQUI VICIOSO

b. 1948

Doña Mariana

Translated by Rosabelle White and M. J. Fenwick

I am 63 years old and everything looks dark
we are like a cargo ship
that's listing to one side
if only they'd raise it a little
to allow us to balance ourselves!

Today it's been seven years since the death of Marino
I wanted to say a prayer
but with the news I don't even have the energy to eat
to tell him to come take care of his kids
that it's okay after so many tears!

What good does it do us to be so rich?
we have mines of land, gold, coffee
and when I was a kid the campesino sowed cane
now the planters are the guards
have you ever seen such a thing?

And our cane is so sweet!
they can take it with them on the plane
when they leave . . . if they leave
. . . if they don't leave
Doña Mariana.

Some day they will all go to the mountains
Ah! I like to raise pigs and chickens!
I kill one, I roast it and I put it on a tray
I cover it with a lot of folded linens and sheets . . .
and I tell them
that I am the washerwoman of Mr. So-And-So . . .

And there, above, the boys giving themselves a banquet!
. . . that business of the mountain isn't used anymore Doña Mariana
You better believe it!
one day this town will rise up like a dove
and there won't be any guards!

And I probably won't see that
you boys will see it
the ants will tell me about it
the earth will tell me, Marino will tell me
. . . and smiles will flourish Doña Mariana!

JOHN AGARD
b. 1949

Pan Recipe

First rape a people
simmer for centuries

bring memories to boil
foil voice of drum

add pinch of pain
to rain of rage

stifle drum again
then mix strains of blood

over slow fire
watch fever grow

till energy burst
with rhythm thirst

cut bamboo and cure
whip well like hell

stir sound from dustbin
pound handful biscuit tin

cover down in shanty town
and leave mixture alone

when ready will explode

Limbo Dancer at Immigration

It was always the same
at every border/at every frontier/
at every port/at every airport/
       of every metropolis

The same hassle
from authorities

the same battle
with bureaucrats

a bunch of official cats
ready to scratch

looking limbo dancer up & down
scrutinising passport with a frown

COUNTRY OF ORIGIN: SLAVESHIP

Never heard of that one
the authorities sniggered

Suppose you got here on a banana boat
the authorities sniggered

More likely a spaceship
the authorities sniggered

Slaveship/spaceship/Pan Am/British Airways/Air France
It's all the same
smiled limbo dancer

Now don't give us any of your lip
the authorities sniggered

ANY IDENTIFYING MARKS?

And when limbo dancer showed them sparks
of vision in eyes that held rivers
    it meant nothing to them

And when limbo dancer held up hands
that told a tale of nails
                    it meant nothing to them

And when limbo dancer offered a neck
that bore the brunt of countless lynchings
                    it meant nothing to them

And when limbo dancer revealed ankles
bruised with the memory of chains
                    it meant nothing to them

So limbo dancer bent over backwards
                    & danced
                    & danced
                    & danced

until from every limb
flowed a trail of red

& what the authorities thought
was a trail of blood

was only spilt duty-free wine

so limbo dancer smiled
saying I have nothing to declare
& to the sound of drum disappeared

BRIAN CHAN
b. 1949

To a Daughter

He never hoped for you, he never not:
it was you who gave birth to a father.

A baby, you wanted often to play
with the only friend you had all day long

but the drug of Work would pull him away
to a desk, piano, easel or stove.

If he felt you were keeping him from other
life like salt running out, he might bark

Leave me alone, in the anger of fear,
and he would feel his voice quiver your spine.

But you never stopped running to embrace
him, teaching how gratuitous is love.

Your father's love for you, shadowed by pain,
clouded by duty, was never as free.

Yet though you're now 'tall as a lantern-post',
you still sit on his knee and hug his neck;

but that he once frightened you still frightens him
should he snap Leave me alone, meaning now Don't.

VICTOR QUESTEL

1949–1982

Judge Dreadword

I am a murderer; I wring words by the rough of their necks.
I misplace commas and abuse silent W's. I use folk-
lift to get from one idea to the next.

I stab thoughts at people without
first preparing them by word of mouth.
I have language in a vice all my own. But today,
I appear before the country's chief judge and word protector:

Judge Dreadword. Yes I. Confess your atrocious crimes
to this Word Court. I am Judge Dreadword—I don't
brook silence in my court.

You are accused of lynching the word 'money' by
its second syllable; you violated a full-stop, you
stabbed three vowels when they weren't

looking. You exploded a bomb in the face of two
young phonemes. You copulated with the letters P and Y
. . . these acts make me blue

with rage, and I'm a hard man. I deal with your kind
every day. How do you plead Rude boy Q?
Guilty or not guilty? What should I do?

Not guilty sir. Take four hundred years. We must rid
society of your kind—insensitive word merchants like you
must be punished. You have no tradition, no lineage, no big

models. Don't write in this court. Take another two
hundred years. Rude boy Q have you heard of Johnson,
Cavafy, Eliot, Whitman, Lorca, Pasternak, Mandelstam?

Li Po? No your Dreadness. I thought so; a mere literary shim-sham.
Don't cry. This court is a product of a proven tradition
of oil and its related cultural benefactors—

BP, CIA, IMF, IOU, the UN, PNM—letters that matter
in the world. You want to destroy all that? Hush up.
I hear you detractors harbour vile thoughts against

foreign socio-linguists and visiting psycho-linguists—you
draw crude lop-side effigies of Chomsky, you hunt and burn
the manifestos of British dialectologists and American politicians.

You dare to write letters to the press. Don't interrupt.
I heard you were tough, but you snivel in my court.
Take another four hundred years. How dare you corrupt

our language? Why don't you dot your i's? Don't talk. I
do all the talking here. This is my court. Leave me.
Court is adjourned. Nail him to the cross of a T.

Grandad

I

That shoe-maker tapping
leather
believes in the little boy he is
talking to

has his faith tacked
firmly
in his sole
ability to survive

feels that the future
can be brought to heel,
controlled by one so young.

The shape of things to come
tightens on
his last . . .

The boy is six fingered
and borne the wrong
way
by decisions he did not make.

II

No longer a boy,
he says goodbye to the empty
house

even as the hills exhale smoke.

There on the truck is
his old school grip
with his clothes, books
and testimonials

as he levels a look at
the road
and its beginning returns to
him

returns to the day he
first left
after gripping his mother

His things then included
a brunswick stove, a wooden plaque that
stared at him from the blank of its eyes
and a framed water colour
print.

Demons of flight fought
and won his sole
possession

his need to move beyond
himself

to ever-
last-
ing
heights

to claim a window in the world
as his

III

The shoe-maker's eyes
are blurred

he looks at the child in
front of him
darkening his shuttered
shop
and named him.

His thoughts criss-crossed
slanted
sank
beneath the child's skin

the child is still
the old man's search is
urgent
the situation is urgent

the face hardens to a glowing
mahogany

the sky screams
the horsemen
pursue him

he feels the suicidal im-
pulse
of his wrist

he jeers

taunts the hooves.

Still;

his thin voice is trapped in his
rib
cage
it is fixed as a dancer's
practised smile.

Now
a sigh pulls at the corners of his lips
evens
the triangle of himself

child
and child's future

as he tacks his hopes on him

JULIA ALVAREZ

b. 1950

Bilingual Sestina

Some things I have to say aren't getting said
in this snowy, blond, blue-eyed, gum-chewing English:
dawn's early light sifting through *persianas* closed
the night before by dark-skinned girls whose words
evoke *cama, aposento, sueños* in *nombres*
from that first world I can't translate from Spanish.

Gladys, Rosario, Altagracia—the sounds of Spanish
wash over me like warm island waters as I say
your soothing names: a child again learning the *nombres*
of things you point to in the world before English
turned *sol, tierra, cielo, luna* to vocabulary words—
sun, earth, sky, moon. Language closed

like the touch-sensitive *moriviví* whose leaves closed
when we kids poked them, astonished. Even Spanish
failed us back then when we saw how frail a word is
when faced with the thing it names. How saying
its name won't always summon up in Spanish or English
the full blown genie from the bottled *nombre.*

Gladys, I summon you back by saying your *nombre.*
Open up again the house of slatted windows closed
since childhood, where *palabras* left behind for English
stand dusty and awkward in neglected Spanish.
Rosario, muse of *el patio,* sing in me and through me say
that world again, begin first with those first words

you put in my mouth as you pointed to the world—
not Adam, not God, but a country girl numbering
the stars, the blades of grass, warming the sun by saying,
¡Qué calor! as you opened up the morning closed
inside the night until you sang in Spanish,
Estas son las mañanitas and listening in bed, no English

252

yet in my head to confuse me with translations, no English
doubling the world with synonyms, no dizzying array of words
—the world was simple and intact in Spanish—
luna, sol, casa, luz, flor, as if the *nombres*
were the outer skin of things, as if words were so close
one left a mist of breath on things by saying

their names, an intimacy I now yearn for in English—
words so close to what I mean that I almost hear my Spanish
heart beating, beating inside what I say *en inglés*.

Last Trees

When I think of my death, I think of trees
in the full of summer, a row of them
describing a border, too distant yet
for me to name them, posted with rusting boards
everyone but the faint of heart ignores.
(By then, I hope not to be one of them.)
I want to go boldly to the extreme
verge of a life I've lived to the fullest
and climb over the tumbled rocks or crawl
under the wire, never looking back—

for if I were to turn and see the house
perched on its hillside, windows flashing light,
the wash plaintive with tearful handkerchiefs,
or hear a dear voice calling from the deck,
supper's on the table—I might lose heart,
and turn back from those trees, telling myself,
tomorrow is a better day to die . . .
Behind me, the wind blowing in the leaves
in my distracted state will seem to say
something about *true love* and *letting go*—

some poster homily which I mistrust,
and which is why I break into a run,
calling out that I'm coming, *wait for me,*

thrashing and stumbling through the underbrush,
flushing out redwing blackbirds, shaking loose
seeds for next summer's weeds from their packed pods—
only to look up, breathless, and realize
I'm heading straight for those trees with no time
left to name my favorites, *arborvitae,*
maple, oak, locust, samán, willow, elm.

MERLE COLLINS
b. 1950

Nearly Ten Years Later
For Grenada

nearly ten years later
look me here analysing
still distraught and debating
sympathising synthesising
regretting and remembering
and time
just passing

who in the prison frustrating
who done dead disappearing
who alive remonstrating
nuff people still mix up and hesitating
and time
just passing

Grannie used to say
when you ask the question why
child forget that
and then it sound like she
just rambling
child forget that
think bout this

miss nancy etticoat
in a white petticoat
and a yellow nose
the longer she stands
the shorter she grows

Child, you see it?
is the candle
the candle of life

Watch Miss Nancy Etticoat
Look the white petticoat
See the burning nose!

And the white petticoat
Just melting
Disappearing
time passing

Child, forget that
think bout this
the shorter she grows
time passing

who in the prison frustrating
who done dead disappearing
who alive remonstrating
nuff people still mix up and hesitating
and time
just passing

like miss nancy etticoat
in she white petticoat
and she yellow nose
the longer she stands
the shorter she grows

time passing

some shouting for hanging
and we wanting an accounting
but watching the children
and dreading more bleeding

the shorter she grows
time passing
the shorter she grows

Like our prophets have asked
who will judge the judges?

child, today for policeman
tomorrow for thief
you see it?
time passing

watch the candle
miss nancy etticoat
and she yellow flame nose
the longer she stands
the shorter she grows

Perhaps the children will judge the judges?
you retreating, they advancing
the shorter she grows

time passing
time passing

GRACE NICHOLS

b. 1950

The Fat Black Woman Remembers

The fat black woman
remembers her Mama
and them days of playing
the Jovial Jemima

tossing pancakes
to heaven
in smokes of happy hearty
              murderous blue laughter

Starching and cleaning
O yes scolding and wheedling
pressing little white heads
against her big-aproned breasts
seeing down to the smallest fed
feeding her own children on Satanic bread

But this fat black woman ain't no Jemima
              Sure thing Honey/Yeah

Blackout

Blackout is endemic to the land.
People have grown sixthsense
and sonic ways, like bats,
emerging out of the shadows
into the light of their own flesh.

But the car headlamps coming towards us
make it seem we're in some thirdworld movie,

throwing up potholes and houses exaggeratedly,
the fresh white painted and grey ramshackle
blending into snug relief.

And inside, the children are still hovering,
hopeful moths around the flickerless Box
immune to the cloying stench of toilets
that can't be flushed. The children,
all waiting on electric-spell to come
and trigger a movie, the one featuring America,
played out endlessly in their heads.

While back outside, coconut vendors decapitate
the night, husky heads cutlassed off
in the medieval glow of bottle lamps.

And everywhere there are flittings
and things coming into being,
in a night where footfall is an act of faith—
A group of young girls huddled in a questionable
doorway;
The sudden dim horizontal of an alleyway;
And the occasional generator-lit big house,
obscenely bright—
hurting the soft iris of darkness
in this worn-out movie, slow reeling

Under the endless cinema of the skies.

GUSTAVO PÉREZ-FIRMAT

b. 1950

Lime Cure

I'm filling my house with limes
to keep away the evil spirits.
I'm filling my house with limes
to help me cope.
I have limes on the counters, under the sink,
inside the wash basin.
My refrigerator is stuffed with limes
(there's no longer any space for meat and potatoes).
Faking onionship, they hang from the walls.
Like golf balls, they have the run of the carpet
(but I would not drive them away).

I stash them in flowerpots.
I put them on bookshelves.
I keep them on my desk, cuddling with my computer.
I have two limes in every drawer of every chest
of every room.
I don't bathe, I marinade.

At night, I think of their cores, plump and wet.
I imagine myself taking off the peel and squeezing
until they burst in my hands.
I taste the tart juice dripping on my tongue.
I shudder.
Then I sleep peacefully inside green dreams of lime
and when I wake, I bask in the morning's lime light.

Were it not for limes, I would not know
what to do with myself.
I could not bear this loneliness.
I would burst. But there is a wisdom in limes, an uneventfulness
that soothes my seething, and whispers to me:
think, be still, and think some more,
and when the night arrives, dream of juice.

MARILENE PHIPPS

b. 1950

My Life in Nérètte

Me too I'll have a child, me too I want a son!
Me too, me too . . . Ika is pregnant. She's my woman.
You know her, skinny sixteen, tough. We are dirt
poor in Nérètte. No running water in these slums.
Most people over there will kill
over water in the ravine: it's a trickle
and getting some is not like in America—
you get a ticket and wait in line.
Midday sun down there bakes your brains,
sweat blinds you, eyes stung pink like a Zombie's.
Ika's skirt's just a piece from a rag; her bucket
overflows with water, bathing
her face, makes it glow like new shoes.

Ika's proud! Pain does not stop her, just makes her more mad.
Five a.m., you see her going down hill
to the *Croix-des-Bossales* market, in town.
She sells roadside food: plantain, sweet potato, pork.
But neighbors have bought bad magic
against us; *magie! Magie!* wherever you turn!
Thing is, the more we sell, the less money we have.
It's called *rale koo*—Ika's real mad! What does she do?:
Smashes all our wares, starts throwing
rocks at people's houses. Neighbors
all come out to defend their walls.

In no time, stones are flying like
bad birds in all directions. But
nothing can touch my happiness:
me too I'll have a son! I want a son! Me too!
We live in a one-room mud house!
Inside, I covered the walls from top to bottom;
all photos from a magazine *Madan* Blan gave

to my nephew Augustin. That magazine's name
is *Nasional Geografik*. Animals called
elephants! Tigers! Zebras, *m'gin tout bèt*—I have
every animal! Even a big poster of a giraffe!
In there, it's Paradise! But, *Sezon la pli vini*—
come rainy season, this is what happens to us:

the stream down the ravine swells up like a river
with arms that pull everything down to its red mouth.
Soon the giraffe in our room has water up
to its neck. Our mattress is making its way
out the door. *Ika!? Ika!? Run! Water's washing
away all our things!* She is playing dominos
with our neighbor Pic-et-Coeur, a Rara gang chief;
he wears dark sunglasses even inside his room.

My son is born in Augustin's red *tap-tap* bus.
He painted all the same animals I have on his bus.
His *tap-tap*'s called *Merci Saint Yves*. Never made it
to the hospital. My son's whole life lasts two months—
diarrhea kills him. His life is washed away.
We watch him. Don't know what to do. *Me too, me too*
I wanted my very own son—*pitit gason moin!*
Ika comes after me with two knives: *fout kaka!*
Salopri! Sa ou vin chache! M'rayi ou!!!
It's in Nérètte she learnt to speak to me like that:
Worthless shit! She yells, *go back to your mother!
I hate your guts!!!* I hit her with a chair. That stops her!
Ika goes to her mirror, puts rouge on her cheeks, lipstick,
adjusts an old red wig on her head, slams the door,
walks up to the road with red high heel shoes, sits on
a milestone, back straight, hands posed on her knees, legs closed,
like a mermaid queen. She chooses to ignore me.

LILLIAN ALLEN
b. 1951

Mrs

In the waiting room
a routine checkup
a technician came in
called me by what
she made my name
Mrs
I didn't answer but knowing
it was I, mumbled
and made my way
in a pace of my own
in a tempo earned
from struggle and long places
of silences
I no longer engage words
or meanings such as
Mistress Miss Mrs Missus

Mistress
rhymes with distress

Miss
missed nothing

Mrs
misses rarely with words

Missus
miss us, ourselves
when we answer to words
others name us

HONOR FORD-SMITH

b. 1951

Swimming Lesson

My mother is teaching me to swim
staying afloat in the clear aqua
is a struggle for her   she wants me
to be better than her   stirs up
the sand when she goes   darkens
the clear and swims like one a them trapped
blue marlin   butting and butting my uncle's boat
thrashing the line of the Sunday deep sea killers
trawling in the blood past the reef
one hand on their rods, the other on their Chivas Regal.

In the water where she can stand
she says   swim to me now
and I begin the crossing
clumsy   laborious   spluttering
banging my little bones
the disparate pieces of arm
leg   shoulder   against the angles
of the deep water, pausing
gulping between splattering on
longing to reach her body's harbour.

As I am about to reach, to rest
'Come on, come come come man,' she laughs
and moves further off again
I am tired. Kicking angry. Shicoom. Shicoom.
glugging up through the bubbles
the hard blue for air and the misty sands
blur the water   so I never reach the end
this homeless groundless body
struggling not to fight
the water   not to thrash
to flash streamlined like the conquering
trawler gliding into port.

Lala the Dressmaker

In memory of Lascelles Tate, 1897–1967

Across from Chang's Green Emporium,
at Halfway Tree, near the fish fry sidewalk
where the men now sit to play at winning
crown and anchor—the dress shop circled her.
Inch measure of her life's scramble—
mountain range of checkered scraps
scent of fabric satin and taffeta—
on the wheels of the foot machines
tread-treading on the raw edges of
parties, teas and mothers' unions socials,
she was drawn into town, moving yard
by yard on the trains of bridal gowns,
fashioning a living from these things.
There was nothing else to do.

The rack of finished dresses, hanging, linings out,
concealed the beadwork her fingers were known for.
(A bald pink mannequin stood in the window—
Issa's had made it necessary.)
She, seated behind the children's magic mahogany
and glass case, cargo of the trade's beads, buttons,
zippers, a bangle, pencil, candle—even fruit,
finished collars. The firm fat of her hands
dissolved by time into a skein of thin brown linen.
One son. No husband. In silence
she stitched the distant canefield's cotton trees,
her shame-mi-lady face half-hidden by the shoulder length
crisp straightened hair. Occasionally, laughter
like a sluice-gate crinkled the black black eyes.

~

Once, before, in the town's taboo, Mohammed's
secret raft of tissue paper and bamboo stood among the
indentured ready to float back to him,
the Indian women chanting
'Allah man say husseh'

She earned her name Lala mingling with the chant
then breaking, climbing, tearing at the women's work
to see the forbidden centre of the thing.

And afterwards, the dry red heat of malaria,
journeying, fighting, fighting through the hot cloth
covering a sea of seaweed, to the place where
years later, behind the hidden patterns in the stripped
backroom of the shop, between rough walls
across the naked cedar table, she gambled on futures
staring into the muddled Darjeeling leaves
calling the good fortunes of the women to life.

～

When Lala died
in the backroom of the shop
the girlchildren she had clothed,
whose futures she chose from those cupped in her hand
unpicked the beaded dresses to find what she hid
stitched in the lining.
They put the beads in the locks of their hair
their needles flashing (dangerous and quick)
collecting the light
opening
opening
their laughter strikes the centre of the clock
at Halfway Tree and the flames of the alleys
lick the rotten wooden walls.

TATO LAVIERA

b. 1951

AmeRícan

we gave birth to a new generation,
AmeRícan, broader than lost gold
never touched, hidden inside the
puerto rican mountains.

we gave birth to a new generation,
AmeRícan, it includes everything
imaginable you-name-it-we-got-it
society.

we gave birth to a new generation,
AmeRícan salutes all folklores,
european, indian, black, spanish,
and anything else compatible:

AmeRícan, singing to composer pedro flores' palm
          trees high up in the universal sky!

AmeRícan, sweet soft spanish danzas gypsies
          moving lyrics la espanola cascabelling
          presence always singing at our side!

AmeRícan, beating jibaro modem troubadours
          crying guitars romantic continental
          bolero love songs!

AmeRícan, across forth and across back
          back across and forth back
          forth across and back and forth
          our trips are walking bridges!

          it all dissolved into itself, the attempt
          was truly made, the attempt was truly
          absorbed, digested, we spit out

the poison, we spit out the malice,
we stand, affirmative in action,
to reproduce a broader answer to the
marginality that gobbled us up abruptly!

AmeRícan, walking plena-rhythms in new york,
strutting beautifully alert, alive,
many turning eyes wondering,
admiring!

AmeRícan, defining myself my own way any way many
ways Am e Rícan, with the big R and the
accent on the í!

AmeRícan, like the soul gliding talk of gospel
boogie music!

AmeRícan, speaking new words in spanglish tenements.
fast tongue moving street corner 'que
corta' talk being invented at the insistence
of a smile!

AmeRícan, abounding inside so many ethnic english
people, and out of humanity, we blend
and mix all that is good!

AmeRícan, integrating in new york and defining our
own destino, our own way of life,

AmeRícan, defining the new america, humane america,
admired america, loved america, harmonious
america, the world in peace, our energies
collectively invested to find other civili-
zations, to touch God, further and further,
to dwell in the spirit of divinity!

AmeRícan, yes, for now, for i love this, my second
land, and i dream to take the accent from
the altercation, and be proud to call
myself AmeRícan, in the US sense of the
word, AmeRícan, America!

JUDITH ORTIZ COFER

b. 1952

Under the Knife

My aunt wipes blood from her knife
across a kitchen towel, spilling
the thick contents of a just decapitated
hen into the sink.
I feel slightly nauseated but must
forbear for her sake. Childless
family martyr, renowned for her patience
with human frailty, and her cooking.
Her man drinks, she has failed three times
at childbearing. She squeezes the last
of the blood from the neck and a blue button
falls into her hand. Rinsing it, she drops it
into her apron pocket. And as she places the
pale carcass and the knife before me, she explains
how to cut the pieces with even, forceful
strokes: no hacking. She is under
no obligation to be kind.
The mothers and the daughters
have given her a lifetime license to mourn,
and like a queen in exile she acknowledges
nothing as a privilege. The pale fingers
of my aunt work with precision over
the pink flesh, showing me just how
to separate the tough from the tender.

KENDEL HIPPOLYTE
b. 1952

Revo Lyric

sweet chile
dem will say dat
dis eh revolution, stop it
dem go talk about
de People an' de Struggle
an' how in dis dry season
t'ings too dread, too serious
for love

as though
love not a serious t'ing
serious like war, frightenin'
tightenin' de heart strings an'
beatin' a rhythm up a twistin' road
all o' we fraid to dance on

love is a serious t'ing
bringin' you back
to baby-helpless trusting nakedness
whether you want or not
if in truth, in real truth
you love

a serious, serious t'ing:
is walking a high high edge
where looking down or back
would end you
yet forward and up
so dark wid no end
love is—o god sweetheart, dey mus' know!
dey can see!
dis instrument we tryin' to make—society

economics—wood and string
den politics—de major key
but de real, real t'ing
de reason an' de melody
de song we want to sing
is love
is love

come doudou, sing wid me . . .

Bedtime Story, W.I.

watching television
cornflakes cars and clothes
the children finally chose

heaven was on the other side
behind the white screen
so all made a decision

they left this hell
and walked right through
into a commercial about beans

they swallowed that too
then, for the first time, looked
at this new world they'd entered:

coiled quiet monsters watched them
strange cubes like blocks of empty buildings
were crackling a million voices

the twentieth century had outfoxed them
they lost the way home, tried another
then an MGM Lion roared and charged

they panicked—some ran into wires
their green eyes burned out from the sparks
some disappeared into transformers

the children scattered, bawling for Batman
looking for Sesame Street
seeking the little house on the prairie

but they were behind god's eye
and it was snowing on the screen
plus, a commercial break was on

a shower of cornflakes fell
some struggled, but you can't beat Kellogs
then it was all over

only one boy returned
into the living room:
now, alone, he stares at his own vision

LINTON KWESI JOHNSON
b. 1952

Sense outta Nansense

di innocent an di fool could paas fi twin
but haas a haas
an mule a mule
mawgah mean mawgah
it noh mean slim

yet di two a dem in camman share someting

dem is awftin canfused an get used
dem is awftin criticised an campramised
dem is awftin villified an reviled
dem is awftin foun guilty widoutn being tried

wan ting set di two a dem far apawt dow
di innocent wi hawbah dout
check tings out
an maybe fine out
but di fool
cho . . .

di innocent an di fool could paas fi twin
but like a like
an love a love
a pidgin is a pidgin
an a dove is a dove

yet di two a dem in camman share someting

dem is awftin anticipated an laywaited
dem is awftin patronised an penalised
dem is awftin pacified an isolated
dem is awftin castigated and implicated

wan ting set di two a dem far apawt dow

di innocent wi hawbah dout
check tings out
an maybe fine out
but di fool
cho . . .

di innocent an di fool could pass fi twin
but rat a rat
an mouse a mouse
flea a flea
an louse a louse

yet di two a dem in camman share someting

dem is awftin decried an denied
dem is awftin ridiculed an doungraded
dem is sometimes kangratulated an celebrated
dem is sometimes suprised an elated
but as yu mite have already guess
dem is awftin foun wantin more or less

dus spoke di wizen wans af ole
dis is a story nevvah told

Dread Beat An Blood

brothers and sisters rocking,
a dread beat pulsing fire, burning;

chocolate hour and darkness creeping night.

black veiled night is weeping,
electric lights consoling, night.

a small hall soaked in smoke:
a house of ganja mist.

music blazing, sounding, thumping fire, blood.
brothers and sisters rocking, stopping, rocking;
music breaking out, bleeding out, thumping out fire:
burning.

electric hour of the red bulb
staining the brain with a blood flow
and a bad bad thing is brewing.

ganja crawling, creeping to the brain;
cold lights hurting, breaking, hurting;
fire in the head and a dread beat bleeding, beating fire:
dread.

rocks rolling over hearts leaping wild,
rage rising out of the heat of the hurt;
and a fist curled in anger reaches a her,
then flash of a blade from another to a him,
leaps out for a dig of a flesh of a piece of skin.
and blood, bitterness, exploding fire, wailing blood,
and bleeding.

JANE KING
b. 1952

Fellow Traveller

You hear the rain crossing the valley?
You know it will strike us quite soon?
You know how this damn roof is leaking?
Well, of course you must know.
for you holed it yourself
when the wind start to blow
on the day that you said
the damn walls hold you in
and you feel like you dead
and you gone on the roof there, to dance.

You said how you were sure
if you climbed right up high
felt the sun right above you,
your hair in the sky,
you would see far far.
That the walls block you up,
that the walls 'paw' you in
and you danced and you laughed.

Now, I was afraid you would fall down.
You said No, and, So what if I do?
Is just safety you want?
I have things I must see
and I can't keep on thinking about you.

But you knew I would stay here inside it.
You knew I would wait for you.
Now I wait and have waited and will wait
but my dancer, the rain's coming in,
and you see how that big storm is brewing?
Where's my shelter?
I drowning again?

You see you, dancer,
big smile on your beautiful mouth?
You see you, seeker?
Fix the roof.
Or is I moving out.

MUTABARUKA

b. 1952

dis poem

dis poem
dis poem
shall speak of the wretched sea
that washed ships to these shores
of mothers crying for their young
swallowed up by the sea
dis poem shall say nothin new
dis poem shall speak of time
time unlimited
time undefined
dis poem shall call names
names like
lumumba
kenyatta
nkrumah
hannibal
akenaton
malcolm
garvey
haile selassie
dis poem is vex
about apartheid
racism
facism
the klu klux klan
riots in brixton
atlanta
jim jones
dis poem is revoltin against
first world
second world
third world
division

manmade decision
dis poem is like all the rest
dis poem will not be amongst great literary works
will not be recited by poetry enthusiasts
will not be quoted by politicians
nor men of religion
dis poem is knives . . . bombs . . . guns . . .
blazing for freedom
yes dis poem is a drum
ashanti
mau mau
ibo
yoruba
niahbingi warriors
uhuru . . . uhuru
namibia uhuru
uhuru
soweto
uhuru
afrika!
dis poem will not change things
dis poem needs to be changed
dis poem is the rebirth of a people arising . . . awaking . . . overstanding
. . . dis poem speak
is speakin . . . has spoken
dis poem shall continue
even when poets have stopped writing
dis poem shall survive . . . u . . . me
it shall linger in history
in your mind
in time . . .
forever
dis poem is time
only time will tell
dis poem is still not written
dis poem has no poet
dis poem is just a part of the story his-story . . . her-story . . . our-story
the story still untold
dis poem is now ringing . . . talking
irritatin

making u want to stop it
but dis poem will not stop
dis poem is long
cannot be short
dis poem cannot be tamed
cannot be blamed
the story is still not told about dis poem
dis poem is old
new
dis poem is copied from
the bible
your prayer book
the new york times
readers digest
the c.i.a. files
the k.g.b. files
dis poem is no secret
dis poem shall be called
boring
stupid
senseless
dis poem is watchin u
tryin' to make sense from dis poem
dis poem is messin up your brains
makin u want to stop listenin to dis poem
but you shall not stop listenin to dis poem
u need to know what will be said next in dis poem
dis poem shall disappoint you because
dis poem is to be continue
in your mind . . .
in your mind . . .
in your mind . . .

OKU ONUORA

b. 1952

Pressure Drop

hunga a twis man tripe
jus sey 'eh' man fight
man nerves raw
man tek a draw   c o o l
man jook up a tek in de scene
garbage   dead-dawg   fly
'cho! but dis nu right'
man ready fi explode
man cyan bear de load
                    pressure drop

dawta sigh
'lard! hear de pickney dem a cry'
man a pass sey dawta fat
dawta smile   but dawta cyan check dat
dawta haffi a check fi food fi put ina pat
dawta sey all man want a fi get im han unda skirt
bam!   she sey she a breed
im vanish like when yu bun weed
dawta wan wuk   dawta willin fi wuk
but is like sey dawta nu have nu luk
or dem nu have enough wuk?
dawta sey she naw ketch nu men
she sey she naw falla nu fren
dawta confuse
too often dawta get use
dawta bawl
'lard! wey mi a go do?'
                    pressure drop

man flare
ina de slum man haffi live mongs rat, roach, fly, chink
'cho! de place stink'
man willin fi wuk

281

man nu wan fi bun gun ina man gut
man nu jus wan fi jook up an chat
man nu wan fi pap lack
but when hunger twis tripe an pickney bawl
time dred
eart tun red
curfew
man screw
gun blaze
knife flash
man run hot   when pressure drop

REINA MARÍA RODRÍGUEZ

b. 1952

When a Woman Doesn't Sleep

Translated by M. J. Fenwick

when a woman doesn't sleep
the magic has been sprinkled between her breasts
and you should fear her attentions
to that myth that begins
between sleep and obscurity.
there will be no spells or spirits.
she is filling herself with the honey of silence
and she has returned again to the time of her summer hats
to reconcile with the clouds
and all the air will contain the danger of her eyes
hunters of stars.

last night I didn't sleep and I warn you:
when a woman doesn't sleep
something terrible can wake you.

DIONNE BRAND

b. 1953

Return

I

So the street is still there, still melting with sun
still the shining waves of heat at one o'clock
the eyelashes scorched, staring the distance of the
park to the parade stand, still razor grass burnt and
cropped, everything made indistinguishable from dirt
by age and custom, white washed, and the people . . .
still I suppose the scorpion orchid by the road, that
fine red tongue of flamboyant and orange lips
muzzling the air, that green plum turning fat and
crimson, still the crazy bougainvillea fancying and
nettling itself purple, pink, red, white, still the trickle of
sweat and cold flush of heat raising the smell of
cotton and skin . . . still the dank rank of breadfruit milk,
their bash and rain on steps, still the bridge this side
the sea that side, the rotting ship barnacle eaten still
the butcher's blood staining the walls of the market,
the ascent of hills, stony and breathless, the dry
yellow patches of earth still threaten to swamp at the
next deluge . . . so the road, that stretch of sand and
pitch struggling up, glimpses sea, village, earth
bare-footed hot, women worried, still the faces,
masked in sweat and sweetness, still the eyes
watery, ancient, still the hard, distinct, brittle smell of
slavery.

II

From here you can see Venezuela,
that is not Venezuela, girl, that is Pointe Galeote
right round the corner, is not away
over that sea swelling like a big belly woman
that must have been a look of envy

every eye looking out of its black face many years
ago must have longed to dive into the sea woman's
belly swimming to away only to find
Pointe Galeote's nubbly face
back to there and no further than the heat flush

every woman must have whispered
in her child's ear, away! far from here!
people go mad here walking into the sea!
the air sick, sibylline, away! go away!
crashing and returning against Pointe Galeote

From here envied tails of water swing out
and back playing sometimeish historian
covering hieroglyphs and naming fearsome artifacts,
That is not footsteps, girl, is duenne!
is not shell, is shackle!

MARGARET GILL
b. 1953

Poem for a Migrant Worker

This isn't a poem to sunrise,
or hurricanes, or seaweed
draped around the keels
of abandoned fishing boats.

This isn't a poem to carnival
or the people, or even a chant
for the ungrateful dead.
This poem merely wants to vibrate
Along your inner ear.

Tell me, this night,
can I bring you away
to my house in the lane
which neighbours the sea?
I want to unclothe you
as I would a poem by Walcott
and reveal the essential stamen.
[the pistil I will especially savour,
amazed as I am at its rare nurturing].

In my sanctuary I would immerse you
in tides of healing surf,
knowing as I do how your exile in Babylon wounds you.
Then I would seed the ocean
with your recollected corolla
and harvest a hurricane.

In the meanwhile, Armatrading
would be holding on with:
'Is it tomorrow yet' and
'I can't wait to see you step across the room . . .'

MBALA

b. 1953

The History of Dub Poetry

di sun it all aready
from flappin dadaist
to dub poet
amusing bemusin
confusin di centre
from griot to
rockin minstrel rollin into court
an village
wile wid laaf an colour
dancehallin towards yu conscience
an yu hardly
feel di barb
as di bard
slip it to yu
thru di space dem
between yu laafta
as slow an invisible
ova centries
di rapso man
calypso man
sad yu
laaf yu
to tears dat melt weh yu walls
an di sun si it all
again
burnin thru
slang and syntax
thru di dub of
tabla an cello an talkin drum
as di bline chanta
in di artic ice
bogle wid a piece a
holy blubba

and
plug een
electric
to supp'm wid
whole heap a name an no name
an di snow sun
di desert sun
di sun si it all again
flappin dadaist
dub poet
amusin
bemusin
confusin
dancehallin
towards yu soul

OPAL PALMER ADISA

b. 1954

Madness Disguises Sanity

Sometimes
I mutter
as I walk
people
stare and pass by
on the far side

To be one
of those
desolate men
who lounge in
stink alleyways
forever talking
to the wind
their words
bullets
people shy from

But I am woman
conditioned
to nurse
my scream
like a mute child

So I write

MAHADAI DAS

1954–2003

They Came in Ships

They came in ships
    From far across the seas
        Britain, colonising the East in India
            Transporting her chains from Chota Nagpur and the Ganges Plain.
          Westwards came the Whitby
        Like the Hesperus
       Alike the island-bound Fatel Rozack.

       Wooden missions of young imperialist design.
       Human victims of Her Majesty's victory.

        They came in fleets of ships.
        They came in droves
        Like cattle.
        Brown like cattle.
        Eyes limpid, like cattle.

         Some came with dreams of milk and honey riches.
         Others came, fleeing famine
         And death,
         All alike, they came—
         The dancing girls,
          Rajput soldiers—tall and proud
          Escaping the penalty of their pride.
          The stolen wives—afraid and despondent.
         All alike,
         Crossing dark waters.
         Brahmin and Chammar alike.
         They came
         At least with hope in their heart
         On the platter of the plantocracy
         They were offered disease and death.

        I saw them dying at the street-corners
        Alone and hungry, they died
        Starving for the want of a crumb of British bread
       And the touch of a healing hand.

       Today, I remember my forefather's gaunted gaze.
        My mind's eye sweeps o'er my children of yesterday
        My children of tomorrow.
      The piracy of innocence.
      The loss of light in their eyes.

     I stand 'twixt posterity's horizon
    And her history.
I, alone today, am alive,
Seeing beyond, looking ahead.

I do not forget the past that has moulded the present.
The present is a caterer for the future.
I remember logies
Barrack-room ranges
Nigga-yards.
My grandmother worked in the field.
Honourable mention.

Creole gang, child-labour—
Second prize.
I remember Lallabhagie.
Can I forget how Enmore rose in arms
For the children of Leonora.

Remember one-third quota
Coolie woman.
Was your blood spilled so that I might reject my history
Forget tears in shadow—paddy leaves.

Here, at the edge of the horizon
I hear voices crying in the wind.
Cuffy shouting—Remember 1763.
John Smith—At least, if I am a man of God
Let me join forces with black suffering.
Akkarra—I too had a vision
Before I lost it.
Atta—in the beginning, I was with the struggle.
And Des Voeux cried
I wrote the queen a letter
For the whimpering of the coolies
In their logies would not let me rest.

Beaumont—Had the law been in my hands
And the cry of the coolies
Echoed around the land.
They came in droves
At the door of his office
Beseeching him to ease the yoke off their burden
And Crosby struck in rage
Against the planters
In vain
He was stripped naked of his rights
And the cry of the coolies continued.

The Commissioners came
Capital spectacles with British frames
Consulting managers
About the cost of immigration
They forgot the purpose of their coming.
The Commissioners left
Fifty-dollar bounty remained.
Dreams of a cow and endless calves
And endless reality, in chains.

MAGGIE HARRIS

b. 1954

Doors

convent door slamming, hollow
through the years
wakening shadows on migrant faces
shadows that once fell on grassland
flattened by Dutchmen, running Blackmen
racing souls that melt like water
on hot dusty roads
child watches Mummy running
racing thru corridors
to the sound of the giro falling
from the letterbox to the floor
what does she care about Dutchmen
or women that they stole
from shackled Ashanti Blackmen
who fell crying through convent doors?

MICHAEL SMITH

1954–1983

Give Me Little Dub Music

Give me little dub music
right ya so
tonight

Give me little dub music
right ya so
tonight

A have dis haunted feelin
so meck we bat een
an ketch a reasonin

No bodder talk bout anyting too tough
Skip de usual stuff
dat yuh out a luck
a look fi wuk
an meck we seat up

We no mourners
We naw go watch weself
go down de road
like witherin flowers

An jus
give me little dub music
right ya so
tonight

Give me little dub music
right ya so
tonight

For we search we head an we heart
down to we very soul
an we still waan someting else fi hold
We naw go stop
an come off a Brutas Pass
We waan something
dat will last

An de more dis-ya system-ya squeeze we
fire boun fi gush outa we

So jus excuse me
an give me pass
an meck a chat to yuh boss
for im a rock out me
for im a rock out me
me rass

fi jus
give me little dub music
right ya so
tonight

Give me little dub music
right ya so
tonight

dat anytime we have a power cut
a no lies an deceit an hypocrisy
full up I-man gut

So jus
give me little dub music
right ya so
tonight

Give me little dub music
right ya so
tonight

Me Cyaan Believe It

Me seh me cyaan believe it
me seh me cyaan believe it

Room dem a rent
me apply widin
but as me go een
cockroach rat an scorpion
also come een

Waan good
nose haffi run
but me naw go siddung pon high wall
like Humpty Dumpty
me a face me reality

One little bwoy come blow im horn
an me look pon im wid scorn
an me realize how me five bwoy-picni
was a victim of de trick
dem call partisan politricks

an me ban me belly
an me bawl
an me ban me belly
an me bawl
Lawd
me cyaan believe it
me seh me cyaan believe it

Me daughter bwoy-frien name Sailor
an im pass through de port like a ship
more gran-picni fi feed
an de whole a we in need
what a night what a plight
an we cyaan get a bite
me life is a stiff fight
an me cyaan believe it
me seh me cyaan believe it

Sittin on de corner wid me frien
talkin bout tings an time
me hear one voice seh
'Who dat?'
Me seh 'A who dat?'
'A who a seh who dat
when me a seh who dat?'

When yuh teck a stock
dem lick we dung flat
teet start fly
an big man start cry
me seh me cyaan believe it
me seh me cyaan believe it

De odder day
me a pass one yard pon de hill
When me teck a stock me hear
'Hey, bwoy!'
'Yes, mam?'
'Hey, bwoy!'
'Yes, mam!'
'Yuh clean up de dawg shit?'
'Yes, mam.'

An me cyaan believe it
me seh me cyaan believe it

Doris a modder of four
get a wuk as a domestic
Boss man move een
an bap si kaisico she pregnant again
bap si kaisico she pregnant again
an me cyaan believe it
me seh me cyaan believe it

Deh a yard de odder night
when me hear 'Fire! Fire!'
'Fire, to plate claat!'
Who dead? You dead!

Who dead? Me dead!
Who dead? Harry dead!
Who dead? Eleven dead!
Woeeeeeeee
Orange Street fire
deh pon me head
an me cyaan believe it
me seh me cyaan believe it

Lawd
me see some blackbud
livin inna one buildin
but no rent no pay
so dem cyaan stay
Lawd
de oppress an de dispossess
cyaan get no res

What nex?

Teck a trip from Kingston
to Jamaica
Teck twelve from a dozen
an me see me mumma in heaven
Madhouse! Madhouse!

Me seh me cyaan believe it
me seh me cyaan believe it

Yuh believe it?
How yuh fi believe it
when yuh laugh
an yuh blind yuh eye to it?

But me know yuh believe it
Lawwwwwwwwd
me know yuh believe it

PEGGY CARR
b. *c.*1955

Flight of the Firstborn

He streaks past his sixteenth year
small island life stretched tight
across his shoulders
his strides rehearsing city blocks
college brochures
airline schedules
stream excitedly through his
newly competent hands
his goodbyes like blurred neon
on a morning suddenly gone wet

I'm left stranded
on a tiny patch of time
still reaching
to wipe the cereal from his smile

DAVID DABYDEEN

b. 1955

Coolie Odyssey

For Ma, d. 1985

Now that peasantry is in vogue,
Poetry bubbles from peat bogs,
People strain for the old folk's fatal gobs
Coughed up in grates North or North East
'Tween bouts o' living dialect,
It should be time to hymn your own wreck,
Your house the source of ancient song:
Dry coconut shells cackling in the fireside
Smoking up our children's eyes and lungs,
Plantains spitting oil from a clay pot,
Thick sugary black tea gulped down.

The calves hustle to suck,
Bawling on their rope but are beaten back
Until the cow is milked.
Frantic children call to be fed.
Roopram the Idiot goes to graze his father's goats backdam
Dreaming that the twig he chews so viciously in his mouth
Is not a twig.

In a winter of England's scorn
We huddle together memories, hoard them from
The opulence of our masters.

You were always back home, forever
As canefield and whiplash, unchanging
As the tombstones in the old Dutch plot
Which the boys used for wickets playing ball.

Over here Harilall who regularly dodged his duties at the
    marketstall
To spin bowl for us in the style of Ramadhin

299

And afterwards took his beatings from you heroically
In the style of England losing
Is now known as the local Paki
Doing slow trade in his Balham cornershop.
Is it because his heart is not in business
But in the tumble of wickets long ago
To the roar of wayward boys?
Or is it because he spends too much time
Being chirpy with his customers, greeting
The tight-wrapped pensioners stalking the snow
With tropical smile, jolly small chat, credit?
They like Harilall, these muted claws of Empire,
They feel privileged by his grinning service,
They hear steelband in his voice
And the freeness of the sea.
The sun beams from his teeth.

Heaped up beside you Old Dabydeen
Who on Albion Estate clean dawn
Washed obsessively by the canal bank,
Spread flowers on the snake-infested water,
Fed the gods the food that Chandra cooked,
Bathed his tongue of the creole
Babbled by low-caste infected coolies.
His Hindi chants terrorised the watertoads
Flopping to the protection of bush.
He called upon Lord Krishna to preserve
The virginity of his daughters
From the Negroes,
Prayed that the white man would honour
The end-of-season bonus to Poonai
The canecutter, his strong, only son:
Chandra's womb being cursed by deities
Like the blasted land
Unconquerable jungle or weed
That dragged the might of years from a man.
Chandra like a deaf-mute moved about the house
To his command,
A fearful bride barely come-of-age
Year upon year swelling with female child.

Guilt clenched her mouth
Smothered the cry of bursting apart:
Wrapped hurriedly in a bundle of midwife's cloth
The burden was removed to her mother's safekeeping.
He stamped and cursed and beat until he turned old
With the labour of chopping tree, minding cow, building fence
And the expense of his daughters' dowries.
Dreaming of India
He drank rum
Till he dropped dead
And was buried to the singing of Scottish Presbyterian hymns
And a hell-fire sermon from a pop-eyed bawling catechist,
By Poonai, lately baptised, like half the village.

Ever so old,
Dabydeen's wife,
Hobbling her way to fowl-pen,
Cussing low, chewing her cud, and lapsed in dream,
Sprinkling rice from her shrivelled hand.
Ever so old and bountiful,
Past where Dabydeen lazed in his mudgrave,
Idle as usual in the sun,
Who would dip his hand in a bowl of dhall and rice—
Nasty man, squelching and swallowing like a low-caste sow—
The bitch dead now!

The first boat chugged to the muddy port
Of King George's Town. Coolies come to rest
In El Dorado,
Their faces and best saris black with soot.
The men smelt of saltwater mixed with rum.
The odyssey was plank between river and land,
Mere yards but months of plotting
In the packed bowel of a white man's boat
The years of promise, years of expanse.

At first the gleam of the green land and the white folk and the Negroes,
The earth streaked with colour like a toucan's beak,
Kiskidees flame across a fortunate sky,
Canefields ripening in the sun
Wait to be gathered in armfuls of gold.

I have come back late and missed the funeral.
You will understand the connections were difficult.
Three airplanes boarded and many changes
Of machines and landscapes like reincarnations
To bring me to this library of graves,
This small clearing of scrubland.
There are no headstones, epitaphs, dates.
The ancestors curl and dry to scrolls of parchment.
They lie like texts
Waiting to be written by the children
For whom they hacked and ploughed and saved
To send to faraway schools.
Is foolishness fill your head.
Me dead.
Dog-bone and dry-well
Got no story to tell.
Just how me born stupid is so me gone.
Still we persist before the grave
Seeking fables.

We plunder for the maps of El Dorado
To make bountiful our minds in an England
Starved of gold.

Albion village sleeps, hacked
Out between bush and spiteful lip of river.
Folk that know bone
Fatten themselves on dreams
For the survival of days.
Mosquitoes sing at a nipple of blood.
A green-eyed moon watches
The rheumatic agony of houses crutched up on stilts
Pecked about by huge beaks of wind,
That bear the scars of ancient storms.
Crappeau clear their throats in hideous serenade,
Candleflies burst into suicidal flame.
In a green night with promise of rain
You die.

We mark your memory in songs
Fleshed in the emptiness of folk,

Poems that scrape bowl and bone
In English basements far from home,
Or confess the lust of beasts
In rare conceits
To congregations of the educated
Sipping wine, attentive between courses —
See the applause fluttering from their white hands
Like so many messy table napkins.

ANTHONY KELLMAN
b. 1955

After the Rain

After the rain withers to fine spray,
wind sweeps in, fresh and reviving,
down on the banana, coconut, casuarina.
They rock and wave victorious arms
and you think: After all that rain who
would believe such emergence could be true?

After the spray effervesces into nothing,
the soaked leaves of my mango tree let fall
their weighty excess that taps
my soil with its rhythmic patter.
And the dark clouds dance off-stage
and the white clouds enter and grow
cottonwooling across such blueness
as never the eye had seen, and you think:
No wonder Columbus went blind at the sight.

After my mango stops weeping, I
can still hear drainage-drops plop-
ping into the low lateral grass.
Two blackbirds cut across the sky,
Others wed with doves in this earth-fresh air
thrilling on electric and telephone cables
poles, on roof-tops . . .
The sun devours its reluctant veil
and sits on the throne,
my eyes eat the scene . . . alone,
Doctor Boobie mauls my ixora with his sword
in this dancing light of the burning god.

In the kingdom of life all things spring
quickly. I raise my head
and my neighbours' windows reopen.

Cocks are crowing on this early morning,
Two lizards leap across a soursop branch,
Four yellow butterflies lead a kitten

to that light, emigrant ants journey
across my window-ledge
to some unknown and distant country
and the voices of the children come to play
and though their naked feet
will be watered by indifferent pools,
they laugh and go dancing down the street
bare feet high in the sun-drenched air.

The sun's deep rays keep coming
and, hearing the final drainage-drop,
you drink the warm air
and forget the rain.

RACHEL MANLEY

b. 1955

Memory

The afternoon belongs to my grandfather.
You cannot take it away
though the mind darkens
and the children's laughter
has strayed like messages.
I am near the verandah,
lost in my nets of thought
which I brought from age six,
a very long way.
You cannot sentence memory to death,
it returns through the years
lulled into hymns.
If I close my eyes
Time will forget me;
I hear an old lady reading from Rilke,
she finds the best line
and explains
that poets don't have to rhyme anymore.
If I close my eyes
my hands will forget me,
I'm up in the plum tree
near to the sky;
if I leave, I'll never come back.
Here in this distance birds fly,
they fly, but they do not sing.
The night waits in the house
safe and peaceful as candles
or carts pulled by trusty mules;
my grandfather waits in the house.
You know, the moon is just a violin
that longs to be repaired.

ROI KWABENA

b. 1956

Letter from Sea Lots

'. . . . . only five pounds yuh send?
bread, sugar an' milk gone up . . . . .
buses doh run. . . water still go
now severe-threat in charge ah de water in maraval
so we looking out fuh poison . . .

money hard to come by . . . . we down here suffering
sure. . we have gas, oil, menthanol. . . .
. . . . steel, an' sugar exporting . .
buh mangrove still vamping . . .
factories not hiring . . . . . even race horse protesting . . . .
crime rampant as jurors hunted
laws improvising an' english q—cees hustling . .
buh teachers' money still owing . . .

yuh ask for news? any news is sad news . . . .
doubles-man an' market vendors still on de run
kidnapping an' family murders add to dis shame
while meh OLE gran still worried sick 'bout she pension . . .

cable an' wireful, wid sure-hell come back . . .
even powertake an' brit grasp follow fashion
buh maxi still accept short change
yet parts expensive. . so only insurance profittin'
as *sprangers* still roam in de night

de only difference is de den opposition
must now salute for de independence parade . . .

senator . . ah sure yuh would ah like tha . . . .'

JEAN 'BINTA' BREEZE

b. 1957

Riddym Ravings
(The Mad Woman's Poem)

de fus time dem kar me go a Bellevue
was fit di dactar an de lanlord operate
an tek de radio outa mi head
troo dem seize de bed
weh did a gi mi cancer
an mek mi talk to nobady
ah di same night wen dem trow mi out fi no pay de rent
mi haffi sleep outa door wid de Channel One riddym box
an de D.J. fly up eena mi head
mi hear im a play seh

Eh, Eh,
no feel no way
town is a place dat ah really kean stay
dem kudda—ribbit mi han
eh—ribbit mi toe
mi waan go a country go look mango

fah wen hungry mek King St. pavement
bubble an dally in front a mi yeye
an mi foot start wanda falla fly
to de garbage pan eena de chinaman backlat
dem nearly chap aff mi han eena de butcha shap
fi de piece a ratten poke
ah de same time de mawga gal in front a mi
drap de laas piece a ripe banana
an mi—ben dung—pick i up—an nyam i
a dat time dem grab mi an kar mi back a Bellevue
dis time de dactar an de lanlord operate
an tek de radio plug outa mi head
den sen mi out, seh mi alright
but—as ah ketch back outa street

308

ah push een back de plug
an ah hear mi D.J. still a play, seh

Eh, Eh,
no feel no way
town is a place dat ah really kean stay
dem kudda—ribbit mi han
eh—ribbit mi toe
mi waan go a country go look mango

Ha Haah . . . Haa

wen mi fus come a town
mi use to tell everybady 'mawnin'
but as de likkle rosiness gawn outa mi face
nobady nah ansa mi
silence tun rags roun mi bady
in de mids a all de dead people dem
a bawl bout de caast of livin
an a ongle one ting tap mi fram go stark raving mad
a wen mi siddung eena Parade
a tear up newspaper fi talk to
sometime dem roll up
an tun eena one a Uncle But sweet saaf
yellow heart breadfruit
wid piece a roas saalfish side a i
an if likkle rain jus fall
mi get cocanat rundung fi eat i wid
same place side a weh de country bus dem pull out
an sometime mi a try board de bus
an de canductor bwoy a halla out seh
'dutty gal, kum affa de bus'
ah troo im no hear de riddym eena mi head
same as de tape weh de bus driva a play, seh

Eh, Eh,
no feel no way
town is a place dat alh really kean stay
dem kudda—ribbit mi han
eh—ribbit mi toe
mi waan go a country go look mango

so country bus, ah beg yuh
tek mi home
to de place, where I belang

an di dutty bway jus run mi aff

Well, dis mawnin, mi start out pon Spanish Town Road,
fah mi deh go walk go home a country
fah my granny use to tell mi how she walk fram wes
come a town
come sell food
an mi waan ketch home befo dem put de price pon i'
but mi kean go home dutty?
fah mi parents dem did sen mi out clean
Ah!
see wan stanpipe deh!
so mi strip aff all de crocus bag dem
an scrub unda mi armpit
fah mi hear de two mawga gal dem laas nite
a laugh an seh
who kudda breed smaddy like me?
a troo dem no know seh a pure nice man
weh drive car an have gun
visit my piazza all dem four o'clock a mawnin
no de likkle dutty bwoy dem weh mi see dem a go home
wid
but as mi feel de clear water pon mi bady
no grab dem grab mi
an is back eena Bellevue dem kar mi

seh mi mad an a bade naked a street
well dis time de dactar an de lanlord operate
an dem tek de whole radio fram outa mi head
but wen dem tink seh mi unda chloroform
dem put i dung careless
an wen dem gawn
mi tek de radio
an mi push i up eena mi belly
fi keep de baby company
fah even if mi nuh mek i

me waan my baby know dis yah riddym yah
fram before she bawn
hear de D.J. a play, seh

Eh, Eh,
no feel no way
town is a place dat ah really kean stay
dem kudda—ribbit mi han
eh—ribbit mi toe
mi waan go a country go look mango

an same time
de dactar an de lanlord
trigger de electric shack
an mi hear de D.J. vice bawl out, seh

Murther
Pull up Missa Operator!

Ratoon

it's the eyes that haunt me most

young men
grown old
too quickly

last sugar stick
surrrounded by dry leaves
no water reaches roots

the eyes
forced ripe
and plucked
long before the coming

some deep worm
now growing old

a rubbed out reddening
of old age
with nothing

there are no pensions here
and careless days
in cane passion
don't outlast a dewdrop
in this heat

and the eyes
sunken now
and blinded with
dead dreams

but even that needs youth
to be cut down
and the joints
now withering
spirit burning
flesh done

any growth is singed
by want of rum

asked for one more smiling
to the sun

cane cracks

these eyes cannot lie
about the heart

the wind laughs
a dry sound
of parched stones
in the bed

where waters once
cooled desire

smoke rises
out of a chestful
of gravel

one with fire
we perspire
to our loss
clutch the tales
of rags to riches
somewhere
over Lotto's horizon
replant me Lord
and send a visa come

already
all around
the next ratoon
is coming

old cane eyes
burnt out
watching them
unspeaking

rising in their heat

MARTÍN ESPADA

b. 1957

Colibrí

For Katherine, one year later

In Jayuya,
the lizards scatter
like a fleet of green canoes
before the invader.
The Spanish conquered
with iron and words:
'Indío Taíno' for the people
who took life
from the rain
that rushed through trees
like evaporating arrows,
who left the rock carvings
of eyes and mouths
in perfect circles of amazement.

So the hummingbird
was christened 'colibrí.'
Now the colibri
darts and bangs
between the white walls
of the hacienda,
a racing Taíno heart
frantic as if hearing
the bellowing god of gunpowder
for the first time.

The colibrí
becomes pure stillness,
seized in the paralysis
of the prey,
when your hands
cup the bird

and lift him
through the red shutters
of the window,
where he disappears
into a paradise of sky,
a nightfall of singing frogs.

If only history
were like your hands.

Imagine the Angels of Bread

This is the year that squatters evict landlords,
gazing like admirals from the rail
of the roofdeck
or levitating hands in praise
of steam in the shower;
this is the year
that shawled refugees deport judges
who stare at the floor
and their swollen feet
as files are stamped
with their destination;
this is the year that police revolvers,
stove-hot, blister the fingers
of raging cops,
and nightsticks splinter
in their palms;
this is the year
that darkskinned men
lynched a century ago
return to sip coffee quietly
with the apologizing descendants
of their executioners.

This is the year that those
who swim the border's undertow

and shiver in boxcars
are greeted with trumpets and drums
at the first railroad crossing
on the other side;
this is the year that the hands
pulling tomatoes from the vine
uproot the deed to the earth that sprouts the vine,
the hands canning tomatoes
are named in the will
that owns the bedlam of the cannery;
this is the year that the eyes
stinging from the poison that purifies toilets
awaken at last to the sight
of a rooster-loud hillside,
pilgrimage of immigrant birth;
this is the year that cockroaches
become extinct, that no doctor
finds a roach embedded
in the ear of an infant;
this is the year that the food stamps
of adolescent mothers
are auctioned like gold doubloons,
and no coin is given to buy machetes
for the next bouquet of severed heads
in coffee plantation country.

SASENARINE PERSAUD

b. 1958

Postcard to a Sister in South America

This lilt of light in rain
clouds swarming sun over woods
bleached of leaves except the spruces'
sticking of sky in answer to rusting
oaks remaining willows ripening
like August oranges bowing down
limbs catching blessings of finch
kiskadee blue-sakie bunting

This lilt of light in last night's
cotton wicks in oil in diyas
marking *Ram's* returned to *Awadhpuri*
with his bride—yes the waiting
for the last jay-calls to go south
sparrows chirping chickadees tweeting
the tip of the days of the long nights

To meet again off *karahi*-holed roads
clasping the dust from wings of sugar
cane stalks the thousand limbed coconuts
swirling Shiva's dance over browntongued
creeks nipping the ocean your sons celebrate
not this lilt of autumn light; the blooded
childhood sunshine of cannotleavebehind.

GEOFFRY PHILP
b. 1958

Standpipe

Tonight rain comes like forgetting;
pine needles scrape against jalousies

like the recurrent dream that rouses conscience
from sleep, for the rain brings no relief,

but urges only flight: the need to forgive
or to be forgiven. Vain acts stalk the ghetto

like revolution, and the rain keeps falling.
Standpipe's children still live unsheltered,

and you keep wishing the rain will wash
their anguished tears away. No such luck.

Raging gullies remain unchanged,
Remembering only the vague pledge of fire

Repeated across the sky as zinc fences
Shiver, and the water quietly flows.

LASANA M. SEKOU
b. 1959

Liberation Theology

in para,
brazil,
a lawyer said
military police invaded the house
of a peasant farmer,
raped his daughter
forced the family to watch
and made him, the farmer,
whose father could as well been a carpenter—
carry a heavy cross for four miles
until he collapsed
with exhaustion

and still
you mean to tell me
that you have not seen the nazarene?

in cuba
before the triumph of the revolution
before marti
and before *madre* mariana's conception of maceo
lived jose antonio aponte
who rose phoenix-clad *macheteros*
against the death-white tyranny of slavery
in a sparkling sun-dawn battle
they called the *conspiracion de aponte*

he was captured
he was quartered
his head placed on exhibit
and his hands nailed to a tree
and you will tell me
that you have not heard of this

of this messiah who came
and lived till death for us?

and did you not see
when we people
like flaming tongues of palm sunday branches
raised a savior on high
passing over the streets of st. george's
proclaiming the science and faith
in the fifth year morning of a second coming
before sadducee sentence
festered a thorn-crown of bullets
and nailed maurice to a bitter cross?

did you not weep then too,
stinging-nettle-laced-tears of vinegar blood
when green beetle soldiers,
the imperial horde
and their impudent soiled spots of oecs,
garyseaga and the other failures too
made buzzard swoops
and cast treacherous lots to see
who would wear
the seamless innergarment of that christ?

and when they stabbed
jesus christ in guyana
wasn't it father darke who bled to death?
then when they slaughtered the archbishop in san salvador
was it not the son of man who lay there
riddled for our silence?
and when they shot lionel laine

did you not hear how jesus
was gunned down in a haitian slum?
and when they bombed him to kingdom-come
didn't we bear rodney's body from the cross?
and when che passed over
didn't you hear
how they tortured the christ in higuera?

¿so when they hanged poet maloise
in south africa
didn't you see adoni
dangling there?

and when they killed sandino
whose father was a small farmer
whose name could as well been joseph—
didn't you hear him say
tyrants do not represent nations,
and liberty is not won with flowers?

unto caesar what is caesar's then
and unto the people the wealth of their labor

and when jacquiline fell
under a crucifix of mutinous guns
didn't you see christ fall
and grace the thirsting earth
with blood and water?
and didn't you hear the child,
as a rainbow arching from within her womb,
the child people said she carried for him, within her,
didn't you hear that child say:
        it is done,
        still, i&i live
                to come again
                like a thief in the night
                like a guest-unannounced
                like a double-edged sword
            like a light that shineth into the darkness
                to proclaim
                the glory of true liberty
                to sing the peoples' praises
            to shout showering hosannas of living rain

and still, you mean to tell me
that you have not yet seen
the likes of the nazarene?

FRED D'AGUIAR

b. 1960

Frail Deposits

For Wilson Harris

1. *The Trench Revisited*

We're being driven past when you point to
Where you'd pushed in a friend long, long ago,
Into what was a trench, to test its depth.
You say it taught you how a civilisation,
Feeling a blow or tug may still not know
A hand's involved, so can't feel indebted.
I was falling, horizontally, just
To keep up and lucky to win your trust.

Push him again, he'll fall on land that's dry
This time and think nothing of it, and you'll
Bank all that knowledge lifted from the sight
Your friend made clad in mud, convinced totally
That he slipped and your hand on his ribcage
Was your brave, unlucky, one-hand-clap save!

2. *A Jealous God*

The light on our first morning at breakfast
Is such that three women as many hundreds
Of yards away in pleated, cotton frocks as
Blinding as if the green, yellow and red
Are light sources and we're in some studio
Within touching distance of them; we look
Their way, quiet and still, more like study
Than look, they are grouped close, signing their talk.

The sun is a jealous God are your words.
Suddenly nothing means much anymore;

Watching those three women, a timeless world
Regards us as much as we regard her:
We feed like enraged Ugolino fed,
Though captive, on his captured jailer's head.

3. *Bone Flute*

'This your son?' enquires the curator
As we waltz in for our official tour.

You finger the thousand year flute of bone
As if about to burst out with a tune.

You tell how the bone came from an enemy,
Morsels of whose flesh is consumed by them.

When air is blown into the fashioned bone,
The enemy's knowhow and plans are summoned.

The flute I'm trying to blow a tune on
Belongs to you, got by me over years from

Stringing your thoughts sentence by sentence,
Or what must stand for you in your absence:

Having to check when I've said something
To see if it's yours since it has your ring.

4. *Seawall*

You explain rudimentary quantum theory:
The frailty of us jetting above weather
From one world touching down in another
With a wheel-screech equalling our surprise.

Ah, to leave marks in this life that survive!
That outstrip the skids of a jet's tyre!
The stretch of seawall we walk looks breached.
A man who seems too fit to beg wants change.

The sea is muddy, loud and creased in the distance.
We have to lean a little into a welcome breeze,
Our heads bowed from the direct beat of sun.

The soldiers in barracks reach us in waves
Dictated by the wind's direction and pace;
Dear God, I think, don't let this moment pass.

JOSÉ MÁRMOL

b. 1960

Abdication

Translated by Ian Craig

God is like fire, whose passion redeems,
Like the powerful wind, whose ardour unmakes all.
God, fear and strength to follow him or hound him,
Like time, like sleep and like the sacred bath of the pagan spas.
God is like fire, his love devours and creates.
Where to look for God and not to look in vain?
Whether in the marvel of your body and your voice,
In the slow sigh of animals and breezes,
In the distance joined by the grasses and the stones,
In the soft folds of the sea, which is the skin of the sky
Or in the mute word of sterile prayer.
God, perpetual seeking,
Transparent form of that which never is?
God is like the water, whose skin rots us,
A knife revealing the centre of dreams
And the deeper the blade, the more fecund, the brighter the animal
    that issues forth.
God is the torment of belief and unbelief,
Dimension of the vast and trivial simultaneously,
Sense of the deft, the ungraspable,
Immutable balance of design and chance,
Content without essence unless it is that of my voice.
God no longer falls sick. God, whose destiny terrifies and
    perturbs him.
Then God dreamed of a body to dress, delicacies on the table,
Of children's stories (how terrible to be born immense!).
God is like a chant, whose vowel deepens
And gathers vast distances within its echo.
God, he who loves all without knowing tendernesses,
Never having been the clean surface of a kiss.
The furious, the sober God who has wept blasts of stupidity and
    tedium.

God is like fire, whose passion consumes,
Like torrential rain, whose crime gives life.
God is like the air, unseen he embraces all,
God is like me and in my words burns the light that hides him.

MARCIA DOUGLAS

b. 1961

The Ascania *Docks in Southampton, circa 1955*

All that's left now is a black and white photo from an old Daily Mirror
One thousand West Indian immigrants on board the Ascania—
mostly men in felt hats.
Flooding the decks, they lean over the rails,
their shoulders pressed together.
On the far left is someone's Uncle Morris.
He has left behind half an acre of yellow yam
and a girl with a pretty black mole on her upper lip.
The dream in his eyes shines like the lighted window far away,
where by candle light,
the girl washes her hair in a plastic basin.
Wearing new shoes and a relative's old wedding suit,
the young man behind him searches the dock for the Queen.
Certainly, she will come to greet him,
her gloved hand waving like the white wing of a dove.
Short men. Tall men. Husky men. Frail men.
Men with five pounds in their pockets
and a cardboard suitcase with a broken latch.
Come to the Mother Country
The Mother Country needs you.
The cry crossed the Atlantic,
ringing from Trinidad and Tobago
and along the curve of the Leewards,
past Anguilla and on to the Cockpit Country of Jamaica.
Brave men. They packed their bags,
their ancestors' fear of ships already strained from their blood,
the Atlantic spread before them like a banquet table.
Now on the upper deck, the fifth person from the right—
a man smiles, rubbing his chin.
Union Jacks are stuffed in the bags beneath his eyes.
Later, he will take a train to Victoria Station.
In the cold and the rain, there will be no one to meet him.
He will work in an asbestos plant,

rent a flat with a mattress
and a clothes lines strung from one corner to the other.
He will dream of children playing on warm rocks by the Martha Brae,
their mothers bathing silently in the water.

KWAME DAWES

b. 1962

Shook Foil

1

The whole earth is filled with the love of God.
In the backwoods, the green light
is startled by blossoming white petals,
soft pathways for the praying bird
dipping into the nectar, darting in starts
among the tangle of bush and trees.
My giddy walk through this speckled grotto
is drunk with the slow mugginess
of a reggae bass line, finding its melody
in the mellow of the soft earth's breath.
I find the narrow stream like a dog sniffing,
and dip my sweaty feet in the cool.
While sitting in this womb of space
the salad romantic in me constructs
a poem. This is all I can muster
before the clatter of school-children
searching for the crooks of guava branches
startles all with their expletives and howls;
the trailing snot-faced child wailing perpetual—
with ritual pauses for breath and pity.
In their wake I find the silver innards of discarded
cigarette boxes, the anemic pale of tossed
condoms, the smashed brown sparkle of Red Stripe
bottles, a melange of bones and rotting fruit,
there in the sudden white light of noon.

2

How quickly the grandeur fades into a poem,
how easily everything of reverie starts to crumble.
I walk from the stream. Within seconds
sweat soaks my neck and back, stones clog my shoes,

flies prick my flaming face and ears;
bramble draws thin lines of blood on my arms.
There is a surfeit of love hidden here;
at least this is the way faith asserts itself.
I emerge from the valley of contradictions,
my heart beating with the effort, and stand looking
over the banking, far into Kingston Harbour
and the blue into grey of the Caribbean Sea.
I dream up a conceit for this journey
and with remarkable snugness it fits;
this reggae sound: the bluesy mellow
of a stroll on soft, fecund earth, battling the crack
of the cross stick; the scratch of guitar,
the electronic manipulation of digital sound,
and the plaintive wail of the grating voice.
With my eyes closed, I am drunk with the mellow,
swimming, swimming among the green of better days;
and I rise from the pool of sound, slippery with
the warm cling of music on my skin,
and enter the drier staleness of the road
that leads to the waiting city of fluorescent lights.

Sunday Morning

Bougainvillea spills its tongues of yellow
and specked blood on the outdoor ballroom
floor and the steel drums rust in the puddles

from August rains. Here, on the aqua tiles,
now fading, the water pools in the sinking foundations;
the dry upper ground is strewn with

goatshit where the goats shelter from the deluge;
bramble lies scattered like debris of sea-
carved wood on a fresh Friday beach.

Here, with the six o'clock morning cloud cover,
the cool breeze licks the shak-shak pods.
Prayers turn heavenward. In the makeshift

chapel-sometimes-gymnasium (where on weekdays
sweating first-years play;
their symphony of ping-pong

dropping like rain: soft sponge,
plastic on wood, their soles squeaking
on the slick floors), the folding

glass windows are stained. The janitor
says the water seeps into the double plate
and stays preserved like that for years. In the yard

behind the building, strewn with bloated plastic
chemical bottles, old film, and the stench of sulphur,
cows graze in the gungu vines and mud,

penned in by the stripped coconut stems and bamboo
strangled by plaits of barbed wire. The soil
is always soft; clay is splattered on the walls

beneath the dripping air conditioner, jutting its
rusting mechanics into the elements. Through
the glass, the avenue of pines sheds

its yellow cones; coolie-plum trees drop
a squishy pungent carpet of fermenting yellow fruit
and dizzy bees. The crooked trees, like starved

acolytes, reach for the praise of song and raised hand.
The campus is overrun by butterflies on Sunday mornings
and, as the sermon flames its tongue of deliverance

in the fanning flurry of the congregation for Christ,
this is the distraction that swallows my wandering eye.
Dreaming is easy in this dream window

landscape and, if I stare long enough,
(pushing back the tambourines and tongues, the muttering
and grunts of possession and release)

at the play of green, yellow and ochre of the wild gungu
vines, I sometimes come away, like David from the wilderness
of olives and eucalyptus green, glowing for my indulgence.

This romantic interim in the passion of gospel reverie
is sometimes all there is to keep you rooted there
in the clamour of your sins, your falling, your remorse.

On Sundays, sometimes, they think I have died inside,
unfeeling to the prophecy coming like the wind,
the bright red blood of Christ in the crystal decanter,

when my eyes dance the leap and dip of yellow butterflies
turning around the cakes of green, fresh, fly-thick
cow shit. The sky winks through the leaves,

and in the precious glass-bowl silence, caught in my
own life-giving bubble of indulgence, the voice carries
clear over water. I am saved again without a shot being fired.

Liminal

I should have been born in the epoch of flesh
mongering, the time of moral malaise, to hear
the blues crawling from the steaming dungeons
of first blues folk; their lyric moaning
against the encroaching gloom;
I should have heard the iambic ebb and roll
of sea lapping against an alien shore,
the boom of wind in sails, the quick-repeat
auctioneer's scatology, that maddening knocking.
But I've arrived in this other time, waiting
upon an old woman's prayer, to carry the tears and laughter
so long preserved in the tightly knotted hem
of her skirt where she keeps herbs, a broken tooth,
cowrie shells, kola nuts, and the soft lavender

of a wild flower's petals; aged good and strong.
I am gathering the relics of a broken threnody,
lisping psalms—all I have—and crying salt and wet.

VIRGIL SUÁREZ

b. 1962

Diaspora

For Nancy Morejon

To tell the truth
I used to think the word
meant some kind of fungus

like the mold that attacks bread,
something that survives a hostile
environment, no matter.

You say that the word
cannot embrace those Cubans
who left the island to seek

exile elsewhere, many in cold
places, that the word only applies
to the cruel punishment inflicted

on African slaves. Okay. But
I have seen Cubans everywhere,
scattered from Tierra del Fuego

to Iceland. I have seen the ones
perishing in snow, these wounded
fish and when I look into their eyes,

Nancy, like when I look into yours,
I see the possibility of reconciliation,
not the fixed gaze of hatred, but like mold

we have taken root where exile threw
us, like these persistent and determined
growths, we will prevail. We hang on.

The longing in our faces cannot end
until both shores unite, yours and mine,
the sting of these subtle twists of definitions.

JENNIFER RAHIM

b. 1963

Leaving the Coast

Leaving the coast behind,
tastebuds still tied to the
sea's salt-heavy hand
will feel the bland of absence
as familiar coastlines fade

Travelling through the unseasoned air
of inner spaces, tastebuds may kick
against resolutions to steer inwards
as mouths flooded with longings
for the old dishes draw steps backwards

To find the centre,
tastebuds must learn to live
in the absence of accustomed flavours,
and practice the art of relearning
to taste life without the pleasures of salt

CLAUDIA RANKINE

b. 1963

She

Daybreak, pon de continent she recall
how once she a farmer, a woman born
(St. Ann's Parish) in time (June 12, 1943)
with she gaze, brown-brown eyes,
favoring, perhaps, that of a dreamer,
though she surely been tried,
fi de English (dem ginnals) lived
in de hinterland, ruled pon de coast.
But lef that alone. Chickens ran yellow
flecks between de trees in them yard:
a mango, two coconuts, a guava.
And from de verandah—what she watched
since girl-time—de big belly sea.

NAOMI AYALA

b. *c*.1965

Personal History

When your history gets too big
to keep fitting in the wagon
you've been pulling all your life
your sleep is thin as water
you zigzag up hills
rely on a ladder to climb into your hammock
flush the toilet with a stick
pick tomatoes with a long steel hook

open beans up with a knife
cut the flowers in your garden with your pride.

There is no Spring like another Spring,
no lover like another come before,
and dreams, they all have a familiar sound
like a song on the radio,
a new pair of shoes,
a phone call in the middle of the night

When your history gets too big
to keep fitting in the wagon
you've been pulling all your life
you leave your keys
where you meant never to go back,
remember what you wanted to forget—
a stranger on the street
selling songs for a dime,
like you his face, his eyes,
his song, his story—

because you are kin with all things now:
the man you kicked into the wall,
the car you crashed,

the food you cannot eat,
the whisper of countries
that open before you in the street,
the mechanical laughter behind the prime
time of your day, somebody else's dreams.
When your history gets that big
you walk backwards as you pull,
run after things that fall out on the street
forget exactly what it is you carry
in that wagon but live your life
as if you knew, always looking
for the sides of things that slope
down smoothly from a straight line across,
the memory that fits
so easily in your pocket.

PATRICK SYLVAIN
b. 1966

Flash Back

After a hot afternoon of photographing the dead,
my darkroom mind printed a life size picture
of three men riddled with bullets. One of them,
Guy Malary, the justice minister, fifty years old.

I flicker my eyes to erase memory, but
the visions remain. Bodies spread
On the sidewalk with blotches of blood
On their clothes and the pavement.

I cannot cope with this grammar of hate,
syntax of violence. Yet, I am pulled by
this senseless savagery. The soldiers
with their machine guns, I with my camera.
Fingers on the triggers—We shoot.

The people are frenzied birds surrounded
by metal. I watched them flutter toward the port
while the outstretched mouths of police guns
spat bullets, struck five. Dead.

In the distant horizon, dark clouds of
dust rose as street merchants hurried
hands grabbing baskets pregnant
with fruit and sun-bruised plantains.

I quickly switched focus when an angry mob of military
attachés spilled out of an army truck like wolves
descending on prey. They dashed toward the port
and some toward journalists. Huffing raw liquor.

I snatched my PBS badge from my neck,
packed my camera and melted in the heat
of slaps, kicks and swinging gunbutts.

ADRIAN CASTRO

b. 1967

Canto of the Tyrant Who Hangs Himself

We purchased a piece of thunder
a ki-lack-um of ilú/tambor
We caught the thundercelt
in its rapid descension to
the dance of flames

We've seen the face of power
inside the inverted pilón
mortar con(secretos)
There were certain shadows
of caudillos on white horses—
Trujillo before his last date with the mistress
Batista entering one of his casinos
Barrientos posing with el Ché
Diaz Ordáz & corpses of 300 students
Videla surrounded by Plaza de Mayo mothers
Somoza slipping on a banana from United Fruit
Rios Montt wearing the cloth of countless massacred indios
Fidel is surfing the Gulf on a raft with his favorite cow
There were certain shadows
of the ceiba tree where they hung themselves
within the inverted pilón

mortar con(secretos)
After the tyranny
there are so few places to go
places to sing
eat gourds of quimbombó y kalalú
kalalú y quimbombó

We purchased a pinch of
ka-ki-li-ka-ki-li-ka-ki-li-kack
Who would be struck by red thunder
being summoned by goatskin?

And how would the first flame
arrive at the throne?

A palma showed us its kingdom—
We were smiling like red-vested mummies
like dancing worms
in a puddle of stones
pile of water
streams of smoke
smoke of streams sending signs
estamos vivito y coleando
this culture is still burning fresco
cool y caliente like guaguancó/columbia/yambú
Muñequitos de Matanzas style
like bomba y plena
Cepeda style
like merengue
Ventura style

There were certain shadows
of the imprisonment of Masayá
of the day he found Olufina's horse
on the path to the big mortar
on his way to greet him
The horse had been missing for some time
But just as Masayá was approaching the throne
Olufina's guards saw him riding the stolen horse
(ki-ti-tack ki-ti-tack ki-ti-tack)
saw him as a thief
(ki-ti-tack ki-ti-tack)

saw him prisoner
(ko-ko-koooo)
Don Masayá stated his case to small burned stones
He remained prisoner with a pen as a pillow
& white cloth
Yet mothers were giving birth to death
crops wilted the river
was now a snake of clay

A poet with yellow n'green tongue & wrists beaded
told Olufina there was someone
wrongly wrapped in iron boxes
someone of some relation
This retribution
was the source of much trouble
Masayá would later brand a poem
unto the turtle's shell
offer it to Olufina—
'. . . so long you kept me hidden
& never saw my face
When would you've realized that I
did not steal yr horse
that I came to yr land to greet you
& bring you a gift . . .'

El pueblo dice: Masayá Obakosó o
& drums summon thunder
dicen: Obakosó o
& stones rain from the sky
dicen: Obakosó o
& the caudillo dangles from a ceiba
dicen: Obakosó o
& the old memory is the new
dicen: Obakosó o
& the new memory crackles
dice Masayá: Obakosó o
& odu burns beyond

VAHNI CAPILDEO

b. 1973

In Cunaripo

The first time I saw the giant Pandit in his peach-hued kurta,
his whole bulk bespoke his kindness, as he gentled his voice's
    soundwaves
to play with his terrified baby nephew (himself large for his age—
some time after, other children would run away, take fright in their
    turn,
when the big little one cooed down at them, gently proffering his toys);
so, what happened with the caymans was entirely in character.

It was the family night
of a festival day.
They opened the door.
Sporting in the ravine
maybe a dozen
baby caymans
and their pianolength mother.
Alligator laughter
splashing and boiling
through their proper element,
sparking off water.
No happier sight.

He scattered consecrated sweets to the beasts,
and the little wedgemouths, delighted, gave chase.
(The mother ignored him, however.) He admired them feasting,
how human and animal could live so close.

Who knows why
he filled in the ravine
later that year,
when he decided
to earth it up.
It is doubtful they died.

Their preferred method
of getting through drought weather
is to be dried into mud.
And even if they did,
who knows how they're reborn.
What a chance. After such blessed food,
perhaps they live in India.
Perhaps they are kalarippayattu masters.

Was it since one small cayman, jagged-jawed, lunged, backed off,
      lunged, backed off,
at his beautiful daughter, when she went out to see to the flowers?
Not necessarily.
Should you agree blood is thicker than water.

MIRLANDE JEAN-GILLES

b. 1973

My Grandmother Danced

My grandmother danced on duvalier's head
with one red shoe and one blue
I come from coconut groves
where men's heads hang like ripe mangoes
no matter what the season
My grandmother would sing these men down
bless the back of their necks with aloe and comfrey
but they would not respond

We watched public burnings,
embers blamed no one
but danced their fiery dance
Grandma had herbs, money and gun powder stuffed into her brassiere
Murder tucked demurely within the folds of her skirt
At five she sang me redemption lullabies
and I dreamt war, blood red

We were hungry
and papa doc was taking the food
from between our teeth
grabbing our real papas in the darkness
and the flames
and their screams
would illuminate midnight
outshine the moon

My grandmother danced on papa doc's skull
with one red shoe and one blue

We played on human bones in Haiti
death left on our swings
in our schools
random fingers as bookmarks in our bibles

And the white god laughed
his crucifix too heavy on our necks
drowned us during baptisms
we couldn't fly any more
couldn't astral project our bodies to tree tops or foothills
they got weapons for that now

Unlike past slave revolts
where entire cargo would disappear
(ya'll never heard about that)
lightening during sunshine
rivers and tidal waves
white babies speaking in tongues
after sucking black breast
did you hear of the slave master
trying to rape
woman black
and she laughed and laughed
turned to jackal, to donkey
then she turned into his own daughter

Men who knocked on doors with heads tilted far left
and cords still wrapped around their necks
tongues eggplant
eyes blasted
(ya'll never heard that stuff)
but you understand
transportation was provided
first class to Paris
to those that peeled the richness of their people
renamed our magic, voodoo
cloaked us in embargoes
signed over revolution and land
our families pay rent on homes that they own
they want our children to pay for the freedom their parents took
want to open Gap factories and Disney pays my aunt three dollars a
    day
for fourteen hours
fills my cousins with birth control
empties them with hysterectomies

They're not afraid of us anymore
now that they got their language tattooed to the roof of our mouths
got us singing gospels to heaven
we forgot we were heaven
they're not afraid of us anymore
got us running to bleach

but ain't all of us scared
We've got spirits forcing us off roofs
making us find our wing span
practicing camouflage on the A train
and finding herbs in Prospect Park at four a.m.

We've got little Clinton dolls in our coach purses
if we could only find some hair samples . . .
masking drum beats in hip hop
spells written between the lines of text books

I now dance on Clinton's head with one red shoe and one blue

NOTES ON CONTRIBUTORS

Adisa, Opal Palmer (Jamaica, b. 1954) Opal Palmer Adisa was born in King-ston, Jamaica but has lived in the USA since the 1980s. She has a PhD from the University of California, Berkeley, and is a Professor at the California College of Arts and Crafts. Her poetry, stories, and articles have been anthologized widely, and she is the author of *Pina, the Many-Eyed Fruit* (1985), *Bake-Face, and Other Guava Stories* (1986), *Traveling Women* (1989), *Tamarind and Mango Women* (1992), *It Begins With Tears* (1997), and *Leaf-of-Life* (2000).

Agard, John (Guyana, b. 1949) John Agard worked as a journalist in Guyana before settling in the UK in 1977. He has had great success as a poet, broad-caster, and teacher, including a period as Writer in Residence at the BBC. He won the Paul Hamlyn Award for Poetry in 1997 and has travelled extensively throughout the world performing his poetry. His published poetry includes *Man to Pan* (1982), which won the Casa de las Américas Prize, *Mangoes and Bullets: Selected and New Poems 1972–84* (1985), *From the Devil's Pulpit*, which won the Guyana Prize in 1998, and *Weblines* (2000). He is also the author of many children's books, including *Lend Me Your Wings* (1987), which was shortlisted for the Smarties Book Prize.

Allen, Lillian (Jamaica/Canada, b. 1951) Lillian Allen was born in 1951 in Spanish Town, Jamaica, and moved to North America in 1969. She studied at the City University of New York, and York University in Toronto. Lillian Allen teaches creative writing at the Ontario College of Art and Design in Toronto. Her first two dub poetry recordings, *Revolutionary Tea Party* (1986) and *Condition Critical* (1988), won Juno awards and a third, *(We Shall Take Our) Freedom & Dance*, was released by Vancouver's Festival Records. Her publications include *Rhythm An' Hardtimes* (1983), *Women Do This Everyday* (Women's Press, 1994), and *Psychic Unrest* (Insomiac Press, 1999).

Allfrey, Phyllis Shand (Dominica, 1908–1986) The founder of the Domi-nica Labour Party and an important figure in West Indian politics in the middle decades of the twentieth century—she was the only female minister in the government of the short-lived Federation of the West Indies. As a writer, Phyllis Shand Allfrey is best known as the author of *The Orchid House* (1954), a novel often compared with Jean Rhys's *Wide Sargasso Sea*. She was also a talented poet, but her work was mostly published in very limited edition pamphlets and has only recently become available to a wider audience.

Alvarez, Julia (Dominican Republic, b. 1950) Although Julia Alvarez was born in New York City, her parents returned to their home in the Dominican Republic shortly after her birth. She remained there until she was ten, when her family left the island because of the political situation, and they settled back in America. Her work as both poet and novelist draws on that dual experience. She has published four novels, including *How the García Girls Lost Their Accent* (1991) and *In the Name of Salomé* (2000). She has published three collections of poems, including, in 1996, *Homecoming: New and Collected Poems* and *Seven Trees* (1999). Julia Alvarez teaches creative writing in the English Department at Middlebury College.

Arion, Frank Martinus (Curaçao, b. 1936) After growing up in Curaçao, Frank Martinus Arion travelled to Holland to study Dutch literature. After his studies he taught in Holland for several years and began to publish poetry and fiction. He then spent some time in Surinam before returning to Curaçao in 1980, where he is the Director of the Instituto Lingwistiko Antiano. Among his scholarly works, his study *The Kiss of a Slave* (1996) has become a standard work on the development of Papiamento and other Caribbean creole languages. Although he has won several prizes for his poetry, he is perhaps best known as a novelist; his novel *Double Play* (1973 in Dutch, 1998 in English) has been translated into German and Danish as well as English.

Arrillaga, Maria (Puerto Rico, b. 1940) Maria Arrillaga teaches in the Spanish Department at the University of Puerto Rico. Long active as a feminist writer and critic, Maria Arrillaga has published poetry and fiction in both Spanish and English. Her publications include a novel, *Mañana Valentina* (1996), and a major volume of her selected poems, *Yo Soy Fili Mele: Obra Poetica* (1999).

Ayala, Naomi (Puerto Rico, b. *c.* 1965) Poet, educator, and community activist, Naomi Ayala is the author of one book of poetry, *Wild Animals on the Moon* (Curbstone, 1997), which was selected by the New York City Public Library as one of 1999's Books for the Teen Age. Her poetry has appeared in many journals and anthologies around the US and beyond—including *Callaloo*, *The Village Voice*, *The Caribbean Writer*, and *The Massachusetts Review*. She received the year 2000 Dr. Martin Luther King, Jr. Legacy of Environmental Justice Award.

Baugh, Edward (Jamaica, b. 1936) Poet and scholar, Emeritus Professor of English and Public Orator at the University of the West Indies, Jamaica, Edward Baugh has published two collections of poems, *Tales from the Rainforest* (1988) and *It Was the Singing* (2000), as well as several works of criticism including *Derek Walcott: Memory as Vision: Another Life* (Longman, 1978). In 1998 the University of the West Indies Press published *Chancellor, I Present*, a collection of his addresses made as Public Orator at Honorary Degree ceremonies.

Bell, Vera (Jamaica, b. 1906) Vera Bell grew up in Jamaica and then studied at universities in New York and London. She was very active among the Focus group of writers in Jamaica in the 1930s and 1940s. She later emigrated to England. She published stories and wrote a pantomime, as well as publishing many poems in Jamaican magazines and anthologies. A poetry book, *Ogog*, appeared in 1971.

Bennett, Louise (Jamaica, b. 1919) The Hon. Louise Simone Bennett-Coverly, folklorist, writer, and performer. In the persona of 'Miss Lou', she has travelled the world promoting the culture of Jamaica. Her poetry and stories have been published in many collections, including *Jamaica Labrish* (1966) and *Selected Poems* (1982). Among many recordings are: Jamaica *Folksongs—Folkways* (1953), *Miss Lou's Views* (1967), and *Yes Me Dear* (1983). She lived in Jamaica for most of her life, but in recent years settled in Canada.

Berry, James (Jamaica, b. 1924) James Berry grew up in a coastal village in rural Jamaica. At seventeen he went to work in America, and in 1948 he migrated to Britain. He worked for many years as a telephonist in London but was always writing and gradually established a reputation as a poet and short story writer. In 1976 he edited *Bluefoot Traveller*, and then *News from Babylon*, the first anthologies of what he described as West-Indian-British poetry. His own poetry is collected in several volumes published over the last thirty years, including *Chain of Days* (1985) and *Hot Earth, Cold Earth* (1995). In recent years James Berry has gained an international reputation as a writer of poems and stories for children. He was awarded an OBE for his services to poetry and an Honourary Doctorate by the Open University.

Brand, Dionne (Trinidad, b. 1953) Dionne Brand grew up in Trinidad before moving to Toronto in 1970. A poet, short story writer, novelist, essayist, and film-maker, Dionne Brand has always been active in feminist and black politics. Her poetry and other writing reflects her political involvements. Her publications include the collections of poems *Winter Epigrams* (1983), *No Language is Neutral* (1990), and the novels *In Another Place Not Here* (1997) and *Land To Light On* (1997). She has also published *Sans Souci* (1988), a collection of short stories, and *Bread Out of Stone* (1994), a volume of essays.

Brathwaite, Kamau (Barbados, b. 1930) One of the great poets of the Caribbean, Kamau Brathwaite is also an important historian, cultural critic, editor, and teacher. After working for many years at the University of the West Indies in Jamaica he is currently Professor of Comparative Literature at New York University. He also spends much of his time back in Barbados. His reputation was founded on the epic vision of his first trilogy, published as *The Arrivants* (1973). His recent work includes the monumental *Barabajan*

Poems (1994) and *Words Need Love Too* (2000). A selection of his essays on Caribbean literature, *Roots*, was published by the University of Michigan Press in 1993, and his re-worked second trilogy, *Ancestors*, appeared in 2001. Brathwaite has received the Neustadt International Award for Literature, the Casa de Las Américas Prize for poetry and for literary criticism, as well as fellowships from the Guggenheim Foundation, the Fulbright Foundation, and the Ford Foundation.

Breeze, Jean 'Binta' (Jamaica, b. 1957) Jean 'Binta' Breeze studied at the Jamaican School of Drama with Michael Smith and Oku Onuora. She began to write poetry in the 1970s, performing and recording first in Kingston then in London. She has worked as a director and scriptwriter for theatre, television, and film. Her poetry collections include the books *Riddym Ravings* (1988), *Spring Cleaning* (1992), and, most recently, *The Arrival of Brighteye and Other Poems* (2000). Several recordings of her work are available, including *Hearsay* (1994) and *Riding on de Riddym* (1996). She has also published a collection of stories, *On the Edge of an Island* (1997).

Brièrre, Jean (Haiti, b. 1909) Born in Jérémie, long known as 'the city of poets', Jean Brièrre served as a teacher, education officer, and cultural worker in Haiti. A member of the 'indigenist' movement, his radical and militant politics resulted in more than one spell in prison. His publications include the collections of poems *Le Drapeau de demain* (1931) and *Black Soul* (1947). He also published a novel, *Les Horizons sans ciel* in 1953.

Brown, Wayne (Trinidad, b. 1944) Wayne Brown, a Trinidadian writer who teaches creative writing at the University of the West Indies, has published two books of poetry. The second, *Voyages* (1989), includes a reprint of his first collection, *On the Coast* (1972), which won the Commonwealth Literature Prize in 1972. He has also published a biography of the Jamaican sculptor Edna Manley, and a collection of short stories, *The Child of the Sea* (1989).

Burgos, Julia de (Puerto Rico, 1914–1953) Julia de Burgos was one of the most important poets to come out of Puerto Rico in the twentieth century. Emerging from very poor social circumstances, she lived a passionate, committed, and controversial life which informs all her poetry. She worked as a teacher and later as a journalist. She lived for parts of her life in Cuba and later settled in New York, where she died in tragic circumstances in 1953. In English translation her work is most accessibly available in *The Complete Poems of Julia de Burgos, Obra Completa Poetica*, translated by Jack Agueros (1997).

Cairo, Edgar (Surinam, 1948–2000) Born in Paramaribo, Edgar Cairo moved to Amsterdam in 1968 to study. A prolific writer, he published eight collections of poems, as well as novels and collections of essays. His books include *Lelu! Lelu! Het lied der vervreemding* (1983), *Het Koninkrijk Ijmond/Ba kuku ba buba* (1985), and *Nymane/In mensenmaan* (1986).

Campbell, George (Jamaica, 1916–2002) Born in Panama, George Campbell became one of the most important voices in the Jamaican cultural rennaisance of the 1940s and 1950s. His work is always associated with the journal *Focus*, founded and edited by the sculptor Edna Manley, which promoted ideas of cultural nationalism in those pre-independence decades. Campbell published his volume *First Poems* in 1945, a collection he saw republished—with an introductory poem by Derek Walcott—in 1981 by Yale University's Garland Press. *Earth Testament*, a collection of new poems by Campbell and illustrated by Edna Manley, was published in Jamaica in 1982. He lived for many years in the USA and died in New York in 2002.

Capildeo, Vahni (Trinidad, b. 1973) Vahni Capildeo was born in Port of Spain and grew up in Trinidad before moving to Britain to study in 1991. She currently holds a research fellowship at Girton College, Cambridge. She published her first collection of poems, *No Traveller Returns*, in 2003.

Carbet, Marie-Magdeleine (Martinique, b. 1902) Marie-Magdeleine Carbet is a prolific writer in a variety of genres. She grew up in Martinique before studying at the University of Paris in the 1920s. She became a schoolteacher, and later founded the first Caribbean theatre in Paris. She has published several novels, including *Au sommet de la sérénité* (1980) and several books of poems, including *Rose de ta grace* (1970) and *Mini-poèmes sur trois méridiens* (1977). She was awarded the Grand Prix Humanitaire for services to arts and letters.

Carr, Peggy (St Vincent, b. *c.*1955) A journalist and poet in St Vincent, Peggy Carr's poetry has been published in several anthologies of Caribbean writing, including *Creation Fire*, *Women Poets of the Caribbean*, and *Caribbean Poetry Now*. She has published two collections of poems, *Echoes from a Lonely Nightwatch* (1989) and *Fresh Tracks in an Ancient Land* (1996).

Carter, Martin (Guyana, 1927–1997) One of the great poets of the twentieth-century Caribbean who chronicled the journey from colonial struggle through the dream of independence to the post-colonial/neo-colonial realities. His early poems have become classics of socialist literature, translated into many languages, and are among the foundation stones of West Indian poetry. His later work, while it never lost its political edge, was more oblique and cerebral than the overtly political poems of his youth. It sits most comfortably alongside that of his fellow South American poets Valejo, Neruda, and Paz. His poems are most accessibly available in his *Selected Poems* (revised edition 1997).

Casal, Lourdes (Cuba, 1938–1981) Born in Havana, Lourdes Casal lived in

New York City from 1962 to 1979. Writer and critic, she founded *Arelito*, a magazine offering an alternate perspective on US Cuban culture. She was also a professor of psychology at Rutgers University. A collection of her poems, *Palabras Juntan Revolution*, was published in 1981.

Castro, Adrian (Cuba, b. 1967) Adrian Castro is a poet, performer, and interdisciplinary artist. He was born in Miami of Cuban and Dominican heritage, a cultural dynamic that shapes his poetry. His work addresses the migratory experience from Africa to the Caribbean to North America, and the inevitable clash of cultures. His work is widely anthologized and he has published a collection of poems, *Cantos to Blood and Honey* (1997).

Causse, Jesus Cos (Cuba, b. 1945) Born in Santiago de Cuba, Jesus Cos Causse is Director of International Relations at Casa del Caribe, where he runs the annual 'Festival of Fire'. He has published several books, including *Concierto de jazz para un angel súbitamente humano* (1994), *Los años, los sueños* (1995), and *El poeta también estaba en la fiesta* (2000). His work is included in several anthologies of Caribbean writing.

Césaire, Aimé (Martinique, b. 1913) One of the great poets of the twentieth century, Aimé Césaire was one of the founders—with Leopold Sedar Senghor of Senegal and Léon Damas of French Guiana—of the philosophy of Negritude. Always active in radical politics, Césaire was for many years mayor of Fort de France, the capital city of Martinique, and a member of the French parliament. A prolific poet and playwright, internationally Césaire's most famous work is the long poem *Cahier d'un retour au pays natal*, translated as *Return to My Native Land*, first published in 1956. His poetry is published in numerous volumes, most accessibly—in English translation—in *Aimé Césaire: The Collected Poetry* (1983), translated by Eschleman and Smith.

Chan, Brian (Guyana, b. 1949) Brian Chan grew up in Guyana before settling in Canada in 1970. His first collection of poems, *Thief With Leaf* (1988), won the 1988 Guyana Prize. His work is experimental, exploring not only experience, but the fictions we create in making sense of experience. His second collection of poems, *Fabula Rasa*, was published in 1994. He is a musician (clarinetist) and accomplished painter. He works as an art gallery curator in Alberta.

Charles, Faustin (Trinidad, b. 1944) Faustin Charles settled in Britain in the 1960s, where he has established a reputation as writer, performer, and cultural historian. He has published four collections of poems including, in 2004, a volume of his selected poems, *Children of the Morning*. He has also published two adult novels, collections of Caribbean folk stories, and several works for children of different ages, including the classic picture book *The*

Selfish Crocodile, which has sold over 100,000 copies. Since 1997 he has been the Community Literacy Officer for Enfield.

Cliff, Michelle (Jamaica, b. 1946) Michelle Cliff was born in Jamaica and grew up there and in the United States. She was educated in New York City and at the Warburg Institute at the University of London, where she completed a PhD on the Italian Renaissance. She is the author of several novels, including *No Telephone To Heaven* (1987), and *Free Enterprise* (1994), the books of short stories *Bodies of Water* (1990) and *The Store of a Million Items* (1998) as well as the poetry collections *The Land of Look Behind* (1985) and *Claiming an Identity They Taught Me to Despise* (1980). Michelle Cliff now lives in Santa Cruz, California.

Cofer, Judith Ortiz (Puerto Rico, b. 1952) Judith Ortiz Cofer is the Franklin Professor of English at the University of Georgia. She is a prolific author in several genres, her publications include the collections of essays *Woman in Front of the Sun: On Becoming a Writer* (2000) and *Silent Dancing* (1990), a book of stories *An Island Like You: Stories of the Barrio* (1999); two novels, *The Line of the Sun* (1991) and *The Meaning of Consuelo* (2003), and three books of poetry, *Terms of Survival* (1995), *Reaching for the Mainland* (1995) and *The Latin Deli* (1993). In 1998 she published *The Year of Our Revolution: New and Selected Stories and Poems*.

Colimon, Marie-Thérèse (Haiti, 1918–1988) Marie-Thérèse Colimon began her writing career as a playwright, publishing five plays between 1949 and 1960. She published her first novel, *Fils de misère*, in 1974. She has also published poems, essays, and books for children. Her much-acclaimed collection of short stories, *Les Chants des sirens*, was published in 1979.

Collins, Merle (Grenada, b. 1950) Merle Collins grew up in Grenada and studied at the University of the West Indies in Jamaica. After graduating in 1972, she returned to Grenada, where she worked in education. She was deeply involved in the Grenadian revolution, but left Grenada for Britain in 1983. Her first collection of poetry, *Because the Dawn Breaks*, was published in 1985. In 1987, she published her first novel *Angel*; this was followed by a collection of short stories, *Rain Darling*, in 1990, and a second collection of poetry, *Rotten Pomerack*, in 1992. Her second novel, *The Colour of Forgetting*, was published in 1995. *Lady in a Boat*, her latest collection of poems, was published in 2003.

Collymore, Frank (Barbados, 1893–1980) An actor, teacher, and editor as well as the author of several collections of poems and short stories, Frank Collymore was a key figure in the development of modern West Indian literature. He edited the literary journal BIM through four decades. His *Collected Poems* was published in 1959 and again in 1971. His stories were collected posthumously in *The Man Who Loved Attending Funerals* (1993).

Craig, Christine (Jamaica, b. 1943) Christine Craig was a member of the Caribbean Artists Movement in London in the 1960s and subsequently worked for the Woman's Bureau in Jamaica. She has published books for children, short stories, film and television scripts, as well as a collection of poems, *Quadrille for Tigers* (1984). Her collection of stories, *Mint Tea*, was published in 1993. She now lives in the USA.

Craig, Dennis (Guyana, 1929–2004) Linguist, scholar, and university administrator, Dennis Craig taught for many years at the University of the West Indies in Jamaica before becoming Vice Chancellor of the University of Guyana in the 1990s. Dennis Craig published poems in Caribbean literary journals and anthologies over several decades but only published his first collection, *Near the Seashore*, in 1999 after the manuscript was awarded the Guyana Prize for Poetry in 1998.

D'Aguiar, Fred (Guyana, b. 1960) Fred D'Aguiar was born in London in 1960 to Guyanese parents. He lived in Guyana until he was 12. Back in England he trained as a psychiatric nurse before taking a degree at the University of Kent. His first collection of poetry, *Mama Dot* (1985), established his reputation as one of the most exciting poets of his generation. His second collection, *Airy Hall* (1989), won the Guyana Prize in 1989 and was followed by *British Subjects* (1993). His first novel, *The Longest Memory* (1994), won the Whitbread First Novel Award. His plays include *High Life*, which was produced in London in 1987, and *A Jamaican Airman Foresees His Death*, first performed in 1991. Other publications include the novels *Dear Future* (1996), *Feeding the Ghosts* (1997), and *Bethany Bettany* (2003). Recent poetry includes *Bill of Rights* (1998), *Bloodlines* (2000), and *An English Sampler: New and Selected Poems* (2001). Fred D'Aguiar is Professor of Creative Writing at the University of Newcastle.

Dabydeen, Cyril (Guyana, b. 1945) Cyril Dabydeen was born in the Canje, Guyana, in 1945. In the early 1970s he left Guyana for Canada to study, eventually gaining an MA and an MBA at Queens University. He has written eight books of poetry, five collections of short stories, and three novels. He has also edited two anthologies. He is a former Poet Laureate of Ottawa, where he teaches at the University of Ottawa. His collections of poems include *Discussing Columbus* (1997).

Dabydeen, David (Guyana, b. 1955) Scholar, poet, and novelist. Professor of Literature at the University of Warwick, UK, where he is Director of the Centre for Caribbean Studies, David Dabydeen has published widely on Caribbean literature and cultural history and written several novels and collections of poetry, most recently *Turner: New and Selected Poems* (1994) and his novel *A Harlot's Progress* (1999). His first book, *Slave Song* (1984), a collection of poetry, won the Commonwealth Poetry Prize and the Quiller-Couch Prize. He is also Guyana's Ambassador-at-Large and a member of UNESCO's Executive Board.

Damas, Léon-Gontran (French Guiana, 1912–1978) Born in Cayenne, French Guiana, where he received his primary education, Léon Damas later moved to Martinique where he shared philosophy classes with young Aimé Césaire, and the two started what would become a lifelong friendship. Later, as students in France, along with Leopold Senghor, they laid the foundations for what is now known as the Negritude movement. Damas was the first of the triumvirate to publish a volume of poetry, *Pigments* (1937), reflecting the values of Negritude. After a varied career in politics, radio, and with UNESCO, in 1970 Damas settled in Washington DC, where he became Professor of African Literature at Howard University. He published many collections of poems after *Pigments*, including *Névralgies* (Paris: Présence Africaine, 1966) and *Veilles noires* (Ottowa: Leméac, 1972).

Das, Mahadai (Guyana, 1954–2003) Mahadai Das was born in Eccles, East Bank Demerara, Guyana in 1954. She wrote poetry from her early school days at Bishops High School, Georgetown. She did her first degree at the University of Guyana and received her MA at Columbia University, New York, and then began a doctoral programme in philosophy at the University of Chicago. Das became ill and never completed the programme. She was a dancer, actress, teacher, and beauty-queen. She published three collections of poetry, including *I Want to Be a Poetess of My People* (1977) and *Bones* (1988). In 2004 Peepal Tree Press published a volume of her selected poems, *A Leaf in His Ear*.

Dawes, Kwame (Ghana/Jamaica, b. 1962) Born in Ghana, Kwame Dawes moved to Jamaica in 1971, where he remained until 1987. He has also lived in Britain, Canada, and currently the USA, where he is Professor of English at the University of South Carolina. A musician, poet, playwright, storyteller, and essayist, Dawes has published several acclaimed collections of poems in recent years, most recently *Shook Foil* (1998), *Midland* (2001), and *New and Selected Poems* (2002). His major scholarly work is *Natural Mysticism* (1999), a study of the reggae aesthetic which critically grounds the anthology of reggae poems he edited in 1998, *Wheel and Come Again*. He has also published a collection of short stories *A Place to Hide* (2002), and a biography, *Bob Marley: Lyrical Genius* (2002).

Dawes, Neville (Jamaica, 1926–1984) Poet, novelist, and literary scholar (father of Kwame—see above). He taught for some years at the University of Ghana and was Director of the Institute of Jamaica in the 1970s. Author of *In Sepia*, a collection of poems, in 1958 and two novels, *The Last Enchantment* (1960) and *Interim* (1978).

Dépestre, René (Haiti, b. 1926) René Dépestre's work as novelist and poet has been widely published around the world, but his poetry is still not well known in English translation. His first volume of poetry, *Sparks (Eincelles)*, was published in Port-au-Prince in 1945. Other publications include *Végétation de clartés*, with a preface by Aimé Césaire (1951) *Un arc-en-ciel pour l'occident chrétien poème mystère vaudou* (1966), and more recently *Anthologie personnelle* (1993) and *Actes sud*, which received the Prix Apollinaire. In 1988, his novel *Hadriana dans tous mes rêves* won the Prix Renandot. His work has appeared in many French and Spanish anthologies, while his best-known works in English translation are probably the collection of poems *A Rainbow for the Christian West* (1972) and the novel *The Festival of the Greasy Pole* (1990).

Dixon, McDonald (St Lucia, b. 1945) McDonald Dixon is a banker by profession but has long been a respected writer in St Lucia, where he has lived all his life. Dixon is best known for poetry, although he is also an accomplished novelist, painter, and photographer. In 1993, he recieved the St Lucia Medal of Merit for his contribution to literature and photography. He has published a collection of poems *The Poet Speaks* (1980 and 1993) and two novels, the most recent being *Season of Mist* (2001).

Dobru, Robin (Robin Ravales) (Surinam, 1935–1983) Robin Dobru was a writer, performance poet, and political/cultural activist in Surinam from the 1960s until his death. He was well known in literary circles across the Caribbean and is particularly associated with the pan-Caribbean Carifesta festival of the arts. His publications include the poetry collections *From Revo and Love in the Sun* (1981) and *Boodschappen uit de zon: gedichten 1965–1980* (1982).

Douglas, Marcia (Jamaica/UK, b. 1961) Marcia Douglas was born in the UK of Jamaican parents, but grew up in rural Jamaica. She left Jamaica in 1990 to study for a Master of Fine Arts in Creative Writing at Ohio State University and was awarded a PhD in African-American and Caribbean Literature in 1997. Her first collection of poems, *Electricity Comes to Cocoa Bottom* (1999), won a Poetry Book Society recommendation. In 2000, she published her first novel, *Madam Fate*, with The Women's Press. She currently lives in Boulder, Colorado.

Ecury, Nydia (Aruba, b. 1926) Born in Aruba, Nydia Ecury has lived in Curaçao for many years. A teacher by profession, she has been involved in theatre and film work there as both actress and director. She has also published stories for children. She has published five collections of poems, including a volume written in both Papiamento and English, *Kantika Pa Mama Tera / Song For Mother Earth* (1984). She was awarded the Order of Oranje Nassau in 2000.

Escoffery, Gloria (Jamaica, 1923–2002) A painter, poet, teacher, and arts critic, Gloria Escoffery lived all her life in Jamaica except for brief periods studying in Canada and the UK. Best known as a painter, her work is included in the National Collection in Jamaica and was exhibited internationally throughout her lifetime. She was also an original and idiosyncratic poet. Her poetry publications include *Landscape in the Making* (1976), *Loggerhead* (1988), and *Mother Jackson Murders the Moon* (1998). Her poems have been included in many anthologies of Caribbean verse. Gloria Escoffery was awarded the Order of Distinction in 1977 and the Institute of Jamaica's Silver Musgrave Medal in 1989 for services in the field of art.

Espada, Martín (Puerto Rico, b. 1957) Poet and educator, Martín Espada was born in Brooklyn, New York, to Puerto Rican parents. His latest collection of poetry is *Alabanza: New and Selected Poems 1982–2002* (2003). Espada's other books of poetry include *A Mayan Astronomer in Hell's Kitchen* (2000) and *Imagine the Angels of Bread* (1996), which won an American Book Award. He has edited several anthologies including *El Coro: A Chorus of Latino and Latina Poets* (1997) and *Poetry Like Bread: Poets of the Political Imagination* (1994). His collection of essays *Zapata's Disciple* was published in 1998. His honours include the PEN/Voelker Award for Poetry, the Paterson Poetry Prize, and two fellowships from the National Endowment for the Arts. Martín Espada is an Associate Professor of English at the University of Massachusetts-Amherst.

Fergus, Howard (Montserrat, b. 1937) Sir Howard A. Fergus was born at Long Ground in Montserrat. He has served Montserrat in a variety of roles, as Chief Education Officer (1970–73), Acting Permanent Secretary, from 1975 Speaker of the Montserrat Legislative Council, and De Facto Deputy Governor from 1976. Since 1974 he has been the Extra-Mural Resident Tutor of the University of the West Indies, in Montserrat. He was awarded a CBE in 1995 and knighted in 2001 for his outstanding sevices to Montserrat. His poetry began appearing from 1976, with *Cotton Rhymes; Green Innocence* in 1978 and he has published *Lara Rains and Colonial Rights* (1998), *Volcano Song: Poems of an Island in Agony* (2000), and *Volcano Verses* (2003).

Ferland, Barbara (Jamaica, b. 1919) Barbara Ferland grew up in Jamaica, where she wrote and published poems from an early age. She wrote many of the songs for the first all-Jamaican pantomime, and one of those songs, 'Evening-time', is still used as a signature tune by Radio Jamaica. Her poems have appeared in numerous anthologies and she published a collection, *Without Shoes I Must Run*, in 1994.

Figueroa, John (Jamaica, 1920–1999) One of the Caribbean's most outspoken men of letters until his death in 1999, the Jamaican poet, critic, educationalist, broadcaster, and scholar John Figueroa edited important anthologies of Caribbean literature, including *Caribbean Voices* (1971) and published several collections of his own poems, most recently *The Chase: A Collection of Poems 1941–1989* (1991). He taught at the University of the West Indies, the University of Jos in Nigeria, and for the Open University in Britain. He was well known as a writer and commentator on cricket.

Ford-Smith, Honor (Jamaica, b. 1951) Honor Ford-Smith was founding Artistic Director of the Sistren Theatre Collective, a Jamaican women's theatre and cultural organization for which she wrote and directed several plays until the early 1990s. Her work with Sistren toured widely in Europe, North America, and the Caribbean and earned her several awards, including Jamaica's Musgrave Medal. She is co-author and editor of Sistren's collection of oral biographies *Lionheart Gal: Lifestories of Jamaican Women*. She is also a well-established poet, her work appearing in several regional anthologies and in the collection *My Mother's Last Dance* (1996). She teaches at the Institute of Women and Gender Studies at the University of Toronto.

Gilkes, Michael (Guyana, b. 1933) Guyanese playwright, critic, and poet Michael Gilkes taught for many years at the University of the West Indies in Barbados and then at the University of Guyana. He has lived in St Lucia for several years now. He has made films, directed theatre, and published literary criticism and poetry. His play on Edgar Mittelholzer, *A Pleasant Career*, won the Guyana Prize for Drama in 1996 and his book on Wilson Harris, *The Literature Imagination* (1989) is very highly regarded. His first collection of poems, *Joanstown*, won the 2002 Guyana Prize for Best Book of Poetry.

Gill, Margaret (Barbados, b. 1953) Of her background as a poet Margaret Gill writes, 'I grew up in a family of ten, with very few opportunities . . . but with a mother who wrote poems for children to "recite" at Sunday School, and with a father who saw to it that the whole family attended church. Acknowledgement of those early imparted tenets of education, creative expression and attention to the spirit helped to create those opportunities which led to my present life.' Her poems have been published in several regional anthologies and literary journals and her first collection, *Alternate Songs from the Kingdom of the Lily*, won the first Frank Collymore Literary Endowment Award in 1999.

Glissant, Édouard (Martinique, b. 1928) Édouard Glissant grew up in Martinique, where he came early under the influence of Aimé Césaire, before going on to study philosophy at the Sorbonne and ethnology at the Musée de l'Homme, in Paris. He worked for some years for UNESCO before taking up a position as a Professor of Literature at the City University of New York. He has published many novels, collections of poetry, and cultural criticism, although until quite recently his work was hardly available in English translation. His recent publications include the novel *The Fourth Century* (2002), a collection of his essays *Caribbean Discourse* (1992), and a book of poems, *Black Salt* (1998).

Gonzalez, Anson (Trinidad, b. 1936) As teacher, editor, and broadcaster Anson Gonzalez played an important role in the development and promotion of Caribbean writing through the last decades of the twentieth century. He edited the literary magazine *The New Voices*, which was published continuously for 20 years. He also published collections of poems by individual writers and was a founding member of the Writers Union of Trinidad and Tobago. As a poet Anson Gonzalez's work is widely anthologized and collected in several volumes, including a *Collected Poems* (1979), *Moksha: Poems of Light and Sound* (1988), and *Merry-Go-Round* (1992). A collection of his prose-poems, *Crossroads of Dream* was published in 2004.

Goodison, Lorna (Jamaica, b. 1947) An artist as well as a poet, Lorna Goodison's collections of poems—and her readings from them—have won international acclaim. Her books of poetry extend from *Tamarind Season* (1980) to *Guinea Woman* (2000) and *controlling the silver* (2005). She also published two collections of short stories, most recently *Fool Fool Rose is leaving Labour-in-Vain Savannah* (2005). Her work is widely anthologized and is included in the new *Norton Anthology of Modern and Contemporary Poetry* (2003). She is at present Associate Professor of English at the University of Michigan. Lorna Goodison has received many awards and honours for her writing, including the Musgrave Gold Medal in 1999.

Goulbourne, Jean (Jamaica, b. 1947) A novelist and short story writer as well as a poet, Jean Goulbourne is a teacher and has worked in the Ministry of Education in Jamaica. She has published three collections of poems, *Actors in the Arena* (1977), *Under the Sun* (1988), and *Woman Song* (2002). She has also published a novel, *Excavation* (1997). She was the recipient of a James Michener Fellowship and an honorary fellowship at the Iowa Institute of Writing Programme.

Gray, Cecil (Trinidad, b. 1923) Cecil Gray was born and lived all his working life in Trinidad. He taught for many years at the University of the West Indies, training secondary teachers in the teaching of English. His important anthologies for schools helped shape the literary taste of a generation of Caribbean students. In 1976 he was awarded the Medal of Merit, Class One, Gold, by the Trinidadian Government for his meritorious service in education and culture. His own poetry was long scattered through many journals and anthologies, but since his retirement in 1988 and his move to Canada he has published several much-admired collections, including *The Woolgatherer* (1994), *Lillian's Songs* (1996), *Leaving the Dark* (1998), *Plumed Palms* (2000), and *Careenage* (2003).

Greaves, Stanley (Guyana, b. 1934) Stanley Greaves was born in Guyana. He studied art in the UK and was Head of the Division of Creative Arts at the University of Guyana for several years. He left Guyana in the 1980s and has been resident in Barbados since that time. He is one of the Caribbean's most distinguished artists, with major exhibitions in the UK and Europe as well as throughout the Caribbean. In addition to his poetry and painting, he is also an accomplished classical guitarist. His first collection of poems, *Horizons* (2002), won the Guyana Prize for Poetry.

Guillén, Nicolás (Cuba, 1902–1987) One of the great poets of the Caribbean, Nicolás Guillén was an Afro-Cuban writer, journalist, and social activist. His first collection of poems, *Cerebro y Corazón* [*Brain and Heart*] appeared in 1922. In 1930 he published *Motivios de son*, eight short poems inspired by the Son, a popular Afro-Cuban musical form. Written in a version of an Afro-Cuban vernacular and reflecting the injustices endured by Afro-Cubans in the prevailing social order, the collection established Guillén as an original and important figure in the development of a distinctively Cuban literature. Over the next fifty years Guillén became a major cultural figure in the Caribbean and across the world, becoming President of the Union of Writers and Artists of Cuba in 1961. He published many collections of poetry, including *Tengo* (1964), *El gran Zoo* (1967), and *Sol de Domingo* (1982). In English translation his most accessible collection is the new edition of *Man-Making Words: Selected Poems of Nicolás Guillén* (2003).

Harris, Claire (Trinidad, b. 1937) Claire Harris grew up in Trinidad but has lived in Canada since 1966. She studied in Ireland, Jamaica, and Nigeria before taking a teaching post in Calgary. Her first collection of poetry, *Fables from the Women's Quarters* (1984), won the Commonwealth Prize for Poetry for the Americas Region. Since then she has published at least eight volumes, including *Drawing Down a Daughter* (1992), and *She* (2000), a novel in poetry and prose poetry. Her work has been included in many anthologies and has been translated into German and Hindi.

Harris, Maggie (Guyana, b. 1954) Born in Guyana, Maggie Harris has been living in the UK since 1971. An artist and teacher as well as a poet, she won the Guyana Prize for Literature for her first collection *Limbolands* (2000). She has performed her poetry in the UK, Europe, and the Caribbean. She is Festival Director of the Inscribing the Island Literature Festival in Kent.

Harris, Wilson (Guyana, b. 1921) Although a long time resident of the UK, Wilson Harris's experience growing up in Guyana and working as a surveyor in the rainforest still informs his imagination. Best known as a novelist and cultural critic, Wilson Harris began his literary career as a poet. One of the major figures in late twentieth-century literature in English, he has published more than a dozen novels, three collections of poems, and several critical works. His latest novel is *The Mask of the Beggar* (2003) and a collection of his *Selected Essays*, edited by Andrew Bundy, was published by Routledge in 1999. His poetry collection *Eternity to Season* (1954) is still in print.

Helman, Albert (Surinam, 1903–1996) Born in Paramaribo, Albert Helman was the pseudonym of Lodewijk, or Lou, Lichtveld, author, historian, diplomat, and journalist. He is regarded by many critics as the most accomplished Surinamese author of the twentieth century. He wrote mostly in Dutch but was also one of the first writers to publish poetry in Sranan. He lived much of his adult life away from Surinam, initially in Holland but for many years towards the end of his life in Tobago. That said, he was Minister of Education in Surinam from 1949 to 1951. The publication in 1923 of his first collection of poems *De glorende dag* [The Dawning Day] is regarded as a key moment in the development of Surinamese literature, and Helman went on to establish a huge body of work in various genres, though little is available in English translation.

Hendriks, A. L. (Jamaica, 1922–1992) A. L. Hendriks was a broadcaster and media executive, a much-travelled poet who finally settled in the UK. He published eight collections of poems over the years, including *Madonna of the Unknown Nation* (1974) and *To Speak Simply: Selected Poems 1961–86* (1988). He co-edited, with Cedric Lindo, the *Jamaica Independence Anthology*.

Hippolyte, Kendel (St Lucia, b. 1952) A dramatist and cultural activist as well as a poet, Kendel Hippolyte worked for some time at the Folk Research Centre in Castries and now teaches at the Sir Arthur Lewis Community College. His poetry is included in most of the major regional anthologies and he has published four collections, most recently *Birthright* (1997). He was a co-founder of the Lighthouse Theatre Company, one of the Caribbean's most important theatre groups.

Hopkinson, Slade (Abdur-Rahman) (Guyana, 1934–1993) Slade Hopkinson was a Caribbean man of letters, journalist, teacher, poet, and playwright/actor/director. He worked for some time with Derek Walcott's Trinidad Theatre Workshop and in 1970 founded the Caribbean Theatre Guild. He lectured for a time at the University of Guyana before settling in Canada, where he acted as the Guyanese Vice-Consul. He published several plays and two pamphlet collections of poetry, and in 1993, shortly after his death, *Snowscape with Signature*, effectively a selection of poems 1952–1992, was published.

Itwaru, Arnold Harrichand (Guyana, b. 1942) Poet and scholar and painter, Arnold Harrichand Itwaru has lived in Canada since 1969. He has published several novels, including *Shanti* (1988) and *Home and Back* (2001), as well as widely admired collections of poetry, including *body rites* (1991). He is the author of scholarly books on issues of power and mass communication as well as works of literary criticism. In Guyana he received two national awards for his poetry. He is currently a lecturer at the University of Toronto.

James, Cynthia (Trinidad, b. 1948) Born in Sangre Grande, Trinidad, Cynthia James has a PhD from Howard University and has lectured both there and in the Department of English at the University of the West Indies in Trinidad. A prize-winning poet and playwright, she has published three collections of poems, including *La Vega and Other Poems* (1995), a collection of stories, *Sooth Me Music* (1990), and a novel, *Bluejean* (2000).

Jean-Gilles, Mirlande (Haiti, b. 1973) Mirlande Jean-Gilles was born to Haitian immigrant parents and was brought up in New York City. Her work has been published in *The Caribbean Writer* and *New Millennium Writing*. She has read her work at the Barnes and Noble Jazz Festival, Rutgers University, Baruch College, and Brooklyn Moon Café. She is the recent recipient of the Toni Cade Bambara Award for Fiction, The Frederick Douglas Fellowship for Young African American Writers, and the Bronx Writer's Center's Van Lier Fellowship.

Johnson, Amryl (Trinidad, 1944–2001) Amryl Johnson spent her early childhood in Trinidad but emigrated to Britain when she was eleven. An inspirational teacher of creative writing, she was best known as a poet, and her collection *Long Road to Nowhere* (1985) won wide acclaim. She also published an autobiographical essay, *Sequins on a Ragged Hem* (1988). Her other poetry publications included *Gorgons* (1992) and *Calling* (2000).

Johnson, Linton Kwesi (Jamaica/UK, b. 1952) Born in Chapelton, Jamaica, Linton Kwesi Johnson came to Britain in his teens. A radical activist—journalist, broadcaster, record producer—as well as a poet and musician, Linton Kwesi Johnson has become a major cultural figure internationally. He has published several collections of poetry and many records and CDs of his work. His most substantial collection of poems as text is *Mi Revalueshanary Fren: Selected Poems* (2002). His recent work on disc includes *LKJ a capella live* (1995), which is an unaccompanied reading of a selection of his best-known poems, and *More Time* (1998), which includes his setting of Martin Carter's 'Poems of Shape and Motion'.

Keane, E. Mc.G. 'Shake' (St Vincent, 1927–1997) Born Ellsworth McGranahan Keane in St Vincent. After studying literature at London University, 'Shake' (after 'Shakespeare') went on to become an internationally acclaimed jazz musician, teacher, and highly original writer. In 1972 he returned to St. Vincent as Director of Culture, then became Principal of Bishop's College, Georgetown. His poetry collection *One a Week with Water* won the Casa de las Américas Prize in 1979. Although many of his poems remain uncollected, he also published several pamphlet collections, including *The Volcano Suite* (1979). Keane moved to New York in 1980 and began to play jazz again. His last recording, *Real Keen: Reggae Into Jazz*—a collaboration with Linton Kwesi Johnson and the Jamaican reggae musician Dennis Bovell—was released in 1992.

Kellman, Anthony (Barbados, b. 1955) Anthony Kellman grew up in Barbados and studied at the Cave Hill campus of the University of the West Indies. In 1987 he left Barbados for the USA, where he studied for an MFA degree in creative writing at Louisiana State University. In 1989 he moved to Augusta State University, Georgia, where he is a professor of English and Creative Writing. He has published several books of poetry, including *The Long Gap* (1996) and *Wings of a Stranger* (2000), and two novels, most recently *The Houses of Alphonso* (2003). In 1992 he edited the first full-length US anthology of English-language Caribbean poetry, *Crossing Water*. A recipient of a National Endowment for the Arts fellowship, his poetry, fiction, and critical essays have appeared in journals all over the world.

King, Jane (St Lucia, b. 1952) Born in Castries, Jane King won a St Lucia island scholarship to study at the University of Edinburgh. Since 1976 she has taught at the Sir Arthur Lewis Community College in Castries. Her poems and stories are widely published in regional journals and anthologies, and she has published two collections of poems, *Into the Centre* (1993) and *Fellow Traveller* (1994), which won both the Commonwealth Writers Prize (Caribbean and Canada) and the James Rodway Memorial Prize.

Kwabena, Roi (Trinidad, b. 1956) Roi Kwabena is an historian, drummer, and cultural activist, currently living in Britain, where he was appointed Poet Laureate of Birmingham in 2001. For some time he was a senator in the Trinidad and Tobago parliament. He has lived and travelled in Africa and performed his poetry internationally. His most recent book is a collection of poems, *Whether or Not* (2001), and his work is collected on the CD *Y24K* (2000).

La Rose, John (Trinidad, b. 1927) Poet, publisher, and cultural activist, John La Rose has been based in London since the 1950s. He was one of the key figures in the Caribbean Artists movement and he founded New Beacon Books, which has published the work of many West Indian and black British writers. His own poetry is published in two collections, most recently *Eyelets of Truth Within Me* (1992).

Laleau, Léon (Haiti, 1892–1979) Léon Laleau published his first book of poems, *A Voix Basse*, in 1920. His work anticipated the concerns of the Negritude movement, and has been hugely influential on generations of Caribbean and African American poets. A diplomat and minister in the Haitian government in later years, Laleau published novels and several further collections of poems, but in English translation his work is really only available in anthologies, perhaps most accessibly in Ellen C. Kennedy's *The Negritude Poets* (1989).

Laviera, Tato (Puerto Rico, b. 1951) Tato Laviera was born in Puerto Rico and has lived in New York City since 1960. A second-generation Puerto

Rican writer, poet, and playwright, as his poem here illustrates he is commit-ted to the cultural development of Puerto Ricans in New York. He teaches creative writing at Rutgers University. His poetry collections include *La Carreta Made a U-Turn* (1976), *Enclave* (1981), and *Mainstream Ethics* (1988).

Lee, John Robert (St Lucia, b. 1948) Drama critic, preacher, librarian, teacher, editor, poet, and general 'man of letters', Robert Lee has lived almost all of his life in St Lucia. His poetry is widely published and anthologized and he has published several collections of poems, most recently *Artifacts: Collected Poems* (2000). He edited *Roseau Valley and Other Poems for Brother George Odlum*, an anthology of St Lucian writing, in 2003.

Lucie-Smith, Edward (Jamaica, b. 1933) Edward Lucie-Smith grew up in Kingston, Jamaica, but moved to Britain in 1946. He has made his reputation as a prolific and influential art critic, having published more than sixty books on aspects of art history—including *Albert Huie: Father of Jamaican Painting* (2001). He is also a photographer and a poet. He has published several volumes of poetry, including *Changing Shape: Collected Poems* (2002). *Flesh and Stone*, a book of his photographs, was published in 2000.

Lyons, John (Trinidad, b. 1933) John Lyons is a Trinidadian-born painter and poet who settled in England in 1959 and studied painting there. His poetry is widely anthologized and he has published three collections, *Lure of the Cascadura* (1994), *Behind the Carnival* (1995), and *Voices from a Silk Cotton Tree* (2002). He has exhibited his paintings internationally.

Mais, Roger (Jamaica, 1905–1955) Roger Mais was an unconventional and controversial figure in his lifetime—he was imprisoned by the colonial authorities during the Second World War for writing a newspaper feature regarded as seditious. He published three important novels exploring Jamai-can identity and spirituality, *The Hills Were Joyful Together* (1953), *Brother Man* (1954), and *Black Lightning* (1955). A collection of his stories, *Listen, the Wind*, was published in 1986. His poetry has never been collected in a single volume but is represented in many anthologies of West Indian poetry.

Malé, Belkis Cuza (Cuba, b. 1942) A prolific poet, essayist, and journalist, Belkis Cuza Malé was famously married to the poet Heberto Padilla (see below) and went with him into exile in the USA in 1979. She lives in Miami where she founded, along with Padilla, the famous cultural review *Linden Lane Magazine*. Her books include *El Clavel y la rosa* (1984), a biography of the nineteenth-century Cuban poet Juana Borrero, and *Woman on the Front Lines* (1987), a collection of poems in English translation.

Malik (Delano Abdul Malik De Coteau) (Grenada, b. 1940) Malik is a poet and cultural activist, associated with the black power struggles in Trinidad in the late 1960s. He was later a leading figure in development of a voice/performance poetry movement in Trinidad, where he lived for some time. He currently lives and works in London. His most accessible collection is *Whirlwind* (1988).

Manley, Rachel (Jamaica, b. 1955) Rachel Manley was born in Cornwall, England, and grew up in Jamaica; a graduate of the University of the West Indies, she is a teacher, poet, and writer. She now lives between Toronto and Jamaica and is working on the third book of an autobiographical trilogy which includes *Drumblair: Memories of a Jamaican Childhood* (1996) and *Slipstream—A Daughter Remembers* (2000). She also edited *Edna Manley: The Diaries* (1989). Her poetry collections include *A Light Left On* (1992).

Markham, E. A. (Montserrat, b. 1939) After a boyhood in Montserrat, E. A. Markham settled in Britain in the mid-1950s. Poet, critic, playwright, dramatist, and editor, he has published many collections of poems, including *A Rough Climate* (2002) and *Human Rights: Selected Poems 1970–1982* (1984). He edited the *Penguin Book of Caribbean Short Stories* (1992) and the poetry anthology *Hinterland* (1989). Other recent publications include his novel *Marking Time* (1999) and the collection of stories *Taking the Drawing Room through Customs* (2002). He is Professor of Creative Writing at Sheffield Hallam University.

Mármol, José (Dominican Republic, b. 1960) A poet and essayist who has taught philosophy and linguistics at several universities in the Dominican Republic. In 1987 he won the Salomé Ureña national prize for poetry with his collection *La invención del día*, and in 1992 he won the Pedro Henríquez Ureña prize with *Lengua del paraíso*. Recent publications include *Amigo del hogar* (1999) and *Premi-sas para morir* (1999).

Marson, Una (Jamaica, 1905–1965) Regarded as the first serious woman poet of the Anglophone West Indies, Una Marson came to London from Jamaica in 1932. She worked for the BBC and later served as an assistant to Emperor Haille Sellasi during his exile in London. On her return to Jamaica she helped establish a local publishing house. She published several collections of poems, all now long out of print, but in recent years her work has undergone a serious re-examination and her poems appear in many anthologies of Caribbean writing.

Mathews, Mark (Guyana, b. 1937) After the traditional 'sound colonial education' in Guyana, Mark Mathews worked in broadcasting as a producer and presenter through the 1950s. He was also a tutor in drama at the Cyril Potter Teachers Training College. In the 1960s he was in London as a freelance reporter, involved with the UK Black Power movement and alternative theatre productions. He was closely involved with the Caribbean Artists movement. His first collection of poems, *Guyana My Alter*, won the 1987

Guyana Prize for Poetry and a second collection, *A Season of Sometimes*, was published in 1992.

Matos, Luis Palés (Puerto Rico, 1898–1959) A radical poet and essayist, Luis Palés Matos was an early exponent of what became known as Afro-Antillean poetry, which explored the African roots of Caribbean culture and the potential of Afro-Puerto Rican creole as a vehicle for poetry. The major collection of his work is *Poesias, 1915–1956* (1957).

Mbala (Michael Bailey) (Jamaica, b. 1953) Dub and performance poet Mbala has been active in Jamaica since the 1970s, and has performed in venues around the region and internationally. He works in theatre as a designer for several Jamaican theatre companies, including Sistren. In Jamaica he works with musicians in various combinations, including the drum group Akwaaba de Drummers and The Papiumba Big Band. His poetry is included in several recent anthologies and has been collected on CD. He is Vice-President of the Poetry Society of Jamaica.

McDonald, Ian (Trinidad/Guyana, b. 1933) Ian McDonald grew up in Trinidad but has lived in Guyana for more than forty years. A poet, novelist, essayist, and editor in his literary life, he is also the Chief Executive Officer of the Sugar Association of the Caribbean. His novel *The Hummingbird Tree* (1969) was made into a BBC television film. He has been the editor of the leading Guyanese literary journal *Kyk-Over-Al* for more than a decade. His poetry is widely anthologized and he has published several collections in recent years, including *Essequibo* (1992), which won the Guyana Prize and *From Silence to Silence* (2003). His early work is collected in *Jaffo the Calypsonian* (1994). In 1998 he was awarded an honorary doctorate by the University of the West Indies in recognition of his contribution to West Indian literature.

McFarlane, Basil (Jamaica, b. 1922) A journalist and art critic as well as a poet, Basil McFarlane was also active in Jamaican theatre. He published a pamphlet collection of poems, *Jacob and the Angel*, in A. J. Seymour's Miniature Poets series in 1952. His poems have appeared in regional magazines and anthologies and his poem here, 'Arawak Prologue', has become a foundation poem of West Indian poetry.

McKay, Claude (Jamaica, 1889–1948) Claude McKay became famous as a figure in the Harlem Renaissance in the 1920s but in terms of Caribbean writing he had already made an important impact with his two volumes of 'dialect verse', *Songs of Jamaica* and *Constab Ballads*, both published in 1912. The poems in those two collections represent the first serious attempt, in the Anglophone Caribbean, to represent and use versions of the 'language of life' in the islands as a vehicle for literature. McKay went on to write novels, stories, travelogues, essays, and several collections of poetry. His poetry is most accessibly available in *Claude McKay: Selected Poetry* (1999), edited by Joan R. Sherman.

McNeil, Anthony (Jamaica, 1941–1996) Anthony McNeil studied creative writing at Johns Hopkins University and the University of Massachusetts. He worked as a journalist, radio producer, and writing tutor. He co-edited, with Neville Dawes, the Carifesta anthology *The Caribbean Poem* (1976). His poetry collections include *Reel from 'The Life Movie'* (1972), *Credences at the Altar of Cloud* (1979), and *Chinese Lanterns from the Blue Child* (1998) which won the 1995 Una Marson Literary Award.

McWatt, Mark (Guyana, b. 1947) Mark McWatt is Professor of West Indian Literature at the University of the West Indies in Barbados. He has published two collections of poetry, *Interiors* (1989) and *The Language of Eldorado* (1994), which won the Guyana Prize. He has published many essays and articles on aspects of West Indian literature in academic and literary journals. He co-edited, with Hazel Simmons-McDonald, the anthology for Caribbean schools *A World of Poetry* (1995).

Miller, Jeanette (Dominican Republic, b. 1944) Jeanette Miller is an art critic and curator as well as a poet. Her publications include many critical studies of art history and architecture, including *Modern and Contemporary Art of the Dominican Republic* (1996). She has also published several collections of poetry, including *Identification Tags* (1985).

Mir, Pedro (Dominican Republic, 1913–2000) The son of a Puerto Rican mother and a Cuban father, Pedro Mir was born in 1913 in San Pedro de Macorís. Opposed to the dictatorship of Trujillo, Mir went into exile as a young man and only returned to live in the Dominican Republic in 1968. His poem *Hay un país en el mundo* [There is a Country in the World] was published in Cuba in 1949, and his most admired work, *The Countersong to Walt Whitman*, was first published in Guatemala in 1952. In addition to his poetry, Mir is the author of political essays, a study of aesthetics, and a novel, *Cuando amaban las tierras comuneras* [When They Loved the Communal Land]. In the late 1960s and early 1970s, Pedro Mir's poetry readings drew huge crowds and he came to be regarded as the poet laureate of the Dominican people.

Monar, Rooplal (Guyana, b. 1945) Rooplal Monar grew up on a sugar estate in Guyana and has worked as a teacher, an estate book keeper, a journalist, and a healer. He has published several novels, collections of stories, and a collection of poetry, *Koker* (1987). His most recent publications include two popular novels, *Ramsingh Street* (1999) and *Tormented Wives* (1999). In 1987 Rooplal Monar's contribution to Guyanese writing was recognized by the judges of the Guyana Prize for Literature.

Mordecai, Pam (Jamaica, b. 1942) A freelance writer, publisher, editor, teacher, and children's author, Pam Mordecai is also an accomplished and original poet. She has edited several anthologies of Caribbean writing, including *Her True-True Name* (1999), which she co-edited with her sister Betty Wilson. She also runs the Sandberry Press, a small press devoted to publishing Caribbean poetry. Her own collections of poetry include *Journey Poem* (1989) and *Certifiable* (2001). Pam Mordecai was awarded the Institute of Jamaica Centenary Award. She now lives in Toronto.

Morejón, Nancy (Cuba, b. 1944) Described by one critic as 'the best-known black woman poet in Spanish America' Nancy Morejón is one of Cuba's most accomplished contemporary poets. Often described as the poet of Havana and its people, she studied French language and literature at the University of Havana and has published several critical works and volumes of translation. Nancy Morejón has been publishing poems since the early 1960s and has travelled the world giving talks and readings. She has published many books of poems, including, most recently, the bilingual collection *Looking Within/Mirar Adentro: Selected Poems, 1954–2000* (2003), edited by Juanamaría Cordones-Cook. Among many other prizes Nancy Morejón was awarded the 2001 National Prize for Literature.

Morris, Mervyn (Jamaica, b. 1937) Poet, critic, and editor, Mervyn Morris recently retired as the Professor of West Indian Literature at the University of the West Indies, Jamaica. Editor of several important anthologies of Caribbean writing, including *Voiceprint* (1989) and *The Faber Book of Caribbean Short Stories* (1990), he has published several collections of his own poems, including *Examination Centre* (1995). He also published a collection of his literary essays, *Is English We Speaking* (1999), which won the Una Marson Literary Award.

Mutabaruka (Jamaica, b. 1952) A performance poet and musician, Mutabaruka is the most prolific member of a generation of poets—including Michael Smith and Oku Onuora—who have established a popular audience for a voiced poetry grounded in the lived experience of 'ordinary' Jamaicans. He has published several collections of poetry and his work is available on record and video. His recent CD collections include *Mutabaruka: The Ultimate Collection* (2000) and *Check It* (2001).

Narain, Jit (Surinam, b. 1948) Growing up in rural Surinam in a Hindu community, Jit Narain has become an important voice for that cultural experience in the literature of Surinam. After completing his secondary education in Paramaribo, he went to the Netherlands to study medicine. He lived in the Netherlands for more than twenty years, working as a doctor but also beginning to write in Sarnami, the language of the Hindu community of Surinam. He established a writers' group, published a journal, and in 1978 published his first volume of poetry, *Dal bhat chatni* [Rice, Yellow Peas, Chutney]. In 1991 he returned to Surinam, where he continues to work as a doctor. He has published several more books of poems, some written in Dutch, some in Sarnami.

Nichols, Grace (Guyana, b. 1950) A novelist, childrens' author, and poet, Grace Nichols has lived in Britain since 1977. Her first book of poems, *i is a long memoried woman* (1983), won the Commonwealth Literature Prize and established her reputation. She also published *The Fat Black Woman's Poems* (1984) and *Lazy Thoughts of a Lazy Woman* (1989). Her most recent collection, *Sunris*, won the 1996 Guyana Prize for Poetry. Her novel, *Whole of a Morning Sky* (1986), is based on her remembered childhood in Guyana. In 2000 she received a Cholmondeley Award from the Society of Authors.

Onuora, Oku (Jamaica, b. 1952) Oku Onuora was among the founders of the dub poetry movement in Jamaica. Released early from a prison term, in part because of the success of his writing, Oku Onuora (at that point still using the name Orlando Wong) published his first collection of poems, *Echo*, in 1977. His first recording, *Reflection in Red*, soon followed. Since then he has established an international reputation as a powerful performer. In 1998 a new collection of poems, *Fuel For Fire*, appeared, and his recent CDs include *Dubbin Away* (1999) and *Overdub: Tribute to King Tubby* (2000).

Padilla, Heberto (Cuba, 1932–2000) Heberto Padilla was a controversial figure in Cuban literature. An outspoken critic of Fidel Castro, he was exiled—with his wife, the poet Belkis Cuza Malé (see above)—to the USA in 1979. His most celebrated and daring book was *Fuera del Juego* [Out of the Game], published in 1968, which won Cuba's leading literary prize but was condemned by the government and led to Padilla's eventual imprisonment. In exile, Padilla published a novel *En mi jardín pastan los héroes* [Heroes Graze My Garden] in 1984. He also wrote a memoir of his two decades under Castro, *La mala memoria*, published in English as *Self-Portrait of the Other* (1990). In English translation his poems were published as *Legacies: Selected Poems* (1984) and *A Fountain, A House of Stone: Poems* (1992).

Perez-Firmat, Gustavo (Cuba, b. 1950) Gustavo Perez-Firmat migrated to the US from Cuba in 1961. A poet, fiction writer, and scholar, he is the David Feinson Professor of Humanities at Columbia University. His many books of cultural and literary criticism include *The Cuban Condition* (1989), *Life on the Hyphen* (1994), and *Cincuenta Lecciones de Exilio y de Sexilio* (2000). His poetry is collected in *Bilingual Blues: Poems, 1981–1994* (1995).

Persaud, Sasenarine (Guyana, b. 1958) Award-winning poet, novelist, and essayist Sasenarine Persaud left Guyana for Canada in his early twenties. He has published two novels and several collections of poems, including *A Surf of Sparrows* (1996), *The Hungry Sailor* (2000), and *A Writer Like You* (2002).

The title story of his collection of stories, *Canada Geese and Apple Chatney* (1999), is included in *The Oxford Book of Caribbean Short Stories*. He received the 1996 K. M. Hunter Foundation Emerging Artist Award for his fiction and the 1999 Arthur Schomburg Award for his pioneering of Yogic Realism and outstanding achievement as a writer. He now lives in Miami.

Perse, Saint-John (Marie René Auguste Alexis Léger) (Guadeloupe, 1887–1975) Marie René Auguste Alexis Léger was born on St Léger des Feuilles, a small family-owned coral island in the French overseas department of Guadeloupe. His father, Amédée Léger, was a lawyer. The family of Perse's mother were plantation owners. The first ten years of his life Perse spent in and around Guadeloupe. In 1899 the family moved to France and Perse became deeply embedded in French culture. His first collection of poems, *ÉLOGES*, which appeared in 1910, celebrates his lost Caribbean childhood. A much-travelled and complicated man, he published several further—widely acclaimed—collections of poems. He was awarded the Nobel Prize for Literature in 1960.

Philip, Marlene Nourbese (Trinidad, b. 1947) Born in Tobago, Marlene Nourbese Philip is a poet, playwright, and novelist who now lives in Toronto. She did her first degree at the University of the West Indies and then moved to Canada for postgraduate studies at the University of Western Ontario. Although primarily a poet, Marlene Nourbese Philip also writes both fiction and non-fiction. She has published several books of poetry, including *Salmon Courage* (1983) and *She Tries Her Tongue; Her Silence Softly Breaks* (1988) which won the Casa de las Américas Prize. Her novels include *Harriet's Daughter* (1988) and *Looking for Livingstone: An Odyssey of Silence* (1991). She has also published collections of essays, including *Genealogy of Resistance and Other Essays* (1997).

Philoctète, René (Haiti, 1932–1995) René Philoctète was born in Jérémie (Haiti). He was one of the founders of the 'Spiralisme' movement in Haitian poetry and an important figure in twentieth-century Haitian literature. His work is collected in the volumes *Caraïbe: Poème* (1995) and *Poèmes des îles qui marchent* (2003). His work has not been widely translated into English.

Philp, Geoffry (Jamaica, b. 1958) A Jamaican-born novelist, poet, and short story writer, Geoffry Philp is the author of a novel, *Benjamin, My Son* (2003), and four poetry collections, including *Florida Bound* (1998) and *Xango Music* (2001). He has also written a book of short stories, *Uncle Obediah and the Alien* (1997). Philp has won many awards for his work, including a James Michener Fellowship at the University of Miami, where he earned his Master of Arts in Creative Writing.

Phipps, Marilene (Haiti, b. 1950) An artist and poet of Haitian/French heritage, Marilene Phipps spent her early life in Haiti. She studied anthropology at the University of California, Berkeley and is an MFA graduate of the University of Pennsylvania, Philadelphia. An award-winning painter, exhibiting internationally, Marilene Phipps has also written six books of poetry, including *Crossroads and Unholy Water* (2000) which won the 1999 Crab Orchard Review Poetry Prize.

Polius, Joseph (Martinique, b. 1942) A radical poet and cultural activist, Joseph Polius, who works as a social security officer in Martinique, has been publishing poems in journals and anthologies since the 1960s. Among other books, he has published two collections of poems, *Bonheur de poche* (1968) and *Martinique debout* (1977).

Pollard, Velma (Jamaica, b. 1937) Velma Pollard is a retired senior lecturer who taught in language education at the University of the West Indies, Jamaica. Her poems and stories have appeared in many regional and international journals and anthologies. She has published a novel, two collections of short fiction, and three books of poetry, including *The Best Philosophers I Know Can't Read or Write* (2001). Her novella *Karl* won the Casa de las Américas Prize in 1992.

Portalatin, Aida Cartagena (Dominican Republic, 1918–1994) Aida Cartagena Portalatin was a short story writer, poet, novelist, literary critic, feminist scholar, and educator. During her lifetime she published more than twenty books. Her novel *Escalera para Electra* (1969) won the Premio Seix Barral in Barcelona. A bilingual edition of her poem *Yania Tierra* was published in the USA in 1995. She was awarded the Medal of Merit for Women by the President of the Dominican Republic.

Questel, Victor (Trinidad, 1949–1982) One of Trinidad's most promising young writers, Victor Questel was a dramatist, poet, and literary critic. He died tragically in 1982 at the age of 33, just a year after finishing his PhD. His poetry is widely anthologized and his collections of poetry include *Score* (1972), with Anson Gonzalez, *On Mourning Ground* (1979), and *Hard Stares* (1992).

Rahim, Jennifer (Trinidad, b. 1963) Jennifer Rahim's first collection of poems, *Mothers Are Not the Only Linguists*, was published in 1992, followed by *Between the Fence and the Forest* (2002). She also writes short fiction and criticism. She currently lectures in English at the University of the West Indies in Trinidad.

Ramkissoon-Chen, Rajandaye (Trinidad, b. 1936) Rajandaye Ramkissoon-Chen is a gynaecologist and obstetrician who began writing in the 1980s. Her poems have been published in journals and anthologies across the region and she has published two collections, *Ancestry* (1997) and *Mirror Eye* (1998).

Rankine, Claudia (Jamaica, b. 1963) Claudia Rankine was born in Jamaica in 1963. She earned her BA in English from Williams College and her MFA in poetry from Columbia University. She is the author of three collections of poetry, including *PLOT* (2001), *The End of the Alphabet* (1998), and *Nothing in Nature is Private* (1995), which received the Cleveland State Poetry Prize. Her work has appeared in the *Boston Review*, *jubilat*, the *Kenyon Review*, and numerous other journals. Claudia Rankine teaches English at Barnard College and lives in New York.

Retamar, Roberto Fernández (Cuba, b. 1930) One of the most renowned Cuban poets of his generation, Roberto Fernández Retamar is a prolific essayist and cultural critic. He has been closely associated with the development of the Cuban revolution. He began publishing poetry in 1950 and quickly established a reputation by winning the National Poetry Prize in 1952. Retamar was the Cuban Cultural Attaché in Paris in the late 1950s. Returning to Cuba, he became the director of the cultural organization Casa de las Americas, a position he held for many years. He is the author of several volumes of poems, including *Here* (1994) and *Verses* (2000). He has received many awards and honours for his work.

Roach, Eric (Trinidad and Tobago, 1915–1974) Eric Merton Roach was born at Mount Pleasant, Tobago. A poet, playwright, teacher, and journalist, Eric Roach stayed almost all his life in Tobago, struggling to make a career as a writer, and refused offers of university scholarships which would have taken him abroad. Finally disillusioned by the struggle, the lack of tangible success, and the direction he saw West Indian literature taking, he committed suicide in 1974. Although his poems were published in journals and anthologies across the region, there was no collection of Roach's poems in his lifetime. In 1992 his collected poems were published as *The Flowering Rock: Collected Poems 1938–1974* by the Peepal Tree Press. He was awarded the Trinidad and Tobago National Hummingbird Gold Medal posthumously in 1974.

Rodríguez, Reina María (Cuba, b. 1952) Born in Havana, Reina María Rodríguez studied Latin American literature at the University of Havana. A prolific writer and cultural critic, she has published several volumes of poetry, including *Para un Cordero Blanco* (1984) and *La Foto del Invernadero* (1998), both of which won the Casa de las Americas prize, and *On the Dark Day of the Tracks* (2002). In English translation her work is collected in *Time's Arrest/La detención del tiempo* (2001) and *Violet Island and Other Poems* (2003), both translated by Kristin Dykstra. Reina María Rodríguez now edits *Azoteas*, a magazine of poetry and poetics.

Roumain, Jacques (Haiti, 1907–1944) Jacques Roumain was one of the generation of Haitian/Caribbean writers who first looked to Africa to connect with their cultural roots. In 1934 he founded the Haitian Communist Party, but was forced into exile. He returned only in 1941, just three years before his death. His novel *Masters of the Dew* was published posthumously and is recognized now as one of the great Caribbean novels of the period. Roumain's poetry is collected in the anthology *When the Tom-Tom Beats: Selected Prose and* Poetry (1995).

Royes, Heather (Jamaica, b. 1943) Born in Kingston, Jamaica, Heather Royes studied journalism and mass communications at the University of the West Indies and at universities in the USA. Beginning her career as a journalist and media professional, she lived and travelled in various countries. She has also been a diplomat and—since 1989—a consultant to international agencies in project design and development for social issues and recently for HIV/AIDS. Her poetry has been appearing in journals and anthologies since 1977 and won various literary prizes. Her collection *The Caribbean Raj* was published in 1996.

Salkey, Andrew (Jamaica, 1928–1995) A novelist, poet, anthologist, and critic, Andrew Salkey was one of that generation of West Indian writers who came to Britain in the 1950s to find publishers and an audience. He published many books across the whole range of Caribbean letters, including his *Georgetown Journal* (1972) and, most recently, the posthumous collection of his previously uncollected stories *In the Border Country* (1998). His poetry is collected in several volumes, including *Jamaica* (1974), *Away* (1980), and *In the Hills Where Her Dreams Live* (1981). Andrew Salkey moved to the USA in 1976, where he was Professor of Writing at the University of Amherst.

Sarduy, Pedro Pérez (Cuba, b. 1943) A poet, writer, journalist, and broadcaster living in London, Pedro Pérez Sarduy is the author of *Surrealidad* (1967) and *Cumbite and Other Poems* (1990). He co-edited, with Jean Stubbs, *Afro-Cuba: An Anthology of Cuban Writing on Race, Politics and Culture* (1993). Pedro Pérez Sarduy and Jean Stubbs also co-edited the critical anthology *Afro-Cuban Voices* (2000).

Scott, Dennis (Jamaica, 1939–1991) A playwright, actor, dancer, critic, and teacher, as well as being a fine poet, Dennis Scott was a powerful force in Jamaican cultural life. His poetry is collected in the Commonwealth Literature Prize-winning volume *Uncle Time* (1973), in *Dreadwalk* (1982), and in *Strategies* (1979). His plays are published in various collections of West Indian drama.

Sekou, Lasana M. (Aruba/St Martin, b. 1959) Lasana M. Sekou is the pen name of H. H. Lake. He was born on Aruba of parents from St Maarten, but he grew up on the partly French, partly Dutch island of St Martin. He studied at the State University of New York and at Howard University. He has published poetry, short stories, and works of cultural history. His poetry publications include *Mother Nation: Poems from 1984 to 1987* (1991), *Quimbe:*

Poetics of Sound (1991), and *Big Up St. Martin—Essay and Poem* (1999). He is also active as publisher with the House of Nehesi Publishers, which he founded. In 1994 Lasana M. Sekou was awarded the James Michener Fellowship by the University of Miami's Caribbean Writers Institute, and in 1998 the University of St Martin honoured Sekou with its Heroes and Heroines Award for Poetry.

Senior, Olive (Jamaica, b. 1941) Olive Senior grew up in rural Jamaica and much of her work grows out of that experience. She has been the editor of *Jamaica Journal*, and published several works on aspects of Caribbean culture, including most recently the magnificent *Encyclopedia of Jamaican Heritage* (2003). She is the author of three books of short stories—*Summer Lightning* (1986), *Arrival of the Snake-Woman* (1989), and *Discerner of Hearts* (1995)—and two books of poetry—*Talking of Trees* (1985) and *Gardening in the Tropics* (1994). In 1987, she won the inaugural Commonwealth Writers Prize for *Summer Lightning*. Olive Senior was awarded the Institute of Jamaica Centenary Medal for creative writing. She now lives in Canada.

Seymour, A. J. (Guyana, 1914–1989) Guyanese poet, editor, and critic, and one of the great men of West Indian letters. A. J. Seymour was the founder and editor of the literary journal *Kyk-Over-Al* and publisher of the Miniature Poets series in the 1950s. A prolific poet in his own right, his work is included in most of the region's anthologies, but his collections of poems—most of which were self-published—are much harder to find. A posthumous volume of his *Collected Poems 1937–1989* was published in New York in 2000.

Sherlock, Philip (Jamaica, 1902–2000) Sir Philip Sherlock was an historian, folklorist, and university administrator. Son of a Methodist minister, Philip Sherlock graduated from the University of London in 1927 with a first-class honours degree. He later served on Jamaica's pre-independence Legislative Council. In the late 1940s he was a member of the committee that established the University College of the West Indies, serving as its principal and later as vice chancellor when it became the University of the West Indies. He published poems in Caribbean journals and anthologies over several decades, but never published a collection. He died in Florida, aged 98.

Simmons-McDonald, Hazel (St Lucia, b. 1947) Hazel Simmons-McDonald studied at the University of the West Indies in Jamaica before gaining her MA and PhD from Stanford. She taught linguistics at Stanford for some time before joining the University of the West Indies in Barbados, where she is currently Dean and Senior Lecturer in Linguistics. Her poems have been published in regional journals and anthologies, and her first collection of poems is *Silk Cotton and Other Trees* (2004). She co-edited, with Mark McWatt, the anthology for Caribbean schools *A World of Poetry* (1995).

Simpson, Louis (Jamaica, b. 1923) Louis Simpson grew up in Jamaica but he emigrated to the USA at the age of seventeen. He studied at Columbia University, then served in the US airforce in the Second World War. His first book of poems, *The Arrivistes*, was published in France in 1949. He worked for some time in a publishing house in New York, before becoming a distinguished literary academic, teaching at Columbia, the University of California at Berkeley, and the State University of New York. His many poetry publications include *The Owner of the House: New Collected Poems, 1940–2001* (2003) and *At the End of the Open Road, Poems* (1963), for which he won the Pulitzer Prize. His critical works include *Ships Going Into the Blue: Essays and Notes on Poetry* (1994). Louis Simpson lives in Setauket, New York.

Smith, Michael (Jamaica, 1954–1983) Perhaps the best known and most subtle of the dub poets, Michael Smith graduated from the Jamaica School of Drama with a diploma in theatre arts in 1980. He represented Jamaica at the Barbados Carifesta in 1981. In 1982, Smith performed at the Black Book Fair and he was filmed by BBC Television performing 'Mi Cyaan Believe It' for the documentary *From Brixton To Barbados*. He also recorded his *Mi Cyaan Believe It* album for Island Records. He died in tragic circumstances in Jamaica at the age of 29. A collection of Michael Smith's work, *It a Come*, edited by Mervyn Morris, was published in 1986.

St. John, Bruce (Barbados, 1923–1995) Bruce St. John was a multi-talented figure who trained as a classical singer, and took a diploma in physical education, before he became a lecturer in Spanish at the University of the West Indies in Barbados. A man of the theatre, he was one of the region's wittiest writers, his poetry exploring the voices and characters of Barbados in ways that anticipate the concerns and strategies of a later generation of West Indian writers. His poetry collections include *Bumbatuk* (1982) and *Joyce and Eros and Varia*. His work is included in several regional anthologies.

Suárez, Virgil (Cuba, b. 1962) Virgil Suárez left Havana for the USA in 1974. He holds an MFA in creative writing (1987) from Louisiana State University and is currently a professor of creative writing at Florida State University. He has written several novels, and published many short stories, essays, and collections of poetry. His recent publications include *Guide to the Blue Tongue: Poems* (2003), *Infinite Refuge* (2002), and *Banyan: Poems* (2001). He was the recipient of an award from the National Endowment for the Arts in Poetry, in 2001–2002.

Sylvain, Patrick (Haiti, b. 1966) Patrick Sylvain grew up in Port-au-Prince, moving to the USA at the age of fifteen. He completed graduate studies at Harvard and lives in Cambridge, Massachusetts, where he works as a bilingual public school teacher and develops educational materials. He is also a video-photographer and has published three volumes of poetry, a play, a short story collection, and a novel. He was a founding member of the Haitian American Writers' Coalition.

Telemaque, Harold M. (Trinidad, 1909–1982) Although born in Tobago, Harold Telemaque spent virtually all his adult life in Trinidad, where he was a teacher. Co-author—with A. M. Clarke—of an early collection of poems, *Burnt Bush*, which was published in 1947, Telemaque is one of that cultural-nationalist generation of West Indian poets whose concerns laid the ground for the development of an 'independent' West Indian literature. His work is acknowledged in many of the studies of the evolution of West Indian literature in the twentieth century.

Thompson, Ralph (Jamaica, b. 1928) Ralph Thompson was born in the USA, but his Jamaican mother returned to the island when he was three. After earning his Doctor of Law degree at Fordham University in New York, he served for two years as an officer in the US Air Force in Japan, after which he returned to Jamaica and started his career as businessman, painter, and poet. He is a regular broadcaster and panelist on Jamaican radio and contributor of articles to Jamaica's press. He has published three collections of poems, *The Denting of a Wave* (1993), *Moving On* (1998), and *View from Mount Diabalo* (2003), which won the 2001 Jamaican National Literary Award. He was awarded the CD (Commander of Distinction) in the Jamaican National Honours of 1988.

Tirolien, Guy (Guadeloupe, 1917–1988) Guy Tirolien was born and educated in Pointe-à-Pitre. After university studies in France—where he met and worked with Leopold Sedar Senghor and Aimé Césaire—he then served in the French diplomatic corps in Africa for more than thirty years. He published two major collections of poetry, *Balles d'or* (1961) and *Feuilles vivantes au matin* (1977).

Trefossa (H. F. De Ziel) (Surinam, 1916–1975) Trefossa was the first poet from Surinam to publish a collection, *Trotji* (1957), in Sranan, the vernacular creole language of the country. His work was taken up by the cultural nationalist movement and was much admired, but has hardly been available in translation. He settled in Holland, where he died, in 1975.

Vaughan, H. A. (Barbados, 1901–1985) Politician, judge, and historian, Hilton A. Vaughan was one of the pioneer generation of West Indian poets whose work set the scene for the development of a self-consciously Caribbean poetry. He was for some time the Barbados ambassador to the USA and UN. He published the collection *Sandy Lane* in 1945, and it was reprinted in 1985. Several of his poems are regarded as classics of early West Indian writing and have been included in various regional anthologies.

Vicioso, Chiqui (Sherezada) (Dominican Republic, b. 1948) Poet, dramatist, and essayist, Chiqui Vicioso has published several collections of poems, including *Viaje desde el agua* (1981), *Un extraño ulular traía el viento* (1985), and *Internamiento* (1992). She has also published literary essays including *Salomé Ureña: A cien años de un magisterio* (1997) and *Algo que decir: ensayos sobre literatura feminina, 1981–1997* (1998).

Virtue, Vivian (Jamaica, 1911–1998) Vivian Virtue was a poet, translator, and broadcaster. He belonged to the Poetry League of Jamaica and published a substantial collection of poems, *Wings of the Morning*, in Kingston in 1938. Virtue migrated to Britain in the 1960s and continued to write, though he published relatively little through the rest of his life. A posthumous collection, *Wings of the Evening: Selected Poems*, edited by A. L. McLeod, was published in 2002.

Walcott, Derek (St Lucia, b. 1930) Poet, painter, dramatist, and essayist, Derek Walcott has received many literary honours including the Queens Gold Medal for Poetry and, in 1992, the Nobel Prize for Literature. His recent poetry publications include *Tiepelo's Hound* (2000), *Collected Poems 1948–1984* (1985), and *Omeros* (1992). A collection of his essays, *What the Twilight Says*, was published in 1998.

Yañez, Mirta (Cuba, b. 1947) Mirta Yañez is a prize-winning writer and professor of Latin American literature at the University of Havana in Cuba. She has edited numerous collections of short stories, poetry, and critical essays. Her poetry publications include *Las visitas y otros poemas* (1986) and *Algún lugar en ruinas* (1997). Her works have also appeared in many anthologies of Caribbean writing.

SOURCES AND
ACKNOWLEDGEMENTS

Opal Palmer Adisa: 'Madness Disguises Sanity' from *Tamarind and Mango Women* (Sister Vision Press, 1992)

John Agard: 'Pan Recipe', © 1982 by John Agard, and 'Limbo Dancer at Immigration', © 1982 by John Agard, from *Weblines* (Bloodaxe, 2000), reprinted by permission of John Agard c/o Caroline Sheldon Literary Agency

Lillian Allen: 'Mrs' from *Utterances and Incantations: 12 Female Dub Poets from the Black Diaspora*, edited by Afua Cooper (Sister Vision Press, 1999), reprinted by permission of the author

Phyllis Shand Allfrey: 'Love for an Island' from *Palm and Oak* (1973; private publication), © Phyllis Shand Allfrey, reprinted by permission of Curtis Brown Ltd, London, on behalf of The Phyllis Shand Allfrey Estate

Julia Alvarez: 'Bilingual Sestina' from *Sisters of the Caliban: Contemporary Women Poets of the Caribbean—A Multilingual Anthology*, edited by M. J. Fenwick (Azul Editions, 1996), and 'Last Trees' from *Seven Trees* (Kat Ran Press, 2000), reprinted by permission of Susan Bergholz Literary Services

Frank Martinus Arion: 'I fell in deep snow . . . ' from *Callaloo*, 21: 3 (1998), 533, © Charles H. Rowell, reprinted by permission of The Johns Hopkins University Press

Maria Arrillaga: 'To the Poets of My Generation' from *Sisters of the Caliban: Contemporary Women Poets of the Caribbean—A Multilingual Anthology*, edited by M. J. Fenwick (Azul Editions, 1996)

Naomi Ayala: 'Personal History' from *Wild Animals on the Moon* (Curbstone Press, 1997)

Edward Baugh: 'The Carpenter's Complaint' and 'Sometimes in the Middle of the Story' from *It Was The Singing*. Caribbean Poetry Series No. 8 (Sandberry Press, 2000), reprinted by permission of the publisher (Toronto, Canada and Kingston, Jamaica)

Vera Bell: 'Ancestor on the Auction Block' from *The Independence Anthology of Jamaican Literature*, edited by A. L. Hendriks and C. Lindo (The Arts Celebration Committee of the Ministry of Development Welfare, Kingston, Jamaica, 1962)

Louise Bennett: 'Dutty Tough' and 'Jamaica Oman' from *Selected Poems* (Sangster's Book Store, 1982)

James Berry: 'Cut-Way Feelins' from *Lucy's Letters and Loving* (New Beacon Books, 1982), and 'Letter to My Father from London' from *Hot Earth Cold Earth* (Bloodaxe Books, 1995), reprinted by permission of the author

Dionne Brand: 'Return' from *No Language is Neutral* (McClelland & Stewart, 1998), reprinted by permission of the publisher

Kamau Brathwaite: 'The visibility trigger' from *X/Self* (Oxford University Press, 1987), reprinted by permission of the author; 'South' from *Arrivants: A New World Trilogy* (Oxford University Press, 1973), reprinted by permission of the publisher; 'Milkweed' from *Mother Poem* (Oxford University Press, 1977), and 'from Sun Poem' from *Sun Poem* (Oxford University Press, 1982), reprinted by permission of the author; 'The SilverSands Poem' from *Words Need Love Too* (House of Nehesi Publishers, 2000), reprinted by permission of the publisher

Jean 'Binta' Breeze: 'Riddym Ravings (The Mad Woman's Poem)' from *Riddym Ravings* (Race Today Publications, 1988), reprinted by permission of the author, and 'Ratoon' from *On the Edge of an Island* (Bloodaxe Books, 1997), reprinted by permission of the publisher

Jean Brièrre: 'Here I Am Again, Harlem' from *Callaloo*, 15:3 (1992)

Wayne Brown: 'The Witness' from *Voyages* (Inprint Caribbean, 1989), reprinted by permission of the author

Julia de Burgos: 'To Julia de Burgos' from *Song of the Simple Truth: the Complete Poems of Julia de Burgos*, edited by Jack Agueros (Curbstone Press, 1997), © 1996 Jack Agueros; 'Poem with the Final Tune' from *Callaloo*, 21: 3 (1998), © Charles H. Rowell, reprinted by permission of The Johns Hopkins University Press

Edgar Cairo: 'Child of a New Tide' from *Callaloo*, 21: 3 (1998), © Charles H. Rowell, reprinted by permission of The Johns Hopkins University Press

George Campbell: 'Negro Aroused' from *First Poems* (Garland Publishing, 1981)

Vahni Capildeo: 'In Cunaripo' from *No Traveller Returns* (Salt Publishing, 2003), reprinted by permission of the publisher

Marie-Magdeleine Carbet: 'Would I Deny?' from *Through A Black Veil: Readings in French Caribbean Poetry*, edited by E. Anthony Hurley (Africa World Press, 2000), reprinted by permission of E. Anthony Hurley

Peggy Carr: 'Flight of the Firstborn' from *Fresh Tracks in an Ancient Land* (1996; private publication), reprinted by permission of the author

Martin Carter: 'University of Hunger', 'Poems of Shape and Motion', 'Proem' and 'Being Always' from *Selected Poems* (Red Thread Women's Press, 1997), reprinted by permission of Phyllis Carter

Lourdes Casal: 'Poem' from *Pacific Quarterly Moana*, Volume. 8, No.3 (1983) *One People's Grief*, edited by Robert Benson, reprinted by permission of Outrigger Publishers

Adrian Castro: 'Canto of the Tyrant Who Hangs Himself' from *The Archipeligo: New Caribbean Writing*. Special issue of *Conjunctions*, No. 27 (1996)

Jesus Cos Causse: 'I Could Say' from *Poems from Cuba* (Research and Publications Committee, University of the West Indies, 1977), reprinted by permission of the translator

Aimé Césaire: from *Notebook of a Return to the Native Land* (Wesleyan University Press, 2001), reprinted by permission of Clayton Eshleman and Annette Smith; 'Lost Body' from *Through A Black Veil: Readings in French Caribbean Poetry*, edited by E. Anthony Hurley (Africa World Press, 2000), reprinted by permission of E. Anthony Hurley; 'lagoonal calendar' and 'Wifredo Lam . . . ' from *Aimé Césaire: Lyric and Dramatic Poetry 1946–82* (Caraf Books/University of Virginia Press, 1990), reprinted by permission of Clayton Eshleman and Annette Smith; 'The Automatic Crystal' from *Aimé Césaire: The Collected Poetry* (University of California Press, 1983), reprinted by permission of Clayton Eshleman and Annette Smith

Brian Chan: 'To a Daughter' from *Fabula Rasa* (Peepal Tree Press, 1994), reprinted by permission of the publisher

Faustin Charles: 'The Red Robber' from *Days and Nights in the Magic Forest* (Bogle L'Overture Publications, 1986), reprinted by permission of the author and publisher

Michelle Cliff: 'The Land of Look Behind' from *The Land of Look Behind* (Firebrand Books, 1985)

Judith Ortiz Cofer: 'Under the Knife' from *Hispanic American Literature: a Brief Introduction and Anthology*, edited by Nicholas Kanellos (HarperCollins Publishers, 1995)

Marie-Thérèse Colimon: 'Encounter' from *The Literary Review*, 35: 4 (1992)

Merle Collins: 'Nearly Ten Years Later' from *Rotten Pomerack* (Virago, 1992), reprinted by permission of Time Warner Books Group UK

Frank Collymore: 'Hymn to the Sea' from *Collected Poems* (1959), reprinted by permission of Mrs Ellice Collymore

Christine Craig: 'St Ann Saturday' from *A World of Poetry for CXC*, edited by Mark McWatt and Hazel McDonald-Simmonds (Heinemann, 1994)

Dennis Craig: 'Trader' from *Near the Seashore: Collected Poems* (Education & Development Services, 1999), reprinted by permission of Zellynne Jennings-Craig

Fred D'Aguiar: 'Frail Deposits' from *British Subjects* (Bloodaxe Books, 1993), reprinted by permission of the publisher

Cyril Dabydeen: 'Returning' from *Discussing Columbus* (Peepal Tree Press, 1997), reprinted by permission of the publisher

David Dabydeen: 'Coolie Odyssey' from *Turner: New & Selected Poems* (Jonathan Cape, 1994)

Léon-Gontran Damas: 'S.O.S' from *Through A Black Veil: Readings in French Caribbean Poetry*, edited by E. Anthony Hurley (Africa World Press, 2000), reprinted by permission of E. Anthony Hurley; 'So Often' from *The Negritude Poets*, edited by Ellen Conroy Kennedy (Thunder's Mouth Press, 1989, 1994), reprinted by permission of Ellen Conroy Kennedy

Mahadai Das: 'They Came in Ships' from *I Want To Be a Poetess of My People* (Guyana National Service Publishing Centre, Georgetown, 1977), reprinted by permission of Chandradai Chandler

Kwame Dawes: 'Shook Foil' from *Shook Foil* (Peepal Tree Press, 1997), and 'Sunday Morning' from *Prophets* (Peepal Tree Press, 1995), reprinted by permission of the publisher; 'Liminal' from *Midland* (Ohio University Press, 2001), reprinted by permission of the author and publisher

Neville Dawes: 'Acceptance' from *In Sepia* (1958), reprinted by permission of Kwame Dawes

René Dépestre: 'Ballad of a Little Lamp' from *The Negritude Poets*, edited by Ellen Conroy Kennedy (Thunder's Mouth Press, 1989, 1994), reprinted by permission of Ellen Conroy Kennedy; 'Black Ore' from *Facing the Sea: Selected Writings (CXC)*, edited by Anne Walmsley and Nick Caistor (Heinemann International Literature & Textbooks, 1986)

Mc Donald Dixon: 'Roseau—The Forgotten Village' from *Collected Poems 1961–2001* (Xlibris Corporation, 2003), © Mc Donald Dixon, 2001, reprinted by permission of the author

Robin Dobru: 'Jani (MP)' from *Revo and Love in the Sun* (1981; private publication)

SOURCES AND ACKNOWLEDGEMENTS

Marcia Douglas: 'The *Ascania* Docks in Southampton, circa 1955' from *Electricity Comes to Cocoa Bottom* (Peepal Tree Press, 1999), reprinted by permission of the publisher

Nydia Ecury: 'The Visit', published by permission of the author

Gloria Escoffery: 'Shelling Gungo Peas' from *Mother Jackson Murders the Moon* (Peepal Tree Press, 1998), reprinted by permission of the publisher

Martín Espada: 'Colibrí' from *Rebellion Is the Circle of a Lover's Hands* (Curbstone Press, 1990), reprinted by permission of the author; 'Imagine the Angels of Bread' from *Imagine the Angels of Bread: Poems* (W. W. Norton, 1997), © 1996 by Martín Espada, reprinted by permission of the publisher

Howard Fergus: 'Behind God Back' from *Lara Rains and Colonial Rites* (Peepal Tree Press, 1998), reprinted by permission of the publisher

Barbara Ferland: 'When They Come from the Island' from *Without Shoes I Must Run* (1994; private publication), reprinted by permission of Mark Ferland

John Figueroa: 'Christmas Breeze' and 'This Tree My Time Keeper' from *The Chase* (Peepal Tree Press, 1991), reprinted by permission of the publisher

Honor Ford-Smith: 'Swimming Lesson' and 'Lala the Dressmaker' from *My Mother's Last Dance* (Sister Vision Press, 1997)

Michael Gilkes: 'The Lighthouse' from *Joanstown and Other Poems* (Peepal Tree Press, 2002), reprinted by permission of the author

Margaret Gill: 'Poem for a Migrant Worker' from *Voices: An Anthology of Barbadian Writing* (National Cultural Foundation, Bridgetown, 1997), reprinted by permission of the author

Édouard Glissant: 'November', 'Wild Reading' and 'Slow Train' from *Black Salt* (University of Michigan Press, 1998), reprinted by permission of the publisher; 'Walkway of Lonely Death' from *Through a Black Veil: Readings in French Caribbean Poetry*, edited by E. Anthony Hurley (Africa World Press, 2000), reprinted by permission of E. Anthony Hurley

Anson Gonzalez: 'Tabiz' from *Collected Poems 1964–1979* (New Voices Publications, 1979), © Anson Gonzalez, reprinted by permission of the author

Lorna Goodison: 'For My Mother (May I Inherit Half Her Strength)' from *Guinea Woman: New and Selected Poems* (Carcanet Press, 2000), reprinted by permission of the author and publisher; 'Ground Doves' from *To Us All Flowers are Roses* (University of Illinois Press, 1995), reprinted by permission of the author; 'The yard man: An election poem' and 'Praise to the mother of Jamaican art' from *Controlling the Silver* (University of Illinois Press, 2004), reprinted by permission of the author

Jean Goulbourne: 'Sunday Crosses'

Cecil Gray: 'On the Road' from *Leaving the Dark* (Lilibel Publications, 1998), and 'Threading the Needle' from *Plumed Palms* (Lilibel Publications, 2000), reprinted by permission of the author

Stanley Greaves: 'Knees' from *Horizons* (Peepal Tree Press, 2002), reprinted by permission of the publisher

Nicolás Guillén: 'Senora', 'The Usurers', 'Hunger', 'Cyclone' and 'KKK' from *The Great Zoo and Other Poems*, edited by Robert Marquez (Monthly Review Press, 1981); 'Bars' from *My Last Name* (Mango Publishing, 2004), reprinted by permission of the publisher; 'Ballad of the Two Grandfathers' from *West*

Indies Ltd (1934); 'Wake for Papa Montero' from *Cuba Libre* (1948), reprinted by permission of David Higham Associates

Claire Harris: 'Child   this is the gospel on bakes' from *Drawing Down a Daughter* (Goose Lane Editions, 1992), © 1992 by Claire Harris, reprinted by permission of the publisher

Maggie Harris: 'Doors' from *Limbolands* (Mango Publishing, 1999), reprinted by permission of the publisher

Wilson Harris: 'Behring Straits' from *Eternity to Season* (New Beacon Books, 1978), reprinted by permission of the publisher

Albert Helman: 'Lullaby' from *Callaloo*, 21: 3 (1998), reprinted by permission of E. A. Markham

A. L. Hendriks: 'The Migrant' from *To Speak Simply: Selected Poems 1961–1986* (Hippopotamus Press, 1986), reprinted by permission of the publisher

Kendel Hippolyte: 'Revo Lyric' and 'Bedtime Story, W.I.' from *Birthright* (Peepal Tree Press, 1997), reprinted by permission of the publisher

Slade Hopkinson: 'The Madwoman of Papine' from *The Madwoman of Papine* (Curriculum Development Centre, Ministry of Education and Social Development, Georgetown, Guyana, 1976), reprinted by permission of Nalo Hopkinson

Arnold Harrichand Itwaru: 'body rites (chant five)' from *Body Rites* (TSAR Publications, 1991), reprinted by permission of the publisher

Cynthia James: 'Woman Descendant' from *La Vega and Other Poems* (G.V. Ferguson Ltd., 1995), © Cynthia James, reprinted by permission of the author

Mirlande Jean-Gilles: 'My Grandfather Danced' from *Caribbean Writer*, Volume 12 (1998), reprinted by permission of the author

Amryl Johnson: 'Far and High' from *Gorgons* (Cofa Press, 1992)

Linton Kwesi Johnson: 'Sense outta Nansense' from *Tings and Times: Selected Poems* (Bloodaxe Books, 1996), © Linton Kwesi Johnson, and 'Dread Beat An Blood' from *Dread Beat 'an Blood* (Bogle L'Overture Press, 1975), © Linton Kwesi Johnson, reprinted by permission of LKJ Music (Publishers)

E. Mc.G. 'Shake' Keane: 'Shaker Funeral' from *L'Oubli* (1950), and 'Soufrière (79)' from *The Volcano Suite* (1979; private publication), reprinted by permission of Julian Keane

Anthony Kellman: 'After the Rain' from *Watercourse* (Peepal Tree Press, 1990), reprinted by permission of the publisher

Jane King: 'Fellow Traveller' from *Fellow Traveller*. Caribbean Poetry Series No. 7 (Sandberry Press, 1994), reprinted by permission of Sandberry Press (Toronto, Canada and Kingston, Jamaica)

Roi Kwabena: 'Letter from Sea Lots' from *A Job For The Hangman* (Raka Publications, 1998)

John La Rose: 'Not From Here' from *Foundations* (New Beacon Books, 1966), reprinted by permission of the publisher

Léon Laleau: 'Betrayal' from *The Negritude Poets*, edited by Ellen Conroy Kennedy (Thunder's Mouth Press, 1989, 1994), © 1975 Ellen Conroy Kennedy, reprinted by permission of the translator

Tato Laviera: 'AmeRícan' from *Hispanic American Literature: a Brief Introduction and Anthology*, edited by Nicholas Kanellos (HarperCollins Publishers, 1995)

John Robert Lee: 'Vocation' and 'Lusca' from *Saint Lucian: Selected Poems 1967–1987* (Phelps Publishing Co, 1988), reprinted by permission of the author

Edward Lucie-Smith: 'Your Own Place' from *Changing Shape: New and Selected Poems* (Carcanet Press, 2002), reprinted by permission of the publisher

John Lyons: 'Crusoe's Thursday' from *Behind the Carnival* (Smith/Doorstop Books, 1994), reprinted by permission of the publisher

Roger Mais: 'All Men Come to the Hills' from *Caribbean Voices*, Volume 1 (1977)

Belkis Cuza Malé: 'My Mother's Homeland' from *New England Quarterly/ Broadloaf Review*, Volume VII, No. 4 (Summer 1985)

Malik: 'Instant Ting' from *The Whirlwind* (Panrun Collective, 1988), reprinted by permission of the author

Rachel Manley: 'Memory' from *A Light Left On* (Peepal Tree Press, 1992), reprinted by permission of the publisher

E. A. Markham: 'A History Without Suffering' from *Human Rites: Selected Poems 1970–1982* (Anvil Press Poetry, 1984), and 'Hurricane, Volcano, Mass Flight' from *A Rough Climate* (Anvil Press Poetry, 2002), reprinted by permission of the publisher

José Mármol: 'Abdication', published by permission of Ian Craig

Una Marson: 'Cameo' from *The Moth and the Star* (1937; private publication), © National Library of Jamaica, reprinted by permission of Delia Jarrett-Macauley

Mark Mathews: 'Mortal' from *A Season of Sometimes* (Peepal Tree Press, 1992), reprinted by permission of the publisher

Luis Palés Matos: 'Forbidden Fruit' from *Poesias, 1915–1956* (1957), published by permission of Ian Craig

Mbala: 'The History of Dub Poetry' from *Wheel and Come Again*, edited by Kwame Dawes (Peepal Tree Press, 1988), reprinted by permission of the author

Ian McDonald: 'Forest Path, Nightfall' and 'The Sun Parrots are Late This Year' from *Essequibo* (Peterloo Poets, 1992), reprinted by permission of the publisher

Basil McFarlane: 'Arawak Prologue' from *Seven Jamaican Poets*, edited by Mervyn Morris (Bolivar Press, 1971)

Claude McKay: 'The Harlem Dancer' from *Selected Poems of Claude McKay* (Harcourt Brace Jovanovich, 1953), and 'A Midnight Woman to the Bobby' from *The Passion of Claude McKay: Selected Poetry and Prose 1912–1948*, edited by Wayne Cooper (Schocken Books, 1973), reprinted by permission of the Literary Representative for the Works of Claude McKay, Schomburg Center for Research in Black Culture, The New York Public Library, Astor, Lenox and Tilden Foundations

Anthony McNeil: 'Ode to Brother Joe' from *Reel from 'the Life Movie'* (Savacou Publications, 1975); 'The Kingdom of Myth' from *Chinese Lanterns from the Blue Child* (Peepal Tree Press, 1998), reprinted by permission of the publisher

Mark McWatt: 'Nightfall: Kangaruma' from *The Language of El Dorado* (Dangeroo Press, 1994), reprinted by permission of the author

Jeanette Miller: 'Because Death is This Feeling' from *The Literary Review*, 35: 4 (1992)

Pedro Mir: 'Meditation on the Shores of Evening' from *Countersong to Walt Whitman and Other Poems* (Azul Editions, 1993)

Rooplal Monar: 'The Cowherd' from *Koker* (Peepal Tree Press, 1987), reprinted by permission of the publisher

Pam Mordecai: 'Last Lines' from *Journey Poem*. Caribbean Poetry Series No. 3 (Sandberry Press, 1989), reprinted by permission of Sandberry Press (Toronto, Canada and Kingston, Jamaica)

Nancy Morejón: 'Black Woman' from *Where the Island Sleeps Like a Wing: Selected Poems* (Black Scholar Press, 1985), reprinted by permission of Dr Robert Chrisman; 'April', 'Mother', and 'Grenadian Woman' from *Black Woman and Other Poems* (Mango Publishing, 2001), reprinted by permission of the publisher

Mervyn Morris: 'Valley Prince' from *The Pond* (New Beacon Books, 1973; n.ed. 1997), reprinted by permission of the publisher; 'Peelin Orange', published by permission of the author; 'Muse' from *Shadowboxing* (New Beacon Books, 1979), reprinted by permission of the publisher

Mutabaruka: 'dis poem' from *www.ireggae.com/muta.htm*

Jit Narain: 'Working all day, dreaming at night' from *enAgni ke yád yád ke rákhi/Ter Herinnering aan Agni* (Den Haag/Paramaribo, 1991), © 1991 Jit Narain, translation © Paul Vincent

Grace Nichols: 'The Fat Black Woman ReMembers' from *The Fat Black Woman's Poems* (Virago, 1984), © Grace Nichols, and 'Blackout' from *Sunris* (Virago, 1996), © Grace Nichols, reprinted by permission of Curtis Brown Ltd, London, on behalf of Grace Nichols

Oku Onuora: 'Pressure Drop' from *Echo* (Sangster's Book Store, 1977)

Heberto Padilla: 'In Trying Times' from *Pacific Quarterly Moana*, 8: 3 (1983) 'One People's Grief', edited by Robert Benson, reprinted by permission of Outrigger Publishers

Gustavo Pérez-Firmat: 'Lime Cure' from *Hispanic American Literature: a Brief Introduction and Anthology* by Nicholas Kanellos (HarperCollins Publishers, 1995), reprinted by permission of the author

Sasenarine Persaud: 'Postcard to a Sister in South America' from *The Hungry Sailor* (TSAR Publications, 2000)

Saint-John Perse: 'The Bells', 'The Wall', 'The City', 'Friday', and 'The Parrot' from 'Pictures for Crusoe', in *Eloges and Other Poems*. Bollingen Series (Princeton University Press, 1971), © 1971 by Princeton University Press, reprinted by permission of the publisher

Marlene Nourbese Philip: 'Fluttering Lives' from *Thorns* (Williams Wallace, 1980)

René Philoctète: 'Misery by Sunlight' from *Callaloo*, 15: 3 (1992), © Charles H. Rowell, reprinted by permission of The Johns Hopkins University Press

Geoffry Philp: 'Standpipe' from *Florida Bound* (Peepal Tree Press, 1995), reprinted by permission of the publisher

Marilene Phipps: 'My Life in Nérètte' from *Callaloo*, 19: 1 (1996), © Charles H. Rowell, reprinted by permission of The Johns Hopkins University Press

Joseph Polius: 'There are those who . . . ' from *Through A Black Veil: Readings in French Caribbean Poetry*, edited by E. Anthony Hurley (Africa World Press, 2000), reprinted by permission of E. Anthony Hurley

Velma Pollard: 'Beware the Naked Man Who Offers You a Shirt' from *The Best Philosophers I Know Can't Read and Write* (Mango Publishing, 2001), reprinted by permission of the publisher

SOURCES AND ACKNOWLEDGEMENTS

Aida Cartagena Portalatin: 'A Woman Alone' from *Del desconsuelo al compromiso/From desolation to compromise: a bilingual anthology of poetry of Aida Cartegena Portalatin* (Colección Montesino), edited by Daisy Cocco De Filippis (Taller, 1988), reprinted by permission of Daisy Cocco De Filippis

Victor Questel: 'Judge Dreadword' from *Hard Stares* (New Voices Publications, 1982), © Victor Questel, and 'Grandad' from *Near Mourning Ground* (New Voices Publications, 1979), © Victor Questel, reprinted by permission of the publisher

Jennifer Rahim: 'Leaving the Coast' from *Mothers Are Not the Only Linguists and Other Poems* (New Voices Publications, 1992), © Jennifer Rahim, reprinted by permission of the publisher

Rajandaye Ramkissoon-Chen: 'Still My Teacher' from *Ancestry* (Hansib Caribbean, 1997), reprinted by permission of Hansib Publications

Claudia Rankine: 'She' from *Nothing in Nature is Private*. CSU Poetry Series XLIV (Cleveland State University Center, 1995)

Roberto Fernández Retamar: 'How Lucky, the Normal' from *Revolutionary Poems* (Savacou Publications, 1974), and 'Where's Fernández?' from *Where's Fernández and Other Poems* (Editions Jose Marti, 2000)

Eric Roach: 'Love Overgrows a Rock' and 'The World of Islands' from *The Flowering Rock: Collected Poems 1938–74* (Peepal Tree Press, 1992), reprinted by permission of the publisher

Reina María Rodríguez: 'When a Woman Doesn't Sleep' from *Sisters of the Caliban: Contemporary Women Poets of the Caribbean—A Multilingual Anthology*, edited by M. J. Fenwick (Azul Editions, 1996)

Jacques Roumaine: 'Guinea' from *The Negritude Poets*, edited by Ellen Conroy Kennedy (Thunder's Mouth Press, 1989, 1994), reprinted by permission of David Higham Associates

Heather Royes: 'I No Longer Read Poetry' from *The Caribbean Raj* (Ian Randle Publications, 1996), reprinted by permission of the author

Andrew Salkey: 'History and Away' from *Away* (Allison & Busby, 1980)

Pedro Pérez Sarduy: 'the POET' from *Cumbite and Other Poems* (Center for Cuban Studies, New York, 1990), reprinted by permission of the author

Dennis Scott: 'Uncle Time' and 'Epitaph' from *Uncle Time* (University of Pittsburgh Press, 1973), © Dennis Scott, 1973, reprinted by permission of the publisher; 'Apocalypse Dub' from *Dreadwalk* (New Beacon Books, 1982), reprinted by permission of the publisher

Lasana Sekou: 'Liberation Theology' from *The Massachusetts Review*, Volume 35, Numbers 3 & 4 (1994), © 1994, reprinted by permission of the publisher

Olive Senior: 'Birdshooting Season' from *Talking of Trees* (Calabash Publications, 1985); 'Brief Lives' from *Gardening in the Tropics* (Bloodaxe Books, 1995); 'Thirteen Ways of Looking at Blackbird' from *Review: Literature of the Arts of the Americas*, 68 (Spring, 2004), reprinted by permission of Olive Senior and the Watkins/Loomis Agency

A. J. Seymour: 'There Runs a Dream' and 'Sun is a Shapely Fire' from *Collected Poems 1937–1989*, edited by Jacqueline de Weever and Ian McDonald (Blue Parrot Press, 2000)

Philip Sherlock: 'Trees His Testament', published by permission of Hilary Sherlock

SOURCES AND ACKNOWLEDGEMENTS

Hazel Simmons-Mcdonald: 'Parasite' from *A World of Poetry for CXC* (Heinemann, 1994)

Louis Simpson: 'Working Late' from *Caviar at the Funeral* (Oxford University Press, 1981), reprinted by permission of the author

Michael Smith: 'Give Me A Little Dub Music' and 'Me Cyaan Believe It' from *It a Come: Poems* (City Lights Books, 1989)

Bruce St. John: 'Lighters'

Virgil Suárez: 'Diaspora' from *Callaloo*, 22: 4 (1999), © Charles H. Rowell, reprinted by permission of The Johns Hopkins University Press

Patrick Sylvain: 'Flash Back' from *Callaloo*, 19:4 (1996), © Charles H. Rowell, reprinted by permission of The Johns Hopkins University Press

Harold M. Telemaque: 'In Our Land' from *Burnt Bush* (Kraus, 1973)

Ralph Thompson: 'Dinner Party' from *Moving On* (Peepal Tree Press, 1997), reprinted by permission of the publisher

Guy Tirolien: 'Islands' from *Facing the Sea: Selected Writings (CXC)*, edited by Anne Walmsley and Nick Caistor (Heinemann International Literature & Textbooks, 1986); 'Ghetto' from *The Negritude Poets*, edited by Ellen Conroy Kennedy (Thunder's Mouth Press, 1989, 1994), © 1975 by Ellen Conroy Kennedy, reprinted by permission of Ellen Conroy Kennedy

Trefossa: 'A true poem . . . ' from *Creole Drum*, edited by Jan Voorhoeve and Ursy M. Lichtveld (Yale University Press, 1975), reprinted by permission of the publisher

H. A. Vaughan: 'Revelation' from *Sandy Lane and Other Poems* (BIM Magazine, 1985)

Chiqui Vicioso: 'Doña Mariana' from *Sisters of the Caliban: Contemporary Women Poets of the Caribbean—A Multilingual Anthology*, edited by M. J. Fenwick (Azul Editions, 1996)

Vivian Virtue: 'Landscape Painter, Jamaica' from *Wings of the Evening: Selected Poems of Vivian Virtue* by A. L. McLeod (Sterling Publishers, 2002), reprinted by permission of the publisher

Derek Walcott: 'The Schooner Flight' from *The Star-Apple Kingdom* (Jonathan Cape, 1979), reprinted by permission of The Random House Group Ltd, and Farrar, Straus & Giroux

Mirta Yanez: 'The Duties of Womanhood' from *The Literary Review*, Volume 35, No. 4 (1992).

Although every effort has been made to establish copyright and contact copyright holders prior to printing this has not always been possible. The publishers would be pleased to rectify any omissions or errors brought to their notice at the earliest opportunity.

A–Z INDEX OF CONTRIBUTORS

A–Z INDEX OF CONTRIBUTORS

INDEX OF CONTRIBUTORS
BY COUNTRY

INDEX OF POEM TITLES

INDEX OF POEM TITLES

INDEX OF FIRST LINES

The Journals of

Jean Cocteau

Edited and translated with an
introduction by Wallace Fowlie

Illustrated with 16 drawings by the Author

Indiana University Press
Bloomington

The publishers wish to acknowledge the kindness of the following copyright holders in giving their permission to include selections from these volumes:

Bruckmann Verlag, for selections from *La Démarche d'un Poète* and for the use of the illustrations on pages 44, 47, 58, 72, 83, 109, 133, 158, 205, 225, 235
Editions Bernard Grasset, for selections from *Journal d'un Inconnu*
Editions du Rocher, for selections from *La Difficulté d'Etre*
Librairie Stock, for selections from *Le Rappel à l'Ordre*
Philosophical Library, for selections from *Lettre à Maritain*

Contents

Jean Cocteau

INTRODUCTION

Election to the French Academy is still the highest official honor which France can pay her writers. A writer is elected only after soliciting his candidacy and calling on as many of the living members as possible. The nonconservative writer usually does not seek admittance. In the nineteenth century, Baudelaire, for example, withdrew his candidacy. He remembered that Balzac had been unsuccessful. Proust and Gide did not trouble to apply. Today, such eminent writers as Sartre, Malraux, André Breton and Julien Green, who are far superior to the majority of Academicians, have not yet campaigned for a chair (*fauteuil*) among the forty "immortals."

France, and the literary world outside of France, were startled when Jean Cocteau announced his intention to "run" for the chair of Jérôme Tharaud. He was elected in March, 1955, and welcomed by André Maurois in October, under the dome of the Académie Française, an impressive black structure on the left bank of the Seine, which heretofore he had never entered. It was one of the spectacular ceremonies of recent times, equal in importance and worldliness to Valéry's reception and to Bergson's. Twelve thousand admission cards were requested for a house that seats

1

only seven hundred. The daily press and the weeklies called attention to the sword and the uniform of the new Academician, and to the celebrities who attended the reception. *Le Monde* published the complete texts of Cocteau's speech and of Maurois' answer.

According to tradition, Cocteau was supposed to pay homage in his oration to his predecessor, but Jérôme Tharaud's art is as distant from Cocteau's as black is from white, and he therefore said as little as possible about the literary accomplishment of that defunct writer. He spent most of his time paying ingratiating tribute to the Académie and announcing to his new colleagues that since he was admitted, the august assembly should henceforth open their doors to the "sublime race of bad subjects." He reminded them that if François Villon were alive in Paris today, he would probably not be elected. The entire speech was carefully worded and skillfully organized to give that effect, which Cocteau always gives in his best writing, of brilliant paradox and wit, of easy flow, of incisiveness never completely devoid of images.

Maurois' answer was a combination of welcome and advice. First, he graciously supplied the homage to Tharaud which Cocteau had bypassed, and then he reviewed the career of Cocteau. Without listing the innumerable plays, films, volumes of poetry and criticism and essays, he described the diversity and the achievement and the historical status of the new Academician. There was warmth and admiration and very little reserve in his text. He had seen Cocteau's speech and referred to many points in it. He even promised that if Cocteau proposed to the Académie a new Villon, he would vote for him. As representative of the

Introduction

famous company, Maurois expressed no hope that now the poet would change in manner and temperament. The new accouterments: the green coat, the bicorn hat, and the sword, were not destined to do more than alter the visible appearance of Jean Cocteau on official occasions. The company did not want an additional Academician. They wanted Angel Heurtebise.

On this occasion, ultimate of its kind, Cocteau did not fall into any of the traps of pomposity or intimidation. The "chair" which is now his, a comfortable visible chair, as he called it, did not deny him his customary practice of disappearance, of prestidigitation, of skilled balancing at great heights. The portrait he offered of himself to his new venerable colleagues was fully recognizable and familiar. It contained all the elements of his legend and his vocabulary: the heavy diving suit he wears in order not to rise too fast to the surface, his wanderer's fatigue, his quality of homelessness, his fate as one of those poets called by Verlaine "poètes maudits." His predilection has always been for the hunted rather than the hunter, for Rousseau who did not make the Academy rather than for Voltaire who did. He recalled a moment in one of the films when Chaplin put a lamp shade on his head and became a lamp in order to escape from the police.

Of all the really famous writers admitted to the ranks of the French Academy, Cocteau holds the distinction of probably being the least well known. His name is famous throughout the world, but his works are not familiar. Legend quickly covered up the facts of his existence and made him into an irresponsible prince, a magician of easy tricks, a prestidigitator, a bizarre angel. The truth is quite the opposite, and it

3

has been only recently revealed—in part—in his journals. The real Cocteau turns out to be a serious, laborious worker; a man who, despite his prodigious activity, has never ceased to meditate on the gravest moral problems. Even his early essays on aesthetics and painters were, because of their agile aphoristic style and because of his nascent legend, misunderstood or quite simply neglected. Everything is unexpected in Cocteau, but everything is a coherent part of his character and the result of his particular genius. He has never claimed to be more than he is. This is one of his most sympathetic traits. He has constantly pointed out his own limitations. Man, and especially the poet, is infirm, a prisoner of his own dimensions. The poet, in contrast with the ordinary man, writes on the fourth wall of his prison. This act gives him the illusion of escape.

Cocteau was born just outside of Paris, but comes from a Parisian family, and has lived in Paris all his life. He has never underestimated the role of the city in his career and in the formation of his character. He is Parisian by speech, education, ideas, habits, tastes. The settings in his books are those characteristic of the city: large public gardens, like the Luxembourg; monuments, such as the Church of the Madeleine; avenues, such as the rue de Rivoli; schools, such as Condorcet where he himself studied and where some of the most private elements of his mythology may have had their origin. His family was of the solid Parisian bourgeoisie, cultivated, wealthy, interested in music, painting, and literature. As a young boy, he was favored in every way. Cocteau has written very little on his early childhood memories, and from those pages

Introduction

one has the impression that he does not remember too much of that period, characterized by happiness and a sense of family security and indulgence. The memories he has written down are lacking in sentimentality. He relates, for example, with a tone of detachment and impersonality, a return to his native town, Maisons-Laffitte.

Among his earliest experiences with his family, he has perhaps mentioned the theatre the most often, the Thursday matinees (*les matinées classiques*) at the Comédie-Française, and the strong fascination the "red and gold" theatre held for him: the curtain, the three knocks preceding each act, the glow of the footlights. The theatre never lost its prestige for Cocteau. He has always respected the theatre, but it has intimidated him. In the theatre he is two people: the man submitting to its bewitchment and the child who feels that the control desk where he shows his ticket for the verification of his seat is assigning him to a dark, forbidding world.

Cocteau was first introduced to the literary and artistic world of Paris by his family. Through them he met in his adolescence such celebrities as Rostand, Proust, Catulle Mendès, and Anna de Noailles. Precociously he published his first volume of verse at seventeen. He knew instantaneously a success with a small public who flattered him and applauded the facile brilliance of the poems. He claims that he has never ceased paying for this early fame. And yet almost immediately he was sensitive to a word of warning and reserve in a review of his poems by Ghéon, published in *La Nouvelle Revue Française*. With unusual shrewdness for so young a writer, Cocteau knew that

5

such approbation would not last and that he would have to do far more than merely write with unusual brio for a very young man. In the long run, Cocteau was less sensitive to the occasion when the actor Edouard de Max read his poetry in public than he was to the reserved criticism of Henri Ghéon. In his first meetings with the Ballets Russes and Serge de Diaghilev, he was not totally successful in captivating the attention of the impresario. Diaghilev's famous command addressed to young Cocteau, *"Etonne-moi"* ("Surprise me"), was a salutary interruption in the series of youthful triumphs. It too caused Cocteau to reflect, withdraw, and take account of himself and his accomplishments.

Those few years immediately preceding the First World War initiated Cocteau into the world of art and literature in Paris. They marked the end of Impressionism and the first works of the Fauves, of Cubism and the early interest in Negro art. The paintings of Manet, with their scenes of picnics, straw hats, and shaded gardens speckled with sunlight, gave way to the strong studies of Picasso, Braque, and Rousseau, exhibited in the Salon des Indépendants. These overwhelmingly rich contacts, his ominously easy first triumphs, the first gentle but clear reprimands, ended for Cocteau in a self-imposed exile. He closed himself off from everything and began the writing of his first novel, *Le Potomak,* which he completed in 1913, at the home of Stravinsky in Leysin.

During the last year of the war and the year following, 1917–1919, Cocteau, with three very different works, which defined his three major preoccupations, became again a public figure, but this time with a far

Introduction

deeper sense of his vocation and capacities. *Parade,* of 1917, a ballet performed in Rome, was his first experiment with the theatre. *Le Coq et l'Arlequin,* of 1919, a manifesto against the disciples of Debussy and Wagner, revealed his interest in aesthetics and his perceptive powers as a critic. *Le Cap de Bonne Espérance,* of the same year, a volume of war poems in which he celebrated the acrobatics of his aviator friend, Garros, placed him in the ranks of the best young poets. Poetry, in its deepest sense, was the mark of all three works, the principle which was henceforth to direct the varied activities of Cocteau.

These three works, then, appear today as exercises in which Cocteau tried to define himself and estimate his particular weight. The lesson which he was teaching himself needed and received an exterior example. Raymond Radiguet, a boy of fifteen, called on Cocteau one day in 1918 with an introduction from Max Jacob. He was adopted by Picasso, Cocteau, and their friends, all of whom failed to realize at the beginning that they were welcoming not a disciple but a master. For the Paris artists who had been following the triumphs of Dada and its program of denying and deriding all values, Radiguet appeared as the youthful prodigy who opposed Dadaism and who advised Cocteau not to appear original but to write like everyone else. He died of typhoid in 1923, but during the few years of their friendship he taught Cocteau a profound lesson on independence and on traits of style, conciseness and soberness, which belong to the tradition of French classicism. Cocteau considers the two novels of Radiguet as extraordinary in the realm of the novel, as the poems of Rimbaud are extraordinary in the realm of poetry.

On many occasions, Cocteau has acknowledged his debt to Radiguet and the subtle doctrine of anticonformist conformity he appropriated from his younger friend. For the first time he listened to someone much younger than himself and learned that originality in literature may be achieved by an effort to write as others do but without succeeding in this. In recent years, Cocteau has translated this lesson into the metaphor of walking. He believes he learned from Radiguet how to progress by walking on his own two feet instead of adopting a speed foreign to his own temperament. The serious young writer should always be wary of the pantomime, no matter how intriguing it appears, of hitch-hiking.

The experience of watching Radiguet work, and often of having to force him to work, offered Cocteau a fuller awareness of the poetic temperament and the drama of the youthful poets who appear to society to be culprits and outlaws, Villon, Baudelaire, Rimbaud, who in their various incarnations, limp as they walk on the surface of the earth, as Jacob did after his fight with the angel. Each one of the *sublimes mauvais sujets,* as Cocteau calls them, is the site of a conflict between the clear intellect of their minds and the bizarre angelic appearance of their bodies. The two principal schools of French style have often been ascribed to the predominantly Latin rhetorical style, illustrated in the sermons of Bossuet and the rich periodic prose of Chateaubriand, and to the predominantly Greek tradition where the sentence is brief, concise, sculptured, as in Voltaire and Stendhal. In his Académie speech, Maurois places Cocteau in this second lineage. The form of the Cocteau sentence is fa-

Introduction

mous for its swiftness and articulateness and lucidity, but the content or the meaning is mysterious and enigmatical. Cocteau's style has become a manner of expressing complicated matters with disarming simplicity.

In itself, *Parade* was of limited interest, but it served as preparatory exercise for all of Cocteau's subsequent experiments in the theatre and it permitted him to introduce to Europe *Les Six,* the six composers who were to make important contributions to contemporary French music. The artist's taste underwent a simplification, a deliberate impoverishment in the pantomime-farce of *Le Boeuf sur le Toit,* of 1920, played by the Fratellini brothers, and for which Darius Milhaud wrote the music. *Les Mariés de la Tour Eiffel,* first performed on June 18, 1921, was a parody of bourgeois attitudes at the turn of the century, and a production far more original and subtle than the earlier *Parade.*

But the theatre never occupied Cocteau to the exclusion of other forms of expression. The poems of *Vocabulaire,* of 1922, contained, as the title indicates, the key words of his poetic experience, symbols and characters projected out of his imagination which were to form in time the mythology of Cocteau, episodes, myths, and characters charged with the duty of narrating the poet's drama. The strange personages appeared and disappeared on the pages as if they were looking for their poet: kidnapers, sailors, angels, cyclists. Difficult for the reader to understand, they invade the poems as if they were obsessions of the poet, bodily manifestations or metamorphoses of the poet's models, of the purity Rimbaud spoke of and the angelism for which Cocteau has provided important notations. The companion volume of *Plain-Chant* (1923) is a more directly personal poem on the suffering of love which, because of its intensity, is constantly forcing the poet toward a void or into sleep. This poem unquestionably reflects the moral crisis and anguish which followed the death of Radiguet and out of which Cocteau sought refuge in the use of opium. The exercise of "vocabulary" continues in this volume. The meanings of the words, as the poet studies them, are helping him to understand his real function of creator, not of myths but of his own myth, the recreation of his own life.

The critical writing of Cocteau during these same years contains some of his most difficult pages, but they are indispensable for an understanding of both his approach to art and the aesthetics of modern art. In *Le Secret Professionnel,* of 1922, and the essay on *Picasso,* of 1923, it is obvious that Cocteau is not the professional type of critic. He belongs to the other lineage of critics, those creative writers who have written some of their most profound pages on the problems of art and on aesthetics: Stendhal, Baudelaire, Giraudoux, Gide, and Valéry. Cocteau makes a point, in *Le Secret Professionnel,* of defining style as "a simple way of saying complex things" (*une façon très simple de dire des choses compliquées*). Rimbaud and Mallarmé are constant points of reference on these pages. Rimbaud, especially, is defined as a particular type of angel on the earth. Propositions on the role of poetry follow one another rapidly. Cocteau does not follow an ordered sequence of thought, nor does he build up a strict kind of argumentation. His basic idea, that poetry is not so much the art of saying something as it is a way of being, gives a metaphysical tone to his essay. One realizes at the end that the poet is a man

Introduction

making use of a certain number of secrets which give him his assurance and protect him from being depossessed. The essay is a sustained effort on the part of the poet to see himself in his integrity.

In the next triad of works, Cocteau deepened his contribution of poet, critic, and dramatist. With *L'Ange Heurtebise,* of 1925, the poet engages in a more open and violent combat with the angel, now named, in a definitely circumscribed supernatural ring. The familiar words, in their new combinations, have a more evocative power: statue, rose, marble, angel, snow, shooting, mirror, horse, cock. The text of *L'Ange Heurtebise* is simple and direct, but one senses that Cocteau is using it as an exorcism. He was, in fact, ready to begin another kind of exorcism in his personal life, a cure for the habit of opium. Urged by two admirable friends, the poet Pierre Reverdy and the philosopher Jacques Maritain, he was to enter the sanatorium at Saint-Cloud. This is referred to in his open letter to Maritain (*Lettre à Maritain,* 1926), which, in addition to its discussion of modern aesthetics, analyzes the moral and religious crisis which Cocteau was going through. His solitude, especially since the death of Radiguet, had led him to an impasse. A return to the Church, which he seriously contemplated, appeared to him as his return to a family. But the dogmas themselves he rejected. He acknowledged with gratitude the friendship of Maritain, which has never been impaired.

The play *Orphée,* performed in Paris in 1926, by Georges and Ludmilla Pitoëff, was the first work of Cocteau to reach a fairly wide public. Reinhardt produced the play in Berlin, and Rilke had begun a translation of the text into German just before he died. In the season of 1926–27 the play represented beyond any doubt an example of *avant-garde* writing, but the seriousness of its theme and its intentions made it into much more than a purely experimental play. It marked a definite break with what the French call *théâtre de boulevard,* or the currently popular melodrama and realistic play. It was seen to be an effort of a contemporary to attach the theatre to its origins, to renovate one of the oldest myths of mankind, and to preserve in the new treatment of the myth the secrecy, the mysteriousness, and the suggestiveness which are the constant ingredients of myth. *Orphée* has been translated many times. It is performed constantly by university theatres in various countries and by little theatre groups.

In a general sense, *Orphée* plays a part in the resurrection of tragedy today and in a specific sense it continued and deepened Cocteau's interpretation of the nature of the poet. Here, the poet would seem to be the two characters combined of Orpheus and Angel Heurtebise. Cocteau never forgets that Orphism is religion based upon the magical power of language, even if he forces the myth to take on the strange atmosphere of a supernatural police court. The power of metamorphosis and the rite of exorcism, so integrated with the original forms of tragedy, are in Cocteau's *Orphée* applied to commonplace objects and words. The action of the play is both familiar and esoteric. Orpheus is both poet and hierophant, both husband and priest.

The public for a play is far more limited than the novel-reading public which Cocteau was to reach to

Introduction

some extent at the beginning, and increasingly so in time, with *Les Enfants Terribles,* written in the space of three weeks when he was in the clinic at Saint-Cloud, and published in 1929. During the past twenty-seven years, this book has become a kind of classic, both novel, belonging to the central tradition of the French novel, and document of historical-psychological significance in the study it offers of the type of adolescent referred to in the title. The intertwined destinies of brother and sister, Paul and Elizabeth, with the dark, forbidding figure of Dargelos behind them, offer a revealing picture of adolescence in its action and speech and games.

Written at the end of the twenties, *Les Enfants Terribles* focuses on the adolescent in France as he appeared in the years immediately following the First World War and on the prestige he acquired during that decade, on the special kind of freedom he enjoyed during the early years, and on the disillusionment he felt during the second half of the decade. Cocteau did not invent this adolescent, but he had observed him with extraordinary perceptiveness, and he outlined his basic dramas and characteristics which few writers have attempted. The adolescents of *Les Enfants Terribles* are the boy and girl who impose their personalities on adults without ever resembling adults. If Cocteau did not invent this type of being, he was the first writer to describe the inviolability of their character and those traits which have been called "angelic" because of their absoluteness and their purity, traits which are lost in adulthood with the practices of adjustment, compromise, and search for security. Destiny grants to these adolescents during a precariously limited number of years a life of grace and ease and ingenuous enthusiasm. They are the race of children opposed to the race of grownups, and their fantasies, when prolonged through the years of adolescence, appear blasphemous and provocative and evil. Some of this fantasy had been incarnated in Raymond Radiguet. It is present in Paul and Dargelos of *Les Enfants Terribles,* and reappears in the writings of Aldous Huxley, Gide, Montherlant, and in the type of youthful gangster of Hollywood films and American novels. The sense of freedom felt by adolescents in the early twenties turns into a deep sense of restlessness and insecurity during the later years of the decade. It is the same adolescent, grown slightly older, but still dominating by his charm and seductiveness a part at least of the Paris scene. He was encouraged by the doctrine of the gratuitous act, by the practices of Surrealism, by the new sense of cosmopolitanism in the French.

The novel itself, *Les Enfants Terribles,* is constructed on a rigorous theme: the adherence of the brother and sister, Paul and Elizabeth, to a logical, coherent behavior quite outside the usual moral system which directs the lives of most men. Between the snowball scene with which the story begins and the snow scene with which it ends, there are very few instances of what the world would call human warmth and love. The brother and sister have invented a special game which unites them and which replaces love. Elizabeth is the stronger of the two, and she will cause the death of her brother when he leaves the game and thereby breaks their childhood contract. The brother and sister learn to exist, cut off from any sense of their period in history, and from any relationship with their city, their family, their religion.

At the beginning, the deadly snowball, thrown by Dargelos, hits Paul on the chest. This scene, where schoolboys celebrate their rite of initiation, overshadows the entire story. Dargelos, although he is rarely visible in *Les Enfants Terribles,* grows into the figure of the dark angel who haunts the dreams and the thoughts of the protagonist. The two children escape the usual difficulties and catastrophes of life by retreating from them and enjoying the promiscuity of their room. This is the closed room of childhood, a facile symbol for the ways in which a child tries to construct his own world and live separated from the world of adults. At the end of the story, the poison, sent by Dargelos, is a further symbol of fatality, first represented in the snowball. With the death of Paul and the suicide of Elizabeth, the room is released from its spell.

For the film of *Les Enfants Terribles,* of 1950, Cocteau prepared the scenario and dialogue and the commentaries which he himself speaks. The accompanying music of Bach and Vivaldi fuses admirably with the pictorial beauty of the film. It does not, however, re-create the power of the novel. A melodramatic aspect emerges from the pictures which does not support the oracular tragedy of the book. This is particularly true of the ending of the film which is poignant and striking and noble, but which fails to give Elizabeth the dimensions of Electra, of some criminal goddess dominating the celebration of a religious rite.

In the early thirties, Cocteau enlarged the scope of his work by the creation of his first film, *Le Sang d'un Poète* (1932), and by the writing of what seems to be

15

his greatest play, *La Machine Infernale* (1934). These two major works represent a deepening of the theme of fatality which had never been absent from his earlier works. Cocteau's friends and apologists had always admired his ceaseless activity, his capacity to move from one work to another and to come to each one with renewed freshness and inventiveness. The making of films, with their particular demands of time and technical experimentation, are to occupy from now on a large amount of Cocteau's attention, but he will not neglect his other forms: plays especially, drawings, essays, and poetry. Colette used to say that when she felt inclined toward laziness, she would think of her young friend, Jean Cocteau, who looked upon his labors as if they were pleasures, and whose finished works never gave the impression of having been labored over.

Cocteau was one of the first writers to undertake the making of a film and to understand that the art of the cinema is a legitimate art and one worthy of his imagination and talent. The theme of his first film, *Le Sang d'un Poète,* was an idea close to the romantics a century earlier: the poet writes with his own blood. As with every work of Cocteau, this first film appeared as something new and yet bearing relationship with all the other works. In *Blood of a Poet,* and in the play which is to follow it, Cocteau moved into closer contact with the great myths of humanity. Each of his works is a metamorphosis of the same being, a release of his spirit. The brilliant succession of his works testifies to the accuracy of one of his sentences which has been applied to his method more than almost any other: "I have to be burned alive in order to be reborn." *(Il faut se brûler vif pour renaître.)* The variety of his works, the rapidity with which one has followed the other, their distinctiveness and yet their common bond, all point to the possibility that Cocteau's creative method is the practice of exorcism.

In *Blood of a Poet,* Cocteau made the art of the movies into a kind of writing. In the aesthetic sense, his aim was difficult. He tried not to make poetry the adjunct of the film, not to make a "poetic" film, but to allow the film itself to be the poem. This aim was totally coherent with all that Cocteau had attempted heretofore. He had always looked upon the "poetic" as really anti-poetic. He had always avoided using the fantastic (*le merveilleux*) in the traditional sense, but had found it, as he does in *Blood of a Poet,* in the ordinary objects of everyday life. He believes that he will come upon the fantastic or that it will attack him. Through the generosity of a friend, Viscount Charles de Noailles, he was free to make the film he wanted to. All the episodes of the film, the scene in the artist's studio, the hotel scene, the snowball scene, compose the life and trials of the poet. The film, like any esoteric work, lends itself to multiple interpretations, some of which have puzzled Cocteau himself.

Much later, in the film *Orphée,* of 1950, Cocteau, with an incomparably surer technique, developed this lesson of the poet and borrowed from *Blood of a Poet* and from his play *Orphée.* In *Blood of a Poet* he forced some of the effects, although still today many of them seem startlingly fresh and successful: the plunge through the mirror, the speaking lips on the palm, the living statue. Many of these devices reappear in the film *Orphée,* where the mythical elements are better served by Cocteau's more highly developed technique.

Le Sang d'un Poète and *Orphée* are two esoteric poems for the screen. The first set a style which has been widely imitated, and the second represented the achievement of a style, in its fullest development.

The Infernal Machine (1934), as well as *Orphée*, has become a permanent classic in the *avant-garde* theatre and the little theatre movements. Cocteau's treatment of the Oedipus theme is very much his own. He focuses on the machinations and the ingeniousness of the gods, of Olympus, in destroying man. He moves closer in this play to the Greek prototypes of tragedy than to the seventeenth-century Corneille and Racine. Against the machine of the gods, in its perpetration of woe and death, there is no defense. Each of the earlier plays had been an effort to discover a vocabulary, a situation, and a style which would not contradict the fundamental illusion which the theatre must always provide. The stage is always the scene for something that is not. Dramatic art is illusion and travesty. Very few contemporary playwrights, except Pirandello, Lorca, and Cocteau, have emphasized this doctrine. But the plays of these three writers are largely concerned with this very problem of illusion and reality.

In *La Machine Infernale* Cocteau reached his full power of illusionist, and he has been able to call upon it at will in the major subsequent plays: *Les Chevaliers de la Table Ronde* (1937), *Les Parents Terribles* (1938), *Bacchus* (1951). Oedipus himself is the prototype and the most famous searcher for truth behind the lie and the illusion. The central problem for the hero is how he can know his destiny. Orpheus turns to Death, who appears in the form of a beautiful woman. Oedipus turns to the Sphinx and to Tiresias. Galahad turns to the monster inhabiting him. Michel, in *Les Parents Terribles*, turns to his mother. Hans, in *Bacchus*, turns to Cardinal Zampi. This search and this eternal questioning have never been better illustrated than in the myth of Oedipus, which Cocteau refurbished with his own uncanny sense of situation, enigma, timing, and characterization.

In *Les Parents Terribles* Cocteau turned to tragedy in modern dress, to a form of tragedy in our own age. This work is deprived, therefore, of the poetry of myth, and the tragedy takes place within the hearts of the characters. Twice the productions of *Les Parents Terribles* created a scandal in Paris. It was first forbidden as being "incestuous," and in 1941, during the Occupation, the theatre was closed by the Germans. The revival, in 1945, however, met with unusual success. At that time even the most hostile critics of Cocteau approved of it. The film, made by Cocteau in 1948, used the same actors and the same text. The situation of the play might have turned it into melodrama. The father and son in love with the same woman was a familiar plot for plays of the "boulevard" tradition in Paris, but Cocteau's treatment is so rigorously bare and honest that the tone and atmosphere, the suffering and the dilemma of the characters, relate the work to a strict form of tragedy.

The theme of the play is avowedly the frustration and the impossibility of love. The key words which resound from beginning to end in the text are "order" and "disorder," and they are easily seen to be parallel terms for "reality" and "illusion" in the other plays. Cocteau never moves away from his central preoccupation. He renews the same problem but creates a new

19

work. The play is about three parents: two sisters, Yvonne and Léo, and Yvonne's husband, Georges, who is loved by Léo. The son, Michel, precipitates the crisis of "disorder" by not coming home one night. The girl he has fallen in love with, Madeleine, turns out to be the mistress of his father. The parents try to break their son's engagement: the mother, through jealous love for her son, and the father, through jealous love for his mistress. The aunt, Léo, dominates the family by her wealth and her authority. She is a kind of Tiresias in this bourgeois family but much more involved in the lives around her than the blind soothsayer in the royal family of Thebes.

Cocteau's most recent play, *Bacchus,* produced in December, 1951, by Jean-Louis Barrault at the Marigny, created a minor scandal in the form of an attack by Mauriac. Cocteau has discussed this open letter in his *Journal d'un Inconnu.* The accusations of Mauriac, which were largely of a personal nature, did not affect the success of the play. In reality, he seems to have launched his attack against the legendary Cocteau. Rather than basing his attack on the text of the play which he knew very imperfectly, he revived the traits and misdemeanors of a celebrated figure which have only a partial basis in fact. The action of *Bacchus* transpires in Germany of the sixteenth century. It was written when Sartre was writing his play on the same historical period, *Le Diable et le bon Dieu.* Beyond this same background, the two plays have nothing in common. *Bacchus* is perhaps Cocteau's longest and most argumentative play. Two philosophies are opposed in it: the anarchistic, in the young hero Hans, and the ecclesiastical authority, in Cardinal Zampi,

Introduction

who has been sent from Rome to investigate the rise of heresy in Germany. Hans represents the free man in the face of what he believes to be tyranny in a political and ecclesiastical sense, and Cardinal Zampi, who is sympathetic to the ardor and honesty of Hans, preaches a return to order and a method of calculation and adjustment. The two theories and the two points of view representing revolution and order are exposed especially during the long second act. At the end of the play, Hans becomes the political martyr. He is slain by the populace whom he tried to help.

Literary art, in all of its forms, is always a risk, but the theatre is the greatest risk of all. This sense of precariousness has always been felt and understood by Cocteau. In fact, he encourages this risk and works under its domination. From his earliest *Parade* and *Mariés sur la Tour Eiffel,* through his adaptations of Sophocles where he learned his scales and the form of tragedy, to the major dramatic works of *Orphée, La Machine Infernale, Les Parents Terribles,* and *Bacchus,* he presented experimentation on the stage, with the tireless enthusiasm of a dramatist enamoured of the theatre and of the idea of a spectacle. Because of his irresistible sense of vocation, Cocteau has always felt that each new play is a new beginning and a new risk. The witchcraft and the spell of the theatre are worth this perpetual risk. To borrow a circus image he has often used, he performs his number without the physical and moral support of a net. His courage, despite setbacks of all kinds and attacks from all sides and in all degrees of intensity and maliciousness, has been indomitable.

Cocteau has been courageous in himself and for his

friends. Not least among his many roles is that of impresario and interpreter. Such modern artists as Satie, Braque, Picasso, and Stravinsky owe some of their glory to Cocteau. The group of *Les Six*—Honegger, Poulenc, Milhaud, Taillefer, Auric, Durey—owe him their composite name and the early support they received in Paris. Ever since the time, in the early twenties, when Raymond Radiguet taught Cocteau to go counter to the *avant-garde* fashions, he has been doggedly defining and illustrating a new classicism. The newspaper chronicle of Paris artistic life which he published in *Paris-Midi,* known under its title of *Carte Blanche,* helped to designate Cocteau as a guide and interpreter of his age. He passed quite easily from an histrionic and tumultuous fame in the twenties to a more judicious and more thoughtful central position in the thirties. His friendship with Christian Bérard was important in the new theatrical enterprises. Bérard's sets for *La Machine Infernale* of 1934 were used in the 1954 revival of the play and created the same impression of beauty. The reflections on Chirico in *Essai de Critique Indirecte* became a necessary adjunct to the earlier pages on Picasso. The *Portraits-Souvenir* of 1935 helped to establish the traits of some of the outstanding celebrities of the day. In the travel chronicle written for *Paris-Soir* in 1936, *Mon Premier Voyage,* he described his meeting with Charlie Chaplin. He offered help, whenever it was needed, to painters, composers, actors, poets, and even a boxer! And in turn he was helped by the example of the artists he knew, by the exemplary courage of such men as Stravinsky, Picasso, Satie, Radiguet. Ever since the death of Apollinaire on the day of the Armistice, 1918,

Introduction

Cocteau has occupied in all the domains of French art a more active and more vital position than any other single artist. By comparison, the work, for example, of André Breton was more limited to a given number of years and to one specific artistic movement. Cocteau's activity and participation during the years between the two wars, continued through the years of the Occupation and are still in evidence today, with *Bacchus* and new volumes of poetry and journals. Membership in the Académie Française will hardly slow him down!

The name Cocteau has given to his entire work is *poésie*. Concomitant with poetic creation is the pleasure and the profit of judgment, of calculation, of flashes of wisdom reached swiftly. The ordinary object of his "vocabulary": mirror, snowball, rose, etc., is presented with an elliptical insolence that turns it into something unfamiliar. In his daily life Cocteau is extremely talkative, but as a writer he arrests this natural flow of words and thereby so highlights a few individual words and a few rapidly sketched situations, that his artistic style is synonymous with brevity. Only a spark is saved from the conflagration. He knows instinctively when he has reached his mark and he is able to put a period when he has said what he has to say.

Cocteau refers constantly to the character and the nature of the poet whenever he discusses the nature of poetry and its function and its revelations. On the whole, he maintains many of the familiar romantic conceptions of the poet. The poet is solitary, aloof, *maudit,* inspired. His volumes of poetry have appeared at regular intervals throughout his career. Some of the most recent volumes appear to be among the very best: *Léone, La Crucifixion, Clair-Obscur.* In this last volume, the poet describes himself under the mask of Marco Polo when he is thrown in prison in Venice and when no one believes the stories of his travels. This is one of the poet's principal dilemmas which Cocteau has never ceased referring to. The poet himself knows his voyages but he does not succeed in convincing his public that he ever understood them. Under the guise of one story or another, Cocteau often returns to the ancient solitude of the poet whose speech is not understood. The term of fatality, as it is used throughout his work, is closely associated with this inevitable solitude. But he has learned through the years that it is essential to poetry and that finally it rescues the poet.

Poetry is, then, for Cocteau, an immemorial rite which may appear as mysterious and enigmatic to the reader as the mysteries of religion appear obscure to the believer. And each poet develops his own particular means of protecting his speech. The short, tense, and elliptical lines of Cocteau form a barrier between himself and his reader. The Muses about whom he speaks, with some degree of familiarity, have appeared to him in some of their most extreme roles, as the destructive Bacchantes in the myth of Orpheus, or as the Sisters of tenderness and love, as in *Plain-Chant.* The poet's relationships with the varying and contradictory temperaments of the Muses form his power and originality and provide him with the necessary experiences by which he may approach his status of demigod. Cocteau has not hesitated to make for poets the noblest and most exalted claims. The immortality of the poet is a very special and very real accomplishment for him.

Introduction

The poet's close association with death is not a terrifying experience but a necessary initiation to his immortality. In the earliest works and in the latest, death has been for Cocteau not a unique experience but a daily experience which is his means of knowing truth, his means of coming into contact with truth, his means of understanding the ordinary objects in his life and the daily occurrences which befall him. Death is the total vision for Cocteau, the aggrandizement and the triumph over constriction.

Metaphorically he explains that the relationship between life and death is that between the two sides of the some coin. The first two acts of *La Machine Infernale,* which take place at the same time, he calls the two faces of the same picture or the same medallion, *l'endroit* and *l'envers.* The poet in his greatest moments of illumination knows what transpires on both sides. There is the stage in the theatre for one presentation, but there are also the wings for another, where the characters take off their masks, where the Beast turns into the Prince. In the play *Orphée,* Orpheus and Heurtebise move back and forth between life and death; and in the film *Orphée,* the communications between the two worlds are more constantly established. This moving back and forth between life and death affects, at least to some degree, the features of the angel and of man. One appears more human and one more angelic, but this is the result of the poet's practice.

Angelism, as Cocteau seems to understand it, is a system of contradictions, because it is essentially an explosion of the divine in the human. The supernatural is found to be everywhere, in the most commonplace and ordinary objects. This discovery is not unrelated to Cocteau's fundamental aesthetic. As an artist his goal is perfection found in simplicity. On every occasion when he has defined his integrity, he has stated his distrust of the artificially beautiful and ornamental. Such doctrine seemed an innovation when Cocteau first defined it. But it is always difficult to assess the innovator. During the forty years of Cocteau's career, he has moved from innovator and experimentalist to a classic figure, to the stature of a stylist who represents his age because now his age copies him. Only during the process of his development did he seem to be defiant and shocking.

What critical estimates have been made so far of Cocteau have been largely the work of friends. One senses behind most of the pages not so much a professional motivation as a duty of friendship eager to alter the false legends circulating about the character of the man himself. Unanimously, those writers who know him have explained his need for work and creativity by his eternal youthfulness of spirit and his animation. To this remarkable energy they have joined as a permanent trait of Cocteau's character his kindness, his sense of goodness, and his willingness to help. His friendships have been marked by loyalty. Auric, Maritain, and Picasso are examples of friendships which have continued for many years. His friendship with Radiguet was brief, intense, and productive in that each profited from the other in their careers as writers. In recent years, he has defended publicly and with considerable courage his friend Jean Genet. The world is jealous of such friendship as Cocteau

demonstrates and often his very reputation of friend
has victimized him.

He has given multiple proofs of his versatility. Even
a cursory glance at his bibliography reveals the large
number and diverseness of his publications. These
books have appeared so rapidly during the course of
the past thirty years that even those readers with the
strongest desire to keep abreast of the new writing are
soon left behind. One has the impression that he is
always engaged in the writing of books far ahead of
schedule. Even his readers, to say nothing of the gen-
eral public, came to look upon him as a literary figure
rather than as the writer of books. Even if his gifts
were accepted as authentic, he would not be read, or
listened to, or taken seriously. And the question was
always posed: was he serious himself, or was he mak-
ing fun of his public, largely composed of people like
himself but with less talent and less industriousness?
The words "clown" or "acrobat" when applied to the
writer have pejorative connotations. Even if he risks
his neck on the tight rope or trapeze, the public can
see, or believe they see, the net below.

It has been difficult for Cocteau's public to realize
that his agility and his brio are only masks, and that
his works, rather than being feats or artifices, are seri-
ous projects related to the great problems of the poet
and human destiny.

> *Les choses que je conte*
> *Sont des mensonges vrais*

> (The matters I relate
> Are true lies)

Such a phrase as "true lies" describes the act of the clown who disguises his heart of a man. The very ease of the clown disguises the difficulty of his art. A classical work is one which seems to be easily and clearly constructed: a Molière comedy, a Racine tragedy, a fable of La Fontaine. But this seeming ease of technique, as in the works of Cocteau also, is not applied to ideas or situations of only slight significance. Cocteau's principal desire has always been to rediscover and estimate anew the signs and symbols of his world and hence to re-establish communication between himself and his public.

The work that had once seemed dispersed and facile, now appears unified and coherent. The life that had once seemed theatrical and exhibitionistic now seems controlled by an exceptional self-discipline. Out of seeming inconstancy, Cocteau has built up a work characterized by the trait of constancy. In the past, Cocteau has suffered at the hands of critics who indulged in either vituperation or panegyric. The era of serious criticism of his work began with the essay of Roger Lannes in the *Poètes d'Aujourd'hui* series, published in 1948, and in the May, 1950, issue of the Belgian *Empreintes,* prepared by Robert Goffin and Herman van der Driessche.

The poet in Cocteau has, for a long time, been invisible to other men. But this fact simply substantiates his belief about poetry. His invisibility is assured by the tempo of his writing, by its swiftness, its precision and bareness, by all the traits of this writer's artistic asceticism which is of a spiritual order. His language corresponds to his spirit. He so organizes his words and so projects them that they seem never at rest, always poised, balanced in mid-air where timing is of the greatest importance. The single words he favors can be so detached that they carry more weight and more significance than words more munificently surrounded. Cocteau's persevering will to perfect and sharpen his style has been erroneously called virtuosity. His books, most of them quite brief, now seem necessary and logical. Even his tone of insolence has been misunderstood. It is, in reality, his protection against any false pose of languor and ecstasy and suffering. His essays and journals reveal him now as a kind of doctrinaire. His aphorisms, once looked upon as the expression of a young man's brio, are now seen to be more aggressive and continuously faithful to Cocteau's particular brand of torment, which he has lived through and to which he has given a literary form in his very deliberate break with the literary past.

W. F.

THE JOURNALS OF JEAN COCTEAU

I. Childhood and Early Influences

I was born on July 5, 1889, Place Sully, in Maisons-Laffitte (Seine et Oise).

Maisons-Laffitte is a kind of park for horse trainers. It is dotted with houses, gardens, avenues lined with linden trees, lawns, flower beds, fountains, and squares. The race horse and the bicycle dominated everything else. People played tennis at one another's house, in a bourgeois society divided into two factions by the Dreyfus Case. The Seine, the training track, the wall of the forest of Saint-Germain which you enter through a small door, deserted spots where you could play cops and robbers, the camp down below, the outdoor restaurants with bowers, the town fair, the fireworks, the acrobatics of the firemen, Mansard's château, its weeds and its busts of Roman emperors—all this made for us children a domain which supported the illusion we had of living in unique places in the world.

Last year I had the sorrow of being taken by friends to the Place Sully which was covered by pale-green

flower spikes and wild pinks. I prided myself on show-
ing them my house and even, despite the difficulty, on
sharing with them the memories it awakened in me.
My first sensation was of being lost in space, just as
when we are blindfolded and released in one spot
when we thought we were in another. Was that my
white gate, my trellised fence, my trees, my lawn, the
house I was born in, the window of the billiard room?
A sand path replaced the grass, the pool, and the flower
beds. A high gray building with a barn beside it occu-
pied the site of our house. Grooms were coming and
going, and looked at us suspiciously as we passed by.
I was holding the bars of the newly painted gate, *like
a prisoner outside,* when I felt a staggering pain which
was nothing but memories expelled by thrusts of a
pitchfork, memories unable to find their habits and the
niche where I thought them asleep and waiting for me.
I turned around. Might I perhaps escape to the other
side of the square? You crossed it in the sun to go to
André's yard (named after my uncle). The iron door
groaned and opened on the right onto the heliotrope.
Then you came into Eden. The garden of explora-
tions. For it is under the shadow of lilac bushes, cur-
rant bushes, and coach houses that children try to
understand the secrets of the world of adults.

A still worse surprise awaited me. They had divided
the yard into lots. Small houses of workmen were
everywhere. Grapes in bags, peaches, heavy gooseber-
ries which burst in your mouth, the smell of gera-
niums in the greenhouse, the flagstones of the hen
house, the greengages whose tops split open and spill
gold, the frogs of the pool, dead in operatic poses, with
their hands over their hearts—all these marvels became

at that moment the ghost of a murdered man asking for justice.

We visited avenues less devastated than my square. Gardens and houses were the same, to such a degree that I could have unearthed some object buried there forty years before when we played treasure games. We went beside the fence of the park where Max Lebaudy (the sugar manufacturer) organized *corridas* and washed his carriages in champagne.

You can imagine how such spectacles aroused the cruel and adventuresome souls of children. In 1904, we prowled about this fence and tried to climb over it, standing up on the seats of our bicycles.

Enough of that! Sentimentalizing clouds the mind. You can't communicate that kind of memory any more than the episodes of a dream. It is well to remember that each of us has similar memories and should not force them on others.

If I have complained for too long a time, it is because my memory, having no place to go, had to carry its own luggage. But I have now locked my bags and shall speak of it no further.

WORK AND LEGEND

To be gifted is to be defeated if you do not see clearly enough in time to build up the slopes and not go down them.

To subdue a gift should be the study of the man who finds he has it. And this study is complicated if, through bad luck, you discover it a bit late. I have spent my life, and I am still spending it, in contradicting a wretched endowment. The tricks it has played on me!

And how hard it is to see this clearly, since the gifts of talent marry the first form they encounter and this form risks becoming permanent. My safeguard was to lose my way so deliberately that I could not preserve the slightest doubt.

My family was of no help to me. It judged in terms of success. It was dilettantish and meddling.

Raymond Radiguet during the war (which he called vacation) read, on the Marne, in Parc Saint-Maur, the books of his father's library. My books were among them. I was therefore one of his classic authors. I bored him, of course, and at fourteen he longed to contradict me. When I met him, at Max Jacob's, he got me out of a trap. I was rapidly going God knows where. He quieted me down with his calmness. He taught me the authentic method. That of forgetting one is a poet and of allowing the phenomenon to take place without our knowing it. But his machine was new. Mine was dirty and noisy.

Raymond Radiguet was fifteen at that time. Erik Satie was almost sixty. These two extremes taught me how to understand myself. The one glory I can pride myself on is that of having complied with their teaching. Erik Satie was unrelatable. I mean you cannot tell his story. Honfleur and Scotland were his paternal and maternal origins. From Honfleur he inherited the style of the stories of Alphonse Allais, stories in which poetry is hidden and which bear no resemblance to the stupid anecdotes circulating.

From Scotland he inherited traits of solemn eccentricity.

Childhood and Early Influences

Physically he looked like a civil servant with a goatee, spectacles, umbrella, derby hat.

Egotistical, cruel, finical, he listened to nothing which did not jibe with his dogma and he lost his temper over anything which distracted him from it. Egotistical, because he thought only of his music. Cruel, because he defended his music. Finical, because he polished his music. And his music was tender. He was also, in his own way.

For several years, Erik Satie came every morning, to 10 rue d'Anjou, to sit with me in my room. He kept his coat on (not a single spot would he allow on it), his gloves, his hat almost touching his glasses, his umbrella in his hand. With his free hand he protected his mouth which looked serpentine when he spoke or laughed. He came from Arcueil on foot. There he lived in a small room where, after his death, under a mound of dust, they found all the letters of his friends. He had not opened one.

He used to clean himself with pumice stone. Never once did he use water.

At the period when music floated in effluvia, Satie, cognizant of the genius of Debussy and afraid of his despotism (they were friends and foes up to the end), turned his back on his school and became, in the Schola Cantorum, the familiar caricature of Socrates.

He pumiced himself, countered blows with himself, filed himself down, and forged the vehicle and the small opening through which his exquisite strength had only to flow from its source.

Once liberated, he made fun of himself, teased Ravel, gave, through modesty, to the beautiful music played by Ricardo Vines droll titles capable of alienating on the spot countless stupid people.

That was the man. It would certainly have been easier to follow in the rhetorical swells of Wagner and Debussy. But we needed a regimen at all costs. Each age refuses to be bewitched. Already, in *Le Coq et l'Arlequin*, I had denounced the charms of *Le Sacre du Printemps*. And in his self-refusal Stravinsky was to go further than all of us.

Erik Satie was my schoolteacher. Radiguet my examiner. Contact with them showed me my mistakes without their having to tell me, and if I were not able to conceal these mistakes, at least I knew of them.

It is not easy to form oneself. To reform oneself is harder still. Until the time of *Les Mariés de la Tour Eiffel*, the first work to which I owe nothing to no one, which is unlike any other work and in which I found my code, I had forced the lock and bent the key in all directions.

Orphée, L'Ange Heurtebise, Opéra saved me from that stratagem. It is true that you can fall back into it quickly and that, until the day I succeeded in taking part in nothing, I mean in taking part only in what concerns me, I still had upsets.

My worst defect comes from my childhood, as does almost everything I have. For I remain the victim of the nostalgic rhythms which make children into maniacs, placing their plate in a certain way on the table, crossing only certain grooves of the sidewalk.

In the midst of work, there are the symptoms that take hold and force me to resist what urges me on, and start me out on strange inconsistencies in writing and stop me from saying what I want to say.

Childhood and Early Influences

That is why my style often takes on a willful character which I despise and quickly give up. I suffer from cramps in my body and they reproduce the nervous ticks children indulge in secretly and by which they think they can control fate.

Now even as I explain them, I feel them. I try to overcome them. I knock against them, I am bogged down in them, I lose my way. I wish I could break the spell. My mania is stronger.

Perhaps I flatter myself in being able to give a shape to what I expel and I do it so ill that this force which I expel turns around and gives back the very form of its shape.

This is my definition of the pain of writing from which I suffer and which makes me prefer conversation.

I have few words in my pen. I turn them over and over. The idea rushes ahead, and when it stops and looks back, it sees me dragging along. It grows impatient and goes off. I can't find it again.

I leave the paper, take up something else, open the door. I'm free. That's easily said. The idea comes back at top speed and sets me to work.

The rage of fighting against cramps has made me into a man obscured by the absurdest legends. Invisible because of fables and monstrously visible because of that fact.

A procedure which confuses people soon wearies them. They grow tired following us. They invent one for us, and if we do not conform to this procedure, they hate us for it. It is too late to complain. We seem in excellent health, everyone says. It is dangerous not to correspond to the idea people have of us, because they do not willingly alter their opinion.

At that point where we escape from the world, legend grows fast.

Let a foreign critic judge us, and nine chances out of ten, he is right. He knows us better than our compatriots who trip over us. Space plays here the role of time. Our compatriots judge the work by the man. And since they see only a false image of the man, they judge falsely.

It is a social crime—or so it appears—to want solitude. After one piece of work, I escape. I look for new land. I fear the softness of habit. I want to be free of techniques, of experiment—awkward. I want to be a man of velleity, a traitor, an acrobat, an experimenter. A kind word would be: a magician.

A wave of the wand and books are written, the camera grinds, the pen draws, the actors play. It is very simple. Magician. That word facilitates everything. It is useless to analyze our own work. It was put together without effort.

ENCOUNTERS

My father was an amateur painter. He died when I was ten. My particular memory connected with him is the smell of oils and a palette which I loved. He painted with a great deal of facility. I sat on a chair near his.

My grandfather collected art objects and paintings. He was original and eclectic. For example, he used to buy paintings at the studios of Ingres and Eugène Delacroix. In addition, he owned masks of Antinoüs and Greek statues. The masks scared us. We loved the

Childhood and Early Influences

Venus in the billiard room because she turned on her pedestal. My grandfather's friends were virtuosi, violinists and 'cellists with whom he played quartets. All of that, outside of the mysterious departures of my family for the Opera, for *Faust* or *Götterdämmerung*, formed a mixture of conformity and nonconformity, which provided me with a vague love for painting, music, and the theatre.

The result was that poetry seemed to me a kind of game and the idea of struggle did not occur to me, nor the idea of overcoming the terrible circle of Muses whose beauty I thought of, to the exclusion of everything else.

After quite a long period when success blinded me (from 1910 to 1916), several important encounters opened my eyes. In a way, I was born at the age of twenty, at that age when Raymond Radiguet was to die, who never walked along bad roads and who at fifteen showed us the roads to take. The meetings I speak of, before his which was to teach me so much, were meetings with Igor Stravinsky and Pablo Picasso.

Le Sacre du Printemps totally upset me. Stravinsky, whom I had already known in 1913 in Leysin, was the first to teach me how to insult habits, without which art stagnates and remains a game. Radiguet next was going to lead me still further and teach me how to contradict the visible insult with an unapparent psychological boldness. He owed this spiritual attitude to the fact that we were his classics and that instinctively he was resisting us. I feel I shall always bear the mark of this influence.

With Picasso, the attack on habits runs the risk of imposing this very habit, and he does impose it in some way or other since no one yet has dared to speak back to him or to turn away from him. It is true that his insults have something religious about them and resemble the loving insults which Spaniards address to the Madonna if she is not the Madonna of their parish.

I repeat, Picasso has always insulted habits, and he insults them until this method itself becomes a habit. But it takes a long time to acquire, because he insults rapidly and is always inventing new insults. The man who insults him with a calm response will indeed be strong. And that new insulter will feel a greater resistance since the method of insult will have become habit and since his insult by calmness and silence will not be tolerated. He will know the suffering of the first public insulters, exemplified in Van Gogh.

Picasso taught me to run faster than beauty. Let me explain. He who runs at the speed of beauty will only commit pleonasm and post-cardism. He who runs less fast than beauty will accomplish only something mediocre. As for him who runs faster than beauty, his work will seem ugly, but he forces beauty to join it and then, once joined, it will become beautiful for good.

From the moment I met these men and we became friends, I tried to harmonize their school with Raymond Radiguet's which seemed to teach the opposite of theirs. But in reality he substituted a scornful insult for a provocative insult, and a storm for an intense calm.

Toward the end of his life, he traded his old broken glasses for a monocle, which gave him a distant grin, because he had a hard time keeping it on, and that monocle on his childlike myopic face produced the strangest and the haughtiest appearance.

Another of my masters was Erik Satie, whose melody was opposed to Impressionism in music, and whose spare music, freed from adornment and veils, seemed too simple to the dilettante.

In short, after a long rather ridiculous period, I found myself in an atmosphere favorable to the creation of poems, an atrocious, proud, incomprehensible creation, the passage from night to day, the limping of those who walk with one leg on the earth and the other in space.

Doubtless this struggle with myself and others, these demands of the artist to obey orders of an ego he knows imperfectly, forced me to explain myself and to study my mechanism.

OTHER ENCOUNTERS

In 1912, for a small sum, I rented a wing of the Hôtel Biron, on the rue de Varennes, where Rodin lived. In the center of Paris, five glass doors opened onto a fairy-story park abandoned by nuns at the time of the separation of Church and State.

In the evening, at the corner window of the hotel, I used to see a lamp light up. This lamp was Rainer Maria Rilke's. He was Auguste Rodin's secretary. I was to know only that lamp of his, which should have become a beacon for me. Long afterwards, alas, I learned from Blaise Cendrars who Rilke was; and many years passed before Rilke became acquainted with my play *Orphée*, produced in Berlin by Reinhardt, and before he sent Madame K this touching telegram: "Tell Jean Cocteau I love him. He is the only one to whom is revealed the myth from which he returns tanned as from the seashore." At the time of his death, Rilke had just begun work on the translation of *Orphée*. My good fortune in this and my loss in his death cannot be measured.

My first two contacts with Germany were this telegram from Rilke and a letter from Thomas Mann which reached me in Toulon where I was recovering from typhoid fever: "Take care! You belong to the race of poets who die in hospital."

Another important encounter was with Jacques Maritain, whose friendship had once helped me recover from the habit of opium in which I had begun indulging after the death of Raymond Radiguet, whom I had looked upon as my son. This death had depleted me. Serge de Diaghilev took me to Monte Carlo where he put on *Les Fâcheux* of Georges Auric and *Les Biches* of Francis Poulenc, musicians from the group of Six whose understanding, which never di-

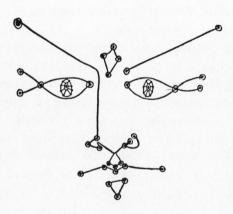

minished, made me, not the leader, but the historian
(*Le Coq et l'Arlequin*).

On coming in contact with the admirable spirit of
Maritain, I conceived the idea of an exchange of let-
ters in which we would extol the primitive power of
Catholicism and in which I would prove to the
younger generation that religion and newness in art
are not incompatible.

My letter, badly understood (it was believed to be
the sign of a conversion, which is ridiculous because
I am a Catholic), forced me subsequently to return to
my belligerent solitude, although I preserved my re-
spect and affection for Maritain. I shall preserve them
as long as I live.

PROUST, GIDE, THE SURREALISTS, APOLLINAIRE

The room of Marcel Proust, on Boulevard Hauss-
mann, was the first dark room where I witnessed al-
most every day—it would be more exact to say every
night, because he lived at night—the evolution of a
powerful work. He was still unknown, and I formed
the habit of looking on him, from my very first visit,
as a famous writer. In that stifling room, full of clouds
of fumigation and dust which covered the furniture
with a gray coating, we saw the activity of a beehive in
which the thousands of bees of memory made their
honey.

My relations with Gide were from beginning to end
a game of blindman's buff, a tentative pursuit of rec-
onciliation, quarrels, open letters, grievances whose
source might well be the incredible group of young

mythomaniacs who went from one to the other of us and amused themselves by confusing all issues.

My break with the Surrealists was to be more complex, more recriminatory, and longer. It arose, first, from my disobedience of official decrees, and second, from an instinct for value, stronger in me than the value itself which at that time I could put into the service of a cause. We were to become reconciled seventeen years later, and during those seventeen years I never stopped believing that certain enemies, troubled by analogous problems, are more friends than mere acquaintances.

All these little wars, skirmishes, duels, and tribunals, taught me more than a peaceful walk would have.

Between Montmartre, where Max Jacob, Reverdy, and Juan Gris lived, and Montparnasse, the "cellar" of rue Huygens, La Rotonde, the studios of Kisling and Modigliani, La Sirène publishing house, where M. Laffitte obeyed the directives of Cendrars and published our books, there was constant movement, supervised by Apollinaire, and led by Picasso, who preceded Dada. The first illumination about Dada came to me in a letter from Tristan Tzara containing a map of Europe on which he had drawn hands with a pointing index finger.

It is wrong to blame those sections of Paris which pride themselves on their crowds and their strollers, which adopt some men and condemn others, because Montparnasse of 1916 was accumulating explosives more secret and more potent than those of the War of 1914.

Each leave (I was with the army in Belgium)

Childhood and Early Influences

plunged me back into that amazing pot of contradictory forces, of inner strife between Cubist painters and writers who upturned a whole order, and substituted for it a new order on the margin of every political belief. A period when "the new spirit" seemed like a disorder, and which was one day to be called the Heroic Period.

It is difficult to understand with the passing of time that the battle of *Parade,* for example, in 1917 (Picasso and I had left to join Diaghilev and his company in Rome) coincided with Verdun, and that behind the lines an exemplary spiritual front had formed.

Apollinaire was to be a victim of those upheavals.

For his wound and his fatigue won out over his charm and thoughtfulness. He died on the day of the Armistice, and we were able to believe, in the confusion of kinds of heroism, that Paris was bedecked in his honor.

WAR AND PEACE

My development took place in the midst of *isms:* Cubism, Futurism, Purism, Orphism, Expressionism, Dadaism, Surrealism, and an avalanche of secrets exposed (this did not prevent them from sinking into the shadows of deep back-shops). It was doubtless due to that instinct of contradiction which controls us, that I decided, as far as the artist decides anything, to put my secrets within me and not to display them.

Boldness in the painter is almost always confused with the boldness of the brush. Baudelaire himself was tricked by this and ascribed to Delacroix traits of boldness which Ingres concealed. Under a very deceptive academic appearance, Ingres deformed, decanted, organized, tipped backwards the necks of women like goiters, murmured in a low voice rather than declaiming, and discovered that the youth of his period had not recognized him and that he would have to wait until the Cubists found him.

Cubism was classicism opposing the romanticism of the Fauves. In 1953, Picasso in *Guerre et Paix* fused the lyric and the peaceful, the *Bain Turc* of Ingres and the *Entrée des Croisés à Constantinople* of Delacroix.

What did Picasso do to upset the young painters? He argued with them, with dramatic force, that the well-done work would betray an aesthetic search and a lack of elegance in the mind. Thus he opened a false door to the lazy who do not bother him and closed it to his opponents who will be taken for aesthetes and latecomers. For he closes all the doors he opens. To follow him is to bump into a door. To paint on that door is to be accused of platitude.

A badly drawn figure of Picasso is the result of endless well-drawn figures he erases, corrects, covers over, and which serve him as a foundation. In opposition to all schools he seems to end his work with a sketch. His destructive enterprise is constructive in the sense that you could not construct anything new without destroying what is. He offers hope if he causes despair. He proves that individualism is not in danger of death and that we are not moving toward a future of termites. Many horns threaten him, but he wars against them with the prodigious agility of a bullfighter.

The schools teach us to start from infinity in order to reach the finite. Picasso moves in the opposite direction. He goes from the finite to the infinite. An infinite object. It is this non-finite, this in-finite which intrigues us and holds us. The adjusting of his opera glasses stops at the blurring. But as this blurring is expressed with precision, it intrigues us still more.

Moreover, each detail of the picture seems to obey different distances between the eyes and what they look at.

Picasso told me that he had seen in Avignon, on the square of the Château des Papes, an old painter, half blind, who was painting the castle. His wife, standing beside him, looked at the castle through binoculars and described it to him. He was painting from his wife.

Picasso often said that painting is a blindman's profession. He paints, not what he sees, but what he feels, what he tells himself about what he has seen. That conveys to his canvases an incomparable imaginative power.

ON MY ESCAPES

The Ballet Russe of Serge de Diaghilev played its part in one of my crises. He splashed Paris with colors. The first time I attended one of his ballets (*Pavillon d'Armide* was being presented), I had a seat reserved by my family. It all took place far off behind the footlights, in that burning bush where the theatre flames for those who do not see behind the stage.

I met Serge de Diaghilev at the home of Madame Sert. Instantly I joined the company. From then on, I saw Nijinsky only from backstage or from the box in which, behind Madame Sert wearing a Persian feather, Diaghilev watched his dancers through a very small pair of mother-of-pearl opera glasses.

What memories I have of them! I could write volumes, but that is not my subject. After the scandal of *Le Sacre du Printemps,* I joined Stravinsky in Leysin where he was caring for his wife. There I finished *Potomak,* which I had begun writing in Offranville, at the home of Jacques-Emile Blanche, under the surveillance of Gide. Returning to Maisons-Laffitte, I decided to extinguish myself or to be reborn. I shut myself in, tortured, questioned, insulted myself. I destroyed myself with contempt.

I kept only my ashes. The war came. By then I was agile in avoiding its traps, in judging what it brings, what it carries away, and how, in its occupations else-

Childhood and Early Influences

where, it rids us of foolishness. I had the good luck to spend the war with the *Fusiliers-Marins* (Marines). They possessed an unbelievable freedom of spirit. I wrote about this in the *Discours du Grand Sommeil* and in *Thomas l'Imposteur.*

Paris was an open city. We occupied it. Our revolution began in 1916.

After Stravinsky, came Picasso. At last I learned the secret without the knowledge of which any mental effort remains ineffectual. A world exists where the artist makes his discovery before he looks, and forever. A world where wars are religious wars. Picasso and Stravinsky were the leaders.

Too much importance is given the word genius. We are too economical with it. Stendhal uses it to say that a woman knew how to get into a carriage. In this respect I had genius and very little talent. My mind intuitively went to the extreme point but did not know how to break the point. You can imagine what the friendship meant to me of the creators of *Les Demoiselles d'Avignon* and *Les Noces*. I elbowed my way through quarrels, disputes, and heresy trials. I was looking for myself. I thought I recognized myself, I lost sight of myself, ran after myself, came upon myself again, out of breath. As soon as I fell under one spell, I trained myself to contradict it.

It is right if young people advance through injustice. For the age of recoil comes very fast. We return to it and can enjoy what we stepped over or trampled on.

The first bell of a period which begins in 1912 and will end with my death, was rung by Diaghilev one night on the Place de la Concorde. We were coming home from supper after the performance. Nijinsky was sulking as usual. He was walking ahead of us. Diaghilev was amused at my behavior. When I questioned him on his reserve (I was used to praise), he stopped, adjusted his monocle, and said to me: "Surprise me." The idea of surprise, so entrancing in Apollinaire, had never occurred to me.

In 1917, the evening of the première of *Parade,* I surprised him.

He was a brave man, but he listened livid to the infuriated house. He was afraid. There was good reason. Picasso, Satie, and myself could not reach backstage. The crowd recognized us and yelled at us. If it hadn't been for Apollinaire, his uniform and the bandage around his head—women, armed with hatpins, would have gouged out our eyes.

Some time after that, Hofmannsthal's *Joseph* was a great success. I was in his box. At the tenth curtain call Hofmannsthal leaned over to Diaghilev: "I should have preferred a scandal," he said to him. And Diaghilev replied, as he had to me when he had said 'Surprise me,' "The fact is—a scandal is not easy."

From 1917 on, Raymond Radiguet, aged fourteen, taught me to distrust a new thing if it seemed new, to oppose the fashion of the *avant-garde.* That was equivalent to putting myself in a bad position. Both right and left were scandalized. But, from a distance, all these opposites are grouped under the same category. Clever is the one who can pick his way out. The young people who visit our ruins only see in them a style. The period called "heroic" demonstrates only its boldness. It is the work of the museum. It equalizes Braque and Delacroix. Matisse and Picasso. Braque and Bon-

Childhood and Early Influences

nard. And I might even say that in a recent revival of *Faust,* the old garden set, by Jusseaume, had become, thanks to dust and subtle resemblances, a magnificent Claude Monet.

But this phenomenon of perspective does not concern the young. They can pretend to this only through the assurance that their projects are the most important and resemble nothing else.

DIAGHILEV AND NIJINSKY

In this book in which I testify to the Socratic trial which Society brings against us, I owe it to myself to express my gratitude to two free men who lived in order to express themselves.

Nijinsky was of a below-average size. Body and soul, he was the exaggeration of his art.

His face, of Mongolian type, was attached to his body by a very high and very wide neck. The muscles of his thighs and calves stretched the cloth of his trousers and gave him the appearance of having legs curved backwards. His fingers were short as if they were cut off at the joints. In a word, you could never believe that this little monkey, with sparse hair, dressed in a wide overcoat, a hat balanced on the top of his skull, was the public idol.

Yet he was the idol, and rightfully. Everything in him was suitable for an appearance at a distance, in stage lighting. On the stage his overdeveloped muscular system appeared supple. He grew taller (his heels never touched the ground), his hands became the foliage of his gestures, and his face radiated light.

Such a metamorphosis is almost unimaginable for those who did not witness it.

In *Le Spectre de la Rose* where he exhibited all his art, he showed irritability from 1913 on. The choreography of *Le Sacre* had seemed scandalous and he disliked being acclaimed and hissed. A heavy weight is in all of us. Nijinsky sought endlessly for some ruse with which to overcome it in himself.

He had noticed that half of the leap which ends *Le Spectre de la Rose* was invisible from the house. He invented a double leap by which he curled up in the air backstage and fell perpendicularly. They caught him like a boxer, with warm towels, slaps, and water which his servant Dmitri threw in his face.

Before the première of *Le Faune,* he surprised us for several days by his movements of a stiff neck. At supper at Larue's, Diaghilev and Bakst were worried. They questioned him but got no answer. Later we learned that he practiced with the weight of real horns. I could cite a hundred examples of this perpetual study for his parts which made him irritable and sulky.

In the Hôtel Crillon (he and Diaghilev migrated from hotel to hotel, expelled by theatre closings) he put on a beach dressing gown, pulled down the hood over his head, and wrote out his choreography.

I saw him create all his roles. His death scenes were poignant. Petrouchka's, in which the puppet becomes human enough to draw tears from us. His role in *Scheherazade,* in which he beat on the floor like a fish in the bottom of a boat.

Serge de Diaghilev seemed to wear the smallest hat in creation. If you put on that hat, it would go down

Childhood and Early Influences

to your ears. For his head was so large that every hat was too small for him.

His dancers called him Chinchilla because of an isolated white lock in his very black dyed hair. He wore a tightly fitting fur coat with an opossum collar and at times he buttoned it up with safety pins. His face was a bull dog's, his smile a very young crocodile's, one tooth on the edge. To grind this tooth was for him the sign of pleasure, or fear, or anger. His mouth surmounted by a small mustache, he munched, seated in the back part of the loge from where he watched his artists to whom he handed on no advice. And his wet eye looking downward had the curve of a Portuguese oyster. He conducted throughout the world a dance company, as confused and multicolored as the fair of Nijni Novgorod. His one luxury was to discover a star. We saw him bring forth from the Russian ghetto the thin, long, glaucous Madame Rubinstein. She did not dance. She appeared, exhibited herself, mimed, walked about, walked off, and at times (as in *Scheherazade*) attempted the beginning of a dance.

One of Diaghilev's triumphs was to present her to the Paris public in the role of Cleopatra. It was like presenting her to Antony. They brought on a roll of cloth and placed it in the middle of the stage. They unwound and unfurled it. And Madame Ida Rubinstein appeared, her legs so thin that you thought you were looking at an ibis in the Nile.

II. The Writer's Character

I am past my fifties. This means that death does not have very far to go to meet me. The play is almost over. Not much dialogue remains. If I look around (at what concerns me), I see only legends which are pure fancy. I avoid stepping in them and getting caught in the glue. Save for the preface of Roger Lannes to my *Morceaux Choisis,* published by Seghers, I see nothing which resembles me (I mean, nothing which uncovers my face). Neither in the praise nor in the blame can I find any attempt to separate the true from the false.

It is true that I find excuse for the silence of those who might unravel my skein. My hair has always grown in every direction and my teeth also and the bristles of my beard. My nerves and my soul must be planted in the same way. That is what makes me insoluble to people who develop in one direction. It is bewildering to those who might rid me of this mythological leprosy. They do not know how to begin explaining me.

My organic disorder is a protection because it scares away the inattentive. Thus I derive some advantage

56

The Writer's Character

from it. It provides me diversity, contrast, a speed in bending now in one direction and now in another, depending on the appeal of this or that object, and in allowing me to catch my balance at the end.

Doubtless this makes my dogma obscure, my cause difficult to support. But since no one comes to my aid, I hasten to it and try to follow myself closely.

For five months, in a terrible state of health, I have been shooting my film *Beauty and the Beast*. After a severe sunburn in Arcachon, I have not stopped fighting microbes and the ravages they provoke in my body.

I am writing these lines on a mountain of snow surrounded by others, under a sulky sky. Medicine insists that microbes die in a high altitude. It seems to me that on the contrary they love it and gather strength at the same time I do.

Suffering is a habit. I am used to it. During the work on the film, they spoke of my courage. It was, rather, a laziness in caring for myself. I let myself fall passively and as heavily as possible into work.

This work distracted me from pain, and since it has been proved that the snow regimen is ineffectual, I derived more profit from persisting in my labors than in exiling myself in a tiresome solitude. Even here, where I should rest my mind and curl up like an animal, I cannot refrain from talking with you.

With whom else could I talk? These hotels receive members of a new society who profit from us and imitate a luxury taught them by films and newspapers. Hence the uproar of children rushing between the tables, children whose families do not know there are other children better behaved. In front of doors, ladies let us go first. I recognize the habit of conducting to

57

the door the clients of very small shops. These ladies and gentlemen move about in the medieval appearance of sport clothes. They put on skis, climb slopes, and gloriously break their legs. I withdraw from them as much as possible, walk in the snow, close the door of my room, and avenge myself on this sheet of paper for not being able to indulge in the one sport I like, which was once called a conference and which is conversation.

The sun is coming out and coloring our world. Far off, from my window, this scene shows me horses and knights, with banners, lances, shields, trumpets, and

grandstands for a white tournament. The summits are spotted with shadows and with snow more dazzling than scarlet. But I converse nevertheless, for I have no pleasure unless I can exchange it with someone. In Morzine I can talk with no one. The inhabitants can scarcely speak. They use their mouths only for eating. Many are departing, called home by the business which is enriching them.

ON MY STYLE

I am neither happy nor sad. But I can be excessively one or the other. If the conversation is spirited, I can forget the sorrows I am leaving behind, the cause for suffering, I can forget myself, such is the intoxication of work for me and the exaltation of ideas. They come to me more easily than in solitude, and often, writing an article is torture whereas I can speak of it effortlessly. This gift for speech might imply a facility I do not have. For as soon as I exercise any control, this facility gives way to painful labor whose realization seems to me arduous and endless. To this is added a superstitious fear about the initial step which I am always afraid of performing badly. This makes me lazy. Psychiatrists call it "worry over the act." White paper and pen and ink terrify me. I feel that they are in coalition against my will to write. If I succeed in quelling them, then the machine warms up, the work excites me, and my mind functions. But it is important that I do not join closely with it, that I half-sleep. The slightest awareness of this mechanism interrupts it. And if I wish to start it up again, I have to wait until it makes up its mind, and not try to convince it by some trap.

That is why I do not use a table which intimidates me and seems too formal. I write at any time, on my knees. For drawing, it is the same process. Of course, I can imitate a line, but that is not what I want, and the real line emerges when it wants to.

My dreams are almost always such serious and detailed caricatures of my actions that they might well be lessons for me. But alas, they parody the very organism of the soul and discourage me rather than provide me with the means of fighting. For no one knows his weaknesses better than I do, and when I happen to read an article directed against me, I believe I could make a surer thrust, and that the blade would sink up to the hilt and that all I would have to do would be to sink down, let my tongue hang out, and kneel in the arena.

One should not confuse intelligence, skilled in tricking its man, with that organ whose seat is nowhere and which teaches us with finality what our limitations are. No one can scale them. The effort would be visible. It would outline all the more clearly the paltry space granted to our vaultings. It is by the ability to move within this space that talent is tested. We can progress only from there. And this progress is of a moral order since each one of our projects catches us unexpectedly. We can count only on rectitude. Any cheating induces further cheating. A simple fumbling would be preferable. The anonymous public jeers at it, but we excuse it. Cheating has its effect in the long run. The public turns away with the lifeless expression of a woman who loved and who no longer loves.

That is why I strove not to lose my strength at school. I allow a hundred mistakes which I fail to correct, since I am lazy in rereading, and I reread only the general idea. When the matter at hand is said, I lose interest. Yet despite this, I possess a method. It consists in being hard, economical in words, in unrhyming prose, in taking aim but not as a hunter, and in scoring the bull's-eye at all costs.

When I reread what I have written long afterwards, I am ashamed only of the ornaments. They are harmful because they turn the interest away from the real center. The public loves them, is dazzled by them, and does not see the rest. I heard Charlie Chaplin complain of having left in his film *The Gold Rush* the dance of the rolls for which he has been so often complimented. He saw it to be a defect which attracted the eye. I also heard him say (about ornamental style) that after making a film, he used to "shake the tree." He added that we should keep only what clings to the branches.

The ornamental often does not come solely from the artist. It comes from an equilibrium. The public looks upon this equilibrium as something superficial and takes solace in not appreciating the foundation. This is Picasso's situation. He is a complete artist, both male and female. He is the site of terrible household quarrels. Never were so many dishes broken. The man always wins out and slams the door behind him. But from the woman there comes an elegance, an inner gentleness, a form of luxury, which offer an excuse to those who fear brute strength and cannot follow the man once he is outside the house.

MY APPEARANCE

My face has never been handsome. Youthfulness took the place of beauty in me. My bone structure is satisfactory, but my skin covers it in a strange way. My skeleton keeps changing and losing its form. My nose, which was straight, is now arched like my grandfather's. I noticed that my mother's nose became hooked on her deathbed. Endless inner upheavals and suffering, periods of doubt, revolts checked by force, setbacks, have marked my forehead, formed a deep line between my eyebrows, twisted them, given me heavy eyelids, softened my hollow cheeks, and lowered the corners of my mouth to such a degree that if I bend down over a low mirror I see my mask come off the bone and make out of a form something formless. My beard comes out white. My hair, in losing its thickness, has maintained its rebellion. It has become a sheaf of locks which fight and cannot be combed. If I flatten them out, I am seedy-looking. If I let them stand up wild, they make me look affected.

My teeth overlap. In a word, my body, neither large nor small, but which is slender and lean, armed with feet and hands that are admired because they are long and very expressive, walks about with a repellent head. It makes me appear arrogant. This false arrogance comes from my longing to overcome the embarrassment I feel at my appearance, and its quickness at dissolving comes from a fear that it might be taken for real arrogance.

What follows this is too rapid a shift from reserve to expansiveness, from assurance to awkwardness. I do

not know hate. I forget offences so easily that I can smile at my enemies when I meet them face to face. Their amazement is like a cold shower and I wake up. Then I do not know what attitude to take. I am surprised they remember the harm they did me and which I had forgotten.

My natural inclination to live in accord with the Gospels separates me from dogma. Joan of Arc is my favorite writer. No one expresses himself more clearly than she does, in both form and content.[1] She would have perhaps lost her poignancy if she had adopted a style. In her original form, she is style itself, and I constantly read and reread her trial. Antigone is my other saint. These two anarchists harmonize with the seriousness I like, which Gide says I do not possess, a seriousness which is akin to me and which is not the same as that kind usually meant by the word. It is the seriousness of poets. Academicians in every period scorn it. If unconsciously they are jealous of it, they may go so far as to commit a crime. Voltaire, Diderot, Grimm are only the names of an attitude as old as the world and which will disappear when the world disappears. It wars against poets and turns against them curved weapons, extremely dangerous at close range.

Rousseau left bloody traces of that manhunt which continued to the time of Hume when the rush for the spoils was to have taken place. Do not believe that

[1] Glory, through the help of a minority, is the prerogative of artists. This method would not count for politicians, but at times pride urges them to take the risk. Lacking unanimity, a majority hurts them. Then they pounce on that minority which, in their reign, could not possibly be strong. The case of Joan of Arc is different. Her vote was meager. She had only three voices. But they counted. Joan of Arc was a poet.

such persistence fades into thin air. Something from it continues. Rousseau will always remain an example of a persecution complex. He had it. But he had reason to have it. It is like reproaching the hunted deer for making his zigzag getaway.

ON BEING WITHOUT BEING

At this time I should like to summarize matters in this house where I am trying to fall asleep. I have cut off all communication with Paris. My letters are opened and I am brought only what is indispensable. I speak with no one. My case of shingles has begun again. Once more I notice it likes to flourish and that it profits from my vegetative existence. My arms, chest, and forehead are affected. Since the cause of this sickness is the same as asthma, I am doubtless incurable, and all I can count on are good and bad days. I carefully avoid the sun which I love. When I walk, I stay in the shade. The rest of the time I stay inside. I read and write. Solitude forces me to be Robinson Crusoe and his island, and to prospect in myself. To this I bring no intelligence but a certain boldness which replaces intelligence.

Incapable of following one course, I proceed impulsively. I cannot follow one idea for long. I let it escape just when I should draw near and seize it. My whole life long I have hunted in that way, but I cannot do otherwise. This deceives those people who interpret my luck as skill, my mistakes as strategy. Never has a man been surrounded by so much incomprehension and love and hate, for if the character they think I am, irritates those who judge me from a distance, those who come close resemble Beauty when she fears a monster and finds a kind Beast who wants only to love her.

I can truthfully say that my best friendships come from this contrast.

The legends about me turn away the fools. The very intelligent are suspicious of me. Who remain after these two categories? The wanderers who resemble me, who change their address more often than their shirt, and who pay with an exhibition for the right of staying where they are. This is why my solitude never seems silent. I appear only at the moment of the act and the parade. I am sorry for those who live in my gypsy wagon and who believe they get the worst of the bargain because they see only my suffering.

Like all vagabonds, I am obsessed with the mania of owning a house. I keep looking for one in the country. When I find one, either its owner refuses to sell it because my enthusiasm opens his eyes to its worth, or the price is too high.[1]

In Paris, I find nothing that suits me. The apartments I am offered seem hostile. I want them to say to me: "I was expecting you."

While hoping for the impossible, I am settling into my little hole.

"I feel a difficulty in existing." (*Je sens une difficulté*

---

[1] Since the printing of this book, I have bought the house which was waiting for me. Here I am correcting these proofs. It is a refuge, far from the bells of the Palais-Royal. It provides me with the spectacle of the ridiculous magnificent determination of growing things. Here I am collecting the memories of old country scenes in which I used to dream of Paris, as later I used to dream in Paris of escaping. The water in the ditches and the sun are painting on the walls of my room their marble-looking mobiles. Spring is radiant everywhere.

d'être.) This is an answer which Fontenelle, aged one hundred, gave on his deathbed to the doctor who asked him: "M. Fontenelle, what do you feel?" Whereas his "difficulty" belonged to his last hour, mine has been going on forever.

It must be ecstatic to live comfortably in one's own skin. From birth, my cargo has been badly stowed. I have never stood upright. This is my balance sheet, on self-examination. And in this woeful state, rather than keeping to my room, I have knocked about the world. From the age of fifteen, I have not stopped one minute. Occasionally I meet someone who speaks to me cordially and whom I am unable to recognize until a strong grasp suddenly pulls up from the dark the setting of a drama in which he played his role and I mine, and which I had completely forgotten. I have been closely associated with so many things that not one but fifty drop out of my memory. A deep undercurrent brings them up to the surface with, as the Bible says, *all that is inside*. It is incredible how few traces remain in me of long periods of time when I must have lived as I always have lived. That is why, when I dig into my past, I first come upon a figure still covered with its earth. If I look for dates, sentences, places, scenes, I overlap, interpolate, soil, move ahead, retreat, and end in confusion.

My principal business is to lead an existence in the present which is my own. I do not boast that it is more rapid than another's, but more to my taste. This present life of mine abolishes time to the extent that I can talk with Delacroix and Baudelaire. When Marcel Proust was unknown, this sense of time allowed me to look upon him as famous and to treat him as if he possessed the fame he was to enjoy one day. When I discovered that this timeless state was my privilege and that it was too late to acquire a better state, I perfected it and grew into it.

But suddenly *my eyes were opened*. I realized I had been using the worst system for emptying my thoughts, that I was wearing myself out in tiresome activities which impeded me and devoured me, that I was bestirring myself for too many things. I persisted in a mechanical way. I had become a slave to the point of confusing an instinct for legitimate defense which inspired me to revolt, with a bad case of fidgeting.

Now I know what to do. As soon as I open one eye, I close the other and take to my heels.

SELF-COMMITMENT

I reap the worst insults and the highest praise, all jumbled together. I left my city and was put in "quarantine" because my commitment was made to myself and not to something outside myself.

I must explain this fashionable word, "commitment" (*engagement*).

An exterior commitment without faith is a sacrilege. I cannot bring myself to do it. I am an anachronism. A free man. I do not know what is under the cards. I imagine it to be, alas, more simple than is believed. But the player who does not know is a dupe. I am willing to be a dupe only in a system which I know or believe I know very well.

The Communist who gives his word without real faith in communism is as guilty as the Catholic who takes communion without faith, by habit.

The Writer's Character

I am well aware of what a man risks who belongs neither to the right nor to the left. He is called an opportunist. For ists and isms are flourishing as usual. I also know that today's disorder has found its order, today's unbalance its balance, and that our modern literature resembles a man falling and turning to stone while he falls. I know that disorder propagates disorder, and that the chain of current events may break the thread of the past which once was the best investment for spiritual funds.

Each day young people are told there is no future. It was worship of the present which forced a young Italian to kill his teacher who had given him a low mark, and a young Frenchman to kill his mother and father who had inconvenienced him. These criminals could see no consequence of their crimes. Immediate matters absorbed them. They gathered their strength into one moment. They were impelled to crime by the suppression of hope.

Despite my wish not to elaborate and lengthen, and my preference to communicate to my words the noble impersonality of figures, I must insist on this drama of the immediate and the current which has infiltrated into our noncurrent activities. Art is threatened by two kinds of danger. Journalism and the digest. I have just learned that for mine workers in the north "novels that can be read standing" (*sic*) have been published. And I have often noticed the scorn shown to enterprises which have little or no connection with party or class struggle.

Every art magazine I know raises on each page the problems discussed by the newspapers. Bossuet judged the century of Louis XIV in these terms: "A mediocre limited century." Yes, each age calls itself mediocre and limited. There is "nothing, nothing, nothing," said Alfred de Musset about his.

But the characteristic of our age is the fear of appearing ridiculous in offering praise, and the certainty of appearing intelligent in criticizing adversely. This does not prevent beauty from being created and growing silently under the curve of the projectiles.

Beauty at its inception is always invisible. A fairy godmother protects it, either saying, "You will appear ugly," or enveloping it in a cloud. This protection has been increased a hundred fold in our age. An impatience for visibility urges some to consider first-class journalism the one valid attitude, and others to run so fast that they see nothing. Not that writers obey orders, but they are caught by a contagion of directives, by a delight in spattering the lonely pedestrian.

The lonely pedestrian is seen less and less. He easily gives up walking, stands on the side of the road, and indulges in the pantomime of hitch-hiking.

When he gets a ride, he is committed (*engagé*), you might say, to an auto not his own, because of simple laziness which keeps him from continuing his walk *on his own feet*.

Solitary walkers are few in number and I am among them. The solitude of my walk is incomprehensible, despite the fact that people ascribe to me bad intentions which they invent, and headlights point me out. I am accused of botanizing on the left and the right of the road, and of collecting plants not listed by the pharmacopoeia. In short, for thirty years now, Paris has had me on trial on a charge similar to that brought by medical schools against quack healers.

The Writer's Character

My housekeeper, Madeleine, is aware of this. At the Palais-Royal, where I live in a very small apartment, she says to me when she drives away the visitors waiting in front of my door: "They must think that Monsieur Jean is a healer."

But I have no magic herb. Like any healer, all I can do is to give to those who come to see me the courage to cure themselves.

WHAT I MEAN BY WALKING IN THE DARK

If, in addition to my books, plays, and films, I have turned my energies of a solitary walker, without any help from the traffic in an eighty-day trip around the world, to chairmanships, articles, prefaces, records, ballets, stage sets, costumes, masks, curtains, tapestries, mosaics, if I was manager for the Negro boxer, Al Brown, and employed clowns, dancers, and acrobats, it was not through any sense of travel or dispersal. I have never carried out the slightest piece of work haphazardly or wantonly. Each time I filled the space I had planned to occupy so that the object of my study would not fluctuate between partitions constructed at a preliminary stage. And even when I seemed to leave my profession, in order to put back into the ring a former world champion, believed to be half dead by the sports world, it was to prove to myself that the poet, like the bad boy, should be capable of everything, that there is no activity forbidden to those who have determination, no effort impossible for intellectual and moral athleticism which comes from a long gymnastics of thought, no inn unworthy of the solitary walker.

71

After his twelve successful fights, under my management, I agreed with Al Brown that it was useless to continue, since the proof was established that even the prestige of an athlete comes from active poetry. I accepted insults for putting him back behind the ropes, because I also withdrew him from the ring. The space I had promised to fill had been filled. The rest of the affair had no importance for him or for me. He had accepted being a link in my chain, one of those problems which I never give up solving until I have made the final computation.

It is said that everything is easy for me. That is not true. It is precisely my lack of talent which fascinates me in one piece of work and blinds me to all others. That is why my work is so diverse and so abundant, why I cannot understand where or how I created it.

The Writer's Character

The one problem which I willingly neglected was financial. I could not simultaneously create and draw benefits. If others have profited, I congratulate them. But there are figures and figures. Mine benefit me in a domain where gold would devaluate my income. To the problem of gold, as to any other, one should be totally devoted, and I admire those men who extract from it a strange kind of poetry. I was born prodigal. And I have said, in my *Journal d'un Inconnu*, there is a race of Who loses-wins, and a race of Who wins-loses. The Who loses-wins implies a visible failure without which no victory is significant. I applaud the amazing negative answer given by India to distinguished minds in 1870, when it realized, but too late, that wisdom is not commerce, and that seeming to lose, it might win the enterprise.

CONFESSION

And now I have to confess the unpardonable and the scandalous, in an age which scorns happiness. I am a happy man. And I am going to tell you the secret of my happiness. It is quite simple. I love mankind. I love love. I hate hate. I try to understand and accept. Every episode provides a dock from which I can set sail and discover something new. The success of a friend comforts me, and I have always been surprised at the situation in which the success of someone else is painful. Egotistically I count on the truth that a pretty woman is more attractive in a group of pretty women than of ugly women. My solitude is illuminated by the spotlight playing on works I approve of and which differ from mine. If I disapprove of a work, I try to

73

The Journals of Jean Cocteau

find in it something that would change my mind. In a word, I am happy I attended a school of friendships so noble that their virtues had the power usually ascribed to vices. The school of those who love as others hate. The school of those who open wide their door for fear of refusing the unknown guest.

I am pessimistic by optimism, by the conviction that all is better than it seems, by a totally mad desire for harmony.

I have passed the age when injustice is a law for self-defense, when love upsets you like an illness which must be cured at any cost. I am at an age when I do not fear being invaded by someone stronger than myself. On the contrary, I try to entertain him like a royal guest. And each night I go to bed happy if I have harmed my neighbor in no way.

I give away freely this secret of happiness, with the way to use it, because it is not for sale, and I still know troubled people who suppose they are given a secret to lead them astray and who perhaps would have more faith in it if it could be bought. Now, my books fall like dead leaves from the hands of those people. I look for the kind of public that is without prejudice, without bristles, without fear.

III. Testimonials

MARCEL PROUST

Marcel Proust's apartment, on Boulevard Haussmann. The table covered with medicine bottles, a theatre-phone (an instrument through which you could hear certain theatres), a pile of school notebooks, and, as on the other furniture, a coat of dust that was never removed, the gas lamp wrapped in cotton cloth, the ebony table in the shadows littered with photographs of notorious beauties, duchesses, dukes, footmen from palaces, the mantelpiece with a false mirror, cloth covers everywhere, and dust, the smell of antiasthmatic powder, the odor of a tomb. This entire room of Jules Verne was a Nautilus crowded with precision instruments where it was fatal to encounter Captain Nemo in person: Marcel Proust, thin, cadaverous, wearing the beard of Carnot in his casket.

Proust put on and took off that black beard of a caliph as fast as the comedians who, in the provinces, imitate statesmen and orchestra leaders. I remember him with a beard, and I have seen him clean shaven as he appears in the painting of Jacques-Emile Blanche, an orchid in his buttonhole and his face looking like an egg.

Proust used to receive me in that closed room. He would be on his bed, dressed, wearing a collar, a necktie, and gloves, in fearful terror of a perfume, a breath of air, an opened window, a ray of sun. "Dear Jean," he would ask me, "didn't you hold the hand of a lady who might have touched a rose?" "No, Marcel." "Are you sure?" And half serious, half joking, he would explain that the phrase from *Pelléas* where the wind passes over the sea was enough to start up in him an attack of asthma.

He lay stiffly across the bed in the wrong way, in a sarcophagus of remains of souls and landscapes and all that had not served him in Balbec, Combray, Méséglise, in the Countess de Chevigné, in Count Greffhule, in Haas and Robert de Montesquiou. He lay just as he did when we looked at his remains for the last time beside the pile of notebooks of his novel which continued to live at his left, like the wristwatches on dead soldiers.

Each night he read to me from *Swann's Way*.

Those sessions added a new chaos to the pestilential disorder of the room, because Proust would read at any point in his manuscript, would miss a page and join two passages, would begin over, would stop to explain that a gentleman's bow in the first chapter would be elucidated in the last volume, and behind his gloved hand he would burst out laughing and drool over his beard and cheeks. "This is too stupid," he would say. "No! I won't read any further. It's too stupid." Then his speech would again become a confused lamentation, a tearful threnody of excuse, politeness, and remorse. "It was too stupid. He was ashamed to force me to listen to such stupid things. It was his fault. Besides, he could never reread anything. He should never have begun the reading. . . ." And when I had convinced him to continue, he stretched out his arm, took the first sheet from the magician's book, and we fell smack into the Guermantes or the Verdurins. At the end of fifty lines, the same scene began over again. He groaned, laughed, excused his bad reading. Sometimes he got up, took off a coat, ran his hand through his black hair, which he himself used to cut and which fell over his starched collar. Then he went into his dressing room where a ghastly light was projected against the wall. There you could see him standing, in his shirt sleeves, a purple vest on the torso of a puppet, holding a plate in one hand, a fork in the other, and eating noodles.

Do not expect me to follow Proust in his night journeys and tell you about them. They took place in the hired cab of Albaret, husband of Céleste, a real night cab of Fantômas. These excursions from which he returned at dawn, with his fur-lined cloak wrapped around him, white faced, his eyes heavily circled with black, a bottle of Evian water sticking out of his pocket, his black bangs over his forehead, one of his button shoes unbuttoned, his derby in his hand, gave to Proust enough figures and calculations to permit him to build a cathedral in his room and grow wild roses there.

Albaret's cab always took on a woeful appearance in the daytime. Proust's daytime excursions occurred once or twice a year. He and I took one together. It was to see the paintings of Gustave Moreau at the home of Madame Ayem, and then in the Louvre, Mantegna's *Saint Sébastien* and Ingres' *Bain Turc*.

·

GUILLAUME APOLLINAIRE

I knew him when he wore a pale-blue uniform, when his head was shaved and a scar on his forehead resembled a starfish. A device of leather and strips of cloth made for him a kind of turban or small helmet,[1] which seemed to be concealing a microphone through which he heard what the rest of us could not hear and by which he kept in secret contact with a magic world. He transcribed its messages. Some of his poems do not even translate the code. We often saw him listen. He closed his eyes, hummed, dipped his pen in the inkwell. A drop of ink formed at the tip. It wavered and fell. It made a star on the paper. *Alcools* and *Calligrammes* were markings of a secret code.

François Villon and Guillaume Apollinaire are the only poets I know who never fall because of the lameness out of which poetry is made and which those who believe they create poetry because they write verse do not even suspect.

The unusual word (and he used many) lost, in Apollinaire's art, all picturesqueness. The banal word became rare. The amethysts, moonstones, emeralds, carnelians, and agates in his poetry, he mounted, no matter where they came from, as a winnower winnows, seated on a café chair. No street artisan was more humble and more alert than this soldier in blue.

He was large without being fat, his Roman face was pale, his mouth with a small mustache over it articulated words in a staccato voice, with a slightly pedantic and panting grace.

---

[1] This was a bandage worn by Apollinaire after an operation. (Translator's note.)

Testimonials

His eyes laughed at the seriousness of his face. His hands of a priest accompanied his speech with gestures which recalled the gesture sailors affect when they drink and when they urinate.

His laughter did not come from his mouth. It rose up from every part of his organism, like an invasion shaking him. Then followed a silent laughter in his eyes, and his body resumed its balance. Wearing socks, without his leather leggings, his knee breeches tight over his legs, he crossed his small bedroom on the Boulevard Saint-Germain, climbed a few steps to the tiny study where we saw the de luxe edition of *Serres Chaudes* and the copper bird of the Beni.

The walls were covered with paintings of his friends. In addition to the portrait of Rousseau with the hedge of pinks, and the young angular-looking girls of Laurencin, there were Fauves, Cubists, Expressionists, Orphists, and one Larionov of the machine period about which he used to say, "it's the gas meter."

He loved art movements and knew, beginning with Moréas and the Closerie des Lilas, the power of names which they bear and which people mysteriously repeat to one another.

His wife's face resembled the pretty goldfish bowl in the shops along the quay, opposite the boxes of books by which, he once wrote, the Seine is supported.

Armistice morning, 1918, Picasso and Max Jacob had come to No. 10 rue d'Anjou. I lived there, with my mother. They told me they were worried about Guillaume, that his heart had been affected, and that we should telephone to Capmas, a physician friend of mine. We called Capmas. It was too late. Capmas begged Apollinaire to help him, to help himself, to

79

find the will to live. His strength had left him. His heavy breathing had grown worse. He was suffocating. In the evening, when I came to the Boulevard Saint-Germain to meet Picasso, Max, and André Salmon, they told me that Guillaume was dead.

His small room was full of shadows and shadowy figures: his wife, his mother, the rest of us, and still others I did not recognize, moving about or meditating. His face illuminated the linen on the bed. A laureate beauty, so radiant that we thought of young Virgil. Death, in Dante's robe, was pulling him, as children do, by the hand.

When he was alive, his corpulence never seemed corpulence. And it was the same with his heavy breathing. He seemed to move in the midst of very delicate things, over earth mined with precious explosives. He moved in a singular, almost underwater fashion, which I associate more with Jean Paulhan.

His remains seemed to fly without moving. The elderberry pith, the marrow of birds and dolphins, of all that dislikes heaviness, left his body, raised it, and made, in contact with the air, a phosphorescent combustion, a halo.

I could see him sauntering down the streets of Montparnasse, strewn with white hopscotch lines, and carrying with him the arsenal of fragile objects I mentioned, avoiding all accidents of breakage, and uttering learned remarks. Such theories as, Bretons being at one time Negroes, Gauls never wearing mustaches, *groom* being an adulteration of *gros homme* pronounced in London where Swiss porters, in imitation of the French, were replaced by small boys.

Then he would stop, raise the finger of a marquess

and say (for example): "I have just reread *Maldoror*. The young today have been more influenced by Lautréamont than by Rimbaud." I quote this sentence from a hundred others because it reminds me of what Picasso told me. Picasso, Max Jacob, Apollinaire, when they were young, roamed over Montmartre, racing down its stairways and shouting: "Long live Rimbaud! Down with Laforgue!" I would say that such meetings were far more significant than those which precede plebiscites.

One morning in 1917 (Picasso, Satie, and myself had just been subjected to the scandal of *Parade*), Blaise Cendrars telephoned me to say that he was reading in the magazine *Sic* a poem signed by me, that he was surprised not to know it, that the poem was not in my style, and that he wanted to read it to me over the telephone so that I might vouch that it was not by me. It was counterfeit. Out of that counterfeit, Apollinaire created a dramatic episode. He became a judge for the cause of literature and enjoyed his rostrum. From café to café, from Montparnasse to Montmartre, from one newspaper edition to another, he questioned, raised doubts, accused everyone, except the guilty man, who later confessed his hoax. This had consisted of sending a poem to Birot, editor-in-chief of *Sic*, of enticing him on with my signature so that he published it without any checkup, because the poem was an acrostic. The capital letters formed the words: PAUVRE BIROT (poor Birot).

Apollinaire asked me once for a poem to print on the program of the first performance of his play *Les Mamelles de Tirésias,* in the Renée Maubel Theatre. I called the poem *Zèbre* and used the word *rue* in the sense of the infinitive, *ruer,* to kick (of animals). The Cubists, with Juan Gris at their head, interpreted *rue* as "street," and after the performance, summoned me to explain the "street," which did not conform to the poem.

At this tribunal, where I was beside Apollinaire, he moved from the role of judge to culprit. He was accused of having compromised dogma in a ludicrous way, by entrusting his sets and costumes to Serge Ferat. I was fond of Gris and he was fond of me. We all loved Apollinaire. I record this episode to show what pinheads we were dancing on. The slightest prank was suspect. It was consigned to experts and usually ended in a condemnation. Gris said, "I put the syphon into painting." (Only the bottles of Anis del Oso were allowed.) And Marcoussis, on leaving the exhibition of the *Fenêtres* of Picasso, at Paul Rosenberg's, said, "He has solved the problem of the *espagnolette*" (the French window fastener).

Do not laugh. It was a noble, distinguished age when such delicacies of meanings tormented the minds of the artists. Picasso is right in saying that a government which would punish a painter for choosing the wrong color or the wrong line would be an impressive government.

I return to Apollinaire. He was embittered by the punishment he received from *Les Mamelles de Tirésias.* He held on to it for a long time as to the string of a kite. In fact, he became a kite. Light in weight, casting about, pulling on the string, dipping, flying to the right and the left. He told me he was "sick and tired of painters." And he added: "I don't give a damn for their architectural designs." That was a surprise

coming from the man who initiated the victory over mimesis in art. But he wanted a wing from Uccello and he wanted painters to graze in a pasture of poisonous colchicum.

Except for Picasso, a ten-headed eagle and supreme ruler in his kingdom, the Cubists ended by measuring their objects. A yardstick in their hand, they obliged it to serve them in a practical way. Others flourished tracing paper and mathematics. Others built up carcasses.

Apollinaire ran from group to group and wore himself out.

This fatigue came doubtless at the beginning of the events which led him to his death. Only extraordinary surprises pleased him. He used to groan. He pitied his generation and claimed it was sacrificed with its backside between two chairs. He used to escape to the studio of Picasso, who was never tired out. He did not suspect for a moment—such is the ignorance of the authentic artist—that he was going to set forth and become a constellation.

That constellation took on the form of his wound, which had been prophesied to him in a painting of Georgio di Chirico.

That is how events take place in our world. Everything unfolds by a system of mathematics unrecognized by mathematicians and which belongs to poets. All things considered, nothing totters in it. And everything totters from beginning to end.

On the rock where soon we will be only a few, escaped from the wreck, Apollinaire sings. Beware, traveling salesman, he's Lorelei.

I do not pretend to study Apollinaire carefully. I prefer to stop with these few lines which sketch a silhouette, and describe an appearance. It is a pin through the living insect, like the profile of Georges Auric whose resemblance I caught in a drawing by replacing the eye with a dot. Others will analyze Apollinaire and his magic, based on the properties of simples. He collected herbs between the Seine and the Rhine. The mixtures he stirred with a spoon in a mess-tin, over an alcohol lamp, testifying to the importance his episcopal personage attached to sacrilege of all kinds. He has been described on his knees serving the mass of the army chaplain, as well as presiding over a black mass, or removing the splinters of a shell from a wound, as well as sticking pins into a wax figure. On the inquisitor's throne as well as tied for burning to a Spanish stake. He is both Duke Alessandro and Lorenzaccio.

Testimonials

RAYMOND RADIGUET

[FROM *Lettre à Jacques Maritain*]

You understand what I call "gloves of heaven." Heaven, in order to touch us without soiling itself, may put on gloves. Raymond Radiguet was a glove of heaven. His form fitted onto the hand of heaven as if it were a glove. When heaven takes its hand out, death comes. To consider that kind of death a real death would be equivalent to confusing an empty glove with a cut-off hand.

I was on my guard. I understood immediately that Radiguet was on loan, that I would have to give him back. But I acted like a fool and tried my hardest to turn him away from his vocation of death.

It was no use. Believing I was weighing him down by wheedling books out of him, I was really unloading him. With each book I could see him setting forth, plunging, overtaking a mystery with which he obviously had a rendezvous.

In the summer I took him to the country.[1] He became a model child and wrote in school notebooks. At times he fumed against his writing, like a pupil against homework in vacation time. I had to scold him and lock him up. Then in a rage he would write out fast a whole chapter. Afterwards, he would correct it.

The winter in the city was terrifying. Why did I keep begging him and why did I change my own life and try to be an example for him? Debts, alcohol, insomnia, piles of dirty linen, hotel rooms one after the

[1] Radiguet, almost an alcoholic, on the day of his arrival in the country without effort began drinking water and milk. We owe his books to this alternating regime.

other, vacated as if they were the sites of crime. These made up the principle of his metamorphosis which took place in a clinic on the rue Piccini, December 12, 1923.

[FROM *La Difficulté d'Etre*]

On meeting Raymond Radiguet, I believe I can say I discovered my star. But I do not know in what way. He was short, pale, and near-sighted. His straggling hair fell to his neck and served as side whiskers. He squinted as if looking at the sun. When walking, he seemed to hop along as if the sidewalks were elastic. He used to pull out of his pockets small sheets of school paper which he had wadded into balls. He pressed them out with the flat of his hand, and still awkwardly holding a cigarette he rolled himself, tried to read a very short poem. He held it up to his eyes.

Those poems were like no other poems of the age I am referring to. Rather, they contradicted the period and reflected no earlier influence. I might say here that his wonderful tact, the solitude of his words, the density of his understatement, the aerial quality of the poems have not yet been recognized in France, and the countless imitations that are on sale do not come close to being even the caricature of Radiguet.

He rejuvenated old formulas. He removed the patina from conventionality. He scoured clichés. When he touched them, his awkward hands seemed to be putting a shell back into water. That was his right. Only he could aspire to this.

"We have to be precious," he used to say, and in

his speech, the word *précieux* took on the meaning of an extremely rare precious stone.

We helped one another continually. He walked everywhere. He lived in Parc Saint-Maur, with his family. Whenever he missed the last train, he went home on foot through the woods, and, since he was a child, dreaded hearing the growl of the lions in the zoo. If he stayed in Paris, he would put up at one of the painters, go to sleep on a table in the midst of brushes and tubes of paint. He seldom spoke. If he wished to inspect a painting or a text, he would pull out from his pocket a pair of broken glasses which he used like a monocle.

Not only did he invent and teach me an attitude of astonishing novelty, which consisted in not appearing original (he used to call it wearing a new suit); not only did he advise me to write "like everyone else" because that precisely is the form in which originality cannot be expressed, but he also gave me the example of working habits. This boy who was lazy (I used to have to lock him up in his room to force him to finish a chapter), this imp who escaped through the window and did his homework in slapdash fashion (he would always go back to it afterwards), had become a Chinese sage bending down over his books. He read a large number of worthless books, comparing them with masterpieces, returning to them, annotating them, and declaring that the mechanism of a masterpiece being invisible could be studied only in books which pretended to be masterpieces and which were not.

His fits of anger were infrequent but terrible. He would grow pale as death. Jean Hugo and Georges Auric will remember an evening in Arcachon where we were all reading around a kitchen table. I was stupid enough to say that Moréas was not too bad. I was reading his poems. Radiguet got up, snatched the book away from me, went down to the beach, and threw it into the water. When he came back and sat down, his face, bearing the expression of a murderer, was unforgettable.

His novels, especially *Le Diable au Corps*, phenomena as extraordinary in their genre as the poems of Rimbaud, have never profited from the help of our modern encyclopedists. Radiguet was too free. It was he who taught me how to lean on nothing.

He doubtless had a plan and a long program ahead to carry out. One day he would have orchestrated his work, and performed, I am certain, all the necessary steps to attract attention to it. He was waiting for his moment. Death took him first.

Since I inherited from him my small amount of clairvoyance, his death left me without guidance, incapable of moving ahead, of promoting my word and providing for it.

JACQUES MARITAIN

My dear Jacques,

Luminous and blind, you inhabit the depths of the sea. Your element is prayer. When you leave that element, you knock into everything. The bond of understanding between us is our awkwardness. The Thomistic machinery deceives the world about yours. Endless errors have caused mine to be called cleverness. We are not shrewd. The Devil would look upon us as traitors.

Testimonials

I am just a bad pupil. In school I won the easiest prizes: drawing and gymnastics. But you are a philosopher. I should be ashamed. But we are natives of the same place: natives exiled from our habitat.

I have to practice flying and keep constantly up in the air. That is how I give a false impression and imitate the liveliness of the spirit. For, unless I fall flat onto things, I am incapable of reaching them through any of the normal channels. But you have no tricks. You avoid no detour. You don't need a machine. You rise like a piece of cork toward the regions which ask for you. But I fly in a machine and progress by falling. One of the reasons for my reserve in the midst of insults is not arrogance but the fear of performing badly in controversy.

Before I knew you, you quoted me in your books. You had met Georges Auric at Bloy's. He must have been fifteen. A few years later, when I understood his budding genius, I dedicated *Le Coq et l'Arlequin* to him. He read to you *Le Cap de Bonne Espérance* and told you about my secret enterprise. You were his Versailles friends, but I did not know which ones. Your friends were so amazed you liked my work, that they believed you were just being kind. "Your friend Cocteau," used to say one of your close friends whom I knew before I knew you. He could not understand that you did not know me, since you were quoting my work.

The deforming heaviness of pretentious prejudice prevents a man from seeing clearly. Nothing comes in between the eyes of a child and what he looks at. But the child needs correctives. The miracle of your vision is the fact that it is pure and trained.

A mind like mine would become confused in calculations and lose its way ten times an hour if it tried to read a map. There was only one method for me, and I adopted it: sincerity. Tell all, reveal all, live openly.

I counted on my miserable limitations to substitute for those which a strong man chooses. I also believe that mystery begins after confession. The hypocrisy and the reticence which are often taken for mystery do not form a beautiful shadow.

My legend was fabulous at the time we met. It protected me. Hearsay destroys the person it invents. Rather than burning us, it burns us in effigy.

For the ordinary spectator a ropewalker's gesticulating in the air must appear comical. With your intuition and your sense of pity, you saw immediately that this behavior was a sickening struggle, that I was looking straight into the face of death.

After the scandal of *Parade* in the Châtelet, in 1917, two remarks flattered me. First, a theatre director crying, "We're too old for Punch and Judy"; and then, a gentleman whom Picasso and I heard say to his wife, "If I had known it was so crazy, I would have brought the children."

I insist that it was the child in you who saw me. The child saw the child. At a table of adults, children, seated at the two ends, devour one another with their eyes.

Yes, dear Jacques, a long time afterwards, seated at your table for the first time in your Meudon dining room, I recaptured the atmosphere of Maisons-Laffitte where I was born, the same chairs, the *same plates* I used to turn about obsessively so that the blue lines would coincide with the glass goblet.

Testimonials

We knew one another under the sign of childhood. I have to repeat it to myself in order to believe myself worthy of your welcome. I wonder if your body may not be a formula of politeness, a piece of clothing quickly thrown over your soul in order to receive your friends.

[FROM *La Difficulté d'Etre*]

My fear of the Church which leads me to Joan of Arc, I trace to her trial and to the *Provinciales* of Pascal. Several men have removed this fear. Among them are Jacques Maritain and Charles Henrion, who inspire such respect and admiration. But the singular part of their spirit is submitted to the order of a plural. Within their narrow rule they find limitless freedom which encourages my trust in them but which creates limitations and prisons at every step. When I saw this tactical exercise which they instinctively obey, I took to my heels as fast as I could and changed sides. Their heart, my faith and my honesty remained with me.

My *Letter to Maritain* testifies to this drama of trust. I thought I could transfer to God's account what is usually deposited in the Devil's. In this, I opposed evil to purity. I referred to an admirable sentence of Maritain. "The devil is pure because he can do only evil." If purity is not tenderness elevating itself, but rather a question of block coalition, why should not so many blocks rejected by tender goodness be adopted by hard goodness and become its attributes? I was naive.

In the gentle hands of priests a bomb does not explode unless they want it to. They caught mine in flight and, by wrapping it in cotton wool, made it an object of conversion, or rather, an example. My enemies saw in it a blow from the right. This thrust of the sword in water brought me only a family and that exterior kind of support which some look for in their family, others in the Church, in sects, at the Ecole Normale, or Polytechnique, or Diplomatic Service, in a political party or in a café. This support upset the long habit I have acquired of leaning on nothing but myself.

Maritain found that I was walking heavily. He wanted to open up another road for me. He opened up his. Alas, to keep up with him, I had neither the wings of angels nor the elaborate spiritual machinery of his soul disguised as a body. Without my legs, I felt only fatigue. I escaped.

PICASSO

Do not expect to find in this essay any of the analogies which it is now fashionable to establish between Bergson, Freud, Einstein and art. This pedantry will pass. If Picasso is a poet-painter, he is exactly the opposite of a literary painter. He finds nothing more ridiculous than the jargon of modern criticism.

Apollinaire used to call Pablo Picasso, *L'Oiseau du Bénin* (the bird of Benin). The superior realism of Picasso must never be confused with the harmonious geometry by which another bird, Paolo Uccello, believed he replaced the representation of the visible world.

We should at the beginning expel the word "Cubism."

Testimonials

Henri Matisse invented it.

"Too much Cubism," he cried out, when looking at paintings of Georges Braque which he had brought up from the south of France.

They showed groups of houses in the form of cubes. It is therefore erroneous to compare the term "Cubism" with the term "Impressionism," the legitimate offspring of a painting of Claude Monet, called *Impression*.

Cubism showed cubes where there weren't any. We should not forget that the spirit of mystification may exist at the beginnings of a discovery. The Muses are ladies accustomed to attentions. If you fail them, they will be avenged. They never indulge in anger. They transform the offense into a prison. I often saw Picasso try to leave their circle, from under their entwined hands. Such attempts are very moving. At those times he draws (in his style) like everyone else. But he quickly returns, with his eyes blindfolded, to take up his central position.

Perhaps the first days of his astonishing enterprise were days of play, like childhood days. That is no one's business. They quickly became school days. But Picasso never professed. He never dissected the doves which flew out from his sleeves. He was satisfied with painting, acquiring an incomparable technique and putting it in the service of chance.

Picasso comes from Malaga. He told me, as a significant characteristic of his city, that he once saw a singing trolley-car conductor slow down and increase the speed of the car in terms of the liveliness or slowness of the song, and sound the bell in cadence.

93

Malaga Picasso does not leave the tracks, and his song abolishes all monotony from the trip.

The world is suspicious of contrasting skills. Picasso, with his profound fantasy, proves how little he has tried to please. It gives his slightest gesture a fairy-like grace.

One day when I was sick, he sent me a dog cut out from a single piece of cardboard, and so skillfully folded that he stood up on his paws, stuck his tail up and moved his head. I recovered immediately.

He is a Spaniard, endowed with the oldest French recipes (Chardin, Poussin, Le Nain, Corot), and in possession of a charm. Objects and faces follow him wherever he goes. Two black eyes devour them and they undergo, between the eyes through which they enter and the hand through which they leave, a strange digestion. Furniture, animals, and persons mingle as if they were bodies of lovers. During this metamorphosis, they lose nothing of their objective power. When Picasso changes the natural order of figures, his final addition is always the same.

As soon as he is in possession of the charm, he uses it. On what will he practice? He is like Midas after Bacchus conferred on him the power of changing what he touches to gold. A tree, a column, a statue intimidate him. He does not dare. He hesitates. So he touches a piece of fruit.

Picasso first tries his powers on what is within reach. A newspaper, a glass, a bottle of Anis del Mono, oilcloth, flowered wallpaper, a pipe, a package of tobacco, a playing card, a guitar, the cover of a song: *Ma Paloma*.

He and Georges Braque, his companion in miracles,

debauch humble objects. What happens when they leave the studio? You find on Montmartre the models which were the origins of their art: custom-made ties in haberdasheries, fake marble, fake zinc, absinthe advertisements, soot and wallpaper of buildings being torn down, hopscotch chalk, tobacco store signs on which two Gambier pipes are clearly painted, tied with sky-blue ribbon.

At first the pictures, often oval, were light-brown monochromes delicately drawn. Then, the paintings became more human and the still lifes began to live with that strange life which is the life itself of the painter.

It is unbelievable when this motorman from Malaga, with his trolley full of surprised clients, paints a woman from Malaga. Without taking his pen from the paper, he draws a *corrida* with a flourish. When he bends a sheet of iron, he composes a plastic poem. In one night, helped by angels, he erects several colossal women, Junos with cows' eyes whose fat broken hands hold a piece of stone linen.

Broken hands? Cows' eyes? I hear you say those women are monsters. It all depends on the use you put them to. A world separates intensity of expression and caricature. For the man who does not realize this, the sculptors of Aegina, Giotto, El Greco, Fouquet, Ingres, Cézanne, Renoir, Matisse, Derain, Braque, Picasso become caricaturists.

A painter who has only talent, a Carolus-Duran, for example, and the Carolus-Durans of every period are given their places in the Louvre, has all the requirements. Other painters, more gifted, less fundamental (a Berthe Morisot), have only the luxuries. A Manet combines the two. But a rich man rarely has much pocket money. Picasso adds pocket money to his wealth. It falls from his hands and lips. If he speaks, his wit shows what he says under cold daylight. If he touches a toy of his son, it ceases being a toy. I have seen him, as he was speaking, manipulate a soft yellow chick that you buy at the department store. When he put it back on the table, it was a chick of Hokusai.

In my house I have under glass a cardboard domino which he cut, folded, and colored. I use it as an experiment. Whoever scorns this little object and pretends he loves Picasso, does not love him for a sound reason.

It is difficult to say at what point for Picasso the superfluous stops and at what point he draws on his capital. A total absence of insincerity places side by side the work done in five minutes and the work labored over one hundred times. The artist's amusement illuminates everything at once. The professors reproach him for this. He cannot be limited. For Picasso nothing is superfluous, nothing is capital. He knows that the girl in sepia, with the transparent colors of barley sugar, the iron guitar, the table in front of the window, have the same value, that they are worthless because he is their mold, and priceless because this mold never makes two copies of the same subject, that they deserve the place of honor in the Louvre, that they will have it one day and that it will prove nothing whatsoever.

For his work is dominated by clairvoyance which could dry up a small spring. It economizes his strength and directs its manifestation. This fertility does not entail any romanticism. The inspiration is not wasted.

Testimonials

Nothing is left over. Harlequin lives in Port-Royal. Each work draws upon an intimate tragedy which results in an intense calm. Tragedy no longer consists of painting a tiger devouring a horse, but in establishing between a glass and the molding of an armchair plastic relationships capable of affecting me without the intervention of an anecdote.

It is easy to see the exceptional qualities of finesse and tact, of proportion, of pious deceit necessary for such a scandal. Without these qualities the artist produces a masquerade where perspectives are distorted, where geometry wears a false nose, where artistic bad taste liberates its monsters.

A fortuitous meeting of circumstances explains this adventure. It is both erroneous to compare Picasso with Mallarmé in terms of their methods, and sound to compare them in terms of Mallarmé's accidental appearance, his historic role, and the disaster of his direct influence.

I write directly because of the service these delightful puns give, with, at the top of the list, the authorization granted my bold plot to win back simplicity.

I hear your objection. Isn't Cubism a fatality in the history of art, just like any other school? Let me answer:

What schools? There are only strong men. Such men open up nothing for others. What they open, they close. They bring their final reckoning. But immediately the school is organized. It both compromises and supports. Doubtless a higher chemistry demands this fringe which feeds on the kernel and consolidates all around it.

Like every major event, the coming of Picasso took

place with simplicity. I hesitate to encumber it with a text. I hesitate first because beauty needs no subtitle, and I hesitate next because the special mysteriousness of this beauty threatens, as soon as a writer takes over, to incriminate with literature the least literary painter of all.

I would not say: the least intellectual. It is impossible to ascribe to Picasso or to use in praising him that aesthetic vocabulary which shocks us especially in a Renoir. If it is a fine thing to paint when heaven has given you the gift of painting, it is a still finer thing not to give any thought to it and to concentrate your genius on the perfecting of talents which will allow others to enjoy it.

I am sorry for the artists who, to recover from disorder, make the journey to Athens. The Acropolis would speak to me in a dead language. I do not dare visit it. I am afraid that meeting place of styles would hypnotize me as it has so many others, that the first column of the Propylaea would send out before my eyes the white ray which puts hens to sleep and would keep me from seeing my Parthenon.

In Montparnasse, then in Montrouge, and now on the rue de la Boëtie, I have taken my trip to Greece. *Snow in predestined hands quickly turns to marble.* I train my vision on respect too much not to grant to new beauty the prestige of distance in time and death.

People guess the respect of my friendship for Picasso and know that I answer his brotherly speech to me with the speech of a Greek to his gods. His heart is not understood. The awkward familiarity of some men comes up against a wall. At times it gives over

Testimonials

lazily to the foolishness of others. This royal politics will have him accused of egoism and cowardice by a casual witness.

On this subject I would let his old friends speak. Consult Gertrude Stein, Guillaume Apollinaire, Max Jacob, André Salmon, Maurice Raynal. You will find they have all the material needed to rebuild the destroyed past.

Besides, what can I add to his legend? A barometer writes out the ideal legend of temptestuous men. Picasso's slightest temper helps to draw a profile which does not resemble him.

This effigy is adopted by fame. It remains deaf to my account.

Nature is too healthy. It pretends it thinks of nothing. And so, we cherish its most secret malady: the pearl; and its deepest calculation: the diamond. Listen to Apollinaire and Jacob. When they are defining their friend's work, one compares it to a pearl, and the other to a diamond. Their two voices sum up the singularity of Picasso.

Tightrope walkers, white mares, emaciated Harlequins, angelic figures—the "blue period" of the painter I pass over quickly since it represents a style he had very early and a lyricism too literary to be written about. Likewise, I pass over the collages, sand and cork, the differences of subject matter at the beginning of Cubism, because they depend on descriptive criticism, a temptation to which I never again wish to succumb.

I am mostly concerned with Picasso as stage designer. I am responsible for his becoming one. His

99

friends did not believe he would consent. Montmartre and Montparnasse were governed by a dictatorship. Cubism prevailed austerely. The objects found on a café table and the Spanish guitar were the only pleasures allowed. Painting a stage set, especially for the Ballets Russes (those pious young people did not know Stravinsky) was a crime. M. Renan backstage did not scandalize the Sorbonne any more than Picasso, the Café de la Rotonde when he accepted my proposition. The worst of it was that we had to join Serge de Diaghilev in Rome and the Cubist code forbade any voyage other than the Paris subway between Place des Abbesses and Boulevard Raspail. The trip took place without mishap, in spite of Satie's absence. Satie did not like to shake up his musical vintage. He never left Arcueil. We were happy to be alive and breathing. Picasso laughed at seeing the figures of the painters grow small as the train left the station.

(Braque and Juan Gris were exceptions. Seven years later they also painted stage sets for Diaghilev.)

We created *Parade* in a Roman cellar which was called Cave Taglioni. We walked in the moonlight with the ballerinas, and visited Naples and Pompeii. We met the happy-go-lucky Futurists.

I will not repeat here the story of the scandal of *Parade* in 1917, and its success in 1920. But it is important to speak of the ease with which Picasso took over the theatre as he had taken over everything else.

I shall never forget the studio in Rome. A small crate held the model of *Parade,* its houses, trees, and its booth. On a table, opposite the Villa Médicis, Picasso painted the Chinaman, the Managers, the American woman, the horse which Mme. de Noailles said

looked like a tree laughing, and the blue Acrobats
which Marcel Proust compared to the Dioscuri.

Parade united the company and Picasso so closely
that Apollinaire, Max Jacob, and I, soon afterwards,
were witnesses at his marriage in the Russian Church
on the rue Daru. Also he did the settings and costumes
of *Tricorne, Pulcinella,* and *Quadro Flamenco.* A con-
fusion over dates, a misunderstanding between the
choreographer Massine and the stage designer, a ballet
completed in Rome which had to be danced in Paris
two days later, prevented Picasso from painting the
correct figures on his set for *Pulcinella.* He improvised
costumes; but they did not correspond to the costumes
and the pantomime he wanted and for which the mod-
els existed. Neapolitan prostitutes and pimps played
the old puppets like music by Pergolese rejuvenated
by Stravinsky. After twenty gouaches in which the
stage represented a theatre with its chandelier, its
boxes, and its setting, Picasso discarded all those de-
tails and fitted out the real stage with the setting of the
model stage. The red velvet was abandoned for the
card tricks of moonlight and a street in Naples.

If you remember the mysteries of childhood, the
scenes it discovers surreptitiously in a puddle, views of
Vesuvius at night, by the stereoscope, Christmas chim-
neys, rooms looked at through the keyhole, you will
understand the soul of that set which filled the stage
of the Opera House without any other artifice save
gray curtains and a house of performing dogs.

The night before the first performance of *Antigone*
in December, 1922, all of us, actors and author, were
seated in the orchestra of Dullin's theatre, the Atelier.

101

A blue curtain of wash-soap bubbles represented the rocky background of a manger. There were openings on the left and right; and in the middle, in the air, a hole, behind which the voice of the chorus spoke through a megaphone. Around this hole I had hung the masks of women, boys, and old men which I had made from Picasso's models and which he and others had painted. Under the mask a white panel was suspended. The problem was to indicate on this surface the meaning of a fortuitous setting which sacrificed precision and imprecision, equally costly, to the representation of a warm day.

Picasso walked up and down.

He began by rubbing red chalk over the board, which, because of the unevenness of the wood, turned into marble. Then he took a bottle of ink and traced some majestic-looking lines. Abruptly he blackened a few hollow spots and three columns appeared. The apparition of these columns was so sudden and so unexpected that we began clapping.

When we were in the street, I asked Picasso if he had calculated their approach, if he had planned on them, or if he had been surprised by them. He answered that the artist is always calculating without knowing, that the Doric column came forth as a hexameter does, from an operation of the senses, and that he had perhaps just invented that column in the same way the Greeks had discovered it.

I wish now to acclaim the example Picasso has been for us. He teaches us not to confuse discipline and fear. Living in isolation is different from being able to cross the street. He proves that personality is not in the repetition of something bold but, on the contrary, in that independence which a bold gesture permits. The reason why Picasso does not exploit any of his discoveries is that they come from him fully developed. Each of us looks for a starting point in them, a seed, a green fruit, and we do not relish them silently. The Frenchman likes tombs. He scorns the young and he feasts on canned goods the day fresh vegetables arrive.

My determination to go straight ahead and not to be sidetracked in small details has kept me on the highways.

Perhaps I have been wrong in neglecting one cross street which serves the square where Picasso and Mallarmé meet. Let me go back to it.

When I refer to the Picasso experiment, I admit that the very minute a painter deliberately leaves his model, painting moves toward Cubism. Cubists were right in claiming Ingres one of their ancestors. The neck of Thetis supplicating Jupiter is large with promise. Cézanne opened one door, and already El Greco's sentence on his view of Toledo contained a warning.

Despite all that, Picasso was the first, courageous enough to pass beyond the monsters born from the marriage between the objective and the subjective, and to hold out to Narcissus a mirror which neither disfigures him nor exposes him to complications.

To realize that Picasso bears on his shoulders the heavy responsibility of having pushed the experiment to the extreme is not to deny that the experiment, whatever the cost, had to be pushed that far.

Accident, accidental, uneven (*accidenté*), apply to the road of art when you count the summits.

We marvel, as we do for Mallarmé, at the career of proofs opened up by Picasso to unripe genius.

The function of the last comer is to clear away the earth and cover it with obstacles. The succession of Picasso is all the more delicate because he excels not only in his chess game, but also in all manner of innocent games.

His calculations could be opposed only by an innocence which would not imitate his.

Since Cubism, I have seen a horn of plenty pour over Europe: hypnoses, fascinating obsessions, insolences, scarecrows, aerogenics, smoke rings, snowdrops, mystery corsets, trick devils, Bengal lights.

But will I see the next broom sweep clean? It is the problem of sons deciding to be fathers who are not like theirs, and who, when they are fathers, adopt the requirements of the situation.

At least, if my eyesight gets bad, my good eyes have had the chance of seeing Pablo Picasso.

IV. Theatre

Since those evenings of my childhood when my mother and father left for the theatre, I have had the "red and gold" sickness. I have never recovered. Each curtain going up brings me back to the solemn minute when, with the Châtelet curtain rising on *The Trip around the World in Eighty Days,* the two voids of darkness and light were joined, separated only by the footlights. The footlights illuminated the base of the painted backdrop. Since this canvas wall did not touch the floor, you could just see a slit of backstage action, a furnace. In addition to this slit, a hole circled with brass was the only opening through which the two universes communicated. The smell of the circus was one thing. The narrow box with the small uncomfortable chairs was something else. As in the rooms of Mena House where the windows open onto the pyramids, the small box opened onto the vast noise of the public, the cry: "Mint drops, caramels, candies" of the ushers, the dark purple cavern, and the chandelier which Baudelaire preferred to the play.

After all this time, the theatre, where I work now, has not lost its prestige. I respect it. It intimidates and fascinates me. I become two persons there. I live in it and become the child whom the ticket-selling tribunal authorizes to descend into hell.

When I produced *La Voix Humaine* at the Comédie-Française, and later, *Renaud et Armide,* I was surprised that my colleagues looked upon that theatre as upon any other and that they produced plays written for any theatre. The Comédie-Française remained for me the palace of marble and velvet, haunted by the majestic ghosts of my youth. Yesterday Marais telephoned me from Paris that they had invited him to return, and this time under the best conditions. He wanted my advice and doubtless wanted me to dissuade him. I had many reasons to do this. But I hesitated. The naive respect which the Comédie-Française calls up in me waved its red cape. In a flash I saw Mounet-Sully cross the stage from right to left, dressed in the livery of young Ruy Blas. He was old. His beard was white. Almost blind, his head sunken between his shoulders, he held a candelabrum. His step was Spanish.

I saw de Max shake his black locks and the train of his robe with a hand covered with rings. I saw that old neckless bird, Madame Bartet, sing Andromaque. I saw Madame Segond-Weber, as Rodogune, emerge poisoned, sticking out her tongue and walking in goose-step fashion.

All that was hardly of a nature to encourage a young man. And yet I put off saying to him, "Refuse." When I had hung up the receiver, the glorious invalids were still moving about before me. My reason said, "This actor has just completed your film. He is acting in your play. He is to act in your next play. He is being offered parts everywhere. And big offers. He is free." My unreasonableness showed me the child I was, led to his seat on Thursday matinee by an usher with a pink

Theatre

bow and a gray mustache, and Marais in that golden frame playing the role of Nero in which he is unmatched.

Such is my spellbound nature, so easily dazzled. I belong to the minute. It falsifies all perspective for me. It shuts me off from diversity. I yield to him who convinces me. I take on onerous duties. That is why solitude does me good. It collects together my mercury.

The sun which had come out is covered with fog. The gaudy-looking families are departing. Everyone is leaving the hotel and now I can write out my vacation exercises. After every page I write, I try to find a title for my play. Ever since finishing the play, the title has escaped me. And the title, *La Reine Morte* (*The Dead Queen*), which would be suitable, irritates me. My queen does not have a name. The pseudonym of Stanislas, Azraël, is suitable, but I am told it would soon become Israël. Only one title is right. It will be —and therefore already is. Time is hiding it from me. How can I turn it up, since it is covered over with a hundred others? It must not contain an image. I have to avoid depicting and not depicting, avoid an exact meaning and an inaccuracy. The flabby and the dry. Neither long nor short. Able to catch the eye, the ear, the intelligence. Easy to read and retain. I have announced several. Even after two repetitions, the newspapers made mistakes. My real title flouts me. It likes its childhood hiding place which is called and is believed "drowned in the pond." [1]

The theatre is a furnace. The man who does not realize this is either consumed in it sooner or later,

[1] This play was *L'Aigle à deux têtes* (*The Two-headed Eagle*).

or burned immediately. The theatre drowns all zeal. It attacks by fire and water.

The public is a billowy sea. It causes nausea. We call it stage fright. There is no good in simply saying: it is the theatre, it is the public. We swear not to be caught by it, but we always go back. It's a gambling den. You play what you have. The torture is exquisite. Unless you are a conceited ass, you feel it. You never get over it.

When I rehearse, I become a spectator. I am bad at rehearsing the actors. I like them and they blind me. I don't heed my own reactions. The night before the performance, all my weak points leap out at me. It is too late. Subsequently, a prey to a kind of seasickness, I wander around the boat, through storerooms, cabins, and corridors. I don't dare look at the sea. Even less would I dare swim in it. I have the feeling that if I joined the public, the boat would sink.

Then I go into the wings and listen. Behind the stage set a room is not painted, it is just outlined. It reveals the mistakes made in its design. I leave. I go to lie down in one of the actresses' dressing rooms. What they leave behind them, when they change their souls, makes a fatal vacuum. It stifles me. I get up. I listen. What scene are they doing? I listen at the door. Yet I know that this sea is controlled by rules. Its waves swell and break in accord with my command. Each new public responds to the same effects. But let one of those effects continue for long and the actor is caught in a trap. Awkwardly he refuses the perch for laughter. This cruel laughter should pain him, but he encourages it. "I suffer and they laugh," he says to himself, "I am winning in the game." The perch is

quickly held out and quickly removed. The author is
forgotten. The ship drifts and moves toward a wreck.
If the actors listen to the sirens, the drama turns to
melodrama and the thread which kept the scenes to-
gether is broken. The rhythm is lost.

From a distance I supervise my crew very badly.
The imponderables escape me. What could I change?
The actors are in charge and they perfect the machin-
ery. There they are, living on the stage and attempt-
ing to conquer the machine. Diderot was too super-
ficial.

I know authors who supervise actors and write them
notes. They obtain a discipline but they paralyze. They
lock the door which a gust of wind might open.

As I write this, I have the impression of being in
the dressing room of my actor, Marcel André, with
whom I like discussing such things. Yvonne de Bray
and Jean Marais are on stage. Their natures comple-
ment one another. I wonder what the mechanics are
by which they respect a dialogue they are living while

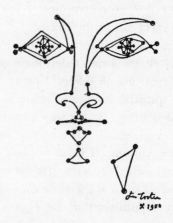

forgetting that the room where they are lacks a wall. Marcel André is speaking. I listen to him. I also listen to the silence of the building. He is expecting the bell which will force him onto the stage. We are only half-existing.

Exquisite minutes of suffering I would not exchange for anything.

Why do you write plays? the novelist asks me. Why do you write novels? the dramatist asks me. Why do make films? the poet asks me. Why do you draw? the critic asks me. Why do you write? the artist asks me. Yes, why? I wonder myself. So that my seed will fly in every direction. I do not know too well the breath that is in me, but it is not tender. It makes fun of the sick. It does not know fatigue. It profits from my aptitude. It tries to give its form to trumpets. It moves against me from all sides. I mean, not breathing in but breathing out. This breath comes from a zone of man where man cannot descend, even if Virgil were to lead him, for Virgil himself would not go down there.

What is my business with genius? It is trying to turn me into an accomplice. What it wants is a pretext to carry out its low deeds.

If my activity is split up, the main thing is not to mix my efforts. I never decide on one of my branches without cutting off others. I prune my tree. It is even rather unusual for me to draw in the margins of a page of writing. That is why I have published albums of drawings which relate to my writings, but not in the same volume. If I did publish them together, the drawings were done long after the writing. In *Portraits-Souvenir*, I drew at the same time as I wrote. The articles were published in *Le Figaro* and that kind of

Theatre

article and drawing could be done with the same ink.

Still less could I conduct simultaneously plays and films, because they go back to back. While I was making my film *La Belle et la Bête,* the Gymnase Theatre was rehearsing my play *Les Parents Terribles.* The actors accused me of being inattentive. Although I was no longer using the camera, I was enslaved to a task where language was visual and was not collected within a frame. I confess I had all the trouble in the world to listen to an immobile text and to devote my attention to it. When one work is done, I have to wait to see if I want to begin another. Completed work does not abandon me quickly. It changes addresses slowly. The wise thing is to change one's atmosphere and one's room. The new material comes to me during walks. Provided I do not see it. If I focus my attention on it, it leaves. One fine day the work demands my collaboration. I give over to it in one stretch. We make the same stops. My pen falters if it falls asleep. As soon as it wakes up, it shakes me. Nothing disturbs it, if I sleep. Stand up, it tells me, I am going to dictate. It is not easy to follow. Its speech is not in words.

I describe, in *Opium,* a liberty I took while writing *Les Enfants Terribles.* Flattered by the activity of my pen, I thought I was free to invent myself. Everything stopped. I had to wait for its convenience.

La Machine Infernale involved another system. It deserted me for very long periods. It waited for other fevers to cease occupying me. It wanted me for itself. If I had one distraction, it turned its back on me. *La Machine à Ecrire* was a disaster. When I thought I was ready to write it, already another theme was in me and dictating *La Fin de Potomak.* I wanted to get back to work on it. I took dictation badly. After the first act, I had my way. Once the play was written, I insisted on rewriting it. In the end, I listened to advice and spoiled the ending. This play should teach me a lesson. I shall never be my own master. I was made to show obedience. A week ago I did not know that I would have to write these very lines I am writing.

Of all the problems which confuse me, that of destiny and free will is the most mysterious. What am I saying? The book is written in advance and yet we can write it. We can change the ending. Truth is different. Time does not exist. It is our bookkeeping. What we think we write afterwards is written as one piece. Time unwinds it for us. My work is already done. And yet I still have to discover it. The surprising thing is this passive participation. There is good reason to be surprised. The public is incredulous. I decide and I do not decide. I obey and I direct. It is a mystery. *La Machine à Ecrire* was not a bad play in the beginning. The fluid left me. I was free. But I am not free to remove the stain I made. It is there.

As I finished my play *Bacchus,* I had the feeling that something would happen, but I could not guess what. I had even jokingly said to Mme. W., in whose house I was working, "Man your boat, we may have to leave in a hurry."

I should have been forewarned by an event, humorous in appearance, in which the medieval style of our period can be recognized.

Santa Claus had just been burned in Dijon, in the public square. The Church accused him of representing a dangerous German custom, capable of leading children into error. If the poor children believed this fable, they would have to be burned alive as heretics.

In a word, I foresaw an imperialistic attack against *Bacchus* of the type: "You disturb me, off with your head." But I could not foresee from what corner the attack would come and from what window they would shoot, since my play offered a large number of targets to all concerned. Moreover, since a play is quite visible, the invisible had to put its defense arsenal into operation.

The marksman was François Mauriac, and quite unexpectedly, because he was an old friend. We went on our first campaigns together, and it would have seemed unthinkable to me that he should turn one of his cannon against me.

A form of imperialism directed the attack: literary imperialism. Under the mask of morals, naturally.

Imprudently the shooter had published shortly before (in *La Table Ronde*) an article in which he justified the free expression of the artist and his right to say everything. But he justified these for his own use.

You will see that the shooter was of the race of those who take aim for a long time. (I speak of his race in *Le Secret Professionnel*.) He misses the clay pipe because he thinks too much of holding a becoming pose and wants to be seen by the mistress of the shooting match.

I was safe in terms of dogma. I had consulted Dominican and Benedictine authorities. From them I had received the *exeatur*. Santa Claus at the stake, and the placing of the first log on mine by Mauriac, risked giving the beast of the Apocalypse the annoying appearance of beast of the good Lord. The finest minds of the clergy disapprove of such initiative. The bishops of Michel de Ghelderode and Sartre do not worry our secular judges. The arrow missed the mark. Sacrilege reassured them in as much as it is a preamble to mysticism (mysticism in a primitive stage). Arthur Rimbaud will benefit from this.

I must be a better Christian than Catholic. *Bacchus* is without any doubt a Christian play. Cardinal Zampi, less orthodox in his heart than Christian.

I confess I was shocked by the vine leaves on the statues in the Vatican.[1] But I would have found it normal for the precious stones of the collection to be hidden by vine leaves. I thought of the sentence of Maurras, quoted by Gide: "I will not leave the learned procession of reverend fathers, councils, popes, and all the great men of modern times, in order to concentrate on the Gospels of four obscure Jews." This is an extreme expression of anti-Semitism.

I was certainly on the wrong side of the fence, as usual. I remember Gide's maxim: "I do not admit that anything can harm me. On the contrary, I intend everything to be of use to me. I mean to profit from everything."

This is the creed of visibility. To obtain the creed of invisibility (mine), these sentences have to be put

---

[1] Dr. M. had just told me that a lady had explained to her small daughter that she forbade her looking at the "shameful parts" of her little brother, cause of all the woes which befall us. That night the little girl, after cutting off the genitals of her small brother with a pair of scissors, ran to awaken her mother and relate her deed. She thought she was a heroine, another Judith. She was amazed when her mother collapsed with grief.

into the negative and these lines of Heraclitus added: "For God everything is good and just. Men, on the contrary, conceive of some things as just and others as unjust."

What can I say? That is the way I am built. I hate only hatred. Yet I can excuse it more easily than frivolity. I find much of that in the attacks of my enemies. I am almost certain that if Mauriac read my play and reread his open letter, he would be ashamed and would go weep on the shoulder of his confessor.

For a long time I had wanted to write *Bacchus*. I had thought of it as a play, a film, a book. I came back to the idea of a play, feeling that the theatre would be a better frame for the story. Ramuz had given me the story. The custom still survives, in Vevey, at the grape harvest.

This custom dates from the Sumerian civilization, about 3,000 years before Christ. "Documents describe ceremonies celebrated on the occasion of the inauguration of the temple of the god Ningirsou. Joyfully the people gave over to real bacchanalias whose origin went back to ancient fertility rites. For seven days a general license reigned over the city. Civil laws as well as moral laws were suspended. No form of authority was shown. A slave replaced the king; the royal harem was put at his disposal, and he was served at the table of the prince by his servants. When the festivity was over, he was sacrificed to the gods so they would pardon the city for its sins and restore prosperity. In the courtyards of the temple, sacred mysteries were performed which will be handed down to Babylon. Saturnalias and mystery plays will persist throughout the

entire history of Mesopotamia. Berosus will see these
in the third century. And Rome itself will see the
celebration of these curious festivities, dating from the
beginning of time, which Christianity will preserve in
the carnival." (J. Perenne, *Civilisation antique*.)

My first version was the story of a dictatorship in
which a village idiot became a monster. I discarded
it very soon. It was too roughly drawn and, also, it was
too difficult. I began treating the theme of the confu-
sion of young people in the midst of dogmas, sects,
and obstacles that face them. A prey to the offers of
service and sentiments, they try to remain free. Their
disorderly freedom glides between obstacles until it
is defeated. It can win only by ruse or a seizure of
power. It lacks the skill which deviousness demands.
Their freedom charges headlong. Its clumsy straight
line, its boldness, its courage, its senses, all do it a

disservice in a society where deviousness reigns, where forms of deviousness crisscross and confront one another blindly.

Hans is all flame and ardor and very naive. His stratagem may deceive the bishop and the duke. It does not deceive the cardinal. He comes from Rome, and is aware of the trick. He pretends to believe in it because he is informed of the upheavals of a Germany where he is prospecting. He likes the duke and his daughter. He senses the worries in family circles brought on by the Reformation. "Pronounce no irreparable words," he advises the duke. He added, in my first version, "Let Christine feel sick, since only fainting is able to silence your family." He is the ancestor of the priests in Stendhal. He is shrewd and warmhearted. He warns Hans, "You are rushing into fire like a night moth." He maneuvers so that the moth will avoid the fire. Unable to catch it in flight, he saves it from the fire even after its death. In his final act, the Church shows her clear vision. Some Catholics saw a lie in the right which Zampi assumes in order to remain worthy of the priesthood and of his heart.

When Sartre and I learned that the setting of our plays was Germany of the sixteenth century, it was too late. He was finishing *Le Diable et le bon Dieu* at Saint-Tropez, and I had finished my first act at Cap-Ferrat. I had made a good start. We decided to meet at Antibes. Our plots had no resemblance whatever. I could continue my work. Since our documentation was similar, Sartre gave me the titles of books I added to those I was studying on Luther. They came to me from every direction.

It was hard to take notes, lock up the files in a chest, forget them, and relive their essence in the speeches of my characters.

They are old sentences, presented in a new style, which seem subversive. They are ascribed to me. It is correct to say that they coincide with what is taking place in 1952. But the coincidences occurred to me long afterwards. Some became apparent to me only when I heard the laughter or the applause in the theatre.

Claudel's *Jeanne au Bûcher* baffles me. The Church is One. Her greatness is in her power of recovery. In condemning Joan of Arc and in canonizing her, she represents for me one person who commits an error and repents. In canonizing Joan, she courageously acknowledges her guilt. I admire in her the nobility of this confession and this self-examination. If the problem concerned Captain Dreyfus, rather than Saint Joan, the reconsideration of the trial of Rennes would not allow a dramatist to jeer at the General Staff. Unless the dramatist were an antimilitarist or an atheist. He could then attack the General Staff and the Church. But not if he respected them. In this alternative, he will praise their capacity to go back on an opinion. Every constituted body should be looked upon as a body endowed with a soul, and fallible like a body and a soul, capable of weakness and repentance.

In watching a performance, I was amazed that the scenes of Claudel jeer at one Church and exalt another without shocking those judges who are so severe on my cardinal and his maneuvers. They would not have allowed the capers of generals.

The blockhead in *Les Mariés de la Tour Eiffel* caused a scandal and prevented a revival of the play. He was nothing more or less than a vaudeville blockhead.

When the play was finished, I gave it first to Jean Vilar. Because my dates did not suit his, I took it next to Jean-Louis Barrault. In one month I worked out the stage directions, the settings, and costumes. The actors in the Marigny Theatre, who were worn out with alternating rehearsals and performances, imagined that my script was easy to learn. They quickly realized that the style *"chasseur sachez chasser sans chien,"* which I use so that the sentences will not flow easily, forced them to respect every syllable. Otherwise, the material gives way. They learned to enjoy this grammatical gymnastics. Jean-Louis Barrault was a magnificent cardinal. He sounded like a prelate from *The Charterhouse of Parma.* He looked like Raphael's young cardinal.

We played first before a public of tradesmen whose reaction was very favorable, then before a gala public whose reaction was predictable, and third, before the real public and the judges. We had that kind of solid triumph in which personalities lose their individualism or leave it at the check room, and concentrate on a collective hypnosis loathed by my judges. In the reverse order, my judges became individualized and closed themselves off through a spirit of contradiction. I should have expected this. On the gala evening, François Mauriac, impelled by some blinding, deafening force, believed he heard and saw a work which was not mine, took offense at it, and left the theatre in a spectacular way when the actors and myself were taking the curtain calls. The next day was Sunday, when the company played *L'Echange*. I was in the country, resting. I presumed that Mauriac was going to write an article and took pleasure in thoughts of answering him.

The next day, the article appeared. An "open letter," a cowardly showpiece which revealed a total misconception of my life and my world. It was the trial of a legend which does not concern me.

A man assaulted on the Rond-point des Champs-Elysées (office of *Le Figaro*) has to defend himself, even if he dislikes doing so. I added a few touches to my preliminary answer, and published it under the title "I accuse you," in the newspaper *France-Soir*. I could not accuse Mauriac for his ancestors and Bordeaux origins. I reproached him for the error of judging beforehand, of usurping the prerogatives of a priest and sitting at the right hand of God.

Mauriac has indeed remained one of those children who want to stay with grownups. You see them in hotels. They are told: "It is late. Go upstairs. Go to bed." They refuse to obey, and disturb everyone. (Mauriac told me himself: "I am an old child disguised as an Academician.") Moreover, the fact he is not in the group he would like to belong to, incites him to write articles on members of the group. With the result that, even if they are at variance, these members join against Mauriac, because of his ceaseless attempts to participate in their inside quarrels and to turn one against the other.

Theatre

François Mauriac went home from the theatre. He sat down at his table. He was to write his "Prayer on the Acropolis." A curious prayer and a curious acropolis. A curious text for the Carmelites. (Mauriac said that his open letter was read there.) It might be said that he turned back, considered the man hunt that was tracking me down, and, to announce the kill, blew into his hunting horn.

Nothing is more serious than to miss the animal. It becomes dangerous. Mauriac missed his animal. But it was not mad and he knew it. When all is said, that is my one reproach.

My answer was deliberately nonliterary. I was not shooting in order to charm the patroness of the shooting match. The sugar of the open letter infuriated me more than its vinegar. It recalled the plays I put on as a child and the group watching them. It showed me tying my old mother to the Marigny column and insulting her. It showed me as an insect, a satellite, a man dressed in a Harlequin costume and carried by angels. Mauriac is not naive, and he knows very well that there is no connection between my work and Apollinaire's or Max Jacob's (with all respect to theirs) and that my play is an objective study of the prodromes of the Reformation. But he likes to bend the wheels of the vehicle so it will turn over. He was indulging in an attempted sabotage.

I suppose that Mauriac expected that his hunting-horn solo, his Harlequinade, would produce a procession. He was wrong. Not only did the clergy not follow him (I had proof of this in Germany), but he called the attention of ridicule to himself.

The noise from this ridicule continued in letters and articles which congratulated me and pestered me, because I am persuaded that Mauriac is very slightly responsible, that he was manipulated by forces which are the object of my study, by a craftiness of shadows struggling against the illumination of footlights and spotlights.

I can hear the retort that the success of the play weakens this theory. Let me answer that it was confirmed when the play was stopped at the time the company went on tour, and that was doubtless one of my motives for going to the Marigny rather than other theatres which were asking for *Bacchus* and which would have played it without the system of alternating plays and interruptions.

Let me add that I doubtless withdrew my play from Vilar because the press was tabooing him with the evil spell of Jean-Louis Barrault, tabooed the day before, de-tabooed in a single day with no reason save the fidgets of a city changing idols and enjoying the destruction of playthings.

It is probable that this transference of powers and the limited number of performances made me decide against all logic and in secret obedience to orders more subtle than the demands of the visible world.

A play is more convincing than a film because a film is a story of phantoms. Movie spectators do not exchange waves with flesh and blood actors. The power of a film is in displaying what I think, and proving it by a subjectivism which becomes objective, by acts which are irrefutable because they are performed before our eyes.

Theatre

One of my correspondents blamed me for my films and considered that I reveal to too many people what should remain hidden. I would say to her that a film immediately sets about confusing its secrets, and reveals them only to a few individuals mingled with the crowd which is distracted by the rapid succession of pictures. I repeat that all religions—and poetry is a religion—protect their secrets by fables and show them only to those who would never know the religions unless they were disseminated by fables.

In the theatre, the spectators, their elbows touching, release a wave which reaches the stage, whence it returns richer, provided the actors are moved by the sentiments they simulate and are not satisfied with being imitators. That would stop the wave surging back.

The actors in my *Bacchus,* stimulated by silly criticism, made every effort to be convincing. They succeeded.

I am convinced that it would be foolish for me to be blinded by success. The misunderstandings which success creates should not affect me more than the misunderstandings which sarcasm directs at me. I should then fall back into the pride of responsibility. I should lose that lofty indifference of a tree, an indifference, I regret to say, I have allowed myself to come down from too often.

The absurd weakness of the soul. Its principal weakness is to believe itself powerful, to be convinced of it, when each experience demonstrates that it has no responsibility for the forces it expels and which turn against it as soon as they put their noses outside.

V. Films

The fantastic is very much discussed today. It would be well to reach an agreement about its meaning. If I had to define it, I would say that it is what separates us from the limitations within which we have to live and that it is like fatigue stretching outside of us to the bed of our birth and death.

There is an error which consists in believing that the cinema is an art capable of putting into operation this faculty of the soul. The error comes from a haste to confuse the fantastic and prestidigitation. It is not a great miracle to pull a dove out of a hat. That kind of trick can be purchased and taught. Such cheap miracles keep up with the fashions. They do not derive from the fantastic any more than algebra does, but present a pleasing and frivolous appearance of the fantastic, less fatiguing for the mind. Does this mean that a film cannot put into one's hands an arm capable of going beyond the target? No. But if it is capable of doing this, it is similar to other arts which show a tendency to exclude it because its youth makes it suspect in a country (France) where it is not taken into consideration save to have it forbidden.

Film-making is fifty years old. My age, alas. That is old for me, but not old for a Muse expressing herself through the intervention of phantoms and a material still in its infancy if it is compared with the use of paper and ink.

It is likely I was advised to "write on the fantastic in the movies" because of the films, *Blood of a Poet* and *Beauty and the Beast,* invented with an interval of twenty years between, and in which many agree on seeing the projection of that curiosity which impels me to open forbidden doors, to walk in the dark and sing to keep up my courage.

Now, *The Blood of a Poet* is only an exercise in introspection, a way of using the mechanics of dreams without sleeping, an awkwardly held candle, often extinguished by some breath, and held over the night of the human body. Acts are linked together in it loosely, under so weak a control that it could not be attributed to the mind. Rather to a manner of somnolence permitting the birth of free memories to be combined, joined, deformed until they take on a consistency without our knowledge and become an enigma for us.

It is unusual for France to have the exercise of this faculty which depends neither on reason nor symbols. Few Frenchmen will enjoy an exceptional event without knowing the source and the aim, and without studying it. They prefer to laugh at it and to cope with it by insult.

A symbol is their last recourse. They give it a wide berth. It still allows them to explain the incomprehensible and to drape with a hidden meaning what derives its beauty from not having any. "Why? Are you joking? Whom are you making fun of?" are the questions with which France undermines an unusual form which a noble soul succeeds in creating when it appears unexpectedly and intrigues a few curious people.

Very soon these few curious people are looked upon as being in league. It happens that snobs who have inherited the flair of kings, follow them blindly. This forms a mixture which the public refuses, incapable of recognizing the signs of a new embryonic conformity, to which it will subscribe tomorrow. And thus it goes. The fantastic therefore would be, since a wonder can be a wonder only in so far as a natural phenomenon still eludes us, not a miracle, sickening in the disorder it creates, but a simple human miracle and very matter of fact, consisting of giving objects and persons an unusual appearance which escapes analysis. Vermeer of Delft proved this for us.

Vermeer certainly painted what he saw, but this exactness, agreeable to all, teaches us how he avoided exactness. For, if he used no artifice to surprise us, our surprise is only more profound in terms of the unique traits which created his solitude and forbade our making any comparison between his work and that of his contemporaries. A painter in the same school paints with the same frankness. It is a pity that his frankness reveals no secret. With Vermeer space is peopled with another world than the world he represents. The subject of his picture is only a pretext, a vehicle by which the universe of the fantastic is expressed.

I wanted to come to this point: that the cinema can bear a relation to the fantastic, as I understand it, if it is satisfied with being a vehicle and if it does not try to produce it. The kind of excitement which moves us when we come in contact with certain works rarely occurs through an appeal to tears or surprise. I repeat that it is rather provoked in an inexplicable way by a sudden opening.

This opening will be made in a film as easily as in a tragedy, a novel, or a poem. The excitement will not come from the facilities it offers to stratagems. It will come from some mistake, some fainting spell, from some fortuitous meeting between the attentiveness and inattentiveness of its author. Why should he behave differently than the Muses? His aptness in deceiving the eyes and the intelligence also deceives us in his titles of nobility.

The cinema is an art. It will free itself of the commercial enslavement whose platitudes do not incriminate it any more than bad pictures and bad books discredit painting and literature.

But it is imperative not to look upon it as a magician. That belongs to the habit of speaking of a worker so as to avoid analyzing his real work. The cinema's privilege is not card tricks. It goes beyond juggling, which is only its syntax. The domain of the fantastic is elsewhere. *The Blood of a Poet* has no magic, nor has *Beauty and the Beast*.

The characters of this latter film obey the rule of fairy stories. Nothing surprises them in a world to which are admitted as normal, matters of which the most insignificant would upset the mechanics of our world. When the necklace of Beauty changes into an old rope, it is not the miracle which revolts her sisters, but the fact that it changes into a rope when they touch it.

If there are some elements of the fantastic in my film, do not expect to find it in such instances, but rather in the eyes of the Beast when he says to Beauty,

"You flatter me as an animal is flattered," and she answers, "But you are an animal."

Laziness, parading as a judge, condemns in my poetic enterprises what it considers not to be poetic, and bases its verdict on the appearance of the fantastic I speak of, and turns a deaf ear to the fantastic if it does not show its attributes.

When you see fairies, they disappear. They help us only in a guise which makes them illegible, and they are present in the sudden unusual grace of familiar objects by which they are disguised in order to keep us company. That is when their help becomes efficacious and not when they appear and dazzle us with light. It is the same with everything else. In *Beauty and the Beast* I did not employ this slope which the public wants to go down with increasing speed without being spared dizziness.

I insist upon repeating: the Fantastic and Poetry do not concern me. They must attack me by ambush. My itinerary must not take them into account. If I imagine that one shady piece of land is more favorable than another for their shelter, I am cheating. For it happens sometimes that an open road in full sunlight shelters them better.

That is why I insist on living just as much in Beauty's family as in the Beast's castle. That is why a fairy-like atmosphere is more important to me than a fairy story in itself. That is why the episode, among others, of the sedan chairs in the farmyard, an episode not deriving from any fantasy, is, for my taste, more significant in its atmosphere than any given artifice in the castle.

In *Blood of a Poet,* the blood flowing through that

film upset my judges. They wondered why they should be disgusted and shocked so deliberately. The blood which sickened them forced them to turn aside and prevented their enjoying the "windfalls" (by this word, they meant: the entrance through the mirror, the moving statue, the beating heart), but I should like to ask what bond exists between these various startling episodes, save the blood which flows and which gives the film its title. What can those who want only to enjoy the ports of call, know of the river? And what would the "windfalls," as they call them, be worth, if they were not the consequence of a plan, even subconscious, and tributary moreover, by means of this bond of blood? They sleep and believe that I sleep and that my waking up awakens them. In a meal, their heaviness condemns them to distinguish only pepper. They are sensitive only to witticisms. That is what inflames them, makes them restless, and forces them to run from place to place.

In *The Eternal Return*, the castle of the lovers seemed to them suitable to poetry. The garage of the brother and sister unsuitable. They condemned it. Strange stupidity. For it was precisely in that garage that poetry functioned the best. In understanding the desertion of the brother and sister, in their innate and almost organic failure to understand grace, I touch poetry and approach the terrible mysteries of love.

This is the result of a few experiments I have made, which I am still carrying out and which form the sole objective of my research. As Montaigne said, "Most of the fables of Aesop have several meanings and interpretations. Those who relate them to mythology choose one aspect which is very suitable to fables; but for the most part, that is the first and superficial aspect. There are others, more vital, more essential, and more central, which they have not reached."

My film (*The Two-headed Eagle*) was not as successful as *Beauty and the Beast*. When the critic on the New York *Times* wrote that he did not understand it and that I should have explained more, a number of letters were sent to the newspaper stating that the function of the critic was to understand and that it was insufferable to treat with such a lack of deference a guest of the city. In New York, newspapers publish this kind of letter and are not afraid of placing their official critic in an awkward position.

I quickly understood the source of the incomprehension over *The Eagle*. New York likes labels. Mine is oddness. *The Blood of a Poet* has been running in New York for more than ten years. In *Beauty and the Beast,* the American public rediscovered the oddness of my old film in a more accessible form. Therefore they liked it. Since *The Eagle* is a story I made up and told, the American judges looked for hidden meanings which are not in it, and hence the film disconcerted them more than an enigma would. It became a flat enigma.

I received in my hotel many exegeses of *Blood of a Poet*. This film, made nineteen years ago, has become a classic among American directors. It has been analyzed, psychoanalyzed, examined by auscultation, turned inside out. It is not understood, but it is a table which attracts the hands of spirits and which they

Films

question. The study which Professor Weiner Wolff made of it seems to me the most enlightening, although he commits a general error, which does not, however, compromise the details. Drawing upon my book *Opium,* the professor ascribes to opium the indirect associations which compose the plot of the film. This is my rhythm, and the behavior and the *awkward gait* of my mind. If the opium, which I took for medical reasons and without the slightest intoxicating effect, was able to facilitate associations and disassociations of ideas to which I give myself over body and soul as soon as I begin a work, it is in nowise responsible for a mechanism to which I have been faithful, even when it is not obvious, for the many years when I have not used the drug.

Each time *Blood of a Poet* is spoken of, the term "Surrealist" is used. It is useful, but it is inaccurate. At that time, Surrealism did not exist, or rather it had always existed and had not yet been named.

Bunuel's film *L'Age d'Or,* begun at the same time as *Blood of a Poet,* pointed in one direction, while mine pointed in the other. We saw our respective films after finishing them. And I was not to know *Le Chien Andalou* until later, although it was made before *L'Age d'Or.* It is therefore useless to look for influences of Bunuel in my film. It is important to understand that analogous waves are registered by certain minds in the same period and that these waves excuse the confusion which sometimes grows between works blatantly different at the time of their creation, and which with time seem related.

American critics have difficulty in imagining that a man can be the site of a real marriage between the

131

conscious and the subconscious. Yet Professor Wolff, author of a book on the subconscious and a book on Easter Island, moves with surprising ease in my world, which is not the world of sleep or of consciousness, and which is inhabited by delightfully ambiguous monsters. He never looked for those symbols which reassure the public and allow it to find an explanation for enterprises whose privilege it is to have no explanations. He never tried to decipher sexual riddles. He even stated, contrary to other interpreters of my cinema art, that the film could not be analyzed from this viewpoint since its line is nonsexual, cold and metaphysical (whereas in France only the sexuality of the film seemed to excite interest).

I can reproach no one for failing to understand a film which I do not fully understand myself, and especially in 1949 when American theatres cut it in order to shorten the program, doubtless because they considered the film means nothing and this "digest" version did not alter it. If this film remains an enigma to me, it is the same with most of my actions. But our actions are joined to one another by a scarlet thread which we can neither stretch nor shorten. College girls reproach me for not making the same kind of film and I have to explain: first, that the commercialization of the movies and the cost of films prevent young people and myself from using this means of confession, and second, that this film, which was looked upon as ridiculous at the beginning, has become sacrosanct and to repeat it would be to profit from one chance rather than taking others, and to bewilder those who like it by enterprises whose boldness is more invisible, since it

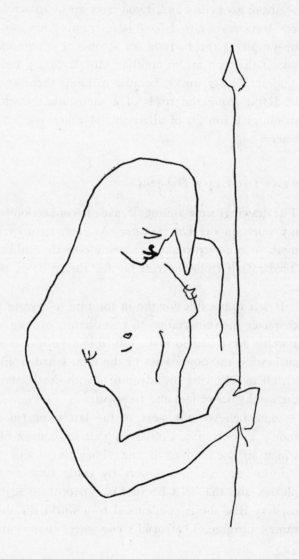

tries to contradict a period when boldness was blatantly displayed.

New Yorkers and Parisians, is it my fault if you do not have my agility and if you treat me as an acrobat? For forty years now I have been training my soul to be supple as the body of an acrobat. I congratulate myself that you are so familiar with my name and so ignorant of my works, because to know them would lead you along the roads of a somnambulist which would give you fits of dizziness and which you would resent.

DRAWINGS FOR *Orpheus*

The drawings were almost all made in connection with my work on the film *Orphée*. As I modernized the myth in order to make it accessible to the public, I freed myself from the real Orphic theme by graphic art.

It was impossible for me in the film to give to the character his importance of an initiator, of lawgiver. I would have had to make him into a politician and go beyond the boundaries of the film. I had to limit myself to following his adventures with death, and to the mechanics of fate and free will.

Some believed the next to the last scene (in the room) a concession similar to that of fantasy films which are ascribed to dreams. They forgot that the Princess exceeds her powers by using time as she pleases, and that it is because of this outrage against mystery that she is condemned to a world that man cannot imagine. That brief scene where time is abolished, where Heurtebise sees this phenomenon and has to reintegrate his death, provides the clue to the work.

It may be wondered whether young Cégeste, abandoned in the other world, does not represent the real poet for whom nothing works out—eternally. Paul Eluard suggested this idea to me after seeing the film. The secret forces depriving Orpheus of his death (of his muse), under the pretext of making him immortal.

FILMS

The cinema is still a form of graphic art. Through its mediation, I write in pictures, and secure for my own ideology a power in actual fact. I show what others tell. In *Orphée,* for example, I do not narrate the passing through mirrors; I show it, and in some manner, I prove it. The means I use are not important, if my characters perform publicly what I want them to perform. The greater power of a film is to be indisputable in reference to the actions it determines and which are carried out before our eyes. It is normal for the witness of an action to transform it for his own use, to disturb it, and to testify to it inaccurately. But the action was carried out, and is carried out as often as the machine resurrects it. It fights inexact testimonies and false police reports.

In short, the ability to translate thoughts into mobile objects impelled me to the use of a vehicle whose industrialization too often limits it to touring or simple means of transportation.

According to the Larousse Dictionary, the man who likes what he does is an amateur. In this respect we are all amateurs, and I dislike amateurs who claim this title because they allow themselves to indulge in habits which paralyze professionals. I wish they would give greater vent to their feelings and use the 16 millimeter camera to confide in us the troubles which torment them and expand only in their dreams.

When years ago I made my first film, *Blood of a Poet,* I knew nothing about the profession of a movie director. I had to invent a technique. The movie professionals thought I was ridiculous. And yet it is my only film still shown throughout the world and which for seventeen years has been shown intermittently in a small New York theatre.

Freedom always finds its reward. However, the desire to reach a large public deceives the producer concerning its endless, diverse, and secret curiosity. It underestimates the vast number of individuals who resemble any one of us. Its enterprise will be brief. Long-enduring is the enterprise which gave little heed to pleasing, which tried to be true, with that truth which seems to me to be the very definition of the beautiful.

VI. Aesthetics

ON READING

I can neither read nor write. When the census asks
for this information, I want to say no.

Who knows how to write? Trying to be understood
is like fighting with ink.

Either you write too carefully or not carefully
enough. You rarely find the middle course along which
you might limp gracefully. Reading is another thing.
I can read. I think I can read. Each time I reread, I
realize I had not read. That is the trouble with a letter.
You find in it what you look for. You are pleased and
you put it away. If you come upon it later, you read
another letter you had not read.

Books play the same trick on us. If they do not cor-
respond to our state of mind, we find them mediocre.
If they upset us, we criticize them, and this criticism
obscures the books and keeps us from reading them
faithfully.

What the reader wants is to read about himself. When
he reads what he approves of, he thinks he might have
written it. He may even dislike the book for taking his
place, for saying what he has not said and what he
believes he would have said better.

The more important a book is for us, the less well
we read it. Our own substance does not collide with

it. That is why, if I wish to read and convince myself that I can read, I read books which I cannot penetrate sympathetically. In sanitariums where I have spent long periods of time, I read whatever the nurse brought me or whatever I picked up by chance. Books by Paul Féval, Maurice Leblanc, Xavier Leroux, and countless adventure stories and detective stories made me into an attentive, undemanding reader. Rocambole, M. Lecoq, the crime of Orcival, Fantômas, Chéri-Biki, while saying to me "you can read," spoke to me in my language so well that I adopted them, without my knowing it, and deformed them to fit my needs. This is so true that you often hear, for example, a tubercular patient say, when speaking of Thomas Mann's *Magic Mountain,* "That book can be understood only by those who have had tuberculosis." But Thomas Mann wrote it without having been tubercular and precisely in order to have tuberculosis understood by those who do not have it.

We are all sick and can read only those books which treat our disease. This explains the success of love stories, because each one thinks he is the only man ever to have been in love. He thinks: "This book was written for me. No one can understand it as I do." Another person says, "What a beautiful book!" when she has been urged to read the book by persons who love her and who believe themselves to be loved by her. But she says it because she loves someone else.

It may be asked whether the function of books, which speak in order to convince, is not to listen and to say what one wants to hear. The reader finds good pasture in Balzac. There's my uncle, he says to himself, my aunt, my grandfather, Madame X., the city where I was born. What does he say when he reads Dostoevski? "That is my fever, my violence, which no one around me suspects."

And the reader believes he reads. The mirror with no silvering on it seems to him a faithful mirror. He recognizes the scene being enacted behind it. How closely it resembles his thought! How clearly it reflects the image of his thought! Between it and him a perfect collaboration, one reflecting the other.

In museums there are paintings with stories in them. I mean paintings which recall stories and which other paintings must look down upon (*Mona Lisa,* Millet's *Angelus,* etc.). Likewise, certain books have stories in them and their fate is different from that of other books, even if they are infinitely more beautiful.

Le Grand Meaulnes (The Wanderer) of Alain Fournier is one of those books. And one of mine, *Les Enfants Terribles,* shares this strange honor. Those who read it and read about themselves in it became, for the reason they believed they were living my ink, the victims of a resemblance which they owed it to themselves to sustain. An artificially created disorder came from this, and the conscious practice of a state of affairs which has only the subconscious as an excuse. Countless letters say to me, "I am your book." "We are your book." The war, the postwar period, a lack of freedom which at first seemed to make a certain way of life impossible, have not discouraged these readers.

In writing that book, in the hospital at Saint-Cloud, I was somewhat inspired by friends of mine, a brother and sister whom I thought the only ones ever to live in that way. I did not expect many sequels, by virtue of the principle I am defining. Who will recognize himself in that book? I asked myself. And even the real models will not, since their charm is not knowing what they are. They were, in fact, as far as I know, the only ones not to recognize themselves. From people like them, if there are any, I shall never hear anything. This book became the bible of mythomaniacs and of those who dream standing up.

Thomas l'Imposteur is a story, but it is not a story which creates difficulties. During the Liberation it almost took on the character of *Les Enfants Terribles*. A number of young mythomaniacs lost their heads, put on disguises, changed their names, and looked upon themselves as heroes. Their friends called them *Thomas l'Imposteur* and told me about their deeds when they themselves were not performing them. But there are few mythomaniacs who are the same as their legend. The others do not like being unmasked. It is in reality quite simple. A book creates misunderstandings immediately or never. *Thomas l'Imposteur* will never have the success of *Les Enfants Terribles*. What would a mythomaniac do with a mythomaniac? It would be like the Englishman playing the part of an Englishman.

The death of Thomas de Fontenoy is mythological. A child plays he is a horse and becomes a horse. A mythomaniac reads *Les Enfants Terribles*. He plays he is a horse and believes he is a horse.

ON WORDS

I attach no importance to what people call style and that by which they think they recognize a writer. I want to be recognized by my ideas, or better, by my bearing. I make every effort to be heard as briefly as possible. I have noticed, when a story does captivate the reader's mind, that he was reading too fast, and gliding down the slope. That is why, in the book, I skirt around the writing which forces me not to glide in a straight line, but to start over again, to reread the sentences in order not to lose the thread.

When I read a book, I marvel at the number of words I find in it and I dream of using them. I note them down. But in my work it is impossible. I limit myself to my own vocabulary. I cannot go beyond it, and it is so restricted that the work becomes a puzzle.

I wonder, at each line, whether I shall go on, whether the combination of the few words I use, always the same ones, will not end up by blocking the way and forcing me to silence. It would be beneficial for everyone, but words are like figures or letters in the alphabet. They are able to reorganize differently and perpetually at the bottom of the kaleidoscope.

I said I was jealous of the words of other writers. It is because they are not mine. Each writer has a bag of them, as in a lotto set, with which he has to win. Except for the style I dislike—Flaubert is the leading example—too rich in words—the style I like, Montaigne, Racine, Chateaubriand, Stendhal, does not spend too many words. It would take no time to count them.

This is the first point to which a teacher in class should call the attention of his students, rather than praise the beautifully flowing sentences. They would quickly learn what richness there is in a certain kind of poverty, and that *Salammbô* is bric-a-brac and *The Red and the Black* a treasure.

Words rich in color and sound are as difficult to use as gaudy jewels and bright colors are difficult to wear. A well-dressed woman does not use them.

I am surprised at the glossaries where footnotes claiming to illuminate a text, miss the point and flatten it out. This happens to Montaigne, who never attempts anything save to say what he means, and he succeeds at any cost but always by twisting the sentence in his own way. To this fashion of twisting the sentence, glossaries prefer a vacuum provided it is well organized.

This does not incriminate the exceptional use of a rare word if it comes in the right place and heightens the economy of the rest. I advise its use, however, only if it does not sparkle too much.

Words should not flow: they become embedded. They draw their zest from a rock garden where the air circulates freely. They demand the conjunction *and* which cements them, as well as *who, which, what, whose.* Prose is not a dance. It is a march. By the manner of the march, one's race is recognized, a balance characteristic of the native whose head carries heavy loads.

This convinces me that beautiful prose is related to the load which the writer carries in his head, and that every other kind of beauty comes from choreography.

Once I wanted to share my taste for a certain kind of prose with people who claimed they did not like it. Read out loud, with the fear of not convincing, this prose exhibited its vices.

Aesthetics

This kind of failure made me suspicious. I distrusted what had first attracted me. Gradually I developed the habit of liking only those writers in whose work beauty resides without their being aware of it and without their worrying about it.

Although the words of another vocabulary do not correspond to mine, I can encounter a technical expression and adopt it. Let me quote one which occurs in nautical books: *by dead reckoning (à mon estime)*. It says exactly what it means and I appropriate it because I cannot find another more suitable.

The French language is difficult. It turns against a certain kind of sweetness. Gide expresses it wonderfully when he calls it a piano without pedals. You cannot blur the chords. It functions dry. Its music is more spiritual than sensual.

What is considered musical in the classical writers is often a mere ornament of the period. The greatest do not escape this, although they surmount it. Its artifice is more visible in the less great writers. Célimène and Alceste seem to speak the same language.

In addition to the meaning words have, they possess a magical power, a *charm*, a form of hypnosis, a fluid which functions outside of meaning. But this functions only when they are grouped together, and it stops functioning if the group they form is only verbal. The act of writing is therefore bound up with several requirements: capturing the attention, expressing, intriguing. A way of intriguing which cannot be taught a writer, since it is his way and since it is vital that the stream of words resemble him in order to function. In short, they replace him and have to fill in for the absence of his glances and gestures and walk. They can act there-

143

fore only on those people vulnerable to such things. For other people, they are meaningless and will remain so.

The magic power of these words grouped together allows me to converse with a writer from any period. They lead me into his presence. I am able to question him. Their inner structure permits me to hear what he would have answered. Unless I find the answer written out, which does happen.

My book has no other purpose than that of engaging in conversation those who read it. It is the opposite of a course in college. I imagine it would teach very little to my friends. It hopes to meet strangers who would like to have known me and talked with me about those enigmas that Europe has ceased to care for and which will become the indistinct words of a few Chinese mandarins.

Aesthetics

The grouping of words is so effective that philosophers whose cosmic system is expelled by another do not remain in the memory of man by what they said but by their manner of saying it. Name one philosopher whose fame does not rest on his writing or at least on the particular lighting effect he projects on an error. We know now that Descartes was wrong, and we read him just the same. It is the word which endures, through a presence it contains and a substance it perpetuates.

I hope I am understood. I am not speaking of the word which is an adornment for an idea. I am speaking of a structure of words, so unusual, so strong, of such perfect conformity with the architect that it preserves its power in translation.

The phenomenon associated with Pushkin is that of not being able to communicate in any language but his own. His *spell* is felt on Russians of every belief. Such a cult cannot depend solely on music, and since the meaning alone seems insipid, some witchcraft must be involved. I ascribe it to a drop of black blood in his veins. Pushkin's drum speaks. If you change the beating, only the drum remains.

The role of words is certainly stronger with poets than with prose writers. But I imagine that some design passes from one language to another if the grouping of the words is tight enough. Shakespeare proves it. That is why Pushkin's case seems unique. I have had him translated twenty times. Twenty times the Russian who tried gave up, telling me that the word *meat,* used by Pushkin, did not mean *meat* but it put the taste of meat in your mouth, and that only he could do this. Now, the word *meat* is only the word *meat*. It can be more only by the words surrounding it and communicating to it a strange power.

Vanity urges us to shoot our pollen to the stars. But now that I think of it, the luxury of a poet must be to belong only to his compatriots. Doubtless what I felt was harmful to Pushkin is really what is protecting him and guarantees for him his cult in Russia.

Prose is less subservient than poetry to the recipes of imitative magic. It is true that the further away it moves from anecdote, the greater chance there is that it will change its idiom. Unless there occurs the providential meeting between Charles Baudelaire and Edgar Allan Poe. That is, between two men equally initiated in the use of herbs, spices, drugs, medicine, cooking, mixtures, and the effect they provoke in the organism.

ON BEAUTY

Beauty is one of the tricks which nature uses to attract one being to another being and to assure their dependence.

It employs it in a great disorderliness. Man calls it vice and it is common to all species whose mechanism functions blindly. Whatever the cost, nature achieves her ends.[1]

We can hardly imagine the principles of such a mechanism in the stars, since the light which reveals them to us comes either from a reflection, or, like any light, from a decomposition. Man imagines that they

---

[1] Bitches mount male dogs. Cows mount one another. This disorder is sometimes an order. Native islanders made it a rule before missionaries came. It was a way of avoiding overpopulation.

serve him as candelabra, but he observes them only when they are diminishing or when they are already extinct.

It is certain that the rhythm of the great machine is cruel.

The most affectionate lovers collaborate in this. Their kiss is a weakened form of the vampire's suction, a rite depicting the act of getting blood from the beloved, of exchanging blood.

This desire for another's blood is expressed even further when lips suck the skin, as a suction cup draws the blood to the surface, and mark it with a blue ring, a spot which adds exhibitionism to vampirism. This spot announces that the person bearing it, usually on her neck, is the prey of the being who loves her to the extent of wanting to seize her essence and mingle it with his.

Flowers remain the innocent trap they were at the beginning. I watch them in an experimental garden where species are crossed. The beauty we procure for them does not exist for the flowers whose color and perfume serve only to point out their presence to the vehicles of their love.

We can imagine, if we forget our size, those knights (the insects) in a translucent palace, with cool vast sweet-smelling rooms.

The *arum maculatum* imprisons the knight, thanks to a portcullis system, until he is covered with sperm and the women's apartment is opened to him.

I should enjoy expatiating on this theme. But have I not said that this book must not be pedantic?

I am interested in the similarity of these erotic spectacles. The world is more simple than our ignorance believes it to be. It seems to me more and more that the machine works in a thoroughly straightforward manner everywhere.

Beauty in art is shrewdness which makes it eternal. She travels about. She may collapse on the way, but she enriches the human spirit. Artists furnish her the vehicle. They do not know her. It is through them and outside of them that she doggedly carries on her life. If they try to take her by force, they produce only something artificial.

Beauty (which is not that for herself, but a simple servant of a marital system) profits from a painter, for example, and does not let him go. This often produces a disaster in the offspring of some creators who claim they procreate carnally and gamble on the painting. Do not believe that beauty lacks a critical spirit nor that she offers proof of it. She is neither one nor the other. She moves swiftly to the extreme point, whatever it is.

She always encounters some who marry her and assure her future.

Her lightning, striking the extreme points, sets fire to the works which scandalize. She avoids the inept representations of nature.

The habit of inept representation of nature is so ingrained in man that he worships it, even in painters where it serves as a simple pretext for taking off. He is revolted when this representation offers him anecdotes from his dreams or his spiritual life, depicted with an equivalent legibility. I mean the anecdote that does not concern him, but *someone else*. His egoism invalidates it for him. He becomes a judge and condemns. The crime is that of wishing to distract him from his own contemplation.

Just as man does not read, but reads about himself, so he does not look except at himself.

Art exists at that very moment when the artist separates from nature. That by which he separates himself gives him the right to live. It becomes an obvious truth.

This separation may take place when it is still unapparent. (I am thinking of Vermeer and certain very young modern painters.) This is the full realization of art. Beauty appears in it secretly. She lays a perfect trap, innocent in appearance as any plant. She will attract the world slyly without creating the fear her Gorgon head always excites.

Diderot irritates me when he describes in detail the anecdotes of Greuze. Baudelaire would unnerve me in describing the stories about Delacroix, if he were not so enriched by the painter. Dante motivated the Delacroix trap. Delacroix motivated the Baudelaire trap. The phenomenon can be seen with the naked eye in the Delacroix-Balzac fecundation (*La Fille aux yeux d'Or*).

Century after century, *Mona Lisa* attracts the beehive of eyes because of the traps which Da Vinci thought he was setting for the sole beauty of his model.

In the cinema, each film, thanks to the absence of color, escapes being platitudinous and accidentally benefits from the privilege of the work of art. Beauty appears there as little as possible. Color would spoil this equivocal condition. Everything would be ugly except the beautiful.

People dislike the film in color because they do not

find it close enough to nature. This is one more example of the divorce by which color will reign, and beauty will use it.

The reproductive instinct urges the poet to project his seed beyond his boundaries.

And I repeat, when the seed is badly transmitted, it is active. Certain species (Pushkin) refuse to be transmitted, but this does not hinder their flying to great distances, and even, when reduced to very little, from being active.

Shakespeare remains the prototype of the explosive plant. His seed has profited from wings and storms. Beauty rushes to it throughout the world on tongues of fire.

If we could measure the distance separating us from those we believe to be closest, we would be terrified. A good understanding is composed of laziness, politeness, lies, a multitude of things which disguise the barriers. Even a tacit agreement involves such a lack of harmony in detail and itinerary that there is good reason to give up and never come together again. If we meet someone with a spirit moved by a mechanism seemingly analogous to ours, and which surprises by its speed in covering areas we are interested in, we then learn he is a specialist, for example, in music, and proves thereby the mirage which seemed to relate him to us. Feeling had estranged his intelligence, which no longer controlled him. A weakness, acknowledged at the start, petted, strengthened, exercised each second, finally developed athletic muscles and stifled all the rest. He was a soul able to understand everything and who understood nothing. The use of what charmed us was of no worth. This able person liked bad music and devoted himself to it. Deaf to real riches, he was not free on this central point. On any other track he would move easily. An atrophied limb was the only one he used and he was proud of the sad spectacle of this atrophy.

An apparent understanding from beginning to end is more serious. This is the kind which permits us to live and which art exploits in convincing us to use it. A work is so specifically the expression of our solitude that I wonder what strange need for contact impels an artist to exhibit it.

A work of art, through whose invention a man exposes himself heroically or unconsciously (another form of heroism), will take root in others thanks to subterfuges comparable to those used by nature in perpetuating herself. Does a work of art exercise an indispensable priestly function, or has not man, by mimicry, submitted finally to the universal method of creation? It is certain he is its slave and that, without realizing it, he clothes his creative power with a decorous gear suitable to announce his presence, to captivate, terrify, seduce, persist, come what may, by signals having no relationship with his mission and by a stratagem similar to that of flowers.

A work bears in itself its defense. It consists of a number of unconscious concessions which permit it to conquer habit and install itself through misunderstanding. Thanks to this hold, it hangs on and its secret seed begins working.

An artist can expect no help from his peers. Any form which is not his must be unbearable to him and upset him at the outset. I have seen Claude Debussy sick at orchestra rehearsals of *Le Sacre du Printemps*.

He was discovering the beauty of that music. The form he had given to his soul suffered from another form which did not match it. No help was possible. Neither from his peers nor from a public incapable of admitting without revolt a violent break with habits it was beginning to form. Whence will the help come? From no one. And that is when art begins to use obscure maneuvers of nature in a reign opposed to it, which even seems to fight it or turn its back on it.

A friend of mine is a typical example. His contribution is tremendous. He is Jean Genet. No one was better armed than he against contacts, no one protected his solitude better. He reached this contact through prison, eroticism, a whole new almost physiological psychology, an arsenal of horrors which intrigue and attract those who seem to be the most in revolt against them. For his genius projects, in wide sweeps, forces which, expelled by talent, would be but picturesque. Secretly he obeys the order of sending out his seed. The trick is performed. Faithful to her ancient method, beauty adopts the mask of a criminal. I think of this as I look at a photograph of Weidmann which Genet gave me. Bandaged, he is of such beauty that it is to be wondered if beauty does not use a universal astuteness and if it is not one of her means to attract what she kills, to exalt her proselytes, to radiate a somber prestige, and thus to perpetuate herself.

Is a man capable of piercing the mystery I am analyzing and becoming its master? No, for the technique itself is a lure. Wilde wisely remarked that technique is individuality. The technicians in my film *Beauty and the Beast* insisted that I was a first-rate technician. I am not. No one is, in fact. What is called technique

Aesthetics

is the equilibrium of each second which the mind instinctively puts into operation in order not to break its neck. Picasso has summarized this admirably: "Technique (*le métier*) is what is not learned."

I reiterate that we have to live closely with people separated from us by a space more funereal than the space between atoms and stars. This is the composition of a theatre public in front of whom we expose ourselves with effrontery. That is the void into which we send poems, drawings, criticism. That is the park where insects buzz getting their food and which the factory of the world deviates to other ends.

Even if you admit that some of these insects have opinions, that does not alter the rule, which is strong enough to stand many failures. It reckons only on numbers. It estimates roughly. It recklessly spends its wealth. It does not know the code. It is no matter if multitudes of its bullets miss their mark. It has so many. It tries to shoot a bullet into the hole.

ON THE BIRTH OF A POEM

> *But the angel whose fist makes*
> *him hit the dust is himself.*
> SARTRE, *Saint Genet*

I was recently the site of a quartering *à la Ravaillac,* pulled by several horses. When I decided to study one of my poems, *L'Ange Heurtebise,* which seemed appropriate for describing the relationship between the conscious and the subconscious, the visible and the invisible, I realized that I could not write. The words dried up and shoved one another, or glued together

153

and rose up like sick cells. When I wrote, they assumed affected positions which kept them from falling in line and making a sentence. I persisted, ascribing the situation to a fictional clairvoyance I try to confront with my ignorance. I came to the point of believing I would never be free, or that age was rusting my machine, which would be worse, since free or not free, I saw myself incapable of undertaking any work. I rubbed out, tore up, began over again. Each time the same impasse appeared. Each time I hit against the same obstacle.

I was going to give up when I found a copy of my book *Opium* on a table. I opened it by chance and read a paragraph which gave me information on my impotence. My memory had played tricks on me, interpolated dates, stripped the gears, twisted the mechanism. A deeper memory revolted, without my being aware of it, and confronted my errors.

A bad perspective showed me one incident coming before another when it really came afterward. Thus our past actions are telescoped as we move back in time, and their orchestration is victimized by one false note, by one false testimony given by him who pleads his own cause.

Before my own poem, *L'Ange Heurtebise,* the symbol "angel" in my work offered no relationship with religious imagery, not even that in which the Greek El Greco gave it the ways of the world and an unusual meaning and called down upon himself in Spain the wrath of the Inquisition.

What approaches it would be what was seen by the crew of the Superfortress Number 42.7353, after dropping the first atomic bomb. They spoke of a purple light and a column of indescribable shades. They could not articulate the spectacle of this phenomenon and it remained locked up inside them.

The similarity between the words angel (*ange*) and angle (*angle*), with the word *ange* becoming *angle* if an *l* (*aile,* wing) is added, is a coincidence in the French language, if coincidence does occur in such matters. But I knew this coincidence is not one in Hebrew where the words angel and angle are synonymous.

The fall of the angels symbolizes in the Bible the fall of the angles, namely, the very human creation of a conventional sphere. Emptied of its geometrical soul, made up of a tangle of hypotenuses and right angles, the sphere no longer rests on the points which guarantee its radiation.

I knew also that it is vital to avoid the fall of that geometrical soul in each of us, and that to lose our angles or our angels is a danger threatening individuals too attached to the earth.

Genesis does not contain the passage relating to the fall of the angels. Those fabulous troublesome creatures fecundated the daughters of men, who gave birth to giants. As a result of this, giants and angels are confused in Hebraic imagination. Gustave Doré shows wondrously the avalanche of bodies in the depths of wild gorges, which they fill with their muscular forms falling backwards.

How did the idea of a visible angel come about? From the human shape of those inhuman creatures? Doubtless from the desire in man to make certain forces comprehensible, to conquer an abstract presence, to incarnate it for greater self-recognition, for less self-fear.

Natural phenomena: lightning, eclipses, floods, would be less terrifying if they were answerable to a visible company, in the command of the Lord.

The units of this company, resembling man, would lose that vagueness disliked by the human spirit, the vague namelessness which frightens children in the dark and sets them screaming until a lamp is turned on.

The Greek gods were born from this sentiment, but without the shadow of the Apocalypse. Each one legitimatized a vice or magnified a virtue. They moved beyond earth and heaven, between Olympus and Athens, as through the floors of an apartment house. They brought reassurance, whereas angels must have been an incarnated fear.

Monsters that were gracious, cruel, androgynous, and excessively male gave me my idea of angels, of *angles that fly,* before I had the proof that their invisibility could take on the image of a poem and become visible, *without risk of being seen.*

My play *Orpheus* was originally destined to be a story of the Virgin and Joseph, of the gossip they had to stand because of the angel (carpenter's aid), and the malevolence of Nazareth over an inexplicable pregnancy which forced the couple to take flight.

The plot involved such intricacies and errors that I gave it up. For it I substituted the Orphic theme where the inexplicable birth of poems would replace that of the Holy Child.

The angel had to play his role in the character of a

window repairer. But I did not write the act until much later, in Hotel Welcome of Villefranche, where I felt free enough to disguise the angel with blue overalls and wings of pane-glass on his back. A few years later, he stopped being an angel and became a nondescript young man who had died, a chauffeur of the Princess in my film. (That is why the critics were mistaken and called him an angel.)

If I anticipate, it is for the sole purpose of explaining that the character of the angel lived in me platonically, and communicated no uneasiness to me before the poem. Once the poem was finished, I found him inoffensive. I only kept his name in the play and in the film. Once he was a poem, he cared very little whether I was or was not preoccupied with him.

Here is the passage in *Opium* which opened my eyes to my impotency on writing this chapter. It dates from 1928. I placed it in 1930.

"One day when I was going to see Picasso, rue La Boétie, in the elevator I felt I was increasing my size to keep up with something terrible and eternal beside me. A voice cried out. 'My name is on the plate.' A jolt awakened me and I read on the brass plate of the control lever: *Elevator Heurtebise.*

"I remember that Picasso and I talked of miracles. He said that everything was a miracle, and that it was a miracle that we did not melt in our bath."

At a distance now, I can see how much this sentence influenced me. It summarizes the style of a play where miracles must not be miracles, but derive from comedy and tragedy, and puzzle as the world of adults puzzles children.

The elevator episode went out of my mind. Suddenly everything changed. My play project altered its form. At night I would go to sleep and wake up with a start, and not fall back to sleep. In the daytime, I fell and stumbled about in a maze of dreams. All this perturbation grew worse. The angel was living in me without my realizing it, and I needed the name Heurtebise, which gradually grew into an obsession, to become fully aware of it.

On hearing that name, hearing it without hearing it, hearing its form, so to speak, and in a zone where man cannot stop his ears, on hearing a silence shout that name, on being tracked down by that name, I recalled the cry in the elevator, 'My name is on the plate,' and I named the angel who was incensed at my stupidity, since he had named himself and I had not given him his name. I hoped he would leave me in peace when I called him by name. I was wide of the

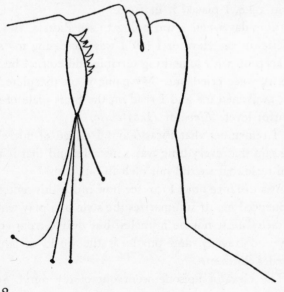

mark. The fabulous creature grew unbearable. He got in my way, spread out everywhere, cut up, struggled like a child in the womb of his mother. I could trust no one and had to bear the torment alone. For the angel tormented me ceaselessly, to such a degree that I used opium, hoping to quiet him down by ruse. But this displeased him, and he made me pay dearly for it.

Today, when all is more clement, it is hard for me to relive the details of that period and its unspeakable symptoms. We have a way of forgetting evil—which is our protection. Only our deep memory is watchful, and that is why we can remember more clearly a gesture of childhood than an action we have just performed. By stimulating this double memory, I can enter a state unbelievable for those who do not practice our priestcraft. And slyly, I who prided myself on being free, in total disobedience toward this priestcraft, I am once more ordained and I write. Nothing stops my pen. I am living on the rue d'Anjou. My mother is alive. I decipher my anxieties in her face. She does not question me. She is suffering. I am suffering. And the angel is delighted. He behaves diabolically. "Have yourself exorcized," they say to me. "A devil is in you." No, it is an angel. A creature looking for a form, one of those creatures who are forbidden entrance to our realm by another realm, who are attracted by curiosity and use every means available to get a footing here.

The angel paid no attention to my revolt. I was merely his vehicle and he treated me as one. He was getting ready to leave me. The intensity of my fits increased. They grew into one seizure comparable to beginnings of birth pangs. A monstrous delivery which would not benefit from maternal instinct and the confidence which comes afterwards. Imagine a parthenogenesis, male and female in one body, and giving birth. At last, after one night when I contemplated suicide, the expulsion took place, on the rue d'Anjou. It lasted seven days, when the nonchalance of that individual exceeded all limits because he forced me to write against my will.

What escaped from me, what was written down on the leaves of a kind of album, had nothing to do with Mallarmé's frigidity, or with Rimbaud's lightning flashes, or with automatic writing, or with anything I knew. It moved about like chessmen, organized as if the Alexandrine rhythm had been broken and was being reconstructed in its own way. It unbalanced a temple, measured columns, arcades, cornices, volutes, architraves, made mistakes, and began over again its computations. It frosted over an opaque windowpane, intersected lines, rectangular triangles, hypotenuses, diameters. It added, multiplied, and divided. It profited from my intimate memories and humanized its algebra. It seized the nape of my neck, bent me down over my paper, and I had to wait for the halts and attacks of an unbearable invader, bow down to the service he demanded from my ink, from the very ink along whose canal he flowed and became a poem. I lived on the hope that he would relieve me of his cumbersome person, that he would become someone else, outside my organism. I did not heed what he was trying to do. The main thing was passive obedience to his metamorphosis. I could not call it help because he seemed to scorn me and expect no help from me. I could neither sleep nor go on living. It was a question of his deliverance and mine, for which he felt no responsibility.

The seventh day (it was seven o'clock in the evening), Angel Heurtebise became a poem and freed me. I was still groggy and looked at the form he had assumed. He was distant, proud, totally indifferent to anything outside himself. A monster of egoism. A mass of invisibility.

That invisibility, constructed on angles which emit fire, that ship caught in ice, that iceberg surrounded by water, will always remain invisible. Angel Heurtebise willed it thus, since his earthly form did not have the same meaning for him as for us. Since then, people have written about him. But then he hides under the exegeses. As you say, he has more than one trick up his sleeve. He wanted to penetrate our realm. Let him stay.

When I look at him, I have no ill-feeling, but I turn away quickly. His big eyes upset me. He looks but does not see me.

It seems remarkable to me that this foreign poem (foreign except to my substance) tells my story and that the angel has me speak of him as if I had known him for a long time and in the first person. This proves that, without my vehicle, the character was unable to take a form, and that, like the genii of Oriental tales, he could only inhabit the vase of my body. The one way for an abstract figure to become concrete and still remain invisible, is to contract a marriage with us, to keep for himself the larger part and to give us an infinitesimal amount of visibility. And the entire amount of reprobation, naturally.

Freed, depleted and quite weak, I settled down in Villefranche. I had just reached a reconciliation with Stravinsky, in a sleeper where we were traveling together. We settled our quarrel which had been rather tense since *Le Coq et l'Arlequin*. He asked me to write the libretto of an oratorio on *Oedipus Rex*.

He had become so Latinized that he wanted the oratorio in Latin. Father Daniélou helped me in this exercise which brought back school memories.

Stravinsky lived in Mont-Boron, with his wife and sons. I remember a wonderful trip to the mountains. February had covered them with rosy trees. Stravinsky had brought along his son Théodore. Our chauffeur spoke in oracles, one finger pointed up. We called him Tiresias.

I wrote *Orphée* at that period and read it in the villa of Mont-Boron, September, 1925. Stravinsky was reorchestrating *Le Sacre* and was composing *Oedipus Rex* for which he said he wanted to write music as curly as Jupiter's beard.

I took him passages as I did them. I was young. There was sunlight, fishing, navy squadrons. After work, I walked home, late at night, without fatigue, to Villefranche. Heurtebise left me alone. He was then only a theatre angel.

Yet I noted down in *Opium* the strange coincidences which occurred with the Pitoëff performances in June, 1926. Coincidences which coalesced and grew serious in Mexico. I quote again from *Opium:* "They played *Orphée* in Spanish in Mexico. An earthquake interrupted the Bacchantes scene, wrecked the theatre and wounded several people. After repairing the damage, they opened with *Orphée*. Suddenly, the stage manager announced that the performance would have to be suspended. The actor playing the part of Orpheus could not come out of the mirror. He had died in the wings."

The play, written in 1925, was scheduled for performance in 1926, after my vacation. The second reading took place at the home of Jean Hugo, on the Avenue de Lamballe. After the reading, in the hallway, I can still hear Paul Morand say to me, as he was putting on his coat, "You opened a mighty strange door. But it isn't strange at all."

The next day, I was to have lunch at Picasso's, on the rue La Boétie. Again I found myself in the elevator. I looked at the brass plate. It bore the name Otis-Pifre. Heurtebise had vanished.

ON A JUSTIFICATION OF INJUSTICE

> *That other defendant, Cocteau. . . .*
> SARTRE, *Saint Genet*

The young are unjust. They owe this to themselves. They fight against the invasion of personalities stronger than themselves. They give themselves over at first. And then, they go on the defensive. In the space of a day they turn against you. The love and confidence they once had, turn into a form of sickness. Their haste in fighting this sickness finds them without weapons. They improvise some. They turn against the object of their confidence and trample on him, but so violently that they injure themselves. Thus they imitate the murderer who keeps hitting his unconscious victim.

It would be ungracious of me to complain about iconoclastic youth. Didn't I, when I was young, accuse my loves? And first of all, *Le Sacre* of Stravinsky, which obsessed me to such an extent that I looked upon it as a sickness and put myself on guard against it. Young men dream of replacing one taboo by another. I have been asked—in fact, Stravinsky asked me—in the sleeper of the chapter, "On the Birth of a Poem"—why I never attacked the Picasso taboo. Stravinsky meant to say, "Since your attack on me was a defense reflex of adolescence, why hasn't Picasso, who also occupied all your attention, aroused this reflex?" The reason is doubtless the fact that Picasso changes quickly his matador leaps, his red cape passing to the right when you believe it on the left, and his *banderilla* thrust unexpectedly into my neck. I loved his cruelty. I loved his belittling of what he loves. I loved his outbursts of affection and wondered what they made up for. No one took better care of his bees, or put on more masks, or made more rumpus to turn away the swarm. All that distracted the enemy which a loving youth carries in himself.

Maurice Sachs had great charm, which is still apparent since his death. I have forgotten how or where I met him. He hardly ever left my house. He came to the hospitals where my bad health forced me to spend long periods of time. I was so accustomed to his fine open face that my memory of him has no dates. If he stole from me, it was to buy me presents. And if I mention thefts, that is because he took pride in them.

When Maurice was without a cent, he stuffed his pocket with toilet paper. He crumpled it and pretended his pocket was full of thousand-franc notes. That gave him a sense of security, he used to say.

I must not complain of having been taken in. No one was to blame except myself. I have always preferred thieves to policemen. It is different to be robbed. There has to be an atmosphere of confidence. There was, with Sachs. I repeat that he gave more than he took, and he took in order to give. This style of theft must not be confused with sordid thieving, no more than with the theft which sets up a kind of inventive genius against which no similar genius protects us.

One year when I was staying in Villefranche, Maurice took away in a cart all my belongings in my Paris room. Books, drawings, letters, manuscripts. He sold them indiscriminately in bundles. He imitated my handwriting to perfection. I was still living on the rue d'Anjou. He went to my mother with a forged letter in which I gave him a free hand.

When he edited a series of books at Gallimard's, volumes of Apollinaire and Proust, on the title-pages of which they had written letters to me, were put on sale. They were exhibited in bookstore windows. Since I was made responsible for the scandal, I told Gallimard the whole story. He called in Sachs and told him he was relieved of his job. Sachs requested a few minutes time. He disappeared and came back with a letter from me, in fresh handwriting. This letter begged him to sell immediately books, correspondence, and manuscripts. "See," said Maurice. "Now I forgive Jean for his fantasies, I will burn his letter." He opened his cigarette lighter and burned it. As he told me of this sleight-of-hand trick, Gaston Gallimard said that he was convinced when he saw the letter burn. And we laughed at Sachs' skill in exonerating himself by destroying a forgery.

Just before leaving for Germany, he telephoned me one morning, after a year's silence. He was at the Hôtel de Castille and was dying. He begged me to go there.

In his hotel room, I found him in bed and very pale. "You are the only one I loved," he said. "Your friendship stifled me. I wanted to escape it. I wrote lies about you and insults. Will you forgive me? I have given the order to destroy them."

Maurice did not die in the Hôtel de Castille. He met his death in Hamburg, under frightful circumstances. His books were not destroyed. On the contrary, some are appearing with the help of our mutual friend, Yvon Bélaval. Others are waiting for publication. Gérard Mille owns them.

I do not share the opinion of my friends who are incensed by these insults. Maurice told me the truth, his truth, which is all anyone can say. I feel that his insults, leveled at me, testify to a deep impression. At least, this is the way I see them. As I said at the beginning of this chapter, he constructed all kinds of weapons and attacked me from every direction. One could see he believed nothing he said. His books are incomprehensible unless one understands his reasons for attacking himself and me. He drew his lifeblood from this blind will to expel what inflated him. His method was defensive and offensive. His plunge to death, which might be considered a flight, was the consecration.

Maurice Sachs was the prototype of the self-defender against an invader. The more he offended, the more he punished himself. He struck his breast in the manner of his coreligionists before the wall of Jerusalem. Today he enjoys a posthumous success and fascinates people because of his self-inflicted punishment. But his cynicism would interest no one if it were only confessions and lies. It is interesting because it is related to passion. Maurice knew the passion of others and of his own character. His books are the scene of the fight he waged between these two sentiments. His youthfulness prevented his arranging for their cohabitation. He had to kill, if he wanted to live. But he aimed only at the visible person. The other escaped.

Devious routes led him to his method. He began friendships with honesty and cordiality. Neither Max Jacob nor I could complain of his friendship. He respected us. He never used *tu* in speaking with me. I used *tu* with him, and usually young people are not sensitive to this slight difference. I was often irked by young poets addressing Max Jacob as *tu*.

At the time of *Potomak,* I decided to construct a moral system for myself. But it was far from being constructed when I engaged an attack. Morals did not exist for Maurice. With great skill he suddenly decided to make a negative system. Morals from an absence of morals. From that moment he used all his active sloth. No one of us suspected that he was writing continuously. We never saw him write. It is true that he began to write when the attitude of my friends forced me to give up seeing him.

Maurice wrote without stopping. He wrote about himself. He dared to take on a sense of importance by the exhibition of what man calls turpitude, and which is merely the obedience to instincts which current morality condemns. As concerns the confessions about his sexual life, nature mixed good and bad morals in his case. It is by a chance use of sex that nature alternates her economy and her prodigality. For if her creatures used the pleasure which accompanies the reproductive act only for that end, she would overcrowd her domain. She instigates visual disorder to protect her invisible disorder. With reservation, young natives accepted the norm, and women gave birth in cow dung so that only the strongest children would survive. Until, of course, Europeans came to establish order, namely to bring dresses, alcohol, sermonizing, overpopulation and death.

When I try to remember Maurice, I do not find him in his books, but in the passionate years when literary politics divided and joined our factions. Maurice moved from one camp to another. He betrayed no one. He listened, laughed, helped, and went to great pains to make himself useful. I scolded him quite often.

When he entered the seminary, I alerted Maritain. I knew that he had gone there to escape his creditors.

Aesthetics

Maritain disregarded my word. His noble-mindedness had hoped for this refuge which would save Maurice from more serious debts which would be canceled. Maurice became a seminarian. We saw him wear the cassock, introduce into his cell American cigarettes and a bathtub. His delightful grandmother, Mme. Strauss, was fearful that no one could wash in the seminary.

One day, at Juan-les-Pins, when he was behaving very badly, I advised him to go back to civilian clothes. He was already bored with his role and he consented gracefully. His charm was such that Father Pressoir, provincial of the seminary, reproached me for my "too premature counsel."

Dear Maurice. If he had not been the *avant-garde* of a period when commandos of all kinds were in fashion, what would be left of him? He was right in giving his weaknesses the appearance of strength. Whether I like it or not, my morals demand that I excuse his and welcome him into my Pantheon.

Claude Mauriac was a second example for me.

His father was the friend of my youthful years. I adopted him therefore as a son. At that time I lived at the Place de la Madeleine. My door was open to him. I let whoever wanted to, come into the house. If he liked it there, he could stay. I refused to predict the future. And if you had asked me what I would take from the house if it burned, I would have answered: the fire.

He had come with me to Versailles, where I had begun work on *La Machine Infernale,* and asked me if I minded if he took notes on my conversations. He was very sorry people had such a wrong idea of me and he was planning to write a book about me. I could stop his taking notes. That displeased me. But I could not stop the book. He offered it to me graciously.

That book has circulated. It is friendly as well as insulting and inaccurate. Claude is a liar and his trump card is to accuse me of lying. To a reporter he will say that he loves me and that it is obvious. He proved this subsequently. We met in Venice, on the Square of Saint Mark's, after a private showing of *Les Parents Terribles*. I pardoned him because quarrels are repulsive to me and because I knew the motives of his action. In the case of Sachs, I had taken the mechanism apart.

Claude praised *Orphée* in two remarkable articles. But the reflex still functioned. He could not bring himself to listen to his heart. He published another article in which he retracted the first two and claimed that *Orphée* loses its value with a cold public. It would have been normal to attack that kind of public, but he attacked the film. However, I am patient, and I hope that his zigzags will lead Claude to his own moral system. That of Sachs would not suit him.

I presume he regretted that last article. A recent letter from him implied this.

The attitudes of Maurice and Claude were not alike and yet they go together. Maurice was talkative. Claude ruminated. In them we find the characteristic of youth closing itself off from enthusiasm. This anguish over enthusiasm is as frequent in young people as "anguish over the act," studied by psychoanalysts. A counterenthusiasm starts in reverse order. It derives its energy from fear of letting itself go and being discovered. Modesty turns into invective. Kindness becomes synonymous with stupidity, unkindness synonymous with intelligence. As Hans says to the cardinal in *Bacchus: the trouble is there.*

Age has brought me a robust health which never worries about invasions. If foreign forces invade me, I can retreat and create a vacuum which they fill without contaminating my forces. I am no longer afraid of admiring contradictory works. I no longer try to triumph over them. They become guests of mine and I welcome them in royal fashion.

Gide obeyed the technique of youth. He remained entangled in it to the very end. I would not speak of him in this chapter if he did not illustrate the meaning of this technique by the use he made of methods which are unconscious in young people and which were perfectly conscious in him. His desire for youthfulness attached him to intrigues where he forgot his age. He behaved then with a fickleness he had to justify subsequently. He will thus provide me with a footnote, as a third example, all the more striking since his defense was crafty and his weapons curved.

In this chapter, where I am trying to excuse my aggressors, I need to enlarge the context and find excuses for Gide when he attacked me in his journal and to define the initial role of the young writers who circulated between us.

I had just published, in 1926, *Le Coq et l'Arlequin.* Gide took offense. He was afraid the young would turn away from his program and that he would lose electors. He called me up before him as a schoolmaster would call a recalcitrant pupil and read me an open letter addressed to me.

I have received quite a few open letters. In Gide's I was described as a squirrel and Gide as a bear at the foot of the tree. I jumped over steps, and from branch to branch. In short, I was being reprimanded, and publicly. I told him I intended answering the open letter. He snorted, agreed, told me that nothing was richer or more instructive than such exchanges.

It goes without saying that Jacques Rivière refused to publish my answer in the *Nouvelle Revue Française*, where Gide had published his letter. I confess mine was severe. Gide had no profit to draw from my answer except to answer it, which he did. He loved notes and counternotes, answers to answers. He replied to mine in *Ecrits Nouveaux*, which had printed it.

I confess that I did not read it. I wanted to protect myself against a reflex action and a terrifying deluge of open letters. Time went by. Montparnasse and Cubism came. Gide kept out of the way. He could forget offenses, especially those he wrote. He telephoned me and asked me to take charge of . . . let us say, Olivier. His disciple Olivier was bored with the books in Gide's library. I would introduce him to the Cubists, to the new music, to the circus where he loved the bands, acrobats, and clowns.

I was cautious in carrying out this order. I knew Gide and his quasi-feminine jealousy. Young Olivier found it amusing to irritate Gide by constantly singing my praises, by declaring he hardly ever left my side and that he knew *Potomak* by heart. I did not know this until 1942, just before leaving for Egypt. Gide confessed and told me he had wanted to kill me (*sic*). It was because of that story he tried to attack me in his journal. At least, he gave it as the reason.

He did not state that I had a hard time convincing him to read Proust. He called him a society writer. Gide was doubtless angry at me for having convinced him, when Proust's cramped handwriting appeared everywhere in the *Nouvelle Revue Française*.

On the day of Proust's death, Gide whispered to me at Gallimard's: "All I will have here now is a mere bust."

In his person Gide combined Jean-Jacques Rousseau botanist and Grimm at Mme. d'Epinay's. He reminded me of that endless harassing hunt after a terrified animal. He had both the fear of the one and the tricks of the others. The pack and the prey were mingled in him.

The posterior of Jean-Jacques was the moon of Freud rising. Such exhibitionism was not distasteful to Gide. But if you passed around him, you found Voltaire's smile.[1]

ROYAL HONEY

If the poet has a dream, it is not of becoming famous, but of being believed. Here begins his calvary. Even if people read him, they are drawn only by what seems to correspond to what they feel. They do not read, they read about themselves. They do not look save at

---

[1] When I asked Genet why he refused to meet Gide, he answered, "A man is a defendant or a judge. I do not like judges who lean over amorously toward the defendants."

themselves. Every work becomes a mirror. Whatever differs from the reader, he conjures away. Of what is secreted, very little is communicated. For the poet's work is really a secretion. Whatever the poet registers and blends, composes a kind of black honey and, in small doses, a substance comparable to the "royal honey" which bees feed to the queen and which used to make the gods immortal.

This substance perhaps gives, in the end, certain works a vague color of immortality.

From these minute doses, where the soul of the artist overflows without being contaminated with impurity, his work draws its greatest power.

Those who read his texts and look at his paintings do not make the distinction, but it is made alone, slowly and mysteriously. Some poets bequeath a visible proof of this because they survive by some poem or stanza which supports the entire structure. Guillaume Apollinaire baptized them "poem-events." *La Chanson du Mal-Aimé* and *Les Colchiques* are examples. And sometimes, only one line is victorious, as in Baudelaire where verses such as *"Et tes pieds s'endormaient dans mes mains fraternelles"* (And your feet went to sleep in my hands of a brother), or *"La servante au grand coeur dont vous étiez jalouse"* (The warmhearted servant you were jealous of) are enough to elevate the entire poem.

In museums, unless we check and consult the catalogue, we feel called by certain signs which reveal to us the effect of this royal substance. Piero della Francesca, Michelangelo, Vermeer, Van Gogh, Corot, Renoir, Cézanne speak to us in a glance, in a gesture, in a balance of forms. They say: "I am here."

Aesthetics

But how rare is this dialogue between spectator and author! The subject is stronger than the object. The pretext by which the artist affirms his presence is more important than the presence. It charms or repulses superficially and does not provoke the great flash which I have already said resembles the principle of sexual mechanics.

That is why, despite the current opinion that art is a luxury, it continues its priestcraft and imposes its necessity by the mediation of those who receive the illumination.

André Malraux, in his work on *The Imaginary Museum* of sculpture, gathers from the centuries the objects most apt to provoke this shock. He proves that plastic characteristics, able to arouse the senses of the soul, are not particularly dependent on individual choice, but on that extreme where civilizations are affirmed, where their truth grows vibrant and reaches its apotheosis without the intervention of aesthetics or the conformity of beauty. A great perspective is needed for such a choice to be made. A large number of leading works of a century were invisible because of the religious or superstitious meaning attached to them.

VII. Moral Essays

OPIUM

[FROM *Lettre à Maritain*]

Opium should not be confused with drugs. I never smoked in company with those who compromise it. A real smoker seeing me suffer handed me his pipe.

You don't try opium. You can't play with it. It marries you. The first contact is disappointing. The profit comes only after a little while and the bliss is felt when it is too late to do without it. I worked harder to acquire the habit than to lose it. The smoke made me sick. I had to go through three months of nausea to grow accustomed to the pitch and roll of the floating carpet. I persisted. I could not admit the discredit cast on opium by literature more than the mockery we are exposed to by snobs. I do not regret the experience and I affirm that opium, if the technique were not so complicated, would prepare many souls for elevation. The difficulty consists in knowing when it ceases to be charitable.

(One of its subtle tricks, which it would be inaccurate to ascribe to anesthesia, is the expansion of touch to the point where the object touched merges with you. A finger falling from the hand of the smoker would not surprise him more than the cigarette he drops which burns his clothing.)

Does opium dictate to us specious reasons for defending it, or does it give us a clairvoyance which disappears in a normal state?

When its noble rites became indispensable for me, I seemed to understand that the prejudice against opium was romanticism: the prejudice of discomfort. Since a remedy acting on the sympathetic nerve suppresses moral suffering or so transfigures it as to make it appealing, no moral suffering exists and that much talked of moral suffering becomes only physical suffering. This led me to conclude that it is foolish to go to the dentist and to refuse the help of opium. The Lorelei continued to whisper: why is suffering a fine thing? Only second-rate poets profit from suffering; great poets work in serenity.

You see the trick. Opium acts as a padding. It carries you along the river of the dead. It disincarnates you and takes you into an airy field. The night of your body swarms with stars, but your happiness is glacial. You become from head to foot a lie. You are mummified and the entire machinery stops working. The organism refuses to obey; temperatures and difficulties have no effect on you. You feel neither cold nor heat.

Neapolitan painters decorate a hotel room in *trompe-l'oeil;* opium is a painter in *trompe-l'esprit* (mental deception). It covers to my advantage all the walls of the room where I smoke. Two and two no longer make four; two and two make twenty-two. A disturbing euphoria takes hold of me. The weak point is this disturbance. Opium quiets one. As soon as any disturbance starts, it is serious.

The Chinese smoke very little and move about very little. They demand of the drug no exceptional services. They respect it and leave it free to extend its waves. We who are not refined try to discover in it sources of an activity which it detests and will always punish. The Chinese smoke in order to draw near to their dead. Invisibility comes from a motionless speed, from speed in its pure form. If the dead diminish ever so slightly their speed, a zone for meeting is formed. Life and death are as far apart one from the other as heads and tails of a coin, but opium goes through the coin.

The Chinese also use opium for less noble reasons. They influence the chances of commerce by offering the pipe of politeness to the European they plan to rob.

Besides, the effects of opium are variable. It is a nerve regulator. It adds whatever is lacking. It attaches cork to some and lead to others. To me it added lead. This diving suit kept me from floating aimlessly and gave me a positive sense of contacts. It never provoked visions. At the most, it put the switchman to sleep. The branch lines were manipulated blindly. The mind glided down a slope. You climbed up it and the mind found itself, with amazement, very far from its point of departure. Sometimes it was able to conquer the resistance of opium and unfold a banal idea. The drug then played the deforming role of water where black divers went down with the complicated majesty of China ink.

These phenomena occur when you smoke alone and close your eyes. In company with others, the effect is dispersed. Then it is possible to instill confidence around the lamp and establish equality among very different people.

But I repeat, in Europe we do not know how to smoke. We do not admit the nausea which the healthy man accepts. The doses are increased. If waking up is painful, we smoke in the morning; and if it is difficult to smoke it at home, we eat the opium. This leaves us far from the goal. You would have to smoke a dozen pipes to equal the effect of a ball of opium, because, when you eat it, you absorb morphine and dross. Troubles begin: sweat, ice-water syphons, yawnings, mucus, tears, a lump in the throat, a catch in the solar plexus. I confess I did not have those symptoms. I was trying to commit suicide and absorbed huge doses. But you can't always commit suicide. The optimism which this imprisonment provides urged me to get out of it. Suicide is cheating. And cheating is impossible for those of us who are clumsy. In a word, I was expelled from the suicide club because I did not know how to cheat.

That is a detour by which I made myself a prisoner, on the rue de Chateaubriand, at the Thermes Urbain, where you were my first visitor after sixty days of seeing no one but my nurse.

Opium resembles religion in the same way an illusionist resembles Jesus. It conjures away suffering, which waits in hiding. You can imagine the bewilderment of my veins and my spirit coming upon this newly made suffering which had been locked up for a year. But the doctors could never make me curse opium. I persist in saying I did not leave it, but it gave me up.

In me this chaste drug became a crime. It developed the charitable tendencies of my spirit. It could fill me artificially with the beatitudes which exalt monks and help us to conquer the senses. It became then the preamble of a real elevation, a uniting of real life and spiritual life. It left in its wake vile tendencies. A faun came out of the wadding. Miraculously I lived without it. The resurrection of the schoolboy was, alas, the first sign of return to normalcy.

Since school, the birth of Venus had attracted me. Now this mythology bores me. Radiguet advised me not to confuse it with the birth of love.

On leaving the Thermes, I was neither proud of myself nor pleased, but I felt my suffering was pleased. It does not like to be used as a distraction and it liked my type.

After my convalescence in Versailles, without extending me a visible prop, without the least proselytizing, you shared your friends with me and your project. You were founding a collection with the publisher Plon, a meeting place for writers of different training but of the same caste. One evening several of us met at your house in order to discuss it. They seemed like children playing adults.

You had announced the possible visit of Father Charles. I knew nothing about him save that he wore the habit of Père de Foucauld and lived as a hermit in the African desert. I also knew that he had met Claudel when he disembarked in Marseille (Claudel was in Aix for the wedding of Darius Milhaud), that he would spend a week in Paris, one or two months in the Vosges, and then go back to his post of prayer, a small hut on the desert sands.

Lightning is disconcerting. It can appear as a very slight red ball, enter a room, move about, and leave without doing any harm.

Jacques, was that your trap? Had you been waiting for that moment? A heart entered. A red heart sur-

mounted with a red cross in the middle of a white
form which moved about, bent down, spoke, shook
hands. That heart hypnotized me, drew my attention
from the face, and decapitated the burnoose. It was
the true face of the white form, and Charles seemed
to be holding his head against his chest like the mar-
tyrs. His head, burned by the sun, seemed a reflection
of his heart, a mirage in the African light. The cheek-
bones and the chin marked the outline and the ex-
treme point. Then I saw his eyes unused to short
distances and his hands of a blindman. I mean, hands
which saw.

I would shock you if I continued. The ease of this
man was the most important trait of all. My ease, com-
pared with his, was the charm of a bad actor. He
smiled, spoke, exchanged memories with Massis.
"Groggy," as boxers say, and stupid, I watched behind
a thick glass the white form moving in the depths of
the sky.

I suppose your wife and guests must have realized
it: the room, the books, the friends, all ceased to exist
for me.

That is when you pushed me, Maritain. With a
shove of your soul, which is an athlete, you pushed me
in the back, and my head went first. Everyone saw that
I was losing my footing. But not one offered me help,
because they knew that to bring me help at that time
would have been fatal. In that way I learned about
the family sentiment which Faith gives to us instan-
taneously and which is not one of the least graces of
God.

After the first spasm from my fall backwards, matters were arranged. A fall from heaven cuts off one's breath, but a fall into heaven attacks the heart.

The earth is a demanding mother. She does not want us to go away. She tries to get us back at any cost; sometimes she does not hesitate to draw back an aviator by force. But even he leaves you free to feel or not to feel its attraction.

Do you know the underwater film of the Williamson brothers? In spite of the polka played by the orchestra, Negroes, deep-sea divers, women divers, seaweed, and octopuses inhabit a silence where our laws do not apply. The slowing down effect of water seemed to mark with a supernatural style things which moved in it, but slow motion of the machine proved that it was always necessary to go beyond. That underwater majesty was a faint outline. My heart stopped beating when it faced the silence of silences, the grace of graces, the slowness of slownesses. I suggest brief slowness to young writers. The water and the camera created a heavy lightness in comparison to which any other movement seemed vile. For no perturbation resists. Plunge it into this revealer and you will see vulgarity and ridicule changed and translated into an idiom capable of moving me.

Slow films taught me that everything is a question of speed. In a rugby match, thirty brutes turn into cigar smoke.

Nothing fascinates me more than the angel which the slow-motion machine forces out of everything like a chestnut out of its bur. Since our centuries, in terms of God, last the space of a wink, our picture is taken in slow motion. Slightly less speed would release all souls and would remove from human intercourse its

ferociousness. Suddenly I understood the secret of
Charles' beauty, and I remembered the sentence, "God
is patient because He is eternal."

Again I was mistaken. There is zeal in the hope for
reward. But here I was contemplating prayer incar-
nated. His hunger for living and survival slept the
sleep of fakirs. He lived underneath a stage whose ma-
chinery could swallow up a distracted character. His
ability to appear and disappear was the reverse of
my distraction. A priest had moved me as Stravinsky
and Picasso had. Thus he provided me with a proof
of the existence of God, for Picasso and Stravinsky
could cover paper with divine signs, but the host was
the one masterpiece which Charles presented to me.
Would his gesture have affected me so deeply if he
had offered only a piece of white paper?

Soon the nobility of that priest's soul was playing
the role of heavy water and calming the puppet, but
without Faith it was a superficial force in speed reduc-
tion.

The surprises at the beginning! I occupied myself,
and I was occupied by that friend, as a country is
occupied by an enemy. God takes charge of every-
thing and thereby our pride is overthrown. Claudel
wrote to me: "As for many of us, the adjustment period
of the new man may be quite disagreeable to you." I
answered him that I was at the moment ashamed of
treading on the dress of the Virgin at each step I took.

Yes, I stumbled. The air was too pure and threat-
ened to put to sleep the man who could not mount
gradually.

On the morning of the feast of the Sacred Heart

of Jesus, in your chapel, in the presence of a few close friends, Father Charles gave me communion.

ON FRIENDSHIP: I

The voyage we make between life and death would be unbearable to me without the blessings of friendship.

Love is still a fringe of the order which nature gives us. Its prodigality misuses the pleasure of an act into which it forces most of us in order to assure its reign. It often seems to misuse it to its own detriment when by sterile loves it protects its economy. Human law calls a vice the great prudence with which nature avoids overpopulation. But perfect friendship is a creation of man, and the very highest.

My sole politics has been friendship. A complex program in a period when politics in the literal sense separates men, when it would not be surprising to read, for example, that the *Ninth Symphony* of Beethoven is a communist hymn. To continue one's friendship is interpreted as opportunistic. You have to subscribe to one or the other camp. You are urged to sever the bonds of the heart if they reach to both sides of the barricade. And yet, it seems to me that I am defending a party of solitary figures who search for one another. Such politics are no longer popular. Opinions destroy sentiments, and it is anachronistic to remain faithful if opinions are divergent. I am stubborn about this and prefer to be condemned for sentimental fidelity rather than for intellectual doctrine.

Unfortunately the forces I am concerned with disapprove of certain friendships which invade my life and which derange their work while distracting me from mine. This doubtless explains my long list of losses, and why friends who lightened my burden were taken away from me. Prudence is necessary in such relationships. Despite my inclination to prefer the duties of friendship to those of my work, I fight it off through fear that all will start up again and I shall be punished for having neglected my solitude to help my friends.

Since friendship is not an instinct, but an art which calls for continual guidance, many nonbelievers try to find in it motivations comparable to those which govern them. Sexual or financial reasons. If friends defend us against its traps, society rises up and decides to isolate us for the sake of protection. It is suspicious of a lack of motivation which remains a dead letter for it. Only animals are praised for that. It is defined as a triumph of serfdom. It becomes then a pretext for touching stories and sentences such as "animals are better than we are." I have heard the story of a police dog who realized it was wearing its muzzle when its young master was drowning in Biarritz in the presence of a powerless nurse. He found a muzzleless dog and sent him to the rescue.

A poodle used to wait for its master each day in front of a railroad station in the provinces. The master died in Paris and the dog continued to wait for him. After several weeks, he too died. And the citizens of the town expressed their *surprise* by erecting a statue to the poodle.

The statue is impressive. I like animals and I know that they teach men lessons. But the art I refer to does not govern them. They become attached to whoever pats them or beats them. We flatter them to flatter ourselves. Each one of us owns the most remarkable animal. This creates reciprocal blindness.

Friendship entails clairvoyance. It acknowledges faults over which love would be blind. That is why friendship with animals is really love. They make us into gods and put forth no effort to correct our faults with courage, in correcting themselves of theirs, nor to correct themselves of theirs in order to be an example to us—which is the epitome of the art of friendship.

The statue of the poodle is Tristan's. It is not Pylades'.

Real friendship does not have quarrels, unless the importance of the quarrel denounces a sentiment which is close to love and imitates the storms of love.

In the friendship between Nietzsche and Wagner, Wagner did not play a noble role. When the demands of Nietzsche were not satisfied, his break and reproaches drew upon all the justice and injustice of passion. This celebrated quarrel was a quarrel of lovers, in the sense that Nietzsche wanted to own Wagner. Wagner wanted to enslave Nietzsche. But Nietzsche tried to transcend in a spiritual realm the mingling of bodies wherein lovers hope to join in a single cry. The difference in quality was apparent in Bayreuth when Wagner refused Nietzsche's manifesto for the collecting of capital, because he reproached him for not sounding clearly enough the call to arms.

Nietzsche's role provides the loftiest testimonial to the experience of solitude which would not be filled by love leading to marriage. This passion characterizes a feminine nature which the world and its pomp attract outside the storm. Péguy's letter to Daniel

Moral Essays

Halévy (*Victor-Marie, comte Hugo*) and the Wagner Case offer two astonishing declarations of love. The slightest grievance proves the passion which dictates them.

I wonder if Nietzsche and Wagner do not demonstrate a new proof of a cold terrifying jealousy over work. I wonder if they are not one of those couples in whom the invisible does not tolerate an invasion which confesses the interests, in whom it imitates those people capable of standing the spectacle of an understanding which expels them. For, when friendship is formed between tempestuous temperaments, it is difficult for the tempest to blow evenly. The wind is divided, and the two winds fear that one will down the other, and that the one down will appear the slave. That is when friendship equates love, and comes to grips, not only with its microbes, but with the exterior obstacles threatening it.

True friendship does not develop in this way. I call it an art because it is self-questioning and self-correcting and signs a peace to avoid the wars of love.

It is possible that when I was a victim of friendship, my friends likewise were victims because I upset the rule. If not, friendship seemed admissible by our undertakings. They exploited it. They found a means to use us better because friendship forces us to give proof, to believe ourselves responsible for this proof, to convince us that we are working for a goal that makes us worthy of our friends. This means is upset as soon as friendship exceeds its prerogative, as soon as one enslavement is added to another and torments our night to the point of disrupting its egoism. In *Tristan and Isolde,* besides Wagner's love for his inspiration, the passion he felt for his own person dictated the passionate style. The work testifies to a couple formed by certain creators, to the fever which destroys the monstrous couple, and to whom a fever of external origin is but a screen of invisibility.

Experience perfected me in this art and in the suffering it inflicted upon me. The meetings which precede the ceremonial should not come from a stroke of lightning, but from a meticulous study of character.

One should not accumulate explosives in one's house.

Only friendship finds the glance or the very simple sentence which binds our wounds—wounds which we aggravate and open with the determination of those who, knowing themselves to be incurable, look for some outlet in the extremity of pain. A force equivalent to ours can do nothing against these wounds except to leave us or follow us to the extremes and perish there with us.

Friendship does not wish to be inspiring. It does not pretend to feed our fire, to pour oil on it, to collaborate on some magnificent conflagration, and to play a role over our ashes.

It watches us without fever. It maintains its equilibrium for the purpose of assuring ours. It is at least from this angle that I recognize its beautiful solemn face.

One can imagine how the absence of a spectacle irritates a world greedy for it and which would like to contemplate our tragedy from their orchestra seats. If we do not offer them tragedy, they look for what is concealed under a good understanding. They imagine an intrigue, and when they tire of this game, they express pity for our calm and rush to more suggestive theatres. There is nothing less exciting for the world than our calm in the face of attacks. It hopes to be the witness of a massacre. I have often met people who deplored my reserve in the trouble over *Bacchus*. They expected more from it. They wanted me to assassinate Mauriac, and his acolytes to assassinate me. The heart of the quarrel did not interest them. They were interested solely in the quarrel and hoped it would land us all in court.

At times, our picadors turn towards victims they imagine less able to defend themselves. That is what happened when, believing they had hung fire with my play, they turned against *Britannicus* at the Comédie-Française, in which Marais played brilliantly. The public was enthusiastic over the performance. But those I speak of wanted to attack me by attacking him and derided him in the hope that the endings of the intrigue would be the same. They had forgotten the friendship which joined us and our ethical codes which are the same. It is true that other arenas turn away spectators from a *corrida* without the slaying of the bull. They direct *banderillas,* pikes, and horses toward beasts less slow in dying.

The group of musicians called *Les Six* is one in which friendship constituted the ethics. I was their historian. They left me full responsibility for my ideas. I did not impose any discipline. That is why, after twenty years, we are again together, bound by the same loyalties in 1952, in a small celebration which the publisher Heugel conducts from capital to capital. Critical attacks and jealousies, which decimated our other friends, have not affected our group, and if they do affect it, professional disputes will never separate us. Friendship grouped us together without constraint. Each one developed according to his aptitude. We never accepted the offer of the countless proposals which would have disunited us.

My friendship with Stravinsky, which has passed through crises, is something else. But I always found it intact when the world hoped it was over.

I live in a fortress whose sentinels protect friendship. This fortress of friendship has been sheltering me since 1949. I regret to say that it will hold and yield only to superior powers against which we have no weapon. It is a fine thing that it held out far away from the major maneuvers. When those major maneuvers come close, we escape on a boat which draws us ever closer together. And if I do leave the fortress and rush imprudently into some skirmish, I return to it, lock myself in, or get onto the boat.

Perfect friendship, which is not poisoned by love, feeds its substance on forces foreign to my studies. I insist on the fact that there is confusion in the frontier lives when secret forces join up. If I speak of an art of friendship, I mean an art where man is free and not an art where he is a slave.

This art relaxes me wonderfully from the other art, and I am happy when no shadow pursues me in it. Yet I have to beware not to infringe on rules outside of which the terrifying machinery would start up again.

Having admitted my responsibility as an artist, I take good care of the responsibilities of my heart. I never allow it to oppose my work. My judges will say, that is a life without fire, a resigned life. I confess I prefer the firebrand to a joyous fire.

A young hostess, an adopted son, and very few visitors form a reduced company. But friendship continues without the explosive boundary marks which Occidental boredom places along its road in order to alleviate the platitude. Friendship's time is Oriental. The mistake of the Orient is perhaps that of having overestimated the West and its fainting fits. It should have sent us missionaries.

It is customary to confuse friendship with comradeship which is its first draft and ought to be the basis of the *Social Contract*. And what can we say of special friendships? Montherlant and Peyrefitte have depicted the shadowy beginnings of those infatuations, at an age when the senses are still unawakened and do not know any prohibitions.

Comradeship and infatuation bear no resemblance to the devotion of Orestes and Pylades, of Achilles and Patroclus. It is regrettable that monks were suspicious of this devotion and destroyed works of Sophocles, Aeschylus, and Euripides which would have enlightened us. Greek love, as understood by moralists, which was an erotic intimacy between pupils and teachers, had nothing to do with such powerful spiritual bonds. And if the heroes exceeded the limitations permitted, no further accusation is added in the trial. The search for this kind of devotion supports wars and attracts a number of men away from their homes where love does not exist and whose dismal atmosphere they cannot abandon without a patriotic pretext.

I have known couples formed by two friends. The faults of one were added to the faults of the other. The first imagined that the second was backing him, when the second was profiting from the first. These couples bear up through a disorder which they elevate to fiction. The title they acquire makes them scorn peace. Drinking keeps them together. They can engage in storms fiercer than those of ordinary couples.

The case of Walt Whitman does not apply to passionate friendship. It is in a category by itself. His interpreters have accused Whitman by camouflaging him. And of what? He is the rhapsodist of a friendship in which the word "comrade" recovers its real meaning. His hymn goes far beyond slaps on the back. He sings of a joining of forces. Whitman is opposed to the contacts which Gide confesses to. It is a pity that in wishing to defend an unfamiliar zone, Gide gives us only a sketch of it. Wilde idealizes it with social grace, and Balzac, when he offers to Wilde (in the dialogue between Vautrin and Rastignac in the garden of the Vauquer pension) the model of the dialogue between Lord Harry and Dorian Gray in the painter's garden, shows us a strong force in the presence of weakness, a weakness which is apparent when Rubempré denounces his benefactor at Camusot's.

Proust set himself up as judge. In this, the beauty of his work loses a lofty meaning. It is regrettable that his pages on maniacal jealousy do not provide fuller documentation.

Let me return to the focal point of this chapter, to friendship, unspoiled by the legends with which society bedecks it. Men and women are elevated by it although women have greater inclination than men to feel jealousy. Jealousy can have no place in friendship. On the contrary, it must serve sentiments foreign to its own record. It does not suspect, nor spy on, nor indulge in reproaches. Its role is to see for those who are blinded by the extravagances of love, to help them in happiness, if they reach it, and in unhappiness if they are so affected. Friendship must act prudently with love, otherwise its support might take on the appearance of strategy for the benefit of its preservation.

Many letters I receive are offers of friendship. People are surprised when I do not welcome these offers and when I answer impetuosity with reserve. I would answer, the art of friendship is summarized in the Chinese formula: "Contract your heart," which does not mean: "Keep from using your heart." It means: "Do not go beyond the chalk circle." I have spent a long time in testing friendships which suit me. One more, and the circle is broken. This wisdom does not mean that I keep three locks on my door. My door is wide open. But it is not the door of my treasure.

It is easy for a man to use the word friendship, to caress and speak familiarly until the slightest circumstance destroys the entire edifice. I keep my real friendships until death takes over. And if to old friendships I add new ones, my first care is to inform them about a past they did not know. Thus old and new can join without a rift, and the new are not kept apart.

Do not believe that friendship is shielded from the test of inclemency. This book lists some of the rebuffs

I have known. I have referred to the long study which precedes friendship. The clairvoyance it gives us, contrary to love, should open our eyes at the moment it spoils, but that is difficult because it is indulgent and it hopes to triumph over its faults. If these faults are not really faults but come from an excess of sensibility, disorder begins without being noticed. No nature is sheltered from a shock which upsets it and marks it with unexpected rules of conduct. When these shocks do not occur, it is through a chance comparable to that of a gambler who wins several times on the same number in roulette.

However, in the long run, we become perspicacious. We help chance in such a way that it serves us without cheating.

The work of friendship would be too simple if it warded off with assurance the obstacles of the labor of artistic works, in which an invisible world alerts its police. We have to carry on the two together, and not confuse one work with the other, and not allow our tasks to believe that friendship is jealous of them.

A fortress is almost indispensable to this balance, insoluble in the midst of the riding, parades, shooting, roller coasters, and swings of a city.

As in the case of wine, I recommend that friendship not allow its bottle to be shaken. Besides, it dislikes being disassociated, even momentarily.

The bishop of Monaco told me that he was responsible for the death of a young woman in the catastrophe of the *Languedoc*. She was in such a hurry to leave, that he exchanged his place with hers. He is the bishop of a rock where a temple rises up: the temple of chance. The bishop was not the friend of the young woman. He was simply doing her a service. If he had been her friend, he would doubtless have wanted to leave with her.

Friendship is looked upon as vain in an age of haste and strong wills. What is friendship for the man who would sacrifice it to a principle? What is friendship in a world which scorns the sentiments of the heart? I don't care an iota, as they say. He who weeps last, weeps best.

ON FRIENDSHIP: II

Prince Polignac said, "Basically I do not like people." But when his wife asked him, "Why are you sad?" and he answered, "I am in love and I am loved," and added, "Alas! it is not the same person," he confessed his solitude. I like people and I exist because of them. Without them, my strength is wasted. Without them, my energy diminishes. Without them, I am a ghost. If I withdraw from my friends, I begin to look for their shadow.

At times, foolishness and ignorance take their place. I am tricked by the slightest civility. But how, then, can I be understood? What I say is not understood. I shall have to find a means to be heard. Do I speak too fast? Is a fainting fit the reason? Aren't the letters of my words big enough? I search, find, speak and am heard. There is no need for practice. It is the love of human contact.

I have said somewhere that I can make friendship better than I can make love. The principle of love is brief spasms. If these spasms disappoint us, love dies.

It is unusual for it to resist experience and become friendship. Between man and woman, friendship is delicate and is a kind of love. There, jealousy is disguised. Friendship is a peaceful spasm. Without greed. The happiness of a friend delights us. It gives us something and takes nothing away. If friendship is offended, it does not exist. It is a hidden love. I believe that this passion for friendship which I have always known comes from the sons I did not have. Because I do not have them, I invent them. I try to educate them. Then I realize they are educating me. Beyond the fact that the young and their presence in my house oblige me never to take one step which will not serve as an example to them, they have weapons suitable for combat for which mine have fallen out of use. I have much to learn from them. There is not much to teach them about myself. Later whatever I am will penetrate and form a soil which they can cultivate. Words are useless. In my classroom you can hear a fly move about. And I am constantly talking.

It is something else to give directions, if I am asked. And yet I am not skillful in that. I speak easily of anything and that is not the way I can be of service.

Max Jacob used to say to me: "You have no sense of comradeship." He was right. Wilde's aphorism, said to Pierre Louÿs, fits me better. Because he did not understand it, he made it into a scandal: "I have no friends. I have only lovers." A dangerous ellipsis if it falls on the ears of a policeman or a writer. He meant that he went only to extremes. I believe in his case that he was attitudinizing. He might have said, "I have only comrades." And if I had been Pierre Louÿs, then I should have been more offended.

Moral Essays

Where would I find the pleasure of being a comrade? At what time of day or night should I go from café to café, from studio to studio, arm in arm with buddies? Friendship takes all my time, and if a piece of work occupies my attention, I dedicate it to friendship. Friendship delivers me from the anguish men feel in growing old.

Youth is not what my friends want from me and their youth interests me in so far as it reflects their shadow. Each one finds what he wants, works at what amuses him, tries to remain worthy of the other. And time flies.

"Our essay of culture had a sad ending," said Verlaine. The failures I have recorded! Enough to make me give everything up. But the soul is tenacious. Destroy its niche and it builds it up again.

Garros' plane burned and fell. Jean Le Roy spread out my letters in a fan shape on his duffel bag. He grabbed his machine gun and died. Typhoid took Radiguet from me. Marcel Khill was killed in Alsace. The Gestapo tortured Jean Desbordes.

I know that I sought the friendship of machines which revolve too rapidly and wear out in dramatic fashion. Today a paternal instinct wards me off. I turn toward those who do not wear the black star. I curse it and detest it. I warm my carcass in the sun.

ON DEATH

I have gone through such tragic periods that death seemed desirable. I have learned the habit of not fearing it and of looking at it face to face.

Paul Eluard surprised me when he said he was terrified at seeing me defy death in the role of the *Baron Fantôme* where I fall into ashes. Living upsets me more than dying. I did not see Garros dead, or Jean Le Roy, or Raymond Radiguet, or Jean Desbordes. My mother, Jean de Polignac, Jean Giraudoux, Edouard Bourdet are the dead with whom I have communed during these last years. With the exception of Jean de Polignac, I made drawings of them, and was left alone for a long time with them. I looked at them closely to see every detail. I touched them, admired them. Death takes great care with her statues. She unwrinkles them. There was no point in telling myself that they were not concerned with what concerned me, that a disastrous distance separated them from me. I felt as close to them as the two sides of a coin which cannot know one another but are separated only by the thickness of the metal.

If I were not saddened by abandoning those I lose and who can still hope for some help from me, I should wait with curiosity for the shadow preceding death to touch me and shrink me. I would not like the ultimate attack and its long work to be continued to the extreme where it takes pleasure in finishing us off. I should like to say farewell to my friends and see my works happy to take my place.

Nothing which relates to death disgusts me except the pomp which goes with it. Funerals are not pleasing to my memory. At Jean Giraudoux's funeral I said to Lestringuez, "Let's leave? He did not come." I thought he might be playing billiards in some basement of the Palais-Royal.

Bourdet's funeral was glacier-like. It was freezing,

and the photographers climbed up the pulpit to take our pictures and set off the flash bulbs.

My mother's death was a beautiful experience for me. She had not fallen into childhood. She had gone back to hers and saw me a child. She believed I was at school, spoke in detail of Maisons-Laffitte and felt no worry. Death had only to smile at her and take her by the hand. But I dislike Montmartre Cemetery, which is ours. They practically put you in the garage. The drunks crossing the bridge urinate on you.

Yesterday I visited a mountain cemetery. It was under snow, with very few graves. It overlooked the chain of the Alps. I know it is ridiculous to choose a last resting place for oneself, but I thought of my hole in Montmartre and I wished I could be planted on the mountain.

After the death of Jean Giraudoux, I published a farewell letter which ended with, "I shall soon join you." I was scolded for that sentence, which was considered pessimistic and resounding with discouragement. That was not true. I meant that if I had to live to one hundred, it would be a few minutes. But not many will admit that we are busy playing cards in an express train rushing toward death.

Since Mother Angelica feared it in Port-Royal, who can derive benefit from it? It is better to wait for it steadfastly. It is too fawning to think only about death, and ungracious to make excuses for living as if life were an error of death. What will those say who are imprisoned in a cell and are compiling anxiously all the articles of their trial? The jury will not take it into

199

account. Its verdict is decided on in advance. They will only be losing their time.

I like the attitude of the man who used well the time given him and did not try to be his own judge. The duration of human life belongs to those who shape and form the minute and who are not concerned with the verdict.

On the subject of death, I have much more to say. I am surprised that so many people are affected by it since it is in us each second and they should accept it with peace of mind. Why be afraid of a person with whom you live, closely joined with your own substance? We have become accustomed to making death into a legend and judging her from the outside. It would be better to say that at birth we marry her and adjust to her character, despite her roguishness. She is able to have herself forgotten and let us believe that she is no longer living in the house. Each one of us gives lodging to his death and is reassured by what he invents about her, namely that she is an allegorical figure appearing only in the last act.

She is an expert in mimicry. When she seems furthest from us, she is in our very joy of living. She is our youth, our growth, our loves.

The shorter my life becomes, the longer her life grows. She settles down more comfortably. She becomes preoccupied with more things and takes on more banal pieces of work. She troubles less and less about deceiving me.

But her glory comes when we stop. She can then go outside and lock us in.

Moral Essays

ON FRIVOLITY

Frivolity is a crime in that it imitates delicacy, such as that of a beautiful March morning in the mountains. It leads to the disorder of invisible uncleanliness, worse than other disorders, fatal to the harmonious functioning of the organism (such as eczema) by the almost pleasant itching which is spread on the surface of the intelligence by the freakish writer (*fantaisiste*), a terrible individual easily confused with the poet.

If you consult the Larousse Dictionary, you will see that Rimbaud is a *fantaisiste* poet. There is a kind of pleonasm in the intent of the culprit who wrote the article. For most people, the poet is necessarily a *fantaisiste*, unless a low kind of lyricism or false gravity earn him a respect corresponding to his platitudes.

Frivolity is nothing but a lack of heroism and a refusal to expose oneself in any way. It is an evasion looked upon as a dance, a slowness which seems to be speed, a heaviness apparently similar to the lightness I am speaking of and which only the most profound spirits possess.

There are situations—the imprisonment, for example, of Oscar Wilde—which open the eyes of the criminal to his crime and force him to repentance. He admits then that "what is understood is good and what is not understood is bad," but he admits it only because discomfort instructs him. The accident of Pascal's carriage is a similar case. It is startling to see such a spirit as his in love with life to the point of attaching

201

such extraordinary importance to being saved from death.[1]

I consider frivolous any person capable of trying to solve problems of local interest with no sense of ridicule, a sense which would risk causing him to reflect and direct his efforts toward peace, for example, in place of war. For, unless he is criminally frivolous, this dangerous person can find excuses only in a personal interest of commerce or glory. And patriotism is a bad excuse, since there is more nobility in displeasing the masses who are duped by it, than in duping them under a pretext of greatness.

Frivolity, already hateful when it functions in a superficial form, since there are heroes in that domain of a charming levity which frivolity discredits (certain characters of Stendhal, among others), becomes monstrous when it proliferates into drama, and, by the facile charm it exerts on every lazy individual, guides people to a place where real gravity seems a childishness which has to give over to the group of adults.

Then we behold, but impotently, a delirium of catastrophes, papers, controversies, murders, trials, ruins, murderous playthings, at the end of which the frightful frivolity of men returns, dazed and worried, in the midst of a disorder comparable to childhood when it smashed pictures, put mustaches on busts, threw the cat into the fire, and upset the goldfish bowl.

[1] I know it was a question of death in or outside a state of grace. I am particularly fond of the following story. At dinner at Stravinsky's, his son Théodore told us that at a lunch of freethinkers, a guest died at the moment he was insulting the Blessed Virgin. He was lucky, said Stravinsky, because he went straight to heaven. His son asked him why. And Stravinsky answered, "Because he died of shame."

It is true that frivolity quickly recovers, unwilling to be guilty under any pretext. That is the stage when the family quarrels in a corner of the parlor while the furniture is taken away, and the storm of grievances keeps its members from seeing that the pieces of furniture disappear one after the other and that not even a chair to sit down on is left.

I am upset by the person whom everyone in advance thinks I will like because he is freakish (*fantaisiste*). Freakishness and frivolity are related, I repeat. The freakish character, incapable of originality, discovers it in the trouble he causes you by the lack of coherence in his actions. He tries to startle you and only upsets you. He believes he is exceptional. He does not move any of the pawns who decide the game. He is satisfied with confusing the dominoes and cards, with chessmen in a position unsuitable for the mechanics of the game and suitable for surprising players at first glance. He mistrusts time, place, and convention with an insolence which is not even the dandy's. He strikes us down like the drunk disdaining us from his superior world where he scorns what he interprets as our conformity and which is only our embarrassment.

I have known freakish characters whose freakishness was in a way organic and who died from it. In them I felt a kind of benign madness very dangerous for them and for their friends. Despite the respect which any selflesss existence inspires in me, they stirred up uneasiness as well. For these freakish characters are usually mythomaniac and often their purpose is not to try to force our attention but our heart. If they succeed, they are neither frivolous nor freakish, but they give the appearance because of their awkwardness in convincing us, of their modesty which forces them to want to appear exceptional, of their desire to join our system and their remorse at being considered indiscreet. This remorse leads them to escapes, to total disappearances, to punishments they inflict upon themselves and which often are excessively cruel.

The world in which they live makes contact with them very difficult since the slightest word, the slightest gesture on our part (and to which we attached no importance) releases in them unbelievable lines of thought which can lead to suicide.

At the beginning, they must be avoided, no matter what charm they demonstrate in a world where fire is rare and always attractive.

I have not observed often enough this prudence. I considered it unworthy and related to a comfort I refused. A scruple made me fear slamming my door in the face of the unknown guest. I opened it and then did not dare change my mind, so great was my shame of appearing fainthearted. That was the error. Rather than quickly foreseeing the consequences of a weakness injurious to my friends and my work, I took pride in defying all traps and jumping into them with my feet tied. Pride rather than innate generosity motivated me. And I blame myself.

I have referred to the dandy. He should not be confused with those who discovered in his attitude, considered as conclusive, a visible image of their lofty spirit and their revolt. I understood why Baudelaire felt attracted. He moved in reverse order. This dramatist is a drama. He is drama, theatre, actors, public, the red curtain, the chandelier. A Brummell is, contrariwise, the perfect male of the tragedienne without a theatre. He will play his role in the void, and even in the definitive void of an attic where he dies after having the names of all the great of England announced in his presence. His witty statement: "I must not have been well dressed at the Derby, since you noticed me," took on its meaning when Baudelaire was forced to depend on an article in which Sainte-Beuve expresses his admiration only for a single sonnet to the moon. "A hot head and a cold hand," Goethe says somewhere. The dandy is a cold hand and a cold head. I advise

ships to avoid that insolent iceberg. Nothing changes his path. He would kill in order to put on his tie. His imperialism has no basis. He is anointed by himself. One fine day Brummell asked King George to get up and pull the bell cord. This bell was enough to awaken the rightful king from his hypnosis and he showed the king of fashion out the door.

When kings put poets out the door, poets win. When the king of England put Brummell out the door, Brummell was ruined.

Our age is sickly. It invented "escapes." The horrors suffered by the victims of a war's frivolity provide it with a few counterirritants. It is drugged with them through the intervention of its newspapers, and even the atom bomb provides it with a Jules Verne lyricism—until the moment a joker tricks it on the air. Orson Welles announced the arrival of the Martians. A French radio station announced the fall of a meteor. At once our war leaders decided to escape not spiritually but physically. They broke their legs. They got away. They fainted and aborted. They called for help. Finally the government was affected and forbade imaginary broadcasts. Poetry would certainly quiet them down and take them far away from stark reality. That is what they believe and that is what is exploited by hundreds of magazines whose smallest advertisement opens the doors of dreams.

The poet was alone in the midst of an industrial world. Now he is alone in the midst of a poetic world. Thanks to this world, generously equipped for escape as for winter sports, by the theatre, movies, and expensive magazines, the poet at last wins back his invisibility.

206

Moral Essays

I like to be with young people. They teach me much
more than older people. Their insolence and their
seriousness are like a cold shower. They administer
our hygiene. And moreover, our obligation to be an
example to them forces us to walk straight. I under-
stand why many of my contemporaries, unlike myself,
avoid knowing them. They tire one out because they
are always in the breach and do not seem to know
what they want.

Children know what they want. They want to leave
childhood. Trouble begins when they do leave it. Be-
cause the young know what they do not want before
knowing what they want. Now, what they do not want
is what we want. They stay in our company to enjoy
the contrast. When they begin to want something, I
learn what it is before they do. My ears of a circus
horse recognize the music. I keep the score.

I remember when Radiguet took out of his pockets
weapons to fight me with. I used them against myself.
That is what happens with the young whom I dis-
cover. People think that I give to them, and it is they
who give to me. I owe everything to them.

Nothing is more erroneous than the motives im-
puted to my liking of young people. Their faces at-
tract me for what they express. This kind of beauty
inspires only respect.

I demand no respect in return. The young are at
home in my house. I realize they forget my age and I
feel the same surprise as if I were received as an equal
by the hierophants of Memphis.

Erik Satie and Max Jacob shared this privilege. I

always met them with young men, walking arm in arm.

The clairvoyant youth I speak of live in capitals. They know where they should live and discover for themselves a family of anarchist tradition. They adopt this family and grow into it and practice exercises of ingratitude. They wait until they are strong enough to kill off the family and set fire to the house.

The young in the provinces employ another method. They write to me and complain. They call for help. They want to leave one place and go to another which will understand and help them. If they come on foot from Charleville (Rimbaud is still a model), they quickly get in step.

It would therefore be absurd to expect gratitude from the young and take glory from the fact that they seek refuge in my house. They love me in so far as my faults teach them and my weaknesses provide them with excuses and my fatigue puts me at their mercy. From this mixture I derive benefits and I profit from them as much as they do from me. My books are playthings for them. They cut their teeth on them.

It is ridiculous to look at the young in the form of a myth or in one solid group. It is likewise ridiculous to fear them, to put a table between them and me, to slam the door in their face, to take flight as soon as they approach.

It is true they are mythomaniac and overfamiliar and they take my time. But what of that?

Naturally I am caught in the network of their lies. Naturally they put on a mask when they speak to me. Naturally they criticize me to others, and when they do something wrong, they blame me.

Moral Essays

I have to run these risks, for the simple fact that those young men reassure me by proving to me that they avoid politics and transmit the secret of enthusiasm.

Many young men have told me, after a long time, that they had come to me, either because of a bet, or because they had read my name on a poster, or to disobey their family.

Their silence disheartened me. I enriched it with a hundred suppositions. It came only from a fear of speaking foolishly.

This does not keep me from falling again into the trap. For the young intimidate me because I ascribe mystery to them. That is the power of their silence, which I make up for with my own speech. They realize this fairly soon and use it. Their silence becomes systematic. They practice unfettering me.

It is well to look out for this. When they leave, their mortal silence deepens in me and plays havoc. Their victim interprets this as a criticism of what he is doing. He weighs it, approves it, is disgusted and paralyzed. He falls from his tree, his beak open.

I see artists, exposed to this adventure, lose their footing, become unable to straighten out and unable to live without their executioners.

At times the solitude of these young monsters has surprised me. They walk about the streets, when they leave my house, and complain that they meet no one their own age whom they like. Some come from a country district where they live. They do not mention this. They stay on late and miss their train. I take them to the door without knowing what the situation is, and that they can neither afford a hotel room nor go home. Their attitude becomes so strange that I grow afraid they will drown themselves. I don't know what to do and they grow silent. It is impossible to get them out of the hole they are digging for themselves, and away from a fall toward which a terrible force of inertia might induce them.

But they know that all doors are not closed to them, that I see their suffering, that I listen to them and speak if they do not speak, that I give them a few recipes. In short, it is one evening out of the void where they are searching for their way. The worst moment, as I have said, is between childhood and youth.

My own drama, as I remember it, was late in coming and not amusing. My dice were loaded. I proudly walked goose-step fashion onto the parade ground. I had to go back to the starting point and take up training.

People I might have met and did not meet would have perhaps saved the launching. I am perhaps one of them now for the young.

Alas, it is impossible to answer all the letters of appeal and receive all the desperate visits. That would make me president of the suicide club. Those drowning who hold on to me and pull me down are dangerous.

If I answer, another letter comes which demands an answer. To answer curtly is to appear scornful. It is better not to answer, and if I open my door, not to let those come back who are marked with a sign.

This danger is not the least.

Why do young students fail in their duty, and what is this duty? Let me tell them. They should form an army for great adventures of the spirit. But their conformity blinds them. They never hesitate to set in motion against the loftiest enterprises a farcical surface anarchy without the slightest sense of direction. Their ignorance, in addition to the pride they feel in it—they judge themselves infallible—and the pleasure of vigorous opposition, turns them against themselves without their realizing it. When they hiss, they hiss themselves and join sides with their families whose decrees they despise.

Also, the past irritates them. Classical works mean only exams flunked, soiled books, homework. Not one of them takes it into his head to blow away the dust and find the living substance underneath. They would be surprised that Racine (one among many) conceals under a polite exterior a terrifying intensity. Rather than going in a group to the theatre to jeer, they would do better to take it out on the actors who deform his tragedies. But they do just the opposite. A bad tragedian can make them forget their jeering. They acclaim his faults.

These are the young—deaf and blind to what was going on, is going on, and will go on. All they have left is disorder. A hiatus they fill by organizing parades, carrying signs, booing, and stamping their feet in time. I am alone if I wanted to fight. I have no shock troops. And even they would turn against me.

Abbé Morel told me about his lecture at the Sorbonne on Picasso. He was showing slides of the works. The students who filled the hall jeered, stamped their feet, and hooted. Without transition, the abbé showed some masterpieces of Romanesque sculpture. His auditors thought they were Picasso's. They yelled, stamped, jeered. The abbé expected this and he let them have it. The students, so skilled in mystifying and who ascribe this skill to artists, enjoyed the trick which had fooled them and applauded their magician.

Not one of them would have been able to speak and down Picasso with new weapons, or offset his work with something more vital, or run more swiftly than Abbé Morel, or turn about and attack him head on.

I hasten to say that it is not in my power to measure the aptitude of each faculty in coming to our help. I suppose that the faculty of science is more localized in problems, more enamored of precise research than the faculty of letters. More rich in seekers than in pedagogues. I suppose also that heads of the faculty of letters must be at fault save for their excuse that when they wish to excite the spirit of a class, they are faced with its reluctance to leave well-beaten paths, and so give it up.

I do know that politics now plays the first role, and yet I can state that students react very little or badly.

I am not asking for the impossible. I am not concerned with long research in addition to the program, or subtleties of an important politics with which we are worn out. I am asking students for a spontaneous interest in what is outside routine, and to think, as Jacques Rivière said, "that there is a time for us to make fun of others, and a time for others to make fun of us."

I do not want students to cultivate a parliamentary prudence. I wish they were imprudent and excited over what shocks them. I know professors younger than they are.

When I spoke, long ago, at the Collège de France,

I first paid a visit to the dean. The many memories of scoldings slowed me down as I approached his office. I found a charming elderly man, very young in appearance. "Beware of our students," he said to me. "Dates are all they like to note down. They don't want to be disturbed."

But I did disturb them. It's a good method. They remember best a shaking up. But a shaking up demoralizes them for a moment.

In summary, let me say that I am not fool enough to expect that an assembly of students should know miraculously what cannot be taught. I should like them not to be proud of cutting off their antennae as if they were the first hairs of a beard. They would gain by registering the prodigious waves which beauty propagates. Rightly or wrongly.

ON SEXUAL HABITS

Writing is an act of love. If it isn't that, it is handwriting. It consists in obeying the mechanism of plants and trees and of projecting sperm far around us. The world's wealth is in waste. This fecundates and that falls by the wayside. It is the same with sex. The focus of pleasure is very vague although it is very strong. It invites the race to perpetuate itself. This does not prevent it from functioning blindly. A dog seizes my leg. A bitch mounts a dog. A certain plant, which was once high and is now atrophied, still produces for its seed a parachute which falls to the ground before it has the time to open. Women on islands in the Pacific give birth in cow dung in order to allow only the strongest children to grow up. Through fear of overpopulation, the islands allow what is usually called perverse love.

The soldiers, sailors, and workmen who indulge in this see no crime in it. When they do see crime in it, vice has declared itself. For vice, as I have said, begins with choosing. In Villefranche, I once watched American sailors for whom the exercise of love presented no precise form, and who adjusted to anyone for any kind of practice. The idea of vice never entered their heads. They acted blindly. Instinctively they adopted the very confused rules of the vegetative and animal kingdoms. A pregnant woman is deformed when she is used. This proves her nobility and that it is more foolhardy to use her in a sterile fashion than to use a man, who represents a luxury article, for the blind passions of the flesh. I have little or no use for this practice, but since I like to be with young men from whom I have a great deal to learn, and who show nobility of spirit on their faces, the world has decided otherwise. Besides, I find that after a certain age these things are vile and do not permit an exchange, and seem ludicrous in either sex.

In a word, I lead a monk's life. An incomprehensible life in a city where the inhabitants think only of rubbing against one another, of seeking out that kind of pleasure even by dancing, of imputing it to others, of believing every friendship suspect.

It is of little consequence. I must not be on exhibition. The more people are wrong about me, and the more fables they invent, the more I am protected and taught how to live in peace. It is enough if those close by esteem me. What I am in others means nothing to me.

A lady whom I had invited to lunch served me up

Moral Essays

such a description of myself that I got up from the table to ask to be excused. I said to her, "You are sharing the meal of a man I do not know and I should prefer not to know." That lady believed she was being kind. She did not know my real character. She knew another, composed from all kinds of stories which fascinated her.

What is the source of the meaning of beauty, or what impels us toward beauty? Where does it begin and where does it end? What nervous center reveals it to us? The gratuitous practice of sexuality is a torment, whether they know it or not, of all great men. Michelangelo exhibited it. Da Vinci whispered it. Their confessions intrigue me less than numerous indications of an order looked upon as a disorder, which does not go so far as acts themselves. What do acts mean? They have to do with the police. They do not interest me. Picasso is an example. This man who likes women is a misogynist in his paintings. There he takes revenge on the domination which women have over him and on the time they steal from him. He wreaks his revenge on their faces and appearance. On the other hand, he flatters men, and having no complaint against them, he praises them in his writing and in his drawing.

ON RESPONSIBILITY

And now a strange sensation of frustration begins to seize hold of the four cardinal points of my organism and to tie them in a knot in the middle. Is it the sudden heat or a storm or solitude or the dates of my plays which are badly arranged or the prospect of being without a home or simply this book which will not be born? I know these crises of vague depression from having often been their victim. Nothing is more difficult than finding for them a shape which will permit me to look straight at them. From the minute this uneasiness is felt, it governs me. It keeps me from reading, writing, sleeping, walking, living. It encircles me with confused threats. Everything that opened, now closes. Everything that helped me, now deserts me. Everything that smiled, now looks sternly at me. I would not dare undertake anything. Enterprises, suggested to me, wither, grow confused, and collapse one on the other. Each time I am tricked by those advances of destiny which entices me only to turn its back on me more deliberately. Each time I repeat to myself that I have reached a zone of quiet, and paid dearly enough for the right to go down an easy slope and not fall off the cliff at night.

Just when I am comfortable with that illusion, my body recalls me to order. It turns on one of the red lights which mean, "Look out." All kinds of pain which I thought had gone, come back with the anger of those who attempt a false exit and hate me all the more for feeling ridiculous. My eyelids, temples, neck, chest, arms, and finger joints burn. If I recover, then the sickness gathers its strength. It seems that it wants even to attack my mucous membranes, gums, throat, palate. From the machine, it passes to the gasoline in the machine and corrupts that. Distress, eruptions, fever fill me with very painful but faint symptoms. They increase rapidly until they become nausea which I attribute to an outside influence. My condition doubtless colors the world and makes me believe I owe my color to it. This scheming splashes all the more my

outside and inside. Life appears to me insoluble, too
vast, too small, too long, too short. Once I was able
to offset the frequency of these attacks by opium, a
euphoric remedy. I gave it up ten years ago because
of an honesty which may well be foolishness. I wanted
no other resources save my own. This makes no sense,
since my ego is made up of my own food. In a word,
I must submit to their attacks and wait for them to
be over.

The illness in me since yesterday declared itself two
weeks ago by an increased suffering. There is the pos-
sible factor of a heavy atmosphere outside turning to
storm. For five minutes there has been wind and rain.
I remember a paragraph in Michelet's *History* where
he is proud of being insensitive to the wind beating
against his window. Rather, he is comforted by it and
studies in it the rhythm of nature. The gusts of wind
promised fine weather. What fine weather I should
like to know. I should like to be my own tuner, and
restring, as I wish, my nerves which heat and cold put
out of tune. I really mean the slightest moral humidity,
the slightest spiritual temperature.

Should we envy those Goethe-like, or Hugo-like
ogres whose egoism passes for heroism and who suc-
ceed in having such sentences admired as, "Over the
tomb and forward!"? That was the way Goethe wel-
comed his son's death. What is the point of envying
or not envying them? The die is cast. I neither glorify
myself nor glorify them in being of one consistency
or another.

I simply state that my particular makeup turns me
into a vagabond. The place I wanted and where I hide
quickly becomes a trap. I escape—and it begins over

again. I need only to discover the place of a retreat for everything there to become an obstacle and keep me from signing the contract.

Nothing is so real as the rhythm which controls us and which we believe is in our way. Its energy is deceptive. Failure is disguised. It never appears under the same mask. Even if we wait a long time for it, we do not recognize it.

Has the book I am writing completed its curve? I who boast, and in its very chapters, of never being preoccupied with it and of being warned about it only by a shock, question myself for the first time. Can I still speak to you, and keep this journal, which is not really one, in the form of a journal, based on what happens to me? That would be falsifying its mechanism. It would not be writing the book as it comes to me, but another one which I would be forcing. I yield to the trick of the station platforms where you run beside the train, jump onto the car steps, and try to slow down the breaking of the thread twined around your heart and the heart of those leaving. I am torn between my taste for habit and the fate obliging me to sever connections. I had formed a picture of us, your youth like mine, standing in a corner of the street, seated in a square, lying on our stomachs on a bed, our elbows on a table, talking together. And then I leave you. But I don't leave you, of course, since I am close enough to my ink for my pulse to beat there. Don't you feel it under your thumb holding the edge of the pages? That would surprise me, because it jumps from under my pen and creates that inimitable, wild, nocturnal, infinitely complex racket of my heart, recorded in *Blood of a Poet*. "The poet is dead. Long

live the poet." That is what its ink shouts. That is
what its muffled drums beat. That is what lights up
its candelabra in mourning. That is what shakes your
pocket where you put my book and makes those pass-
ing you in the street turn around and wonder what
the noise is. There is the difference between a book
which is only a book and a book which is a person
changed into a book, and crying for help so the charm
will be broken and he will be reincarnated in the
person of the reader. That is the sleight-of-hand trick
I ask of you. Please understand. It is not as difficult as
it seems at first.

You take this book out of your pocket. You read.
And if you succeed in reading without any distraction,
gradually you will feel that I live in you and you will
resuscitate me. You will even risk having unexpectedly
one of my gestures, one of my expressions. Naturally
I am speaking to the youth of a period when I will not
be in the flesh and when my blood will have joined my
ink.

We agree then. Do not forget that it is important

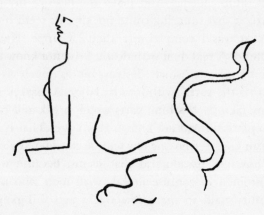

for my downstrokes in their form of printed letters, to find in you their scrolls and unfold them, twisting for a moment my line with yours under such a banner that you will feel the heat from my body.

If you carry out my instructions to the letter, a phenomenon of osmosis will take place thanks to which this rather disreputable book, called a book, will cease being that, and become a pact of mutual help in which the living helps the dead and the dead helps the living. You will bring me as much as I bring you. That is all we need to say.

This evening when I am speaking to the children of the children of our children, I am suffering from hard pain. Between the middle and the ring fingers of my right hand, the skin is peeling. Under my arms there are bundles of nettle. I force myself to write because idleness increases my agony. That is why I move ahead into a period when it will be the time for my pages to suffer. Because they will. An ink as persuasive as mine can never find rest.

How I wish I had good health and could tackle plays, films, poems! And make the flesh of my paper so strong that suffering could not sink its teeth in it!

What was I complaining about? Grippe. Neuritis. Typhoid. A real duel with death. I did not know about that sly plague which destroys us as much as man destroys the earth, with infinite labor. A masked strike in my factory. Machine parts which break and cannot be replaced. I had not known about age. That is all.

Jean Genet, who one day will be considered a moralist, however paradoxical that seems, because we are accustomed to confuse morals with men who preach morality, said to me a few weeks ago this poignant sentence: "It is not enough to watch one's heroes live and to pity them. We have to take on their sins and submit to the consequences."

Who are my real heroes? Sentiments. Abstract figures which have their own life and make extreme demands. That is what I understood as I listened to Genet and saw the destruction perpetuated in him by the crimes of the Egyptian Querelle. He knew he was responsible for them and refused any excuse of irresponsibility. He was ready, not to engage in a lawsuit against the extremes of the book, but to accept the suit which a higher justice might bring against his characters.[1]

Suddenly he threw a great light on the endless trial in which I am caught. Suddenly he explained the reason why I feel no revolt. It is right for this trial, brought against words, attitudes, and fantasies, to be taken on by the author and for him to appear between two policemen. The position is inadmissible of the author who judges, who has a seat on his own jury, and who shows compassion for the guilty. A man is on one side of the bar or on the other. This is the very foundation of our commitment.

If I did not belong to the race of men who are accused and who are awkward in defending themselves, what shame I would have felt with Genet when he told me the secret of his torment. But would he have told me if he had not recognized me long before and in-

---

[1] In order to describe Jean Genet in the Court of Justice (1942), I had to say to the tribunal that I considered him the great writer of France. As can be imagined, this delighted the newspapers of the Occupation. But a Paris tribunal is always afraid of making a new blunder, of condemning another Baudelaire. I saved Genet. And I would not alter my testimonial.

stantly by the signs which permit outlaws to recognize one another. I had seen Genet refuse to be introduced to a famous writer whose immorality *seemed to him suspect.*

It is imperative for me to warn openly that I represent my ideas, however contradictory they be, and that the tribunal of men can blame only me. These ideas, I repeat, have the face of characters. They move about. I alone am responsible for their actions. It would be wrong for me to say, as Goethe did, after the suicides provoked by *Werther,* "That does not concern me."

It is therefore normal for me to take on the judicial errors which ideas, easy to deform and without alibi, will always provoke.[1]

I am not unaware of the terrible risks a spiritual lawyer, a witness for the prosecution, and the distance separating the jurors of a poet, inflict on my work in my person. I pardon the verdict, no matter how insane it is. It would be too simple to circulate freely just outside of laws in a world governed by them.

5 July 1946

---

[1] It happens in this world that a public judicial reparation does occur. Condemned for incest in 1939 by the Municipal Council and in 1941 by the Militia, the pure, childlike mother and son of *Les Parents Terribles* were acquitted unanimously by repeal in 1946.

VIII. France

France is a self-disparaging country. It is better that way because otherwise she would be the most pretentious country in the world. The essential point is that she does not define herself. Whatever defines itself is neutralized. In my novel *Les Enfants Terribles,* I take care to say that the brother and sister did not define themselves. Had they defined their strength in poetry, they would have become aesthetes and passed from the active to the passive. No. They hate one another. They hate their room. They want another life. Probably the life of those who imitate them and lose their privileges for a world which exists only by the certainty that privileges are somewhere else and we never possess one of them.

I own a letter of Musset written in the period richest in geniuses. He complains that there is not one artist, one book, one painter, one play. He says the Comédie-Française is crumbling under the dust, and Madame Malibran is singing in London because the Paris Opéra sings out of tune. Each period in France is so constituted that in the midst of her wealth she sees nothing and looks for her wealth elsewhere.

Those who want her great in words are stupid. "Greatness, purity, constructive works." These form the modern chorus. And during this time, greatness, purity, constructive works are produced in a form which remains invisible and would appear to them to be a disgrace for the country. Critics judge works and do not know they are judged by them. Who gives greatness to France? It is Villon, Rimbaud, Verlaine, Baudelaire. All of them were taken to prison. People wanted to throw them out of France. They were allowed to die in hospitals. I do not speak of Joan of Arc. In her case, it is the trial that counted. Her revenge was sad. Poor Péguy! I was fond of him. He was an anarchist. What would he say of the use his name has been put to?

The attitude of France after the Liberation was quite simple. Controlled by the military, she could not adopt an attitude. Could she say to the world—I did not want to fight. I do not like fighting. I had no arms. I will not have any. I have a secret arm. What is it? Since it is secret, I cannot tell you. And if they insist, "My secret arm is a tradition of anarchy."

That is a strong answer. An enigma to fascinate strong races. "Invade me. I will end by possessing you."

Since this Chinese position was not taken, and we played the blusterers, what chance did we have? The chance to become a village, as Lao-tzu advises. To be no longer enviable except in an invisible power, vaster than the visible, and sovereign.

Lao-tzu, speaking of the ideal empire, says: one should hear cocks crow from one end of the land to the other.

What is France, I ask you? A cock on a manure heap. Remove the manure and the cock dies. That is what

happens when people are foolish enough to confuse a manure heap with a pile of garbage.

France is forever struggling against herself. This has always impressed me. The great French tradition is one of anarchy. The strongest of all traditions. Disorder allows France to live, as order is indispensable to other countries. I am amused by those people who fear that France will become a village. It has always been one. And it always will be. It was that under Louis XIV.

A village with its café du commerce, its newspaper stand, and its tobacco store where each Frenchman argues and fights.

Out of this perpetual argumentation comes the fire which gives France its clear intense light about which Guillaume Apollinaire used to say that the eye can look into its depths tirelessly.

From the outside, this causes consternation and resembles a heavy cloudiness. The foreigner sees only groups opposing one another, personalities contradicting one another, individuals insulting one another. But do people realize it is boiling water and some of the bubbles on the surface have a coloring that can be seen nowhere else?

Everyone is a thinker in France. Even fools think. Everyone is on stage. Almost no one occupies the theatre seats, and it is unusual for my public not to say it could do a better job than I do. But this amazing lack of discipline has its advantages. Today France is perhaps the only country where the public can make a play successful because the critics condemn it. No one is believed, and I might say that the spirit of contradiction, pushed to this extreme, encourages the public to take the opposite view of any judgment and to applaud when the detractors hiss.

IX. New York

Americans, I am writing to you in the plane taking me back to France. I spent twenty days in New York and I did so many things and saw so many people that I am not sure whether I lived twenty days or twenty years in your country. You will say to me that a country is not judged by one city, America by New York, and that my visit was too brief for me to make any judgment. But sometimes the first glance at a face teaches you more about it than a long study. We may become confused in the long run over a person, revise our opinion of the first meeting, and make a mistake in our opinion of the second meeting. The third meeting and subsequent ones mean we live with the person and hence become a bad judge since we judge well only from the outside. If you live with a person, a confused substance is created where two personalities mingle their forms. It also happens that a city which believes it reflects badly other cities, reflects even immense territories where time is not the same, so that night in one is day in another, and one is awake when the other is asleep. I mean that one is occupied by the magnificent absurdity of dreams while the other moves about and is not dreaming. This provokes, without any one being aware of it, a circulation of contrary waves which the soul registers while the mind does not decipher them. It is nonetheless true that these waves circulate and engage in a mysterious work. It is possible that the taste of the inhabitants of New York for a world which wrests them away from their own comes from this tremendous tide of dreams and that the ceaseless questions they oppose to it represent the defense, the wall, the barrage which keep them from being submerged by it.

For the attraction which enigmas possess and the horror of enigmas are the great preoccupation of the American mind.

Everything is paradoxical in New York. You demand something new if you want no change. The temporary failure with which every great enterprise begins is incomprehensible to you and you see only its definitive aspect. You demand success—and that is the drama of the movie business, because all the Muses can wait, and may be painted and depicted in positions of waiting, and grow young finally, rather than old, and because although painting, sculpture, music, poetry can wait and triumph late, after the death of the person in charge, a film cannot wait, it costs too much to wait and has to succeed in monstrous fashion at the very beginning.

I will return to these matters. For the moment, I am letting myself go to the rhythm of the propellers and to the strange regime of memories which live in me. They move like underwater grasses, and each time they touch, they start off in another direction.

People do not sit down in New York. They don't lie down. They stand up, not because of the skyscrapers where numerals (which devour New York) have established their anthill. I speak of a city standing, because if it sat down, it would rest and reflect, and if it lay down, it would sleep and dream; and it wants neither to meditate nor dream, but to divide itself, standing between the two breasts of its mother, one of which gives it alcohol and the other, milk. It wants to remain standing, and forget (what?), forget itself, weary itself, wear itself out, escape, by fatigue and the imperceptible wavering of people who drink, and of skyscrapers whose base is immobile and whose summit moves slightly—escape, I repeat, the question that one asks oneself, which you fear asking yourself, and which you continually ask others.

Man is possessed by a darkness, by monsters of dark zones. He cannot enter those zones, but at times night sends out rather terrifying ambassadors, through the mediation of poets. These ambassadors fascinate you. They attract you and repulse you. You try to understand their language, and not understanding it, you ask the poets to translate it for you. Alas! the poets do not understand it any better and they are satisfied with being the humble servants of these ambassadors, the mediums of these individualistic phantoms who haunt

you and upset you, and whom you would like to unionize.

New York detests a *secret.* It tries to learn the secret of others. It calls its own secret, *ennui,* which it exorcizes by a method of optimism.

New York is an open city and wide open. Its arms are open, its faces and hearts are open, its streets, doors, and windows are open. From this comes a euphoria for the visitor and a draft in which ideas cannot mature. They are tossed about like dead leaves.

I repeat, you refuse to wait and to have wait. In New York everyone arrives ahead of time. You dislike tradition and the new. Your ideal would be *an instantaneous tradition.* The new is immediately attached to a school. Its life is over at that time. You classify and name it, and since you don't allow an artist to experiment, you demand that he repeat himself and you replace him when he tires you. In that way you kill the flies.

I saw in the Museum of Modern Art [1] an unforgettable scene. In a very clean nursery, fifty little girls were painting on tables covered with brushes, inks, tubes, gouache. They were not looking at their work and their tongues stuck out like those of dogs who have been conditioned to look strained on the striking of a bell. Nurses were taking care of these young creators of abstract art, and slapped their hands if by mistake what they painted represented something and dangerously inclined toward realism. The mothers

---

[1] Thanks to Monroe Wheeler, this museum is a model of order and beauty. I saw there, among other marvels, the *Sleeping Gypsy* of Rousseau, and *Guernica* of Picasso, which is waiting to take its place in a new Spain.

(who still admire Picasso) were not admitted. In the galleries, beside masterpieces of Rousseau, Matisse, Braque, Picasso, Bonnard, Vuillard, they exhibit the dirty linen of our young painters, our spots of ink and wine on the old tablecloths of the Rotonde and the Dôme. New York is a tall giraffe, speckled with windows and burdened with relics.

How can I explain to the large number of young people who take notes, that boldness does not necessarily wear the attributes of boldness, that it is only a spirit of revolt, and that we now have to contradict ourselves and again upset the young by new expressions of boldness which they will consider retrogression?

On my right, a lady is sleeping. Orchids surround her face like a beard. On her knees *Life* magazine is open. I believe it is one of the largest publications in America. I close my eyes and relive the events of last Sunday. *Life* magazine had asked permission to take eccentric pictures of me. When I told the editors that my age and my position of a poet (that is, of a worker) did not justify my granting them permission to take eccentric pictures of me, they replied that it was the custom and that their readers liked only that kind of photograph. Since I was the guest of New York, I acquiesced and suggested a few ideas which might satisfy them and would compromise me only to the degree that I am willing to be compromised.

We worked from three in the afternoon until seven. I dined with Jacques Maritain. Then we resumed the work, from eleven until five in the morning. About two, there was a rest. Sandwiches and ginger ale. That is when the reporters and photographers of *Life* said this surprising thing to me, "What will a man in a barbershop, in a Massachusetts town, as he looks at *Life* magazine, get out of these photographs? Aren't you afraid they'll puzzle him?" — "But," I answered, "these extravagances aren't my idea. They're yours." In these men, worry alternated with assurance that their pictures were the one valid kind. Then they raised the serious problem of the text, and asked me how they could explain the inexplicable. I suggested they say they had taken the pictures in the most normal way, and that the camera had played a trick on them, and that machines were becoming dangerous in their resemblance to men. And I said, "Give Rolleiflex some publicity. For example: *Rolleiflex thinks.*"

This anecdote is typical of the American paradox. You are constantly coming face to face with boldness and the fear of boldness. To the extent that in your plays passion must be illusion, either curable or punished at the end. Passion must be presented with an excuse. Passion must come from a disorder brought on by insanity or alcohol. Imagination, in films, must be accounted for by dreams. If a man falls asleep at the beginning of the film and wakes up at the end, the director is free to depict any action in any place.

Since you need excuses, are you therefore guilty? Do you consider yourselves guilty? When your censorship, enslaved to the strange psychosis of the bed associated with shame and symbolic of love and dreams, your two obsessions, reproached me for the scene between the son and the mother in my film *Les Parents Terribles,* weren't you ashamed, as a noble people should be, of a low thought? Don't you feel the repression which forces you to give such a bad interpretation to goodness and innocence?

When you deify Van Gogh, I approve.

But wasn't Van Gogh the typical artist who dies in poverty? Poverty is what New York despises the most.

In this, you are imitating the rest of the world, because if Joan of Arc had not been burned, she would not be a heroine and she would not be a subject for films.[1]

I say "you," but I am not speaking about you, the American people. I am speaking of the rich who are afraid of taking chances and lose their courage, because in the long run chance alone makes money. I speak of the world of money and immediate returns, of the gold curtain which is as hard as the iron curtain, of the gold curtain separating America from America and America from Europe.

The New York public is the best in the world. I have seen it, eager, attentive, amused, enthusiastic, refusing to go at the end, and calling back the actors whom it likes. But the producer loathes this public. He declares it incapable of understanding great works and believes it expedient to present mediocre works. If he does present to the public a great work, he cuts and rearranges it, he twists it and pulls it down to the level of a public he judges by his own capacity, and which does not exist. Of course it does happen that the public makes mistakes. But it has been deceived for a long time and it has some excuse. No effort is made to educate it. The instincts of the public are sound and the producer may pay dearly for his malice.

---

[1] May I point out that the world champion Al Brown, a boxing genius, lives in Harlem, alone, unrecognized, penniless.

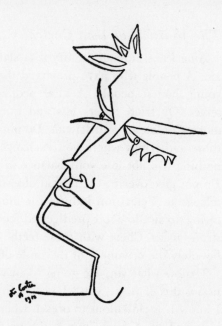

In Hollywood, after endless discussions and in spite of his distaste for composing music for a film, Stravinsky was about to settle the agreement with Mr. G. Mr. G. said that he would also have to pay the arranger. "What arranger?" asked Stravinsky. "The one who will arrange your music."

This habit of arranging everything is your method. A work must not at any cost remain what it is. Hollywood is the source of this phenomenon, which can be explained by the pale blood of an aristocracy of movie men (technicians and artists) whose kingdom does not communicate with the outside and whose race is losing its strength.

This aristocracy, whose blood is becoming very pale, exiled those heads that had been too mysteriously crowned. Greta Garbo and Charlie Chaplin were noble victims of this imperialistic beehive.

Americans, human dignity is at stake. Be what you are. A people who have preserved their childhood. A young honest people. A vital people. Release yourselves. Question others less and question yourselves more. Confide in your friends. Do not be satisfied with those gatherings where you exchange drinks and say nothing. Do not lose your balance in vain enterprises. Do not give over to the mortal obsession of radio and television. Television induces the mind to stop masticating, to swallow soft predigested food. The mind has strong teeth. Chew with those teeth. Do not let them be solely the ornament of the smile of stars.

I know what you are going to answer. "What business is this of yours, you who come from old Europe?" I know it is ridiculous to preach when I deserve to be preached to. I know our faults better than I know yours. But in France there exists a disorder which allows new things and surprises, a manure heap in which our cock anchors its feet and which must not be confused with a refuse pile. An error which our government has often been guilty of committing.

I know that we inhabit a farmyard and that you inhabit a bathroom. But tell me, isn't it pleasant for the man who inhabits a farmyard to go into a bathroom, and for a man who inhabits a bathroom to go into a farmyard? This is the basis of our exchange. This is what I dream of, and I am a man from the old French farmyard, an artisan who makes his article with his own hands and carries it under his arm in your city.

And tell me, isn't it time for you to cease being the specialist you are, and to teach your specialist recipes? Isn't it time to entrust your machines to us to see if we could humanize them, and humanize you by diminishing the prerogatives of your machines, and, in a word, to calm down our individualism and to stir up yours, so that we can all, in close company, rise up against false morality and bad habits?

Richard Wright spoke to the French a few days ago and the things he said were not pleasant for anyone to hear. I know that Bible trumpet which is so precious to Negroes. When Louis Armstrong puts it to his mouth, it joins with the cries of angels. What is the meaning of this cry? Just what I am trying to tell you. It is what comes from my visit to New York. A cry of anguish and love.

And perhaps my words reveal a selfish fear and an instinct of preservation. For the destiny of my country is bound up with yours, and if the values which threaten you triumph, we are lost with you.

Editor's Note

The passages included in this collection have been chosen from six books. They are listed here with their respective publishers, who have granted permission for this volume of translations.

> *Lettre à Maritain.* Stock, 1926
> *Le Rappel à l'Ordre.* Stock, 1926
> *La Difficulté d'Etre.* Morihien, 1947
> *Lettre aux Américains.* Grasset, 1949
> *Journal d'un Inconnu.* Grasset, 1953
> *La Démarche d'un Poète.* Munich: Bruckmann, 1953

The arrangement of the chapters follows subject matter and theme rather than chronology. It was the hope that these pages would comprise a kind of poet's journal, representative of the predilections and preoccupations of Jean Cocteau. Most of the chapters are complete in themselves, but a few have been shortened for the purpose of presenting in each case only those pages which reveal the observations of the poet on his character.

No published book of Cocteau is explicitly or avowedly a journal, but in many of his books the tone is that of a personal diary. To read his publications in their chronological order is to follow not only the evolution of a fervent artistic activity, but the development of a thought which is both personal and abstract. The anecdotal in Cocteau's writings always serves some higher purpose.

Even in the French tradition, Cocteau's style is individualistic and strange. His constant use of ellipsis and his predilection for a sparse, bare vocabulary make his thought difficult to encompass. His sentences seem to move easily and swiftly. The visible form in Cocteau gives a deceptive appearance of facility. If the translator transcribes literally this bleak and apparent simplicity, he runs the risk of emphasizing the initial effect of strangeness. Every translator does some violence to the original. A fairly literal translation seemed often to serve Cocteau better than an effort to recast the original in order to find a style and phrasing more native to English.

The idea of assembling a Cocteau journal was suggested to the publisher and to me by Mr. Donald Allen. I should like to express here my gratitude to Jean Cocteau for the help and encouragement he offered me during the preparation of this volume.

W. F.

Selected Bibliography of Jean Cocteau

I. POETRY

Le Cap de Bonne Espérance. La Sirène, 1919
Vocabulaire. La Sirène, 1922
Plain-Chant. Stock, 1923
L'Ange Heurtebise. Stock, 1927
Opéra. Stock, 1927
Jean Cocteau, poèmes choisis par Henri Parisot, pré-cédés d'une étude par Roger Lannes. Seghers, 1945
Léone. Gallimard, 1945
La Crucifixion. Morihien, 1946
Clair-Obscur. Editions du Rocher, 1954
Poèmes 1916–1955. Gallimard, 1956

II. NOVELS

Le Potomak (édition définitive). Stock, 1924
Le Grand Ecart. Stock, 1923
Thomas l'Imposteur. Gallimard, 1923
Les Enfants Terribles. Grasset, 1929
La Fin de Potomak. Gallimard, 1939

241

III. CRITICISM

Le Coq et l'Arlequin. La Sirène, 1918
Carte Blanche. La Sirène, 1920
Le Secret Professionnel. Stock, 1922
Picasso. Stock, 1923
Le Rappel à l'Ordre. Stock, 1926
Lettre à Jacques Maritain. Stock, 1926
Opium. Stock, 1930
Essai de Critique Indirecte. Grasset, 1932
Portraits-Souvenir. Grasset, 1935
Mon Premier Voyage. Gallimard, 1936
La Belle et la Bête. Janin, 1946
La Difficulté d'Etre. Morihien, 1947
Lettre aux Américains. Grasset, 1949
Journal d'un Inconnu. Grasset, 1953
La Démarche d'un Poète. Munich: Bruckmann, 1953

IV. PLAYS

Parade. Lerolle, 1919
Le Boeuf sur le Toit. La Sirène, 1920
Les Mariés de la Tour Eiffel. Gallimard, 1924
Orphée. Stock, 1927
Antigone. Gallimard, 1928
La Voix Humaine. Stock, 1930
La Machine Infernale. Grasset, 1934
Les Chevaliers de la Table Ronde. Gallimard, 1937
Les Parents Terribles. Gallimard, 1938
Les Monstres Sacrés. Gallimard, 1940
La Machine à Ecrire. Gallimard, 1941
Renaud et Armide. Gallimard, 1943
L'Aigle à Deux Têtes. Gallimard, 1946
Bacchus. Gallimard, 1952

Selected Bibliography of Jean Cocteau

V. FILMS

Le Sang d'un Poète, 1932
Le Baron Fantôme, 1943
L'Eternel Retour, 1944
La Belle et la Bête, 1945
La Voix Humaine, 1947
Ruy Blas, 1947
L'Aigle à Deux Têtes, 1948
Les Enfants Terribles, 1950
Orphée, 1950

VI. BOOKS IN ENGLISH TRANSLATION

Cock and Harlequin, tr. by Rollo Myers. London: Egoist Press, 1921

The Grand Ecart, tr. by Lewis Galantière. Putnam, 1925

Thomas the Imposter, tr. by Lewis Galantière. Appleton, 1925.

Opium, tr. by Ernest Boyd. Longmans, 1932

Orphée, tr. by Carl Wildman. Oxford University Press, 1933

The Infernal Machine, tr. by Carl Wildman. Oxford University Press, 1936

Round the World Again in Eighty Days, tr. by Stuart Gilbert. London: Routledge, 1937

The Eagle Has Two Heads, tr. by Ronald Duncan. Funk and Wagnalls, 1948

Diary of a Film (La Belle et la Bête), tr. by Ronald Duncan. London: Dobson, 1950; and New York: Roy, 1950

The Children of the Game (Les Enfants Terribles), tr. by Rosamond Lehmann. London: Harvill, 1955.

The Holy Terrors, New York: New Directions, 1956

VII. BOOKS ON COCTEAU

Claude Mauriac, *Jean Cocteau ou la Vérité du Mensonge.* Paris, 1945

Roger Lannes, *Jean Cocteau.* Paris: Seghers, 1947

Francis Fergusson, *The Idea of a Theatre.* Princeton University Press, 1949

Empreintes, May-June-July, 1950, Brussels

Wallace Fowlie, *Age of Surrealism.* Denver: Swallow, 1950

Margaret Crosland, *Jean Cocteau, A Biography.* New York: Knopf, 1956

Index

Index

Index

Index

248

Index

Index